— *The Unofficial Guide to*
Walt Disney World ®
& EPCOT ® —

The Unofficial Guide to
Walt Disney World®
& EPCOT®

1994 Edition

Bob Sehlinger

PRENTICE HALL TRAVEL

New York • London • Toronto • Sydney • Tokyo • Singapore

Produced by Menasha Ridge Press

Published by Prentice Hall General Reference
A division of Simon & Schuster Inc.
15 Columbus Circle
New York, New York 10023

PRENTICE HALL and colophon
are registered trademarks of
Simon & Schuster Inc.

ISBN 0-671-86848-9

ISSN 1059-3578

Manufactured in the United States of America

10 9 8 7 6 5 4 3 2 1

For Trent, Marva, and Nicholas:
Goodbye Fantasyland, Hello Adventureland

—— *Declaration of Independence* ——

The author and researchers of this guide specifically and categorically declare that they are and always have been totally independent of the Walt Disney Company, Inc., of Disneyland, Inc., of Walt Disney World, Inc., and of any and all other members of the Disney corporate family not listed.

The material in this guide originated with the author and researchers and has not been reviewed, edited, or in any way approved by the Walt Disney Company, Inc., Disneyland, Inc., or Walt Disney World, Inc.

Trademarks. The following attractions, shows, components, entities, etc., mentioned or discussed in this guide are registered trademarks of the Walt Disney Company, Inc.:

> Adventureland
> AudioAnimatronics
> *Captain EO*
> Disneyland
> EPCOT
> Fantasyland
> Magic Kingdom
> New Orleans Square
> PeopleMover
> Space Mountain
> Walt Disney
> Walt Disney World

New trademarks are applied for almost continuously. These will be recognized as and when appropriate in subsequent editions of this guide.

Contents

List of Maps

— Acknowledgments —

Special thanks to our field research team who rendered a Herculean effort in what must have seemed like a fantasy version of Sartre's *No Exit* to the tune of *It's a Small World*. We hope you all recover to tour another day.

Caroline Blondy
Allison Grizzle
Betsy Amster
Leslie Cummins
Molly Burns
Pid Rafter
Karin Zachow
Trent Sehlinger
Mary Mitchell

Peals of laughter and much appreciation to nationally renowned cartoonist Tami Knight for her brilliant and insightful work.

Mike Jones, Lee Wiseman, Marie Hillin, and Nicole Jones all energetically contributed to shaping this latest edition. Sue Katz is to be credited with pushing everybody to try harder. Psychologists Dr. Karen Turnbow, Dr. Gayle Janzen, and Dr. Joan Burns provided much insight concerning the experiences of small children at Walt Disney World.

Many thanks also to Barbara Williams and Deborah Wong for design and production, and to Alexa Dilworth for editorial work on this book. Tseng Information Systems, and especially Giovanna de Graaff, earned our appreciation for their fine work and for keeping tight deadlines in providing the typography. Cartography was provided by Tim Krasnansky.

Finally, some of John Finley's comments and descriptions, which originally appeared in *Central Florida Attractions* (co-authored by Finley and Bob Sehlinger, Menasha Ridge Press, 1983), are reproduced in this guide.

— The Unofficial Guide to Walt Disney World® & EPCOT® —

How Come "Unofficial"?

This guidebook represents the first comprehensive *critical* appraisal of Walt Disney World. Its purpose is to provide the reader with the information necessary to tour Walt Disney World with the greatest efficiency and economy, and with the least amount of hassle and standing in line. The authors of this guide believe in the wondrous variety, joy, and excitement of the Disney attractions. At the same time, we recognize realistically that Walt Disney World is a business, with the same profit motivations as businesses the world over.

In this guide we have elected to represent and serve you, the consumer. Its contents were researched and compiled by a team of evaluators who were, and are, completely independent of Walt Disney World and its parent corporation. If a restaurant serves bad food, or a gift item is overpriced, or a certain ride isn't worth the wait, we can say so, and in the process, hopefully make your visit more fun, efficient, and economical.

—— The Importance of Being Goofy ——

A group of Disney executives, clean-shaven (because of a company policy banning all facial hair) and impeccably attired in dark suits, gather around a polished black walnut table. There is an almost palpable tension. Everyone speaks in hushed tones, carefully measuring their words:

"I don't want to be blindsided by this at the shareholders' meeting."

"No one's raised the issue yet. Let's just sit on it. The last thing we want is to stir something up."

"Too late, I've heard the *Post* is working on a story. There are even rumors about a paternity suit."

"What's Donald saying?"

"He's stonewalling. Won't return my calls."

"Well, he's going to have to come clean. Our people need to know what to tell the press."

"Right. And we need to know, too. If he doesn't have a brother and he doesn't have a sister, where *did* Huey, Dewey, and Louie come from?"

And so it goes. . . .

What really makes writing about Walt Disney World fun is that the Disney people take everything so seriously. Day to day they debate momentous decisions with far-ranging consequences: Will Goofy look swishy in a silver cape? Have we gone too far with the Little Mermaid's cleavage? At a time when the whole nation is concerned about the drug problem, can we afford to have a dwarf named "Dopey"?

Unofficially, we think having a sense of humor is pretty important. This guidebook has a sense of humor and it is probably necessary that you do too. Not to use this book, but more significantly, to have fun at Walt Disney World. Disney World (in the popular phrasing) is the mother of all tourist attractions. A certain amount of levity is required simply to survive. Think of the *Unofficial Guide* as a private trainer to help get your sense of humor in shape. It will help you understand the importance of being Goofy.

——— *An Apology of Sorts* ———

The first edition of *The Unofficial Guide to Walt Disney World* was considerably less than 200 pages, a mere shadow of its present massive size. In the years since the first edition, Disney World has grown considerably; adding the Disney-MGM Studios, Pleasure Island, Typhoon Lagoon, several new attractions in EPCOT and the Magic Kingdom, and about 12,000 new hotel rooms. The *Unofficial Guide* has grown to match this expansion.

We have no idea where it will all end. In 30 years we may be selling an alphabetized 26-volume edition, handsomely packaged in its own imitation oak bookcase. In the meantime, we offer a qualified apology for the tome that is our current edition. We acknowledge that it may be too heavy to be comfortably carried without the assistance of a handcart, llama, or Sherpa, but defend the inclusion of all the information presented. Not every diner uses the catsup, the A-1 Sauce, and the Tabasco, but it's nice to have all three on the table.

The Death of Spontaneity

One of our all-time favorite letters came from a man in Chapel Hill, North Carolina:

Your book reads like the operations plan for an amphibious landing. . . . Go here, do this, proceed to Step 15. . . . You must think that everyone [who visits Walt Disney World] is a hyperactive, Type-A, theme-park-commando. Whatever happened to the satisfaction of self-discovery or the joy of spontaneity? Next you will be telling us when to empty our bladders.

As it happens, we researchers for the *Unofficial Guide* are a pretty existential crew. We are big on self-discovery if the activity is walking in the woods or watching birds. Some of us are able to improvise jazz without reading music, while others can whip up a mean pot of chili in the absence of a recipe. When it comes to Walt Disney World, however, we all agree that you either need a good plan or a frontal lobotomy. The operational definition of self-discovery and spontaneity at Walt Disney World is the "pleasure" of heat prostration and the "joy" of standing in line.

It's easy to spot the free spirits at Walt Disney World, particularly at opening time. While everybody else is stampeding to Space Mountain, they are the ones standing in a cloud of dust puzzling over the park map. Later, they are the people running around like chickens in a thunderstorm trying to find an attraction with less than a 40 minute wait. Face it, Walt Disney World is not a very existential place. In many ways it's the quintessential system, the ultimate in mass-produced entertainment, the most planned and programmed environment imaginable. Spontaneity and self-discovery work about as well at Walt Disney World as they do on your tax return.

We are not saying that you can't have a great time at Walt Disney World. Bowling isn't very spontaneous either, but lots of people love it. What we are saying is that you need a plan. You do not have to be compulsive or inflexible about it, just think about what you want to do before you go. Don't delude yourself by rationalizing that the information in this bulky guide is only for the pathological and the super-organized. Ask not for whom the tome tells, Bubba, it tells for thee.

How This Guide Was Researched and Written

While much has been written concerning Walt Disney World, very little has been comparative or evaluative. Most guides simply parrot Disney World's own promotional material. In preparing this guide, however, nothing was taken for granted. Each theme park was visited at different times throughout the year by a team of trained observers. They conducted detailed evaluations and rated each theme park with all its component rides, shows, exhibits, services, and concessions according to a formal, pretested rating instrument. Interviews with attraction patrons were conducted to determine what tourists—of all age groups—enjoyed most and least during their Disney World visit.

While our observers were independent and impartial, we do not claim special expertise or scientific background relative to the types of exhibits, performances, or attractions. Like you, we visit Walt Disney World as tourists, noting our satisfaction or dissatisfaction. We do not believe it necessary to be an agronomist to know whether we enjoyed the agricultural exhibits in the EPCOT Center Land pavilion. Disney offerings are marketed to the touring public, and it is as the public that we have experienced them.

The primary difference between the average tourist and the trained evaluator is in the evaluator's professional skills in organization, preparation, and observation. The trained evaluator is responsible for much more than simply observing and cataloging. While the tourist seated next to him is being entertained and delighted by the *Tropical Serenade* (*Enchanted Tiki Birds*) in the Magic Kingdom, the professional is rating the performance in terms of theme, pace, continuity, and originality. He or she is also checking out the physical arrangements: Is the sound system clear and audible without being overpowering; is the audience shielded from the sun or from the rain; is seating adequate; can everyone in the audience clearly see the staging area? And what about guides and/or performers: Are they knowledgeable, articulate, and professional in their presentation; are they friendly and engaging?

Does the performance begin and end on time; does the show contain the features described in Disney World's promotional literature? These and many other considerations figure prominently in the rating of any staged performance. Similarly, detailed and relevant checklists were prepared and applied by observer teams to rides, exhibits, concessions, and to the theme parks in general. Finally observations and evaluator ratings were integrated with audience reactions and the opinions of patrons to compile a comprehensive quality profile of each feature and service.

In compiling this guide, we recognize the fact that a tourist's age, sex, background, and interests will strongly influence his or her taste in Walt Disney World offerings and will account for a preference of one ride or feature over another. Given this fact we make no attempt at comparing apples with oranges. How indeed could a meaningful comparison be made between the priceless historic artifacts in the Mexican pavilion of EPCOT Center and the wild roller coaster ride of the Magic Kingdom's Space Mountain? Instead, our objective is to provide the reader with sufficient description, critical evaluation, and pertinent data to make knowledgeable decisions according to individual tastes.

The essence of this guide, therefore, consists of individual critiques and descriptions of each feature of the Magic Kingdom, EPCOT Center, and Disney-MGM Studios, along with detailed Touring Plans to help you avoid bottlenecks and crowds. Also included are in-depth descriptions and Touring Plans for Typhoon Lagoon, Pleasure Island, and nearby Universal Studios Florida.

—— *Letters, Comments, and Questions from Readers* ——

Many of those who use *The Unofficial Guide to Walt Disney World* write to us asking questions, making comments, or sharing their own strategies for visiting Walt Disney World. We appreciate all such input, both positive and critical, and encourage our readers to continue writing. Readers' comments and observations are frequently incorporated in revised editions of *The Unofficial Guide* and have contributed immeasurably to its improvement. If you write us or return our reader survey form, rest assured that we will not release your name and address to any mailing list companies, direct mail advertisers, or any other third party.

Reader Survey

At the back of this guide, you will find a short questionnaire that you can use to express opinions concerning your Walt Disney World visit. The questionnaire is designed to allow each member of your party, regardless of age, to tell us what they think. Clip the questionnaire out along the dotted line and mail to:

Reader Survey
The Unofficial Guide Series
P.O. Box 43059
Birmingham, AL 35243

How to Write the Author

Bob Sehlinger
The Unofficial Guide to Walt Disney World
P.O. Box 43059
Birmingham, AL 35243

When you write, be sure to put your return address on your letter as well as on the envelope. Sometimes envelopes and letters get separated. It is also a good idea to include your phone number. And remember, as travel writers, we are often out of the office for long periods of time, so forgive us if our response is a little slow.

Questions from Readers

Questions frequently asked by readers in their letters to the author are answered in an appendix at the end of *The Unofficial Guide*.

Field Research Internship

A small number of qualified graduate students are selected each year to participate in a field research internship held in conjunction with semiannual revision work at the Disney parks and in relation to consulting projects at other American theme parks. The internships focus on theme park planning and design, attraction product design and engineering, vehicular and pedestrian traffic engineering, and the functional areas of marketing and operations. Internships are four days to a week in duration. Applicants must be 21 years of age or older and currently enrolled in an accredited graduate program, preferably in a relevant field of study (business, statistics, engineering, architecture, etc.), and be available at one month's notice for dates in June, July, and August. Those selected will be expected to pay all of their own expenses, including transportation to the research site, lodging, and meals. To apply, send vita with cover letter and SASE to:

Field Research Internship
c/o The Unofficial Guide Series
P.O. Box 43059
Birmingham, AL 35243

The Attraction That Ate Florida

Before Walt Disney World, Florida was a happy peninsula of many more-or-less equal tourist attractions. Distributed around the state in great proliferation, they constituted the most perennially appealing vacation opportunity in the United States. There was the Monkey Jungle, the Orchid Jungle, venerable Marineland, the St. Augustine Alligator Farm, Silver Springs, the Miami Wax Museum, the Sunken Gardens, the Coral Castle, and the Conch Train Tour. These, along with Cypress Gardens, Busch Gardens, and others, were the attractions that ruled Florida. Now like so many dinosaurs, those remaining survive precariously on the droppings of the greatest dinosaur of them all, Walt Disney World. With doors still open, the old standbys continue to welcome tourists, thank you, but when was the last time you planned your vacation around a trip to Jungle Larry's Safari Park?

When Walt Disney World arrived on the scene, Florida tourism changed forever. Before Disney (B.D.), southern Florida was the state's and the nation's foremost tourist destination. Throngs sunned on the beaches of Miami, Hollywood, and Fort Lauderdale and patronized such nearby attractions as the Miami Serpentarium and the Parrot Jungle. Attractions in the Ocala and St. Augustine area upstate hosted road travelers in great waves as they journeyed to and from their southern Florida destinations. At the time, Orlando was a sleepy little central Florida town about an hour's drive from Cypress Gardens, and with practically no tourist appeal whatsoever.

Then came Disney, and it was not as if Walt had sneaked up on anyone. To the contrary, he came openly and bargaining hard, asking for improved highways, tax concessions, bargain financing, and community support. So successful had been his California Disneyland that whatever he requested, he received.

Generally approving, and hoping for a larger aggregate market, the Florida attractions industry failed to discern the cloud on the horizon. Walt had tipped his hand early, however, and all the cards were on the table. When Disney bought 27,500 central Florida acres, it was fairly evident that he did not intend to raise cattle.

The Magic Kingdom opened on October 1, 1971, and was immediately successful. Hotel construction boomed in Orlando and Kissimmee and around Walt Disney World. Major new attractions popped up along recently completed Interstate 4 to cash in on the wellspring of tourists arriving to tour Disney's latest wonder. Walt Disney World became a destination, and suddenly nobody cared as much about going to the beach. The Magic Kingdom was good for two days, and then you could enjoy the rest of the week at Sea World, Cypress Gardens, Circus World, Gatorland Zoo, Busch Gardens, the Stars Hall of Fame Wax Museum, and the Kennedy Space Center.

These various satellite attractions, all practically new and stretching from east coast to west coast, formed what would come to be called the Orlando Wall. No longer did tourists pour into Miami and Fort Lauderdale. Rather, they held up at the Orlando Wall and exhausted themselves and their tourist dollars in the shiny modern attractions arrayed between Cape Canaveral and Tampa. In southern Florida venerable old attractions held on by a parrot feather and more than a few closed their doors. Flagship hotels on the fabled Gold Coast went bust or were converted to condominiums for legions of retirees.

When Walt Disney World opened, the very definition of a tourist attraction changed. Setting standards for cleanliness, size, scope, grandeur, variety, and attention to detail, Walt Disney World relegated overnight the majority of Florida's headliner attractions to positions of comparative insignificance. Newer attractions such as Sea World and the vastly enlarged Busch Gardens strove successfully to achieve the new standard. Cypress Gardens, Weeki Wachi, and Silver Springs expanded and modernized. Most other attractions, however, slipped into a limbo of diminished status from which they never recovered. Far from being headliners or tourist destinations, they plugged along as local diversions, pulling in the curious, the bored, and the sunburned for two-hour excursions.

Many of the affected attractions were and are wonderful places to spend a vacation day, but even collectively, as has been sadly demonstrated, they do not command sufficient appeal to lure many tourists beyond the Wall. We recommend them, however, not only for their variety of high quality offerings, but as a glimpse of Florida's golden age, a time of less sophisticated, less plastic pleasures, before the Mouse. Take a day or two and drive three and one-half hours south of Orlando. Visit the Miami Seaquarium or Ocean World, try Vizcaya, Fairchild Tropical Gardens, and Lion Country Safari. Drive Collins Avenue along the Gold Coast. You'll be glad you did.

When EPCOT Center opened in Walt Disney World on October 1, 1982, another seismic shock reverberated through the Florida attractions industry. This time it was not only the smaller and more vulnerable attractions that were affected, but the newer large-scale attractions along the Orlando Wall. Suddenly, with EPCOT Center, Walt Disney World had swallowed up another one to two days of each tourist's vacation week. When the Magic Kingdom stood alone, most visitors had three or four days remaining to sample other attractions. With the addition of EPCOT Center, that available time was cut to one or two days.

Disney ensured its market share by creating the multi-day admission passes which allow unlimited access to both the Magic Kingdom and EPCOT Center. More cost-efficient than a one-day pass to a single park, these passes had the effect of keeping the guest on Disney turf for three to five days.

The Kennedy Space Center and Sea World, by virtue of their very specialized products, continued to prosper following the opening of EPCOT Center. Most other attractions, however, were forced to focus more of their energy on local markets. Some, like Busch Gardens, did very well, with increased local support replacing the decreased numbers of Walt Disney World destination tourists coming over for the day. Others, like Cypress Gardens, suffered badly but worked diligently to improve their product. Some, like Circus World and the Hall of Fame Wax Museum, passed into history.

Though long an innovator, Disney turned in the mid-80s to copying existing successful competitors, except that copying is not exactly the right word. What Disney did was to take a competitor's product concept, improve it, and reproduce it in Disney style on a grand scale.

The first competitor to feel the heat was Sea World when Disney added The Living Seas pavilion to the Future World section of EPCOT Center. Sea World, however, had killer whales, the Shark Encounter, and sufficient corporate resources to remain preeminent among marine exhibits. Still, many Walt Disney World patrons willingly substituted a visit to The Living Seas for a visit to Sea World.

Disney had one of its own products threatened when the Wet 'n Wild water theme park took a shot at the older, smaller, but more aesthetically pleasing River Country. Never one to take a challenge sitting down, Disney responded in 1989 with the opening of Typhoon Lagoon, the largest swimming theme park in the world.

Also in 1989 Disney opened Pleasure Island, a one-admission multi-nightclub entertainment complex patterned on Orlando's successful Church Street Station. In the several years Pleasure Island has been operating, it has robbed Church Street Station of much of its destination tourist traffic.

Finally, and most significant of all, in 1989 Walt Disney World opened the Disney-MGM Studios, a combination working motion picture and television production complex and theme park. Copying from the long-heralded Universal Studios tour in southern California, the Disney-MGM Studios were speeded into construction and operation after Universal had announced its plans for a central Florida park.

This newest of the Walt Disney World theme parks, however, affects much more than Universal's plans. With the opening of Disney-MGM, the 3-Day World Passport was discontinued. Instead, Disney patrons are offered either a single-day pass or the more economical multi-day passports, good for either four or five days. With the three theme parks on a multi-day pass, plus a water park (Typhoon Lagoon), several golf courses, various lakes, and a nighttime entertainment complex, Disney has effectively swallowed up the average family's entire vacation. Break away to Sea World or the Kennedy Space Center for the day? How about a day at the ocean (remember the ocean)? Fat chance.

With the opening of the Walt Disney World Swan and Dolphin hotels, and the Conference Center, Disney took a quantum leap toward monopolizing the business and convention traveler as well. With over 250,000 square feet of exhibit space, the Conference Center is one of the largest in the southeast. Disney has even discussed constructing a monorail to the airport so that visitors will not have to set a single foot in Orlando.

I regret the passing of an era in Florida tourism. The old attractions were more intimate, more personal, more human. The live alligators were more interesting (if less predictable) than the Disney robotic version, and I found I could stomach the pungent odor of a real cougar. Each modest attraction embodied the realization of some maverick's dream, a dream he longed to share with anyone who passed through the turnstile.

But dreams are only as grand as the men who create them, and only the truly visionary endure. Such was the dream of Walt Disney, come to fruition in Walt Disney World. Is his dream a cancer in the breast of tourism? Far from it. It is a testimony to careful planning, harboring of resources, precise timing, and adherence to a standard of quality unprecedented in the entertainment industry. Walt Disney World represents the delivery of a product that amazes and delights, that exceeds the expectations of almost every visitor.

From an entrepreneurial seed, a beloved cartoon mouse, and a California amusement park years ahead of its time has risen an entertainment giant, a giant that sometimes moves clumsily and sometimes with cold hard determination but always with a commitment to quality. Walt Disney World represents the kind of imagination, industry, and farsighted thinking that might have preserved American leadership in steel, automobiles, and electronics. Sure, we all like to see the little guy succeed, and most of us prefer a competitive marketplace. But if giants we must have, would that they all be like Walt Disney World.

Walt Disney World: An Overview

If you are selecting among the tourist attractions in Florida, the question is not whether to visit Walt Disney World but how to see the best of the various Disney offerings with some economy of time, effort, and finances.

Make no mistake, there is nothing on earth quite like Walt Disney World. Incredible in its scope, genius, beauty, and imagination, it is a joy and wonder for people of all ages. A fantasy, a dream, and a vision all rolled into one, it transcends simple entertainment, making us children and adventurers, freeing us for an hour or a day to live the dreams of our past, present, and future.

Certainly we are critics, but it is the responsibility of critics to credit that which is done well as surely as to reflect negatively on that which is done poorly. The Disney attractions are special, a quantum leap beyond and above any man-made entertainment offering we know of. We cannot understand how anyone could visit Florida and bypass Walt Disney World.

—— What Walt Disney World Encompasses ——

Walt Disney World encompasses forty-three square miles, an area twice the size of Manhattan Island. Situated strategically in this vast expanse are two major theme parks, a filmmaking studio and tour, the world's largest swimming theme park, a smaller swimming attraction, a botanical and zoological exhibit, a nightlife entertainment area, several golf courses, hotels, four large interconnected lakes, a shopping complex, a convention center, a permanent nature preserve, and a complete transportation system consisting of four-lane highways, an elevated monorail, and a system of canals.

Most tourists refer to the entire Florida Disney facility as Walt Disney World, or more simply, as Disney World. The Magic Kingdom, EPCOT Center, and Disney-MGM Studios are thought of as being "in" Disney World. Other visitors refer to the Magic Kingdom as

Disney World and EPCOT Center as EPCOT, and are not sure exactly how to label the entity as a whole. In our description we will refer to the total Disney facility as Walt Disney World according to popular tradition, and will consider the Magic Kingdom, EPCOT Center, and everything else that sits on that 43-square-mile chunk of real estate to be included in the overall designation.

— *The Major Theme Parks* —

The Magic Kingdom

The Magic Kingdom is what most people think of when they think of Walt Disney World. It is the collection of adventures, rides, and shows symbolized by the Disney cartoon characters and Cinderella Castle. Although the Magic Kingdom is only one element of the Disney attraction complex, it remains the heart of Disney World. The Magic Kingdom is divided into seven subareas or "lands," six of which are arranged around a central hub. First encountered is Main Street, U.S.A., which connects the Magic Kingdom entrance with the central hub. Moving clockwise around the hub, other lands are Adventureland, Frontierland, Liberty Square, Fantasyland, and Tomorrowland. Mickey's Starland, the first new land in the Magic Kingdom since the park opened, is situated along the Walt Disney Railroad on three acres between Fantasyland and Tomorrowland. Access is through Fantasyland or via the railroad. Main Street and the other six lands will be described in detail later. Three hotel complexes (the Contemporary Resort, Polynesian Resort, and Grand Floridian Beach Resort) are located close to the Magic Kingdom and are directly connected to it by monorail and by boat. A fourth hotel, the Disney Inn, is located nearby, but is not serviced by the monorail.

EPCOT Center

EPCOT (Experimental Prototype Community of Tomorrow) Center opened in October of 1982. Divided into two major areas, Future World and World Showcase, the park is twice the size of and is comparable in scope to the Magic Kingdom. Future World consists of a number of futuristic pavilions, each relating to a different theme concerning man's creativity and technological advancement. World Showcase, arranged around a 41-acre lagoon, presents the architectural, social, and cultural heritages of almost a dozen nations, with each country represented by famous landmarks and local settings familiar to world travelers. EPCOT Center is generally more educationally oriented than the Magic Kingdom and has been repeatedly characterized as a sort of permanent world's fair. Unlike the Magic Kingdom, which Disney spokesmen represent as being essentially complete, EPCOT Center is pictured as a continually changing and growing entity.

There are four EPCOT Center resort hotels: Disney's Beach Club, Disney's Yacht Club, the Walt Disney World Swan, and the Walt Disney World Dolphin. All are within a five- to fifteen-minute walk of the International Gateway entrance to the EPCOT Center theme park. The hotels are also linked to the park by canal and tram. EPCOT Center is connected to the Magic Kingdom and its resort hotels by monorail.

The Disney-MGM Studios

This $300 million, 100-plus-acre attraction, which opened in 1989, is divided into two areas. The first is a theme park relating to the past, present, and future of the motion picture and television industries. This section contains movie-theme rides and shows and covers about a third of the Disney-MGM complex. Highlights here include a re-creation of Hollywood Boulevard from the 20s and 30s, audience participation shows on TV production and sound effects, movie stunt demonstrations, the Star Tours ride, and The Great Movie Ride, which takes guests for a journey through the movies' greatest moments.

The second area, encompassing the remaining two-thirds, is a working motion picture and television production facility comprised of three sound stages, a back lot of streets and sets, and creative support services. Public access to this area is limited except for studio tours which take visitors behind the scenes for a crash-course on movie making, including (on occasion) the opportunity to witness the actual shooting of feature films and television shows.

The Disney-MGM Studios are connected to other Walt Disney World areas by highway and canal, but not by monorail. Guests can park in the Studios' own pay parking lot or commute by bus from EPCOT Center, the Transportation and Ticket Center, or from any Walt Disney World lodging. Patrons staying in the EPCOT Center resort hotels can also reach the Studios by boat.

—— *The Water Theme Parks* ——

There are two major swimming theme parks in Walt Disney World, Typhoon Lagoon and the older River Country. Typhoon Lagoon is the world's largest park of its kind and is distinguished by a wave pool capable of making six-foot waves. River Country, a pioneer among water theme parks, is much smaller but very well done. Since Typhoon Lagoon's opening in 1989, River Country has catered primarily to Walt Disney World campground and resort hotel guests. Both parks are beautifully arranged and landscaped, with great attention paid to atmosphere and aesthetics. Either park can be reached via private vehicle or the Walt Disney World bus system.

—— *The Minor Theme Parks* ——

Pleasure Island

Part of the Walt Disney World Village, Pleasure Island is a six-acre nighttime entertainment center where one cover charge will get a visitor into any of seven nightclubs. The clubs have different themes and feature a variety of shows and activities. Music ranges from pop-rock to country and western to jazz. For the more sedentary (or exhausted) there is a ten-screen movie complex, or for the hungry, several restaurants.

Discovery Island

Situated in Bay Lake close to the Magic Kingdom, Discovery Island is a tropically landscaped, small zoological park primarily featuring birdlife. Small intimate trails wind through the exotic foliage, contrasting with the broad thoroughfares of the major theme parks. Plants and trees are marked for easy identification and the island features an absolutely enormous walk-through aviary, so cleverly engineered that you are essentially unaware of the confining netting.

In the best traditions of Florida, small-attraction tourism, Discovery Island now offers three shows called "Animal Encounters." *Feathered Friends* features cockatoos and macaws in a variety of natural and not-so-natural behaviors. *Birds of Prey* showcases owls, hawks, vultures, and the like (mostly disabled birds that are convalescing at

Discovery Island). The third show, curiously called *Reptile Relations*, introduces guests to alligators, snakes, and other scaly species indigenous to Florida. Informative, interesting, and well presented, all of the "Animal Encounters" are staged in natural surroundings with few props. Seating is in the round on benches set out in the open, not unlike what you might expect at camp. There is little shade and audiences must generally endure whatever Mother Nature is meting out. Showtimes, four for each of the Encounters, are normally scheduled between 10:30 A.M. and 4 P.M., thus insuring that guests will be in the company of "mad dogs and Englishmen" as they sit through presentations during the hottest time of day.

A trip to Discovery Island is fairly pricey (about $8) for three shows, a few birds and animals, and a short stroll through the woods. As for children, they enjoy Discovery Island if allowed to explore on their own, but become bored and restless touring under the thumb of their elders. One deal for seeing Discovery Island is to buy a River Country/Discovery Island combination ticket (about $22). But of course it's only a good deal if you plan to go to both minor parks anyway. Probably the best deal for those spending four days or more at Walt Disney World is the 5-Day Super Duper Pass that in addition to providing admission to the three major parks also provides unlimited admission to Typhoon Lagoon, River Country, Pleasure Island, Discovery Island, and Disney's Boardwalk. Do not spring for the Super Duper Pass, however, unless you intend to take advantage of its features.

There are no lodging accommodations on Discovery Island, but food is available. Access is exclusively by boat from the main Bay Lake docks (Magic Kingdom Dock, Fort Wilderness Landing, Resort Hotels' docks). Boats run about every 15–20 minutes. Dock to dock, it takes about 12 minutes in the boat to cover the distance from the Magic Kingdom to Discovery Island. While you could spend up to three hours on Discovery Island, most folks are ready to split in an hour or two.

Disney's Boardwalk (Expected to open in 1995)

Located along a walkway connecting the Swan hotel with EPCOT Center's International Gateway, Disney's Boardwalk will be an amusement park in the style of Atlantic City and Coney Island. Game arcades, rides, music, food, and bright lights will render a Disney-clean version of America's traditional amusement park. Guests at the Swan or Dolphin hotels, or at Disney's Yacht and Beach Club Resorts, will be able to walk to Disney's Boardwalk. EPCOT Center guests can access Disney's Boardwalk on foot via the International Gateway between France and the United Kingdom in the World Showcase. Others can reach the boardwalk by private automobile or Disney bus service.

—— *Should I Go to Walt Disney World If I've Been to Disneyland in California?* ——

Walt Disney World is a much larger and more varied entertainment complex than is Disneyland. There is no EPCOT Center, Disney-MGM Studios, or Typhoon Lagoon at Disneyland. To be specific, Disneyland is roughly comparable to the Magic Kingdom theme park at Walt Disney World in Florida. Both the Magic Kingdom and Disneyland are arranged by "lands" accessible from a central hub and connected to the entrance by a Main Street. Both parks feature many rides and attractions of the same name: Space Mountain, Jungle Cruise, Pirates of the Caribbean, It's a Small World, and Dumbo, the Flying Elephant, to name a few. Interestingly, however, the same name does not necessarily connote the same experience. Pirates of the Caribbean at Disneyland is much longer and more elaborate than its Walt Disney World counterpart. Space Mountain is somewhat wilder in Florida, and Dumbo is about the same in both places.

Disneyland is more intimate than the Magic Kingdom since it doesn't have the room for expansion enjoyed by the Florida park. Pedestrian thoroughfares are more narrow, and everything from Big Thunder Mountain to the Castle is scaled down somewhat. Large crowds are less taxing at the Magic Kingdom since there is more room for them to disperse.

At Disneyland, however, there are dozens of little surprises: small unheralded attractions tucked away in crooks and corners of the park, which give Disneyland a special charm and variety that the Magic Kingdom lacks. And, of course, Disneyland has more of the stamp of Walt Disney's personal touch.

For additional information on Disneyland, see *The Unofficial Guide to Disneyland*, by Bob Sehlinger, Prentice Hall Travel.

To allow for a meaningful comparison, we provide a summary of those features found only at one of the parks, followed by a critical look at the attractions found at both.

Attractions Found Only at the Magic Kingdom

Liberty Square:	*The Hall Of Presidents*
Tomorrowland:	Dreamflight
	Mission to Mars
	Carousel Of Progress

Attractions Found Only at Disneyland

Main Street:	*Great Moments With Mr. Lincoln*
	The Walt Disney Story
Frontierland:	Sailing Ship Columbia
	Big Thunder Ranch
Fantasyland:	Pinocchio's Daring Journey
	Casey Jr. Circus Train
	Storybook Land Canal Boats
	Alice in Wonderland
	Matterhorn Bobsleds
Tomorrowland:	Star Tours (also at Disney-MGM Studios)
New Orleans Square:	The Disney Gallery
Mickey's Toontown:	Minnie's House
	Goofy's Bounce House
	Miss Daisy, Donald Duck's Boat
	Gadget's Go-Coaster
	Chip 'N Dale's Treehouse and Acorn Ball Crawl
	Jolly Trolley

Critical Comparison of Attractions Found at Both Parks

Main Street

WDW/Disneyland Railroad	The Disneyland Railroad is far more entertaining by virtue of the Grand Canyon Diorama and the Primeval World components not found at the Magic Kingdom.

Adventureland

Jungle Cruise	More realistic AudioAnimatronic (robotic) animals at Walt Disney World, otherwise about the same.
Enchanted Tiki Birds	About the same at both parks.
Swiss Family Treehouse	Larger at the Magic Kingdom.

New Orleans Square

Pirates of the Caribbean	Far superior at Disneyland.
The Haunted Mansion	Slight edge to the Magic Kingdom version.

Critter Country

Country Bear Jamboree	Same production with much less of a wait at Disneyland.
Splash Mountain	Storyline easier to follow at the Magic Kingdom.

Frontierland

Various river cruises (Canoes, steamboats, keelboats, etc.)	Slight edge to the Magic Kingdom in terms of the sights.
Tom Sawyer Island	Comparable, but a little more elaborate with better food service at the Magic Kingdom.
Big Thunder Mountain Railroad	Ride about the same. Sights and special effects better at the Magic Kingdom.
Golden Horseshoe Jamboree/Diamond Horseshoe Jamboree	Similar at both parks.

Fantasyland

Snow White's Adventures	About the same at both parks.
Peter Pan's Flight	Better at Disneyland.
Mr. Toad's Wild Ride	About the same at both parks.
Dumbo, the Flying Elephant	Newer version at Disneyland.
Carousels	About the same at both parks.

Castles	Far larger and more beautiful at the Magic Kingdom.
Mad Tea Party	The same at both parks.
It's a Small World	About the same at both parks.
Skyway	About the same at both parks.

Tomorrowland

Autopia/Grand Prix Raceway	About the same at both parks.
Rocket Jets/StarJets	The same at both parks.
PeopleMover	Edge goes to the Disneyland version.
World Premier Circle-Vision	The same at both parks.
Space Mountain	Vastly superior in terms of special effects at the Magic Kingdom.
Submarine Voyage/ 20,000 Leagues Under the Sea	About the same at both parks.

Walt Disney World Summary

P.O. Box 1000, Lake Buena Vista, FL 32830-1000
Call ahead for opening/closing times   Phone: (407) 824-4321

Admissions

Ticket options	Discounts	
One-Park/One-Day Ticket	Children (3–9)	**yes**
4-Day Super Pass	Children under 3	**free**
4-Day Super Duper Pass	Students	**varies**
5-Day Super Duper Pass	Military	**varies**
Be Our Guest Pass	Senior citizens	**varies**
Annual Passport	Group rates	**yes**
Florida Four-Season Pass		

Credit cards accepted for admission: **MasterCard, American Express**, and **VISA**.
Features included: **All except game arcades**

Overall Appeal*

By age groups	Preschool	Grade School	Teens	Young Adults	Over 30	Senior Citizens
	★★★★★	★★★★★	★★★★★	★★★★★	★★★★★	★★★★★

Touring Tips

Touring time	Periods of lightest attendance
Average: **Full day per park**	Time of day: **Early morning**
Minimum: **Full day per park**	Days: **Friday, Sunday**
Touring strategy: **See narrative**	Times of year: **After Thanksgiving**
Rainy day touring: **Recommended**	**until 18th of December**

What the Critics Say

Rating of major features:
(begins on p. 208)

Rating of functional and operational areas

Parking	★★★★★
Rest rooms	★★★★★
Resting places	★★★★★
Crowd management	★★★★★
Aesthetic appeal of grounds	★★★★★
Cleanliness/maintenance	★★★★★

Services and Facilities

Restaurant/snack bar **Yes**	Lockers **Yes**
Vending machines (food/pop) **No**	Pet kennels **Yes**
Handicapped access **Yes**	Gift shops **Yes**
Wheelchairs **Rental**	Film sales **Yes**
Baby strollers **Rental**	Rain check **No**
	Private guided group tours **Yes**

*Critical ratings are based on a scale of zero to five stars with five stars being the best possible rating.

PART ONE: Planning
Before You Leave Home

Gathering Information

In addition to this guide, information concerning Walt Disney World can be obtained at the public library and at travel agencies, or by calling or writing any of the following:

Important Walt Disney World Telephone Numbers

General Information	(407) 824-4321
Accommodations/Reservations	(407) 934-7639
	or (407) 824-8000
Beach Club Resort	(407) 934-8000
Caribbean Beach Resort	(407) 934-3400
Contemporary Resort	(407) 824-1000
Convention Information	(407) 828-3200
Dining Reservations for Walt Disney World Lodging Guests	
Dining Information	(407) 824-4500
If calling from:	
Home	(407) 824-4500
WDW guest room	Dial 55 for same day
	Dial 56 for 1–3 day advance
WDW campground	Dial 44 for same day
	Dial 45 for 1–3 day advance
Discovery Island Information	(407) 824-2760
Disney Car Care Center	(407) 824-4813
The Disney Inn	(407) 824-2200
Disney's Ocala Information Center	(904) 854-0770
Disney Vacation Club Resort	(407) 827-7700
Disney's Village Resort	(407) 827-1100
Disney Village Marketplace	(407) 828-3800
Dixie Landings Resort	(407) 934-6000
Educational Programs	(407) 354-1855

Fishing Reservations & Information	(407) 824-2757
Fort Wilderness Campground	(407) 824-2900
Grand Floridian Beach Resort	(407) 824-3000
Guided Tour Information	(407) 824-4321
Horseback Tours Reservations	(407) 824-2832
Learning Programs	
Information	(407) 824-7997
Registration	(407) 354-1855
Lost and Found for articles lost:	
Yesterday or before (All parks)	(407) 824-4245
Today at Magic Kingdom	(407) 824-4521
Today at EPCOT Center	(407) 560-6105
Today at Disney-MGM	(407) 560-4668
Medical Care in WDW	(407) 648-9234
Merchandise Mail Order	(407) 363-6200
Movie Information	
AMC Pleasure Island	(407) 827-1300
Disney films at hotels	(407) 824-4321
Pleasure Island Information	(407) 934-7781
Polynesian Resort	(407) 824-2000
Port Orleans Resort	(407) 934-5000
Resort Dining and Recreational Information	(407) 824-4500
River Country Information	(407) 824-2760
Tee Times and Golf Studio	(407) 824-2270
Telecommunication for the Deaf	(407) 827-5141
Tennis Reservations/Lessons	(407) 824-3578
Typhoon Lagoon Information	(407) 560-4141
Walt Disney Travel Company	(407) 828-3255
Walt Disney World Dolphin	(407) 934-4000
Walt Disney World Swan	(407) 934-3000
Yacht Club Resort	(407) 934-7000

Important Walt Disney World Addresses

Walt Disney World Information
P.O. Box 10040
Lake Buena Vista, FL 32830-0040

Walt Disney World Central Reservations
P.O. Box 10100
Lake Buena Vista, FL 32830-0100

Convention and Banquet Information
P.O. Box 10000
Lake Buena Vista, FL 32830-1000

Walt Disney World Educational Programs
Wonders of Walt Disney World (Ages 10–15)
The Disney Learning Adventure (Adults)
P.O. Box 10000
Lake Buena Vista, FL 32830-1000

Merchandise Mail Order
P.O. Box 10070
Lake Buena Vista, FL 32830-0070

Walt Disney World Ticket Mail Order
P.O. Box 10030
Lake Buena Vista, FL 32830-0030

Timing Your Visit

── Trying to Reason with the Tourist Season ──

It is one of the objectives of this book to assist the tourist, when possible, in avoiding crowds. It is useful therefore to understand the overall seasonality and traffic flow of Florida tourism.

Peninsular Florida (all of Florida except the Panhandle) has two peak seasons. One begins just before Christmas and ends just after Easter and is referred to as the "Winter Season" or sometimes just "the Season." The other, known as the "Summer Season" or "Family Season," gets into swing about the middle of June and lasts until late August.

Christmas Week, which effectively kicks off the Winter Season, is Florida's busiest week of the year, with facilities throughout the state (including attractions) being pushed to their limit. Many attractions offer special programs beginning several days prior to Christmas and extending through New Year's Day. Crowds, however, are awesome, with many smaller attractions inundated and long waits in line the norm at larger attractions. Because of the crowded conditions, we do not recommend Christmas Week for attraction touring. If, however, your schedule permits arriving the preceding week (say December 15th or thereabouts) crowds are manageable and sometimes even sparse. Get your touring in by the 22nd and then relax and enjoy the beach over Christmas.

Though the mammoth throngs of Christmas Week dissipate following New Year's Day, the Winter Season remains in full session with heavy attraction attendance through Easter. Easter Week is almost as congested as Christmas Week. During the Winter Season a high concentration of tourists is a fact of life.

The period between Easter and the beginning of the Summer Season in early June is usually slow and is a particularly good time for attraction touring. Activity picks up again toward the middle of June with the arrival of the family vacation traffic. This second season runs through late August when the kids return to school.

Attendance at individual attractions varies, with some attractions more popular with the Winter Season tourist and others more popular with the Summer Season tourist. This is attributable in part to the relatively small number of school-age children present during Winter Season.

September through mid-December is very slow throughout Florida except for the Thanksgiving holiday period. Our research team felt that the nicest time to visit Florida in terms of weather, low-stress touring, and crowd avoidance was the first two weeks in December, just prior to the Christmas crunch.

Holiday weekends throughout the year, as well as special events (Florida Derby, spacecraft launchings, auto races, local festivals, etc.) precipitate heavy attraction attendance in and out of season. On days immediately preceding or following the holiday periods, however, attendance is often extremely light.

The best weather in Florida usually occurs between late fall and mid-April, which coincides, of course, with the busy Winter Season. Attraction touring is pleasant throughout the day, though mornings and late afternoons are best for crowd avoidance during this time of the year.

During the warmer months of the Summer Season, comfort as well as crowd avoidance suggest early day touring.

Rainy days in both the Summer and Winter Seasons often afford excellent opportunities for beating the crowd. Many outdoor attractions offer good protection from the elements and are as enjoyable on a rainy day as on a sunny day. Indoor attractions see their heaviest attendance on rainy days. Here we recommend touring on sunny days during the very hot midday hours (11:30 A.M.–2:30 P.M.).

Off-season (mid-April through early June and September through mid-December) touring is characterized by smaller crowds and by somewhat rainier weather, and is generally an excellent time to visit the state's premier, large-scale attractions. However, since attendance is lightest at these times it is not uncommon for certain major rides, shows, and exhibits to be closed for maintenance or revision. A phone call to the attraction under consideration will obtain information concerning which, if any, key features will be out of action during your intended visit.

The Florida Panhandle has a somewhat abridged Winter Season centered around Christmas and New Year's Day then followed by somewhat of a lull until March and April. The big season for the Panhandle is the Summer Season.

— *Florida Traffic Patterns* —

Attraction touring takes place both while traveling en route and at the tourist's vacation destination. Southern Florida is a destination area; tourists, upon arrival, visit local attractions as a supplement to their vacation itinerary. The Orlando area is both a vacation destination and an en route center of tourism. Many visitors spend their entire vacation in the Orlando area while others visit en route to or from southern Florida. Ocala by contrast is largely an en route center of tourism with most tourists stopping on their way to or from other destinations.

Since most tourists do their traveling to and from their vacation destination on weekends, it is possible to identify patterns of traffic which are useful in avoiding crowds. As an example, a Tennessee family whose primary destination is Walt Disney World may tour Silver Springs at Ocala en route. Departing Tennessee on Friday evening or Saturday morning places them at Silver Springs on Sunday, arriving in the Orlando area on Sunday evening. Since this is a very common itinerary, executed by thousands of tourists every week, a traffic pattern becomes discernible. Silver Springs will show its heaviest attendance on weekends. Walt Disney World, as a destination, will show large crowds on Monday, Tuesday, and Wednesday. Sea World, and other Orlando area attractions will see heavier attendance from Wednesday through Friday when visitors, such as our Tennessee family, have finished seeing Walt Disney World and begin to explore other attractions nearby.

Because of the extended driving distance, the average length of stay in Florida is greater for most tourists whose ultimate destination is southern Florida. An Ohio couple departing Columbus on Friday evening might typically tour St. Augustine or Marineland on Sunday and then proceed directly to their Fort Lauderdale destination or stop again for a day or two to tour Orlando area attractions. This itinerary places the couple at their Fort Lauderdale destination sometime late Monday, Tuesday, or Wednesday. Thus in southern Florida, attraction attendance is heaviest toward the end of the week and, as noted above, since visitors to southern Florida stay longer on the average, attendance remains heavy on weekends.

Thus, by understanding the more common patterns of arrival, departure, en route touring, and destination touring, it is possible to plan an

Visitation patterns of specific centers of Florida tourism

Area	Tourism Classification	Heaviest Attendance	When to Go
Panhandle	Destination	Weekends	Weekdays
St. Augustine, Marineland	En route	Weekends	Weekdays
Ocala	En route	Weekends	Weekdays
Weeki Wachee, Homosassa Springs	En route	Weekends	Weekdays
Orlando, Kissimmee, Cape Canaveral	En route, destination	Monday through Thursday	Friday through Sunday
Tampa	En route, day trip from Orlando and from beaches	Thursday through Sunday	Monday through Wednesday
Clearwater, St. Petersburg	Destination	Winter: Sunday through Tuesday	Wednesday through Saturday
		Summer: Friday through Sunday	Monday through Thursday
Sarasota	En route, destination, day trip from beaches to the north	Varies	Varies
Naples, Bonita Springs	Destination	Varies	Varies
Southern Florida, East Coast	Destination	Thursday through Sunday	Monday through Wednesday
Keys, Key West	Destination, day trip from beaches to the north	Weekdays	Weekends

attraction visitation itinerary which operates counter to the usual traffic flow and places the tourist at each chosen attraction on a day of lighter attendance.

Displayed here in summary form is a guide to the visitation patterns of specific centers of Florida tourism. Note that light and heavy attendance are relative terms, with light attendance in season possibly exceeding heaviest attendance out of season. Also remember that traffic patterns described are based on the norm, and that a specific day, according to the law of averages, will probably but not necessarily approximate the norm.

—— When to Go to Walt Disney World ——

Selecting the Time of Year for Your Visit

Walt Disney World is busiest of all Christmas Day through New Year's Day. Thanksgiving weekend, the week of Washington's Birthday, spring break for colleges, and the two weeks around Easter are also extremely busy. To give you some idea of what busy means at Walt Disney World, up to 92,000 people have toured the Magic Kingdom alone on a single day! While this level of attendance is far from typical, the possibility of its occurrence should forewarn all but the ignorant and the foolish from challenging this mega-attraction at its busiest periods.

The least busy time of all is from after the Thanksgiving weekend until the week before Christmas. The next slowest times are September through the weekend preceding Thanksgiving, January 4th through the first half of February, and the week following Easter through early June. At the risk of being blasphemous, our research team was so impressed with the relative ease of touring in the fall and other "off" periods that we would rather take our children out of school for a week than do battle with the summer crowds.

Though we strongly recommend going to Walt Disney World in the fall or spring, it should be noted that there are certain trade offs. The parks often close earlier on fall and spring days, sometimes early enough to eliminate evening parades and other live entertainment offerings. Also, because these are slow times of the year at Walt Disney World, you can anticipate that some rides and attractions may be closed for maintenance or renovation. Finally, you should know that central

Annual Attendance Patterns at Walt Disney World

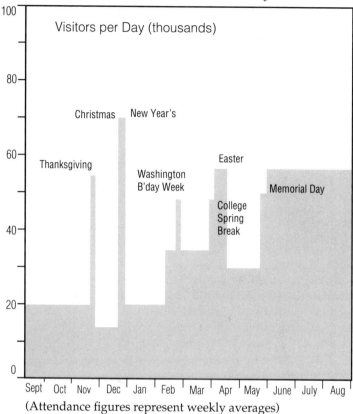

(Attendance figures represent weekly averages)

Florida temperatures fluctuate wildly during the late fall, winter, and early spring; daytime lows in the 40's are not uncommon.

Given the choice, however, we would never go to Walt Disney World in the summer or during a holiday period. To us, small crowds, bargain prices, and stress-free touring are well worth risking a little cold weather or a couple of closed attractions.

Most readers who have tried Walt Disney World at varying times of year agree. A gentleman from Ottawa, Ontario, who toured in early December wrote:

> It was the most enjoyable trip [to Walt Disney World] I have ever had, and I can't imagine going [back] to Disney World

Walt Disney World Weather

	Average Daily Low	Average Daily High	Average Daily Temperature	Avg. Daily Humidity (%)	Avg. Rainfall per Month (inches)	No. Days of Rain per Month
January	49°	72°	61°	74	2.1	6
February	50°	73°	62°	71	2.8	7
March	55°	78°	67°	71	3.2	8
April	60°	84°	72°	69	2.2	6
May	66°	88°	77°	72	3.9	9
June	71°	91°	81°	77	7.4	14
July	73°	92°	82°	79	7.8	17
August	73°	92°	82°	80	6.3	16
September	73°	90°	81°	80	5.6	14
October	65°	84°	75°	77	2.8	9
November	57°	78°	68°	76	1.8	6
December	51°	73°	62°	76	1.9	6

Hurricane Season

when it is crowded. Even without the crowds we were still very tired by afternoon. Fighting crowds certainly would have made a hellish trip. We will never go again at any other time.

Selecting the Day of the Week for Your Visit

Selecting the best day of the week to visit a specific Walt Disney World theme park requires analysis of several variables. Entering into the equation are: (1) The time of year of your visit (holiday, summer, or off-season); (2) Attendance patterns for each day of the week at the respective parks; (3) Whether you are staying in a Walt Disney World hotel or campground (thereby making yourself eligible for early entry to the Magic Kingdom on specified days of the week); and (4) The traveling habits of people coming to Walt Disney World from outside of Florida.

A typical vacation scenario during the summer would be for a family to arrive in the Orlando area on Sunday, visit the Magic Kingdom and EPCOT Center on Monday and Tuesday, visit Disney-MGM Studios on Wednesday, and go to Typhoon Lagoon or a non-Disney area attraction on Thursday. Friday is often reserved for heading home or to another Florida destination. If this was all we had to consider, we could recommend Fridays and Sundays as the best days all year long to avoid crowded conditions at the theme parks.

During the off-season, however, the Disney people initiate dozens of special promotions to attract the local population to Walt Disney World. Because these folks are not on vacation, they tend to visit the theme parks on the weekend. During the fall, late winter, and spring, you might encounter larger crowds on a weekend than on a weekday.

The most significant shift in daily attendance patterns is the result of an early entry program for guests staying at Walt Disney World resort hotels and campgrounds (but not for guests at Disney Village Hotels). Four days a week (usually on Tuesdays, Thursdays, Saturdays, and Sundays) Disney World lodging guests are invited to enter the Magic Kingdom one hour before the general public is admitted. During this hour, the early entrants can enjoy all the attractions in Fantasyland, as well as Space Mountain and the Grand Prix Raceway in Tomorrowland.

The effect of the early entry program on attendance is pronounced at all three of the major theme parks, especially during the busier times of the year. On days when early entry is offered, a vast number of Walt Disney World lodging guests, not unexpectedly, tour the Magic Kingdom. This means that the Magic Kingdom will be more crowded than usual on those days, and that EPCOT Center and the Disney-MGM Studios will be less crowded (because most of the Walt Disney World lodging guests will be at the Magic Kingdom). By the same token, you can expect EPCOT Center and the Disney-MGM Studios to be more crowded on days when there is no early entry at the Magic Kingdom.

If you lodge at a Walt Disney World hotel or campground, you definitely want to take advantage of the early entry program by visiting the Magic Kingdom on a day when the program is in effect. Conversely, if you are staying outside of Walt Disney World (and therefore not eligible for early entry privileges), you want to avoid the Magic Kingdom on Tuesday, Thursday, Saturday, and Sunday, using these days to visit the other theme parks. During less crowded times of the year when attendance is lower, the early entry program will not seriously impact traffic patterns in the major theme parks. During holiday periods and the summer, however, when the Disney hotels are full, the early entry program makes a tremendous difference in the crowd at each of the parks.

Because the Disney people are always changing things, we suggest you call Walt Disney World Information at (407) 824-4321 before you leave home to verify which days of the week will be early entry days during your stay.

Assuming the early entry days do not change, we recommend the following:

For Walt Disney World hotel and campground guests (with early entry privileges to the Magic Kingdom):

Best Days To Visit	Summer		Other Times of Year	
Magic Kingdom	1	Sunday	1	Thursday
	2	Thursday	2	Tuesday
	3	Saturday	3	Sunday
	4	Friday	4	Friday
	5	Tuesday	5	Saturday
	6	Wednesday	6	Wednesday
	7	Monday	7	Monday

Best Days To Visit	Summer		Other Times of Year	
EPCOT Center	1	Sunday	1	Thursday
	2	Thursday	2	Friday
	3	Friday	3	Tuesday
	4	Saturday	4	Sunday
	5	Tuesday	5	Monday
	6	Monday	6	Saturday
	7	Wednesday	7	Wednesday
Disney-MGM Studios	1	Saturday	1	Friday
	2	Sunday	2	Tuesday
	3	Monday	3	Monday
	4	Friday	4	Thursday
	5	Tuesday	5	Sunday
	6	Thursday	6	Wednesday
	7	Wednesday	7	Saturday

For guests staying outside Walt Disney World (without early entry privileges to the Magic Kingdom):

Best Days To Visit	Summer		Other Times of Year	
Magic Kingdom	1	Friday	1	Friday
	2	Monday	2	Wednesday
	3	Wednesday	3	Monday
	4	Sunday	4	Sunday
	5	Saturday	5	Saturday
	6	Thursday	6	Thursday
	7	Tuesday	7	Tuesday
EPCOT Center	1	Sunday	1	Thursday
	2	Thursday	2	Friday
	3	Saturday	3	Tuesday
	4	Friday	4	Sunday
	5	Tuesday	5	Monday
	6	Monday	6	Saturday
	7	Wednesday	7	Wednesday

Best Days To Visit	Summer		Other Times of Year	
Disney-MGM Studios	1	Saturday	1	Friday
	2	Sunday	2	Tuesday
	3	Friday	3	Monday
	4	Tuesday	4	Thursday
	5	Monday	5	Sunday
	6	Thursday	6	Wednesday
	7	Wednesday	7	Saturday

If you visit Walt Disney World over a major holiday period, you can expect huge crowds at each of the parks every day. If you have early entry privileges to the Magic Kingdom (or, as is occasionally in effect, to the other parks), use them. You will need all the help you can get. If you are not accorded early entry privileges, avoid the Magic Kingdom on the days when early entry is in effect. During longer holidays like Easter and Christmas, crowds build almost exponentially as the big day approaches, culminating on the holiday itself.

If Disney changes the early entry days and you have to puzzle this out on your own, remember the following:

1. Weekend days (Friday, Saturday, Sunday) will always be less crowded than weekdays during the summer (except on holiday weekends).

2. Weekends often tend to be more crowded during the off-season, particularly in the spring and fall when the weather is nice. For the most part, however, off-season weekends cannot compare (in terms of crowd levels) to weekdays or weekends during the summer or holiday periods.

3. All days, but particularly weekend days, are crowded during Thanksgiving, Christmas and New Years, and Easter. Also expect huge crowds over three-day weekends for national holidays.

4. Disney lodging guests should always take advantage of early entry privileges.

5. Those of you staying outside of Walt Disney World must balance the least crowded days of the week (for the time of year of your visit) with an estimation of the impact of early entry. As a rule of thumb, off-property guests should not visit the Magic Kingdom on early entry days. It is far better to arrive early on busy non-early-entry days and

stay ahead of a big crowd than to enter the Magic Kingdom on a slower day when thousands of Disney lodging guests have been allowed into the park ahead of you. The ultimate key to efficient touring in any of the parks is to be one of the first guests through the turnstiles.

—— *Operating Hours* ——

It cannot be said that the Disney folks are not flexible when it comes to hours of operation for the parks. They run a dozen or more different operating schedules during the year, making it advisable to call (407) 824-4321 for the **exact** hours of operation the day before you arrive.

—— *Official Opening Time vs.* *Real Opening Time* —— ·

The hours of operation that the Disney folks will give you when you call are "official hours." In actuality the park will open earlier. If the official hours of operation are 9 A.M.–9 P.M., for example, the Main Street section of the Magic Kingdom will open at 8 or 8:30 A.M. and the remainder of the park will open at 8:30 or 9 A.M. If the official opening time for the Magic Kingdom is 8 A.M. and you are eligible for early entry, you will actually be able to enter the park at 6:30 A.M.

Many visitors, relying upon the accuracy of the information disseminated by Disney Guest Relations, arrive at the stated opening time to find the park packed with people. Once again, if you visit the Magic Kingdom on an early entry day and enter the park when the general public is admitted, you will always find the park swarming with Walt Disney World lodging guests.

The Disney folks publish their hours of operation well in advance, but allow themselves the flexibility to react to gate conditions on a day-by-day basis. Based on a survey of local hotel reservations, Disney traffic controllers estimate how many visitors to expect on a given day. To avoid bottlenecks at the parking facilities and ticket windows, the theme parks frequently open early, absorbing the crowds as they arrive.

We recommend arriving 50 minutes before the official opening time at EPCOT Center, the Disney-MGM Studios, or the Magic Kingdom regardless of the time of year of your visit. If you happen to go on a major holiday, arrive an hour and twenty minutes in advance of the official opening time.

At the end of the day, the Disney people usually shut down all rides and attractions at approximately the official closing time. Main Street in the Magic Kingdom remains open a half hour to an hour after the rest of the park has closed.

—— Packed Park Compensation Plan ——

The thought of teeming, jostling throngs jockeying for position in endless lines under the baking Fourth of July sun is enough to wilt the will and ears of the most ardent Mouseketeer. Why would anyone go to Walt Disney World during a major holiday period? Indeed, if you have never been to Walt Disney World, and you thought you would just drop in for a few rides and a little look-see on such a day, you might be better off shooting yourself in the foot. The Disney folks, however, being Disney folks, feel kind of bad about those long, long lines and the basically impossible touring conditions on packed days and compensate their patrons with a no-less-than-incredible array of first-rate live entertainment and happenings.

Throughout the day the party goes on with shows, parades, concerts, and pageantry. In the evening, particularly, there is so much going on that you have to make some tough choices. There are concerts, parades, light shows, laser shows, fireworks, and dance occurring almost continually in all parks. No question about it, you can go to Walt Disney World on the Fourth of July (or on any other extended hours, crowded day), never get on a ride, and still get your money's worth five times over. Admittedly, it's not the ideal situation for a first-timer who really wants to see the theme parks, but for anyone else it's one heck of a good party.

If you decide to go on one of the parks' "big" days, we suggest that you arrive an hour and twenty minutes before the stated opening time. Use the Walt Disney World One-Day Touring Plan of your choice until about 1 P.M. and then take the Monorail to the Walt Disney World resort hotels for lunch and relaxation. Local Floridians visiting Walt Disney World on holidays often chip in and rent a room for the group (make reservations well in advance) in one of the Walt Disney World hotels, thus affording a place to meet, relax, have a drink, or change clothes prior to swimming. A comparable arrangement can be made at other nearby hotels as long as they furnish a shuttle service to and from the parks. After an early dinner, return to the park of your choice for the evening's festivities, which get cranked up about 8 P.M.

A Word About Lodging

While this guide is not about lodging, we have found lodging to be a primary concern of those visiting Walt Disney World. In general, the Magic Kingdom resort hotels and EPCOT Center resort hotels are the most expensive, while rooms at other Walt Disney World hotel properties run slightly less. The least expensive lodging is located outside of Walt Disney World. Also out of the World, however, are some of the area's most luxurious hotels.

In addition to proximity and a certain number of guest privileges, there is special magic and peace of mind associated with staying inside Walt Disney World. "I feel more a part of everything and less like a visitor," is the way one guest described it.

There is no real hardship, however, in staying outside Walt Disney World and driving (or taking the often available hotel shuttle) to the theme parks for your visit. Meals can be had less expensively, too, and there is this indirect benefit: rooming outside "The World" puts you in a more receptive mood toward other Orlando area attractions and eating establishments. Universal Studios Florida, the Kennedy Space Center, Sea World, and Cypress Gardens, among others, are well worth your attention.

Prices for accommodations are subject to change, but our research team lodged in an excellent (though not plush) motel surrounded by beautiful orange groves for one third the cost of staying in the least expensive Walt Disney World hotel. Our commuting time was 17 minutes one way to the Magic Kingdom or EPCOT Center parking lots.

Guest rooms are not all that is expensive at Walt Disney World hotels. Any traveler who makes a lot of phone calls should know that the Walt Disney World hotels charge 75¢ for local calls and tack on a hefty 50% surcharge to all credit card and direct-dial long distance calls.

—— *Staying in the World* ——

The specific privileges and amenities of staying in a Walt Disney World lodging property (listed below) are these:

1. Vastly decreased commuting time made possible by easy access to the Walt Disney World bus, boat, and monorail transportation system. This is especially advantageous if you stay in one of the hotels connected by the monorail or by the lake/canal system (boat service).

2. Preferential treatment in making advance reservations to the *Hoop Dee Doo Revue* and other Walt Disney World dinner shows.

3. The privilege of making lunch and dinner reservations over the phone, one to three days in advance, at EPCOT Center, Disney-MGM Studios, and Magic Kingdom full-service restaurants.

4. Various kinds of preferential treatment at the theme parks. Walt Disney World lodging guests (excluding guests at the independent hotels of the Walt Disney World Village) are invited to enter the Magic Kingdom one hour earlier than the general public on Tuesday, Thursday, Saturday, and Sunday, and sometimes are allowed into the Disney-MGM Studios ahead of other guests. Occasionally Walt Disney World lodging guests are offered special deals on admission, for instance, a passport good for the exact number of days of your visit (a minimum of four) or discounted admission to the water theme parks. These benefits and extras are subject to change without notice and are generally put in effect for a limited time and for a specific purpose, such as promoting a new Walt Disney World theme park or attraction. The Magic Kingdom early entry program, however, is now in its third year.

5. A number of alternatives for baby-sitting, childcare, and special children's programs. Each of the resort hotels connected by the monorail, as well as several other Disney hotels, offers "clubs," or themed childcare centers where potty-trained children, 3 to 12 years, can be left while the adults go out. Also available are the Fairy Godmother and Kinder-Care in-room baby-sitting services (see pages 172–73).

6. Only Walt Disney World resort guests may leave pets overnight in the kennels.

7. On days of particularly heavy attendance, Walt Disney World resort guests are guaranteed admission to the theme parks.

8. There is no extra charge per night for children under 18 sharing a room with their parents.

9. Walt Disney World resort guests with cars do not have to pay for parking in the theme park lots.

10. Walt Disney World resort guests are accorded preferential treatment for tee times at the golf courses.

All Things Considered

1. Ease of Access. Even if you stay in Walt Disney World you are dependent on some mode of transportation. Hotels on the monorail line cut time commuting to the Magic Kingdom, but that's all. You must take a bus everywhere else. The EPCOT resorts provide easy access to EPCOT Center, but only through the International Gateway, located at the opposite end of the park from where you need to initiate your touring. The EPCOT resorts also provide boat service to the Disney-MGM Studios. All other Disney World lodging properties depend on bus service. It may be less stressful to use the Disney transportation system, but with the single exception of commuting from the monorail-linked hotels to the Magic Kingdom, the fastest, most efficient, and most flexible way to get around is usually a car. If you have been touring EPCOT Center, for example, and want to take the kids back to Disney's Grand Floridian Beach Resort for a nap, forget the monorail. You'll get back much faster if you have your own car.

A reader from Raynham, Massachusetts, who stayed at the Caribbean Beach Resort (and liked it very much) described her transportation experience:

> Even though the resort is on the Disney bus line, I recommend renting a car if it [fits] one's budget. The buses do not go directly to many destinations and often you have to switch at the Transportation and Ticket Center. Getting a [bus] seat in the morning is no problem [because] they allow standees. Getting a bus back to the hotel after a hard day can mean a long wait in line.

To present a complete picture, it must be said that the Disney transportation system, particularly the bus system, is about as efficient as humanly possible. No matter where you are going, you will never have to wait more than 15 minutes for a bus, monorail, or boat. While only for the use and benefit of Disney guests, it *is* nonetheless public transportation, with "public" as the operative word. In other words, you are relegated to accepting the inconveniences inherent in any transportation system: conveyances that arrive and depart according to their schedule as opposed to yours; the occasional necessity of transfers; multiple stops; time lost while loading and unloading large numbers of passengers; and, generally, the challenge of understanding and utilizing a large, complex transportation network.

2. Small Children. Although the actual hassle of commuting to most off-World hotels is only slightly (if any) greater than that of commuting to Disney World hotels, a definite peace of mind results from staying in Walt Disney World. If you are traveling with small children and have a few bucks, go for the Polynesian Resort on the monorail line. If the Polynesian is too expensive but you can handle $94–119 a night, try to book the Caribbean Beach, Dixie Landings, or Port Orleans resorts.

3. Splitting Up. If you are in a party that will probably be splitting up (as frequently happens in families with children of widely varying ages), staying in the World offers more transportation options and therefore more independence. Mom and Dad can take the car and return to the hotel for a relaxed dinner and an early bedtime while the teens remain in the park for the evening parades and fireworks.

4. Feeding the Army of the Potomac. If you have a large crew that chows down like cattle on a finishing lot, you might be better off staying outside the World where food is far less expensive.

5. Visiting Other Orlando Area Attractions. If you plan to visit Sea World, Spaceport USA, Universal Studios Florida, or other area attractions, it may be more convenient to stay outside the World.

How to Get Discounts on Lodging at Walt Disney World

There are so many guest rooms in and around Walt Disney World that competition has become brisk, and everyone including Disney is having to wheel and deal to keep the rooms filled. This has led to a more flexible discount policy for Walt Disney World hotels. Actually getting the discounts, however, remains a confusing and somewhat Machiavellian task in the best Disney tradition. In any event, here are some tips which should be of help.

1. Value Season vs. Regular Season. The same room is $20–40 cheaper in Value Season than in Regular Season.*

1994 Value Season   *1994 Regular Season*
January 3–February 12   December 20, 1993–January 2, 1994

April 10–June 11 *	February 13–April 9
August 14–	June 12–August 13
December 18	December 19–January 2, 1995

* Does not apply at the Caribbean Beach, Port Orleans, Dixie Landings, or Disney All-Star Resorts, all of which have year-round rates.

2. Travel Agents. Travel agents, once ineligible for commissions on Disney bookings, are now active players and particularly good sources for information on time-limited special programs and discounts.

3. Disney's Ocala Information Center. The Disney Information Center off I-75 in Ocala, Florida, routinely books Disney hotel rooms at discounts of up to 43%! The discounts are offered as an incentive to walk-in travelers who may not have considered lodging at a Disney property or even going to Walt Disney World. The number of rooms available at specific hotels varies according to date and season, but you can almost always count on getting a good deal. Because the discount program is designed to snare uncommitted, walk-in travelers, you must reserve your room in person at the Information Center. If you call the center in advance, however, and tell them you are on your way down, they will usually tell you what they have available and what the discounts are. The phone number is (904) 854-0770. Finally, as with all things Disney, there is no telling how long this program will last.

4. Disney Shareholder Discounts. The discount program for Walt Disney Company shareholders has been effectively dismantled. Disney shareholders are currently offered only a modest discount on the purchase of a Magic Kingdom Club Gold Card, available to the general public for about $50. For information, call the Walt Disney Company's shareholder relations office at (818) 505-7040.

5. Magic Kingdom Club. The Magic Kingdom Club is offered as a benefit by employers, credit unions, and organizations. Membership entitles you to a 10–30% discount on Disney lodging and a 5–7% discount on theme park tickets, among other things. Almost all state and federal government employees are Magic Kingdom Club members (though a lot of them don't know it). If you work for a large company or organization, ask your personnel department if the Magic Kingdom Club benefit is provided. Those not signed up through their work can buy a two-year individual membership in the Magic Kingdom Club

Gold Card program for about $50. For information call (714) 490-3200 or write:

> Magic Kingdom Club
> Gold Card
> P.O. Box 3850
> Anaheim, CA 92803-3850

6. *Organizations and Auto Clubs*.   As Disney has become more aggressive about selling guest rooms, it has developed time-limited programs with a number of auto clubs and other organizations. Recently, for instance, AAA members were offered 15% savings on Walt Disney resorts and a 20% discount on Disney package vacations. While these deals come and go, the market suggests that there will be more coming than going for the next year. If you are a member of AARP, AAA, or any travel or auto club, check to see if your association has a program before shopping elsewhere.

— *Walt Disney World Lodging** —

Expensive, but most convenient, are the hotels situated around the Seven Seas Lagoon or Bay Lake and connected to the Magic Kingdom and EPCOT Center by monorail. These include the giant A-frame hotel, Disney's Contemporary Resort; Disney's recently renovated Polynesian Resort; and Disney's Grand Floridian Beach Resort, modeled after the fabled Florida grand hotels of the nineteenth century. Accommodations in any of these hotels make touring Walt Disney World easier and more relaxing. Commuting to and from the Magic Kingdom via monorail is quick and simple, allowing visitors to return at leisure to their hotel for a nap or a dip. Additionally, the Seven Seas Lagoon and Bay Lake offer a variety of boating, swimming, and other water sports.

Contemporary Resort
   1,050 rooms   lakefront   monorail service $190–435 per night
Polynesian Resort
    863 rooms   lakefront   monorail service $189–295 per night
Grand Floridian Beach Resort
    900 rooms   lakefront   monorail service $230–440 per night

* Rates vary depending on room location (view) and/or season, and are subject to change.

The best lodging deals in Walt Disney World for the economy conscious are the Caribbean Beach, Port Orleans, and Dixie Landings Resorts. All three offer nice accommodations at nightly rates of $94–119. The Caribbean has a colorful island theme, while Port Orleans and the Dixie Landings blend old New Orleans with a Mississippi River plantation motif. The Caribbean Beach Resort is situated on a 42-acre lake not far from EPCOT Center. The Port Orleans and Dixie Landings Resorts are located side-by-side on one of the Disney canals. Of the three, the Caribbean Beach is the most centrally located and offers the best swimming and play areas for children. While none of the three are serviced by monorail, getting around Walt Disney World is easy by private car or the Disney shuttle bus system.

In 1994, 400 rooms of Disney's new All-Star Resorts will come on line. Current plans call for the eventual completion of nine hotels with sports and entertainment themes offering Disney's version of budget accommodations at about $60 a night. The All-Star Resorts will be connected to the rest of Walt Disney World by bus.

Caribbean Beach Resort
| 2,112 rooms | lakefront | shuttle bus service | $94–119 per night |

Port Orleans Resort
| 1,008 rooms | on canal | shuttle bus service | $94–119 per night |

Dixie Landings Resort
| 2,048 rooms | on canal | shuttle bus service | $94–119 per night |

The Disney Inn (formerly the Golf Resort Hotel), in addition to being near the theme parks, offers 60 holes of golf. One of the most luxurious, and possibly the most sedate and restful of the Disney resorts, the Disney Inn is a particularly good property for seniors and for couples traveling without children. Located near the Grand Floridian, the Disney Inn is accessible by private car or the Disney bus system.

Disney Inn
| 288 rooms | golf course | shuttle bus service | $180–215 per night |

The Walt Disney World Swan, Walt Disney World Dolphin, and Conference Center is one of the largest convention/resort complexes in the southeastern U.S. Built on the shore of a 50-acre lagoon, the complex is connected by canal to the Disney-MGM Studios, and by tram and walkway to EPCOT Center, as well as by bus and highway to other areas of Walt Disney World.

Swan Resort
760 rooms   lakefront   boat/bus service $195–310 per night
Dolphin Resort
1,510 rooms   lakefront   boat/bus service $209–319 per night

Disney's Yacht Club Resort and Disney's Beach Club Resort are located between the Dolphin and EPCOT Center across a lake from Disney's Boardwalk. EPCOT Center is within walking distance and the Disney-MGM Studios can be reached by boat. Other Walt Disney World destinations are serviced by bus.

Yacht and Beach Club Resorts
1,214 rooms   lakefront   boat/bus service $205–370 per night

Disney's Wilderness Lodge Resort, located on Bay Lake, is close to both the Magic Kingdom and the Fort Wilderness Campground, but is not on the monorail line. The newest Disney luxury property, the Wilderness Lodge is modeled on rustic National Park Service lodges erected just before and after the First World War. The Magic Kingdom can be reached by launch. All other Walt Disney World destinations are serviced by bus.

Disney's Wilderness Lodge Resort
725 rooms   lakefront   boat/bus service $205–370 per night

Fort Wilderness Campground is a spacious resort campground for both tent and RV camping. Fully equipped, air-conditioned trailers are also available for rent. Campsites, classified as either "preferred" or "regular," are arranged on loops emanating from three main thorough-fares. The only difference between a preferred and regular campsite is that the preferred sites are closer to the campground amenities, i.e., swimming pools, restaurants, and shopping. All campsites have a 110- and 220-volt outlet, a picnic table, and a grill. Most RV sites have sanitary hook-ups. The campsites are roomy by eastern U.S. RV stan-dards, but will probably feel a little cramped to tent campers. On any given day, about 90% of the campers will be RV folks. When making reservations tent campers should request a campsite on Loop 1500, Cottontail Curl, or Loop 2000, Spanish Moss Lane. The better loops for RV campers are Loops 200, 400, 500, and 1400. All loops have a comfort station with showers, toilets, phones, an ice machine, and a coin laundry.

Aside from economy accommodations, features of Fort Wilderness Campground include a group camping area, full RV hook-ups, evening entertainment, horseback riding, bike trails, jogging trails, swimming, and a petting farm. River Country, a water theme park, is near Fort Wilderness Campground. Access to the Magic Kingdom and Discovery Island is by boat from the Fort Wilderness landing on Bay Lake, or to any other destination in Walt Disney World by private car or shuttle bus.

Fort Wilderness Campground

827 campsites	boat/bus service	$32–49 per night
363 trailers (sleeps 4–6)	boat/bus service	$180–195 per night

The Disney Vacation Club is a new property with an "old Key West" feel that offers nice guest rooms as well as luxurious one-, two-, and three-bedroom homes and villas with full kitchens. The Vacation Club, situated squarely in the middle of Walt Disney World, is a timeshare program; it is possible to acquire partial ownership in the property. Rooms and units not being used by timeshare owners are available for daily rental by non-owners. The Vacation Club has restaurants and other amenities and is serviced by the Disney bus system.

Disney Vacation Club

275 rooms	golf course	shuttle bus service	$185–755 per night

Disney's Village Resort is about six minutes from EPCOT Center by car and close to I-4. A huge entertainment, dining, lodging, and shopping complex, the Disney Village Resort offers a variety of lodging. The villas in this resort are one of two hotel accommodations in Walt Disney World proper that offer kitchen facilities. A not inexpensive grocery is located conveniently in the shopping complex.

Fairway Villas	64 units	bus service	$340–360 per night
Treehouse Villas	60 units	bus service	$320–340 per night
Vacation Villas	119 units	bus service	$240–310 per night
Club Lake Villas	324 units	bus service	$185–280 per night

Walt Disney World Village Hotels. In addition to the Village Resort, seven hotels offering a total of 3,825 rooms and suites are located in the Walt Disney World Village. Although commodious, some rooms are more expensive than the hotels serviced by the monorail. We found few bargains among the Walt Disney Village Hotels, and felt less of that special excitement you have when you stay inside "The World." While technically part of Walt Disney World, it is like visiting a colony instead of the mother country. Early entry privileges to the Magic Kingdom are not accorded to guests at the Village Hotels, nor is free parking at the theme park pay lots. What's more, several of the Disney Village Hotels are dropping their contract with the Disney bus service that provides guest transportation to and from the parks. These developments make lodging at the Disney Village Hotels extremely problematic. If you are considering one of the following hotels, be sure to clarify the transportation situation before making your reservations.

The Hilton	814 rooms	bus service	$135–240 per night
Howard Johnson's Resort Hotel	383 rooms	bus service	$95–115 per night
Hotel Royal Plaza	396 rooms	bus service	$85–118 per night
Guest Quarters Suite Resort	229 rooms	bus service	$139–195 per night
Travelodge Hotel	325 rooms	bus service	$119–159 per night
Grosvenor Resort	614 rooms	bus service	$99–160 per night
Buena Vista Palace	844 rooms	bus service	$110–199 per night
	220 suites	bus service	$255–310 per night

NOTE: Incidentally, the Disney folks call the seven-hotel complex (which includes The Hilton and Buena Vista Palace) by three different names in their brochures and maps. It is referred to as the Walt Disney World Village, Village Hotel Plaza, and Disney Village Hotels. Only complicating matters further is Disney's Village Resort, a separate hotel complex altogether. And you thought you were confused?

Lodging Outside of Walt Disney World

Lodging costs outside of Walt Disney World vary incredibly, as do amenities and services. If you shop around, you can find a nice, clean motel with a pool within 20 minutes of Walt Disney World for as low as $35 a night. You can also find luxurious, plush, expensive hotels with all the extras. Because of the competitive situation, discounts abound, particularly for members of AAA and AARP.

There are three primary "out-of-the-world" areas to consider:

1. International Drive area.   This area about 15–20 minutes east of Walt Disney World parallels I-4 on its southern side, and offers a wide selection of both hotels and restaurants. Accommodations range from $30–200 per night. The chief drawbacks of the International Drive area are its terribly congested roads, countless traffic signals, and inadequate access to westbound I-4. The biggest bottleneck on International Drive is at the intersection with Sand Lake Road. In some sections of International Drive, the horrendous traffic can be circumvented by using local streets one or two blocks to the southeast (i.e., away from I-4).

2. Lake Buena Vista and the I-4 Corridor.   There are a number of hotels situated along FL 535 and north of I-4 between Walt Disney World and I-4's intersection with the Florida Turnpike. These properties are easily reached from the Interstate, and are near a large number of restaurants, including those on International Drive. Driving time to Walt Disney World ranges from 5–15 minutes.

3. US 192.   This is the highway to Kissimmee, southeast of Walt Disney World. In addition to a number of large, full-service hotels, there are many small, privately owned motels in this area that are a good value. Several dozen properties on US 192 are actually closer to the Magic Kingdom and Disney-MGM Studios than the more expensive hotels in Walt Disney World Village and the Disney Village Hotel Plaza (in Walt Disney World). Traffic on US 192 is extremely heavy, but usually moves smoothly without much congestion. Though

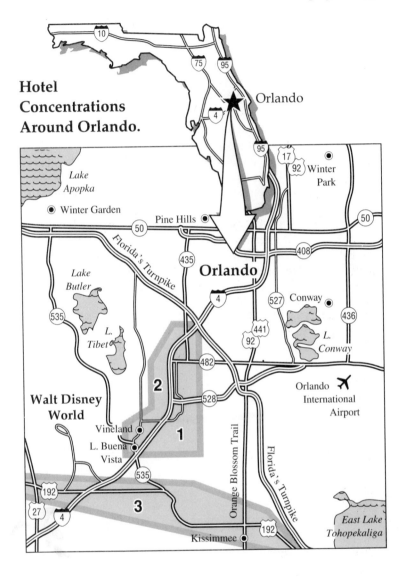

Hotel Concentrations Around Orlando.

the food situation is rapidly improving, US 192 is somewhat inferior to the other areas in terms of number and quality of restaurants.

In the following section, "Hotels and Motels: Rated and Ranked," we compare the hotels situated in these three main areas outside Walt Disney World with those inside Walt Disney World. This critical evaluation will help you identify the best rooms and best values, both in and out of the World.

In addition to Walt Disney World and the three lodging areas, there are also hotels at the intersection of US 27 and I-4, on US 441 (the Orange Blossom Trail), and in downtown Orlando. All of these, however, require more than 20 minutes commuting time to Walt Disney World, and are not included in our comparative ratings. We've also excluded lodging properties south of Siesta Lago Road on US 192.

There has been a tremendous amount of lodging development in and around Walt Disney World. As more and more new rooms become available and the market becomes more competitive, many hotels will have to offer deeply discounted rates to remain in business. One way to discover these bargains is to check out the brochure racks at the Florida state line welcome centers and at the service plazas along the Florida Turnpike.

What's in a Room?

Except for cleanliness, state of repair, and decor, most travelers do not pay much attention to hotel rooms. There is, of course, a discernible standard of quality and luxury which differentiates Motel 6 from Holiday Inn, Holiday Inn from Marriott, and so on. In general, however, hotel guests fail to appreciate that some rooms are better engineered than others.

Contrary to what you might suppose, designing a hotel room is (or should be) a lot more complex than picking a bedspread to match the carpet and drapes. Making the room usable to its occupants is an art, a planning discipline which combines both form and function.

Decor and taste are important, certainly. No one wants to spend several days in a room where the decor is dated, garish, or even ugly. But beyond the decor, there are variables which determine how "livable" a hotel room is. In Orlando, for example, we have seen some beautifully appointed rooms that are simply not well designed for human habitation. The next time you stay in a hotel, pay attention to the details and design elements of your room. Even more than decor, these are the things that will make you feel comfortable and at home.

It takes the *Unofficial Guide* researchers about 40 minutes to inspect a hotel room. Here are a few of the things we check that you may want to start paying attention to:

Room Size.   While some smaller rooms are cozy and well designed, a large and uncluttered room is generally preferable, especially for a stay of more than three days.

Temperature Control, Ventilation and Odor.   The guest should be able to control the temperature of the room. The best system, because it's so quiet, is central heating and air conditioning, controlled by the room's own thermostat. The next best system is a room module heater and air conditioner, preferably controlled by an automatic thermostat, but usually by manually operated button controls. The worst system is central heating and air without any sort of room thermostat or guest control.

55

The vast majority of hotel rooms have windows or balcony doors which have been permanently secured shut. Though there are some legitimate safety and liability issues involved, we prefer windows and balcony doors that can be opened to admit fresh air. Hotel rooms should be odor free, smoke free, and not feel stuffy or damp.

Room Security. Better rooms have locks that require a plastic card instead of the traditional lock and key. Card and slot systems allow the hotel, essentially, to change the combination or entry code of the lock with each new guest who uses the room. A burglar who has somehow acquired a room key to a conventional lock can afford to wait until the situation is right before using the key to gain access. Not so with a card and slot system. Though larger hotels and hotel chains with lock and key systems usually rotate their locks once each year, they remain vulnerable to hotel thieves much of the time. Many smaller or independent properties rarely rotate their locks.

In addition to the entry lock system, the door should have a deadbolt, and preferably a chain that can be locked from the inside. A chain by itself is not sufficient. Doors should also have a peephole. Windows and balcony doors, if any, should have secure locks.

Safety. Every room should have a fire or smoke alarm, clear fire instructions, and preferably a sprinkler system. Bathtubs should have a nonskid surface, and shower stalls should have doors which either open outward or slide side-to-side. Bathroom electrical outlets should be high on the wall and not too close to the sink. Balconies should have sturdy, high rails.

Noise. Most travelers have been kept awake by the television, partying, or amorous activities of people in the next room, or by traffic on the street outside. Better hotels are designed with noise control in mind. Wall and ceiling construction are substantial, effectively screening routine noise. Carpets and drapes, in addition to being decorative, also absorb and muffle sounds. Mattresses mounted on stable platforms or sturdy bed frames do not squeak even when challenged by the most acrobatic lovers. Televisions enclosed in cabinets, and with volume governors, rarely disturb guests in adjacent rooms.

In better hotels, the air conditioning and heating system is well maintained and operates without noise or vibration. Likewise, plumbing is quiet and positioned away from the sleeping area. Doors to the hall, and to adjoining rooms, are thick and well fitted to better keep out noise.

Darkness Control. Ever been in a hotel room where the curtains would not quite come together in the middle? Thick, lined curtains which close completely in the center and which extend beyond the dimensions of the window or door frame are required. In a well-planned room, the curtains, shades, or blinds should almost totally block light at any time of day.

Lighting. Poor lighting is an extremely common problem in American hotel rooms. The lighting is usually adequate for dressing, relaxing, or watching television, but not for reading or working. Lighting needs to be bright over tables and desks, and alongside couches or easy chairs. Since so many people read in bed, there should be a separate light for each person. A room with two queen beds should have an individual light for four people. Better bedside reading lights illuminate a small area, so if you want to sleep and someone else prefers to stay up and read, you will not be bothered by the light. The worst situation by far is a single lamp on a table between beds. In each bed, only the person next to the lamp will have sufficient light to read. This deficiency is often compounded by light bulbs of insufficient wattage.

In addition, closet areas should be well-lit, and there should be a switch near the door that turns on lights in the room when you enter. A seldom seen, but desirable, feature is a bedside console that allows a guest to control all or most lights in the room from bed.

Furnishings. At bare minimum, the bed(s) must be firm. Pillows should be made with nonallergic fillers and, in addition to the sheets and spread, a blanket should be provided. Bed clothes should be laundered with a fabric softener and changed daily. Better hotels usually provide extra blankets and pillows in the room or on request, and sometimes use a second topsheet between the blanket and the spread.

There should be a dresser large enough to hold clothes for two people during a five-day stay. A small table with two chairs, or a desk with a chair, should be provided. The room should be equipped with a luggage rack and a three-quarter- to full-length mirror.

The television should be color, cable-connected, and ideally have a volume governor and remote control. It should be mounted on a swivel base, and preferably enclosed in a cabinet. Local channels should be posted on the set and a local TV program guide should be supplied.

The telephone should be touchtone, conveniently situated for bedside use, and should have on or near it, easily understood dialing instructions and a rate card. Local white and yellow pages should be provided. Better hotels have phones in the bath and equip room phones with long cords.

Well-designed hotel rooms usually have a plush armchair or a sleeper sofa for lounging and reading. Better headboards are padded for comfortable reading in bed, and there should be a nightstand or table on each side of the bed(s). Nice extras in any hotel room include a small refrigerator, a digital alarm clock, and a coffeemaker.

Bathroom.   Two sinks are better than one, and you cannot have too much counter space. A sink outside the bath is a great convenience when two people are bathing and dressing at the same time. Sinks should have drains with stoppers.

Better bathrooms have both tub and shower with a nonslip bottom. Tub and shower controls should be easy to operate. Adjustable shower heads are preferred. The bath needs to be well-lit and should have an exhaust fan and a guest controlled bathroom heater. Towels should be large, soft, and fluffy, and provided in generous quantities, as should hand towels and washcloths. There should be an electrical outlet for each sink, conveniently and safely placed.

Complimentary shampoo, conditioner, and lotion are a plus, as are robes and bathmats. Better hotels supply their bathrooms with tissues and extra toilet paper. Luxurious baths feature a phone, a hair dryer, sometimes a small television, or even a jacuzzi.

Vending.   There should be complimentary ice and a drink machine on each floor. Welcome additions include a snack machine and a sundries (combs, toothpaste) machine. The latter are seldom found in large hotels that have restaurants and shops.

—— *Room Ratings* ——

To separate properties according to the relative quality, tastefulness, state of repair, cleanliness, and size of their **standard rooms**, we have grouped the hotels and motels into classifications denoted by stars. Star ratings in this guide apply to Orlando area properties only, and do not necessarily correspond to ratings awarded by Mobil, AAA, or other travel critics. Because stars have little relevance when awarded in the absence of commonly recognized standards of comparison, we have tied our ratings to expected levels of quality established by specific American hotel corporations.

★★★★★	*Superior Rooms*	Tasteful and luxurious by any standard
★★★★	*Extremely Nice Rooms*	What you would expect at a Hyatt Regency or Marriott
★★★	*Nice Rooms*	Holiday Inn or comparable quality
★★	*Adequate Rooms*	Clean, comfortable, and functional without frills—like a Motel 6
★	*Super Budget*	

Star ratings apply to *room quality only,* and describe the property's standard accommodations. For most hotels and motels a "standard accommodation" is a hotel room with either one king bed or two queen beds. In an all-suite property, the standard accommodation is either a one- or two-room suite. In addition to standard accommodations, many hotels offer luxury rooms and special suites which are not rated in this guide. Star ratings for rooms are assigned without regard to whether a property has restaurant(s), recreational facilities, entertainment, or other extras.

In addition to stars (which delineate broad categories), we also employ a numerical rating system. Our rating scale is 0–100, with 100 as the best possible rating, and zero (0) as the worst. Numerical ratings are presented to show the difference we perceive between one property and another. Rooms at the Ramada Resort Maingate at the Parkway, Sheraton World, and the Holiday Inn Maingate are all rated as three and a half stars (★★★½). In the supplemental numerical ratings, the Ramada is rated an 82, Sheraton an 81, and Holiday Inn a 76. This means that within the three-and-a-half-star category, the Ramada and Sheraton are comparable, and both have slightly nicer rooms than the Holiday Inn.

The location column identifies the area around Walt Disney World where you will find a particular property. The designation WDW means that the property is located inside Walt Disney World. A "1" means that the property is located on or near International Drive. Properties on US 192 (a.k.a. Irlo Bronson Memorial Highway, Vine Street, and Space Coast Parkway) are indicated by a "3." All others are marked number "2," and are located for the most part along the I-4 corridor, though some are in isolated locations that do not meet any other criteria.

Properties along US 192 also carry location designations with their names, such as the Holiday Inn Maingate East. The consensus in Orlando seems to be that the main entrance to Walt Disney World is the broad interstate-type road that runs off of US 192. This is called Maingate. Properties located along US 192 call themselves Maingate East or West to differentiate their positions along the highway. So, coming from Highway 27 toward the maingate area, the properties before you reach the Maingate turnoff are called Maingate West, while the properties after you pass the Maingate turnoff are called Maingate East.

—— *The Nicest Rooms in Town* ——

Cost estimates are based on the hotel's published rack rates for standard rooms. Each "$" represents $30. Thus a cost symbol of "$$$" means a room (or suite) at that hotel will be about $90 a night.

Here is a hit parade of the nicest rooms in town. We've focused strictly on room quality, and excluded any consideration of location, services, recreation, or amenities. In some instances, a one- or two-room suite can be had for the same price or less than that of a hotel room.

If you used an earlier edition of this guide, you will notice that many of the ratings and rankings have changed. In addition to the inclusion of new properties, these changes are occasioned by such positive developments as guest room renovation or improved maintenance and housekeeping. A failure to properly maintain guest rooms or a lapse in housekeeping standards can negatively affect the ratings.

Finally, before you begin to shop for a hotel take a hard look at this letter we received from a couple in Hot Springs, Arkansas:

> We cancelled our room reservations to follow the advice in your book [and reserved a hotel highly ranked by the *Unofficial Guide*]. We wanted inexpensive, but clean and cheerful. We got inexpensive, but [also] dirty, grim, and depressing. I really felt disappointed in your advice and the room. It was the pits. That was the one real piece of information I needed from your book! The room spoiled the holiday for me aside from our touring.

Needless to say, this letter was as unsettling to us as the bad room was to our reader. Our integrity as travel journalists, after all, is based on the quality of the information we provide our readers. Even with the best of intentions and the most conscientious research, however, we cannot inspect every room in every hotel. What we do, in statistical terms, is take a sample: we check out several rooms selected at random in each hotel and base our ratings and rankings on those rooms. The inspections are conducted anonymously and without the knowledge of the property's management. Although unusual, it is certainly possible that the rooms we randomly inspect are not representative of the majority of rooms at a particular hotel. Another possibility is that the rooms we inspect in a given hotel *are* representative, but that by bad luck a reader is assigned a room which is inferior. When rechecking the hotel our reader disliked so intensely, we discovered our rating was correctly representative, but that he and his wife had unfortunately been assigned to one of a small number of threadbare rooms scheduled for renovation.

The key to avoiding disappointment is to do some advance snooping around. We recommend that you ask to be sent a photo of a hotel's standard guest room before you book, or at least get a copy of the hotel's promotional brochure. Be forewarned, however, that some hotel chains use the same guest room photo in their promotional literature for *all* hotels in the chain, and that the guest room in a specific property may not resemble the photo in the brochure. When you or your travel agent call, ask how old the property is and when the guest room you are being assigned was last renovated. If you arrive and are assigned a room inferior to that which you had been led to expect, demand to be moved to another room.

The Nicest Rooms in Town

Hotel	Star Rating	Rating	Cost	Phone (A/C 407)
Disney's Grand Floridian	★★★★★	97	$$$$$$$$$$$+	934-7639
Disney's Beach Club	★★★★½	95	$$$$$$$$	934-7639
Disney's Yacht Club	★★★★½	95	$$$$$$$$	934-7639
The Disney Inn	★★★★½	94	$$$$$$$−	934-7639
Marriott Orlando World Center	★★★★½	92	$$$$$+	239-4200
Stouffer Orlando	★★★★½	92	$$$$$$−	351-5555
Peabody Orlando	★★★★½	91	$$$$$+	352-4000
Villas at Resort World	★★★★½	91	$$$−	238-1700
WDW Dolphin	★★★★½	91	$$$$$$$$	934-7639
WDW Swan	★★★★½	91	$$$$$$$$$−	934-7639
Best Western Buena Vista Suites	★★★★½	90	$$$$−	239-8588

The Nicest Rooms in Town (continued)

Hotel	Star Rating	Rating	Cost	Phone (A/C 407)
Disney's Polynesian	★★★★	88	$$$$$$$$+	934-7639
Homewood Suites Maingate	★★★★	88	$$$$$−	396-2229
Buena Vista Palace	★★★★	87	$$$$+	827-2727
Guest Quarters Suite Resort	★★★★	87	$$$$$+	934-1000
Hawthorne Suites Orlando	★★★★	87	$$$+	351-3300
Hilton Inn Gateway (tower rooms)	★★★★	87	$$+	396-4400
Holiday Inn Lake Buena Vista	★★★★	87	$$$+	239-4500
Hyatt Regency Grand Cypress	★★★★	87	$$$$$$$−	239-1234
Summerfield Suites	★★★★	87	$$$$$+	352-2400
Disney's Port Orleans	★★★★	86	$$$$−	934-7639
Embassy Suites Orlando Int'l.	★★★★	86	$$$$+	352-1400
Embassy Suites Resort	★★★★	86	$$$$$+	239-1144
Disney's Dixie Landings	★★★★	84	$$$$−	934-7639
Sol Orlando Village Resort	★★★★	84	$$$$+	397-0555
Sonesta Villa Resort	★★★★	84	$$$$−	352-8051
Enclave Suites	★★★★	83	$$$+	351-1155
Grosvenor Resort	★★★★	83	$$$$+	828-4444
Disney's Contemporary Resort	★★★½	82	$$$$$$$$+	934-7639
Embassy Suites Plaza Int'l.	★★★½	82	$$$$+	345-8250
Hyatt Orlando	★★★½	82	$$$	396-1234
Radisson Inn Lake Buena Vista	★★★½	82	$$$	239-8400
Ramada Resort Maingate at the Parkway	★★★½	82	$$$+	396-7000
Residence Inn Lake Cecile	★★★½	82	$$$+	396-2056
Clarion Plaza Hotel	★★★½	81	$$$	352-9700
Doubletree Club Hotel	★★★½	81	$$$$+	239-8500
Sheraton World Resort	★★★½	81	$$$$−	352-1100
The Hilton–Disney Village	★★★½	81	$$$$$$+	827-4000
Heritage Inn Orlando	★★★½	80	$$$−	352-0008
Disney's Caribbean Beach	★★★½	79	$$$+	934-7639
Residence Inn Orlando	★★★½	79	$$$−	345-0117
Travelodge Hotel–Disney Village	★★★½	78	$$$$−	828-2424
Courtyard by Marriott	★★★½	77	$$$	351-2244
Holiday Inn Maingate	★★★½	76	$$$−	396-7300
Hampton Inn International Drive	★★★	74	$$$−	345-1112
Howard Johnson Universal Tower	★★★	74	$$$	351-2100
Quality Suites Maingate East	★★★	74	$$$$	396-8040
Hampton Inn Maingate	★★★	73	$$$−	396-8484
Howard Johnson Fountain Park	★★★	73	$$$−	396-1111

The Nicest Rooms in Town (continued)

Hotel	Star Rating	Rating	Cost	Phone (A/C 407)
Comfort Suites Orlando	★★★	72	$$$	351-5050
Hampton Inn Universal Studios	★★★	72	$$$−	351-6716
Holiday Inn International Resort	★★★	72	$$$$−	351-3500
Howard Johnson Maingate West	★★★	72	$$+	396-2500
Ramada Inn Plaza International	★★★	72	$$+	351-1660
Hilton Inn Gateway (garden rooms)	★★★	71	$$+	396-4400
Hotel Royal Plaza	★★★	71	$$$+	828-2828
Quality Inn Maingate	★★★	71	$$+	396-4000
Radisson Inn International	★★★	71	$$	345-0505
Travelodge Suites Eastgate	★★★	71	$$+	396-7666
Days Inn Lake Buena Vista Village	★★★	70	$$−	239-4646
Floridian of Orlando	★★★	70	$$$+	351-5009
Holiday Inn Maingate East	★★★	70	$$$−	396-4488
Howard Johnson Park Square	★★★	70	$$+	239-6900
Holiday Inn Universal Studios	★★★	69	$$$−	351-3333
Howard Johnson–Disney Village	★★★	69	$$$+	828-8888
Orlando Marriott	★★★	69	$$$+	351-2420
Wynfield Inn Maingate	★★★	69	$$+	800-346-1551
Holiday Inn Express	★★★	68	$$$−	351-4430
Ramada Resort Florida Center	★★★	68	$$$−	351-4600
Sheraton Lakeside Inn	★★★	68	$$$+	239-7919
Comfort Inn International	★★★	67	$$+	351-4100
Holiday Inn Maingate West	★★★	67	$$$	396-1100
Radisson Inn Maingate	★★★	67	$$+	396-1400
Ramada Inn Westgate	★★★	67	$$−	800-365-6935
Days Suites Maingate East	★★★	66	$$$$	396-7900
Ramada Resort Maingate	★★★	66	$$$−	396-4466
Wynfield Inn Westwood	★★★	66	$$+	800-346-1551
Days Inn Lake Buena Vista	★★★	65	$$$−	239-4441
Days Inn Lake Buena Vista Resort	★★★	65	$$$+	239-0444
Gateway Inn	★★★	65	$$−	351-2000
International Gateway Inn	★★★	65	$+	345-8880
Riande Continental Royal	★★★	65	$$+	345-0131
Travelodge Maingate East	★★★	65	$$$−	396-4222
Best Western Eastgate	★★½	64	$$−	396-0707
Best Western Plaza Int'l.	★★½	64	$$+	345-8195
Howard Johnson Hotel	★★½	64	$$+	351-1730
Larson's Lodge Maingate	★★½	64	$$−	396-6100
Quality Inn Lake Cecile	★★½	64	$+	396-4455

The Nicest Rooms in Town (continued)

Hotel	Star Rating	Rating	Cost	Phone (A/C 407)
Quality Inn Maingate West	★★½	64	$$+	800-638-7829
Red Roof Inn Kissimmee	★★½	64	$$+	396-0065
Days Inn Orlando Lakeside	★★½	63	$$$−	351-1900
Inns of America International	★★½	63	$$−	800-826-0778
Las Palmas Hotel	★★½	63	$$$−	351-3900
MIC Lakefront Inn	★★½	63	$$−	345-5340
Quality Inn Plaza	★★½	63	$$−	345-8585
Travelodge Orlando Flags	★★½	63	$+	351-4410
Best Western Maingate	★★½	62	$$−	396-0100
Fairfield Inn International	★★½	62	$$+	363-1944
Ho Jo Inn	★★½	62	$+	800-446-5669
Howard Johnson Lodge	★★½	62	$$−	351-2900
Inns of America Maingate	★★½	62	$$−	800-826-0778
Park Inn International	★★½	62	$$+	396-1376
Rodeway Inn Eastgate	★★½	62	$+	396-7700
Days Inn International Drive	★★½	61	$$+	351-1200
Famous Host Inn	★★½	61	$$+	396-8883
Ho Jo Inn Maingate	★★½	61	$$+	396-1748
Quality Inn International	★★½	61	$$−	351-1600
Riande Continental Plaza	★★½	61	$$+	352-8211
Choice Suites	★★½	60	$$+	396-1780
Days Inn Civic Center	★★½	60	$$−	352-8700
International Inn	★★½	60	$$−	351-4444
Rodeway Inn Civic Center	★★½	60	$$+	351-5100
Travelodge Maingate West	★★½	60	$$	396-1828
Wilson World Maingate	★★½	60	$$$−	396-6000
Buena Vista Motel	★★½	59	$+	396-2100
Comfort Inn Maingate	★★½	59	$$−	396-7500
Sleep Inn Maingate	★★½	59	$$−	396-1600
Comfort Inn at Lake Buena Vista	★★½	58	$$+	239-7300
Days Inn Universal Studios	★★½	57	$$$−	351-3800
Knights Inn Maingate	★★½	57	$+	396-4200
Knights Inn Maingate East	★★½	57	$$−	396-8186
Ramada Limited	★★½	57	$$−	396-2212
Econo Lodge Maingate Central	★★½	56	$$−	396-4343
Golden Link Motel	★★½	56	$+	396-0555
Sun Motel	★★½	56	$+	396-2673
Super 8	★★½	56	$$−	352-8383
Central Motel	★★	55	$+	396-2333

The Nicest Rooms in Town (continued)

Hotel	Star Rating	Rating	Cost	Phone (A/C 407)
Econo Lodge Maingate West	★★	55	$$+	396-9300
Motel 6 International Drive	★★	55	$+	351-6500
Red Roof Inn Orlando	★★	55	$$−	354-1507
Traveler's Inn	★★	55	$+	396-1668
Days Inn Maingate East	★★	54	$$$	396-7900
Economy Inns of America	★★	54	$+	396-4020
Embassy Motel	★★	54	$+	396-1144
Key Motel	★★	54	$+	396-6200
Monte Carlo	★★	53	$+	396-4700
King's Motel	★★	52	$+	396-4762
Econo Lodge Maingate Hawaiian	★★	51	$$+	396-2000
Motel 6 Maingate East	★★	51	$+	396-6333
Lakeview Motel	★★	50	$+	396-8282
Red Carpet Inn East	★★	50	$+	396-1133
Days Inn Maingate West	★★	48	$$	396-1000
Motel 6 West	★½	45	$+	396-6427

—— *The Best Deals in Town* ——

Having listed the nicest rooms in town, let's reorder the list to rank the best combinations of quality and value in a room. As before, the rankings are made without consideration of location or the availability of restaurant(s), recreational facilities, entertainment, and/or amenities. Once again, each lodging property is awarded a value rating on a 0–100 scale. The higher the rating, the better the value. You will note, that the Polynesian Resort at Walt Disney World has a relatively low value rating. This is because for the same price you can get a *nicer room* at another property. The Polynesian, however, is one of the most popular hotels in the area and many guests are willing to pay a higher rate for the convenience, service, and amenities.

We recently had a reader complain to us that he had booked one of our top ranked rooms in terms of value and had been very disappointed in the room. We noticed that the room the reader occupied had a quality rating of ★★½. We would remind you that the value ratings are intended to give you some sense of value received for dollars spent. A ★★½ room at $30 may have the same value rating as a ★★★★ room at

$85, but that does not mean the rooms will be of comparable quality. Regardless of whether it's a good deal or not, a ★★½ room is still a ★★½ room.

Listed below are the best room buys for the money, regardless of location or star classification, based on averaged rack rates. Note that sometimes a suite can cost less than a hotel room.

The Best Deals in Town

Hotel	Value Rating	Star Rating	Cost
Villas at Resort World	99	★★★★½	$$$−
Hilton Inn Gateway (tower rooms)	90	★★★★	$$+
International Gateway Inn	84	★★★	$+
Gateway Inn	77	★★★	$$−
Travelodge Orlando Flags	76	★★½	$+
Ho Jo Inn	75	★★½	$+
Days Inn Lake Buena Vista Village	74	★★★	$$−
Best Western Buena Vista Suites	72	★★★★½	$$$$−
Hawthorne Suites Orlando	71	★★★★	$$$+
Holiday Inn Lake Buena Vista	71	★★★★	$$$+
Ramada Inn Westgate	71	★★★	$$−
Radisson Inn International	70	★★★	$$
Golden Link Motel	69	★★½	$+
Quality Inn Lake Cecile	69	★★½	$+
Residence Inn Orlando	68	★★★½	$$$−
Sun Motel	68	★★½	$+
Rodeway Inn Eastgate	66	★★½	$+
Enclave Suites	65	★★★★	$$$+
Heritage Inn Orlando	64	★★★½	$$$−
Buena Vista Motel	63	★★½	$+
Holiday Inn Maingate	62	★★★½	$$$−
Hyatt Orlando	62	★★★½	$$$
Radisson Inn Lake Buena Vista	62	★★★½	$$$
Inns of America International	62	★★½	$$−
Disney's Port Orleans	61	★★★★	$$$$−
Clarion Plaza Hotel	61	★★★½	$$$
Best Western Maingate	61	★★½	$$−
Howard Johnson Lodge	61	★★½	$$−
Inns of American Maingate	61	★★½	$$−
Disney's Dixie Landings	60	★★★★	$$$$−
Comfort Inn International	60	★★★	$$+

The Best Deals in Town (continued)

Hotel	Value Rating	Star Rating	Cost
Hilton Inn Gateway (garden rooms)	60	★★★	$$+
Ramada Inn Plaza Int'l.	60	★★★	$$+
Wynfield Inn Westwood	60	★★★	$$+
Ramada Limited	60	★★½	$$−
Key Motel	60	★★	$+
Sonesta Villa Resort	59	★★★★	$$$$−
Riande Continental Royal	59	★★★	$$+
Courtyard by Marriott	58	★★★½	$$$
Residence Inn Lake Cecile	58	★★★½	$$$+
Howard Johnson Maingate West	58	★★★	$$+
Wynfield Inn Maingate	58	★★★	$$+
Embassy Motel	58	★★	$+
Travelodge Suites Eastgate	57	★★★	$$+
Quality Inn Plaza	57	★★½	$$−
Motel 6 International Drive	57	★★	$+
Quality Inn Maingate	56	★★★	$$+
Radisson Inn Maingate	56	★★★	$$+
Larson's Lodge Maingate	56	★★½	$$−
Quality Inn International	56	★★½	$$−
Motel 6 Maingate East	56	★★	$+
Econo Lodge Maingate Central	55	★★½	$$−
International Inn	55	★★½	$$−
Knights Inn Maingate East	55	★★½	$$−
MIC Lakefront Inn	55	★★½	$$−
Sleep Inn Maingate	55	★★½	$$−
Buena Vista Palace	54	★★★★	$$$$+
Ramada Resort Maingate at the Parkway	54	★★★½	$$$+
Hampton Inn International Drive	54	★★★	$$$−
Hampton Inn Maingate	54	★★★	$$$−
Howard Johnson Fountain Park	54	★★★	$$$−
Howard Johnson Park Square	54	★★★	$$+
Red Carpet Inn East	54	★★	$+
Embassy Suites Orlando Int'l.	53	★★★★	$$$$+
Hampton Inn Universal Studios	53	★★★	$$$−
Comfort Inn Maingate	53	★★½	$$−
Days Inn Civic Center	53	★★½	$$−
Central Motel	53	★★	$+
Economy Inns of America	53	★★	$+

The Best Deals in Town (continued)

Hotel	Value Rating	Star Rating	Cost
Disney's Caribbean Beach	52	★★★½	$$$+
Holiday Inn Maingate East	52	★★★	$$$−
Grosvenor Resort	51	★★★★	$$$$+
Super 8	51	★★½	$$−
Lakeview Motel	51	★★	$+
Traveler's Inn	51	★★	$+
Marriott Orlando World Center	50	★★★★½	$$$$$+
Sol Orlando Village Resort	50	★★★★	$$$$+
Holiday Inn Express	50	★★★	$$$−
Travelodge Maingate West	50	★★½	$$
King's Motel	50	★★	$+
Homewood Suites Maingate	49	★★★★	$$$$$−
Ramada Resort Florida Center	49	★★★	$$$−
Peabody Orlando	48	★★★★½	$$$$$+
Sheraton World Resort	48	★★★½	$$$$−
Travelodge Hotel–Disney Village	48	★★★½	$$$$−
Days Inn Lake Buena Vista	48	★★★	$$$−
Howard Johnson Universal Tower	48	★★★	$$$
Travelodge Maingate East	48	★★★	$$$−
Howard Johnson Hotel	48	★★½	$$+
Red Roof Inn Kissimmee	48	★★½	$$+
Comfort Suites Orlando	47	★★★	$$$
Holiday Inn Universal Studios	47	★★★	$$$−
Famous Host Inn	47	★★½	$$+
Stouffer Orlando Resort	46	★★★★½	$$$$$$−
Riande Continental Plaza	46	★★½	$$+
Ramada Resort Maingate	45	★★★	$$$−
Quality Inn Maingate West	45	★★½	$$+
Monte Carlo	45	★★	$+
Holiday Inn Maingate West	44	★★★	$$$
Embassy Suites Resort	43	★★★★	$$$$$+
Embassy Suites Plaza Int'l.	43	★★★½	$$$$+
Floridian of Orlando	43	★★★	$$$+
Hotel Royal Plaza	43	★★★	$$$+
Best Western Eastgate	43	★★½	$$−
Fairfield Inn International	43	★★½	$$+
Park Inn International	43	★★½	$$+
Rodeway Inn Civic Center	43	★★½	$$+
Summerfield Suites	42	★★★★	$$$$$+

The Best Deals in Town (continued)

Hotel	Value Rating	Star Rating	Cost
Ho Jo Inn Maingate	42	★★½	$$+
Guest Quarters Suite Resort	41	★★★★	$$$$$+
Doubletree Club Hotel	41	★★★½	$$$$+
Best Western Plaza Int'l.	41	★★½	$$+
Choice Suites	41	★★½	$$+
Comfort Inn at Lake Buena Vista	41	★★½	$$+
The Disney Inn	40	★★★★½	$$$$$$$−
Sheraton Lakeside Inn	40	★★★	$$$+
Days Inn International Drive	40	★★½	$$+
Red Roof Inn Orlando	39	★★	$$−
Days Inn Lake Buena Vista Resort	38	★★★	$$$+
Holiday Inn International Resort	38	★★★	$$$$−
Howard Johnson–Disney Village	38	★★★	$$$+
Orlando Marriott	38	★★★	$$$+
Days Inn Orlando Lakeside	38	★★½	$$$−
Knights Inn Maingate	37	★★½	$+
Quality Suites Maingate East	36	★★★	$$$$
Las Palmas Hotel	36	★★½	$$$−
Wilson World Maingate	36	★★½	$$$−
Days Inn Universal Studios	35	★★½	$$$−
Motel 6 Maingate West	35	★½	$+
Disney's Beach Club	34	★★★★½	$$$$$$$$
Disney's Yacht Club	34	★★★★½	$$$$$$$$
Days Suites Maingate East	32	★★★	$$$$
Days Inn Maingate West	31	★★	$$
Econo Lodge Maingate West	31	★★	$$+
WDW Swan	30	★★★★½	$$$$$$$$$−
Econo Lodge Maingate Hawaiian	30	★★	$$+
WDW Dolphin	29	★★★★½	$$$$$$$$$
Disney's Grand Floridian	28	★★★★★	$$$$$$$$$$$+
Hyatt Regency Grand Cypress	28	★★★★	$$$$$$$−
The Hilton–Disney Village	28	★★★½	$$$$$$+
Disney's Polynesian Resort	27	★★★★	$$$$$$$+
Days Inn Maingate East	23	★★	$$$
Disney's Contemporary Resort	22	★★★½	$$$$$$$+

The Best Deals on Four- and Five-Star Rooms

Hotel	Value Rating	Star Rating	Cost
Villas at Resort World	99	★★★★½	$$$−
Hilton Inn Gateway (tower rooms)	90	★★★★	$$+
Best Western Buena Vista Suites	72	★★★★½	$$$$−
Hawthorne Suites Orlando	71	★★★★	$$$+
Holiday Inn Lake Buena Vista	71	★★★★	$$$+
Enclave Suites	65	★★★★	$$$+
Disney's Port Orleans	61	★★★★	$$$$−
Disney's Dixie Landings	60	★★★★	$$$$−
Sonesta Villa Resort	59	★★★★	$$$$−
Buena Vista Palace	54	★★★★	$$$$+
Embassy Suites Orlando Int'l.	53	★★★★	$$$$+
Grosvenor Resort	51	★★★★	$$$$+
Marriott Orlando World Center	50	★★★★½	$$$$$+
Sol Orlando Village Resort	50	★★★★	$$$$+
Homewood Suites Maingate	49	★★★★	$$$$$−
Peabody Orlando	48	★★★★½	$$$$$+
Stouffer Orlando Resort	46	★★★★½	$$$$$$−
Embassy Suites Resort	43	★★★★	$$$$$+
Summerfield Suites	42	★★★★	$$$$$+
Guest Quarters Suite Resort	41	★★★★	$$$$$+
The Disney Inn	40	★★★★½	$$$$$$$−
Disney's Beach Club	34	★★★★½	$$$$$$$$
Disney's Yacht Club	34	★★★★½	$$$$$$$$
WDW Swan	30	★★★★½	$$$$$$$$$−
WDW Dolphin	29	★★★★½	$$$$$$$$
Disney's Grand Floridian	28	★★★★★	$$$$$$$$$$$+
Hyatt Regency Grand Cypress	28	★★★★	$$$$$$$−
Disney's Polynesian	27	★★★★	$$$$$$$$+

The Best Deals on Three-Star Rooms

Hotel	Value Rating	Star Rating	Cost
International Gateway Inn	84	★★★	$+
Gateway Inn	77	★★★	$$−
Days Inn Lake Buena Vista Village	74	★★★	$$−
Ramada Inn Westgate	71	★★★	$$−
Radisson Inn International	70	★★★	$$
Residence Inn Orlando	68	★★★½	$$$−
Heritage Inn Orlando	64	★★★½	$$$−
Holiday Inn Maingate	62	★★★½	$$$−
Hyatt Orlando	62	★★★½	$$$
Radisson Inn Lake Buena Vista	62	★★★½	$$$
Clarion Plaza Hotel	61	★★★½	$$$
Comfort Inn International	60	★★★	$$+
Hilton Inn Gateway (garden rooms)	60	★★★	$$+
Ramada Inn Plaza International	60	★★★	$$+
Wynfield Inn Westwood	60	★★★	$$+
Riande Continental Royal	59	★★★	$$+
Courtyard by Marriott	58	★★★½	$$$
Residence Inn Lake Cecile	58	★★★½	$$$+
Howard Johnson Maingate West	58	★★★	$$+
Wynfield Inn Maingate	58	★★★	$$+
Travelodge Suites Eastgate	57	★★★	$$+
Quality Inn Maingate	56	★★★	$$+
Radisson Inn Maingate	56	★★★	$$+
Ramada Resort Maingate at the Parkway	54	★★★½	$$$+
Hampton Inn International Drive	54	★★★	$$$−
Hampton Inn Maingate	54	★★★	$$$−
Howard Johnson Fountain Park	54	★★★	$$$−
Howard Johnson Park Square	54	★★★	$$+
Hampton Inn Universal Studios	53	★★★	$$$−
Disney's Caribbean Beach	52	★★★½	$$$+
Holiday Inn Maingate East	52	★★★	$$$−
Holiday Inn Express	50	★★★	$$$−
Ramada Resort Florida Center	49	★★★	$$$−
Sheraton World Resort	48	★★★½	$$$$−
Travelodge Hotel–Disney Village	48	★★★½	$$$$−
Days Inn Lake Buena Vista	48	★★★	$$$−
Howard Johnson Universal Tower	48	★★★	$$$
Travelodge Maingate East	48	★★★	$$$−

The Best Deals on Three-Star Rooms (continued)

Hotel	Value Rating	Star Rating	Cost
Comfort Suites Orlando	47	★★★	$$$
Holiday Inn Universal Studios	47	★★★	$$$−
Ramada Resort Maingate	45	★★★	$$$−
Holiday Inn Maingate West	44	★★★	$$$
Embassy Suites Plaza Int'l.	43	★★★½	$$$$+
Floridian of Orlando	43	★★★	$$$+
Hotel Royal Plaza	43	★★★	$$$+
Doubletree Club Hotel	41	★★★½	$$$$+
Sheraton Lakeside Inn	40	★★★	$$$+
Days Inn Lake Buena Vista Resort	38	★★★	$$$+
Holiday Inn International Resort	38	★★★	$$$$−
Howard Johnson–Disney Village	38	★★★	$$$+
Orlando Marriott	38	★★★	$$$+
Quality Suites Maingate East	36	★★★	$$$$
Days Suites Maingate East	32	★★★	$$$$
The Hilton–Disney Village	28	★★★½	$$$$$$+
Disney's Contemporary Resort	22	★★★½	$$$$$$$+

The Best Deals on Two-Star Rooms

Hotel	Value Rating	Star Rating	Cost
Travelodge Orlando Flags	76	★★½	$+
Ho Jo Inn	75	★★½	$+
Golden Link Motel	69	★★½	$+
Quality Inn Lake Cecile	69	★★½	$+
Sun Motel	68	★★½	$+
Rodeway Inn Eastgate	66	★★½	$+
Buena Vista Motel	63	★★½	$+
Inns of America International	62	★★½	$$−
Best Western Maingate	61	★★½	$$−
Howard Johnson Lodge	61	★★½	$$−
Inns of America Maingate	61	★★½	$$−
Ramada Limited	60	★★½	$$−
Key Motel	60	★★	$+
Embassy Motel	58	★★	$+

The Best Deals on Two-Star Rooms *(continued)*

Hotel	Value Rating	Star Rating	Cost
Quality Inn Plaza	57	★★½	$$−
Motel 6 International Drive	57	★★	$+
Larson's Lodge Maingate	56	★★½	$$−
Quality Inn International	56	★★½	$$−
Motel 6 Maingate East	56	★★	$+
Econo Lodge Maingate Central	55	★★½	$$−
International Inn	55	★★½	$$−
Knights Inn Maingate East	55	★★½	$$−
MIC Lakefront Inn	55	★★½	$$−
Sleep Inn Maingate	55	★★½	$$−
Red Carpet Inn East	54	★★	$+
Comfort Inn Maingate	53	★★½	$$−
Days Inn Civic Center	53	★★½	$$−·
Central Motel	53	★★	$+
Economy Inns of America	53	★★	$+
Super 8	51	★★½	$$−
Lakeview Motel	51	★★	$+
Traveler's Inn	51	★★	$+
Travelodge Maingate West	50	★★½	$$
King's Motel	50	★★	$+
Howard Johnson Hotel	48	★★½	$$+
Red Roof Inn Kissimmee	48	★★½	$$+
Famous Host Inn	47	★★½	$$+
Riande Continental Plaza	46	★★½	$$+
Quality Inn Maingate West	45	★★½	$$+
Monte Carlo	45	★★	$+
Best Western Eastgate	43	★★½	$$−
Fairfield Inn International	43	★★½	$$+
Park Inn International	43	★★½	$$+
Rodeway Inn Civic Center	43	★★½	$$+
Ho Jo Inn Maingate	42	★★½	$$+
Best Western Plaza Int'l.	41	★★½	$$+
Choice Suites	41	★★½	$$+
Comfort Inn at Lake Buena Vista	41	★★½	$$+
Days Inn International Drive	40	★★½	$$+
Red Roof Inn Orlando	39	★★	$$−
Days Inn Orlando Lakeside	38	★★½	$$$−
Knights Inn Maingate	37	★★½	$+
Las Palmas Hotel	36	★★½	$$$−

The Best Deals on Two-Star Rooms (continued)

Hotel	Value Rating	Star Rating	Cost
Wilson World Maingate	36	★★½	$$$−
Days Inn Universal Studios	35	★★½	$$$−
Days Inn Maingate West	31	★★	$$
Econo Lodge Maingate West	31	★★	$$+
Econo Lodge Maingate Hawaiian	30	★★	$$+
Days Inn Maingate East	23	★★	$$$

—— *When Only the Best Will Do* ——

The trouble with profiles, including ours, is that details and distinctions are sacrificed in the interest of brevity. For example, dozens of properties have swimming pools and though most are quite basic and ordinary, a few are pretty spectacular.

Because the World tends to be a family-oriented place, and because many of our young readers have let us know that their favorite activity while in Orlando was swimming in the hotel pool, we have included a pool ranking. The pools are evaluated on the basis of size, cleanliness, imagination, and general ambience. Consideration was also given to shade for the parents who will, of course, watch their children at all times.

All of the Disney-owned lodging properties, as well as the Walt Disney World Swan and Dolphin, have extraordinary swimming areas. Some, like the Grand Floridian, the Polynesian, the Beach Club, and the Yacht Club, feature a freshwater lake beach in addition to swimming pools. Because the Disney hotel swimming facilities are so uniformly outstanding, we have grouped them as follows.

The Best Hotel Swimming Facilities

1. Disney's Yacht & Beach Clubs
2. Disney's Port Orleans and Disney's Polynesian Resort
3. Disney's Caribbean Beach Resort
4. WDW Dolphin & Swan and Disney's Grand Floridian
5. Ramada Resort Maingate at the Parkway
6. Hyatt Grand Cypress
7. All other Disney properties*
8. Radisson Inn Lake Buena Vista
9. Radisson Inn Maingate
10. Grosvenor Resort–Disney Village
11. Wynfield Inn
12. Sheraton Lakeside Inn
13. Hilton Inn Gateway

The Best Hotel Swimming Facilities (continued)

14. Quality Suites Maingate East
15. Holiday Inn Maingate
16. Hawthorne Suites
17. Summerfield Suites
18. Homewood Suites Maingate
19. The Hilton–Disney Village
20. Heritage Inn
21. Courtyard by Marriott
22. Wilson World Maingate
23. Hotel Royal Plaza
24. Holiday Inn Maingate East
25. Ramada Inn Westgate

*Includes the Contemporary, Dixie Landings, and Vacation Club.

A few properties on US 192 are located on a lake. While their pool areas may not rank with those above, they do offer jet ski rentals, waterskiing, and other special activities. They are (listed in alphabetical order):

Embassy Motel
Golden Link Motel
Key Motel
King's Motel
Lakeview Motel
Park Inn International
Quality Inn Lake Cecile
Residence Inn Lake Cecile
Traveler's Inn

—— *Lodging Discounts in the Walt Disney World Area* ——

A company called EIG (Exit Information Guide) publishes a book of discount coupons for bargain rates at hotels throughout the state of Florida. These books are available free of charge in many restaurants and motels along the main interstate highways leading to the Sunshine State. Since most folks make reservations prior to leaving home, picking up the coupon book en route does not help much. For two dollars ($5 Canadian), however, EIG will mail you a copy (third class) before you make your reservations. If you call and use a credit card, EIG will send the guide first class for $3. Write or call:

Exit Information Guide
4205 N.W. 6th Street
Gainesville, FL 32609
(904) 371-3948

Condominium Deals

There are a large number of condo resorts and timeshares in the Kissimmee/Orlando area that rent to vacationers for a week or even less. Bargains can be found, especially during off-peak periods. Reservations and information can be obtained from the following reservation services:

Condolink	(800) 733-4445
Kissimmee–St. Cloud Reservations Center	(800) 333-5477

The majority of area condos that rent to visitors also work with travel agents. In many cases the condo owners pay an enhanced commission to agents who rent the units for *reduced consumer rates*. It's worth a call to your travel agent.

Another good source of information is the book *Condo & Villa Vacations Rated*, by Clinton and Ellen Burr, published by Prentice Hall Travel. Recently updated, the $17 guide describes and rates the better condos and timeshares in the Walt Disney World area.

—— How to Evaluate a Travel Package ——

Hundreds of Disney Travel company package vacations are offered to the public each year. Some are created by the Walt Disney Travel Company, others by Delta Airlines or by Premier Cruise Lines, and some by independent travel agents and wholesalers. Almost all Walt Disney World packages include lodging at Walt Disney World and a five-day all parks admission pass. All Delta packages include air transportation. Premier Cruise packages mix a three- or four-day cruise with three or four days at Walt Disney World.

Packages should be a win/win proposition for both the buyer and the seller. The buyer only has to make one phone call and deal with a single salesperson to set up the whole vacation: transportation, rental car, admissions, lodging, meals, and even golf and tennis. The seller, likewise, only has to deal with the buyer one time, eliminating the need for separate sales, confirmations, and billing. In addition to streamlining selling, processing, and administration, some packagers also buy air fares in bulk on contract like a broker playing the commodities market. Buying a large number of air fares in advance allows the packager to buy them at a significant savings from posted fares. The same practice is applied also to hotel rooms. Because selling vacation packages is an efficient way of doing business, and because the packager can often buy individual package components (air fare, lodging, etc.) in bulk at discount, savings in operating expenses realized by the seller are sometimes passed on to the buyer so that, in addition to convenience, the package is also an exceptional value. In any event, that is the way it is supposed to work.

All too often, in practice, the seller realizes all of the economies and passes nothing in the way of savings on to the buyer. In some instances, packages are loaded additionally with extras which cost the packager next to nothing, but which run the retail price of the package sky-high. As you might expect, the savings to be passed along to customers are still somewhere in Fantasyland.

When considering a package, choose one that includes features you are sure to use. Whether you use all the features or not, you will most certainly pay for them. Second, if cost is of greater concern than convenience, make a few phone calls and see what the package would cost if you booked its individual components (air fare, rental car, lodging, etc.) on your own. If the package price is less than the a la carte cost, the package is a good deal. If the costs are about the same, the package is probably worth it for the convenience.

An Example. A popular package offered by the Walt Disney Travel Company is Disney's Deluxe Magic package, which includes:

1. Four nights' accommodation at your choice of the Grand Floridian Beach Resort, Yacht and Beach Club Resorts, Polynesian Resort, Contemporary Resort, The Disney Inn, Disney's Village Resort, Vacation Club Resort, or Fort Wilderness Resort trailer homes. Rates vary with choice of lodging between the Grand Floridian, most expensive, and Disney's Village Resort, least expensive.
2. Five days' use of the Walt Disney World Transportation System.
3. Five days' admission and unlimited use of the three major theme parks.
4. Five days' admission and unlimited use of Pleasure Island, River Country, Typhoon Lagoon, and Discovery Island.
5. Five days' unlimited use of Walt Disney World recreational facilities and activities.
6. Breakfast, lunch, and dinner each day at a variety of Disney World restaurants, gratuities included.

7. Admission to a behind-the-scenes guided tour at EPCOT Center.
8. A Fantasia commemorative clock (one per party).
9. Tips for valet parking and baggage handling both checking in and out.
10. Steve Birnbaum's *Official Guide to Walt Disney World* (one per party).

This package is interesting because it is one of Walt Disney World's most popular packages and is loaded with benefits and amenities. It is also interesting because you can come out a winner or a loser depending on how you use it. The package price varies with your choice of hotel and room. If you chose a room with a view of the pool or marina at the Polynesian Resort, the package cost $1,147 for each adult, two to a room, in July of 1993 when we did our analysis.

Although the package is set up for five whole days, it only provides four nights' lodging. Most visitors will either have to travel on one of those five days or alternatively book an extra night or two at the Polynesian in order to take advantage of their fifth day of benefits.

The five days' use of the transportation system is no big deal. Anyone who buys a regular four- or five-day admission can ride around all day on the buses and monorails.

The package provides five days' admission to the Magic Kingdom, EPCOT Center, Disney-MGM Studios, River Country, Typhoon Lagoon, Discovery Island, and Pleasure Island. Since it takes at least four days to see the major theme parks, that doesn't leave much time to take advantage of Typhoon Lagoon, River Country, Discovery Island, and Pleasure Island.

Another problem with the five days' admission provided in the package is that whatever you don't use you lose. Your admission options are good only for the days of your package, unlike the regular (non package) five-day admission, the 5-Day Super Duper Pass. Unused days on the Super Duper Pass are good forever. If you come back next month or three years from now you will be able to finish using your Super Duper Pass. Not so with the package admission.

The package provides five days of admission to Discovery Island, Pleasure Island, Typhoon Lagoon, and River Country. With the Super Duper Pass you have seven days from the date of purchase to enjoy these four smaller parks.

Unlimited use of Walt Disney World recreational facilities and activities are included in the package. This is a big deal if you want to golf, play tennis, boat, fish, and horseback ride. If you golf all morning, for instance, and visit the theme parks in the late afternoon and evening, you'll be walking on your tongue by the third day, but at least will be taking advantage of the recreational benefits. No matter how you cut it, you can't be in two places at once, and there is not enough time in five days to do all the stuff the package provides.

If you are a big eater, the inclusion of breakfast, lunch, and dinner each day is a major plus. Not only are these meals included, but you can eat as much as you want—appetizers, desserts, the works. Even tips are included (but not alcoholic beverages). You must eat all of your meals in full-service restaurants (no fast-food counter service or room service). While this ensures nicer meals, the time it takes to have a big sit-down breakfast and lunch every day bites into your touring and recreational schedule. On the bright side, you can select dinner shows like the *Hoop Dee Doo Revue* (providing space is available) or Disney character breakfasts as part of your meal package.

As far as the rest is concerned, the Fantasia clock is only available as a gift for package buyers. The behind-the-scenes tours are available to the general public at $20. Finally, the *Official Guide to Walt Disney World* by Steve Birnbaum is available at bookstores if you want to buy it exclusive of the package.

In the final analysis, the World Adventure Vacation package is best suited to vacationers who have lots of energy and big appetites, and who like to play tennis and golf and go boating. It's for people who plan to be on the go from dawn until midnight and visit the theme parks every day. And finally, as you may have figured out, the package is set up in a way that makes it almost impossible not to waste many of its benefits.

Getting Down to Dollars and Cents.   If you leave out the golf, tennis, boating, and other recreational extras provided by the package, here is how the package compares to going it on your own:

Option A: Disney's Deluxe Magic package for two people
sharing room with a view of the pool at
Polynesian Resort. $1,147 per person × 2 $2,294

Option B: Creating your own vacation with the same basic
features as in the Deluxe Magic package.

Polynesian Resort (with same room as in package) for four
nights with tax included.   Total for two adults $1,402

Two 5-Day Super Duper Passes (unlimited admission to three major and four minor parks) with tax	360
$55 per person per day meal allowance ($10 for breakfast, $15 for lunch, and $30 for dinner) for two people for five days	550
EPCOT Center behind-the-scenes tour for two	40
Fantasia clock	30
Arrival and departure gratuities	14
Birnbaum's *Official Guide to Walt Disney World*	12
Grand Total for two people	$2,408
Preliminary amount saved by buying the package	$114

Since only Option A (the package) includes the recreational facilities and activities, you could say that you are getting all the recreational extras at no additional charge. To take maximum advantage of the Deluxe Magic package, however, it would be better to lengthen your stay to at least a week. The additional days would allow you more time to enjoy the recreational activities and facilities. This package would work especially well for a party whose members had different vacation interests. Some members of the party could play golf or tennis while others spent their time at the theme parks.

Testing several other Disney packages for the summer of 1993, we found that packages which included meals generally afforded more savings than those which primarily included lodging and park admissions. The Disney Resort Magic package (which included lodging, admissions, one breakfast, and the Birnbaum book), for example, totaled almost exactly the same as the sum of its individual components. The same was true for Disney's Festival Magic package which included only lodging and admission. With both of these packages, the consumer was better off buying featured items a la carte in order to get the Super Duper Pass (which allows future use of unused admission days).

Another Example.   The simpler the package, the easier to evaluate. Most Delta Dream Vacation packages include air fare, round-trip airport transfers, lodging, and admission to all major and minor theme parks for five days. A Delta Dream Vacation package including the following features cost $2,025 in July of 1993 for a Cleveland, Ohio, couple:

Round-trip coach air fare on Delta from Cleveland

Four nights lodging at the Polynesian Resort (garden view)

Round-trip airport transfers to and from Walt Disney World

Unlimited admission to the three major and four minor
parks for your entire stay

One breakfast at the Walt Disney World restaurant of your
choice

Option A:	Delta Dream Vacation package with room at the Polynesian Resort (garden view). Total for two adults	$2,025
Option B:	Booking the same air fare, room, and admissions yourself.	

Same room at the Polynesian Resort for four nights, tax included	$992
5-Day Super Duper Pass for two with tax	360
Round-trip airport transfers for two from Mears Motor Transportation Service	46
Contemporary Resort character breakfast, buffet for two	23
Total before air fare	$1,421

If you subtract the a la carte (Option B) costs of all components from
the total package price ($2,025 minus $1,421), the remainder ($604)
amounts to what you are being charged for air fare, in this case about
$302 per person ($604 divided by two). If you can fly round-trip to
Orlando from Cleveland for less than $302 a person, the package is
not such a great deal. If air fares from Cleveland equal or exceed $302
per person, then the package makes sense.

Disney Reservationists.   If you buy a package from Disney, do not
expect Disney reservationists to offer suggestions or help you sort
out your options. As a rule they will not volunteer information, but
will only respond to specific questions you pose, adroitly ducking any
query that calls for an opinion. A reader from North Riverside, Illinois,
wrote, complaining:

> I have received various pieces of literature from WDW and it is
> very confusing to try and figure everything out. My wife made

two telephone calls and the representatives from WDW were very courteous. However, they only answered the questions posed and were not very eager to give advice on what might be most cost effective. [The] WDW reps would not say if we would be better off doing one thing over the other. I feel a person could spend eight hours on the telephone with WDW reps and not have any more input than you get from reading the literature.

Another reader, also from Illinois, had this to say:

I called Disney's reservations number and asked for availability and rates. . . . [Because] of the *Unofficial Guide's* warning about Disney reservationists answering only the questions posed, I specifically asked, "Are there any special rates or discounts for that room during the month of October?" She replied, "Yes, we have that room available at a special price . . ." [For] the price of one phone call, I saved $440.

If you cannot get the information you need from the Disney people, try a good travel agent. Chances are the agent will be more forthcoming in helping you sort out your options.

Information Needed for Evaluation.   For quick reference and to save on phone expenses (Walt Disney World's only 800 number is for travel agents), write or call Walt Disney World accommodations reservations (see page 25) and ask that you be mailed a Walt Disney World Resort Vacation Guide and a rate sheet for the Walt Disney World lodging properties that shows the various rooms available at each property with their respective rates. The rate sheet also contains a price list for all Walt Disney World theme park admission options, including Pleasure Island, Typhoon Lagoon, Disney's Boardwalk, Discovery Island, and River Country. This in hand, you are ready to evaluate any package that appeals to you. Remember that all packages are quoted on a per person basis, and there is a 10% combination sales and room tax in Orange County, and a 9% combination sales and room tax in Osceola County. For about everything else you buy in Florida (except groceries and prescription medicine) a 6% sales tax applies. Good luck.

Getting There

Directions

If you arrive by automobile you can reach any Walt Disney World attraction or destination via World Drive, off US 192, or via EPCOT Center Drive, off I-4 (see map, pages 86–87).

If you are traveling *south* on the Florida Turnpike: Exit at Clermont, take US 27 south, turn left onto US 192, and then follow the signs to Walt Disney World.

If you are traveling *north* on the Florida Turnpike: Exit westbound onto I-4 and exit I-4 at EPCOT Center Drive.

If you are traveling *west* on I-4: Exit at EPCOT Center Drive and follow the signs.

If you are traveling *east* on I-4: Exit to US 192 northbound and then follow the signs.

Walt Disney World Village has its own entrance separate and distinct from entrances to the theme parks. To reach Walt Disney World Village take FL 535 exit off of I-4 and proceed north, following the signs.

Getting to Walt Disney World from the Airport

If you are flying, buy a package that includes transportation from the airport to your hotel if you do not intend to rent a car. If not on a package, try to find a hotel which offers shuttle service to the airport. Failing this, try to share transportation to the Disney World area. If you get stuck with a hired shuttle (where you ride with other Disney World bound passengers), expect to pay $22–35 per person round trip. Mears Motor Transportation Service (407) 423-5566 charges $23 per adult round trip. Cabs run about $32–42 *one way*. One option, if there are at least two in your party, is to rent a compact car at a weekly rate (even if you will not need the car for an entire week). For only a few dollars more than the shuttle fee or the cab fare, you will take care of your airport transportation needs and have a car at your disposal to boot.

A Good Map Is Hard to Find

We frequently hear from readers complaining about the signs and maps provided by the Disney people. While it is not difficult to find the major theme parks, it can be quite an odyssey to strike out in search of other Walt Disney World destinations. Many maps supplied by the Disney organization are stylistically rendered and just plain hard to read, while others provide less than complete information. To make matters worse, the maps (all produced by various Disney divisions) do not always agree with each other.

In the 1993 edition of this guide, we recommended that guests contact Walt Disney World Seminar Productions for a good map of Walt Disney World. As it turned out, Seminar Productions had discontinued printing their map, and our recommendation created a great deal of extra work and consternation for their small department. Given that the objective of the *Unofficial Guide* is to reduce, rather than create stress, we feel bad about all the commotion we stirred up. As for a decent map, a new one has been prepared and can be obtained by calling (407) 824-4321. Ask for the Walt Disney World Resort Map that contains maps of the overall resort as well as the three major theme parks and a bus chart.

Magic Kingdom and EPCOT Center Parking

The Magic Kingdom and EPCOT Center have their own pay parking lots (each one the size of Vermont), including close-in parking for the handicapped. In the case of the Magic Kingdom, a tram meets you at a loading station near where you parked and transports you to the Transportation and Ticket Center. Here you can buy passes to both the Magic Kingdom and EPCOT Center. If you wish to proceed to the Magic Kingdom you can either ride the ferryboat across Seven Seas Lagoon or catch the monorail. If you wish to go to EPCOT Center, you can board a separate monorail that connects EPCOT Center to the Transportation and Ticket Center. The various sections of the Magic Kingdom (Transportation and Ticket Center) parking lot are named for Disney characters. Guests are given a receipt with the aisle numbers and names of the parking sections listed on the reverse side. Mark where you have parked and jot down the aisle number in the space provided. Put the receipt in your billfold or some other safe place for referral when you return to your car. Failure to take these precautions will often result in a lengthy search for your car at a time when you will be pretty tuckered out.

If you wish to visit EPCOT Center you can park at the Magic Kingdom (Transportation and Ticket Center) parking lot and commute via monorail, or park directly in the EPCOT Center parking lot. Arrangements in the EPCOT Center lot are essentially the same as described above; a tram will shuttle you from where you park to the EPCOT Center entrance, and you will be given a receipt where you can mark your parking place for later reference. At EPCOT Center the sections of the parking lot are named for pavilions in the Future World area of the park. The big difference between parking for the Magic Kingdom and parking for EPCOT Center is that access to the park is direct from the tram at EPCOT Center whereas to reach the Magic Kingdom you must transfer from the tram to the ferryboat or the monorail at the Transportation and Ticket Center. If you park at EPCOT Center and wish to go to the Magic Kingdom you may do so by taking the monorail from EPCOT Center to the Transportation and Ticket Center and then transferring to a Magic Kingdom monorail.

Disney-MGM Studios Parking

The Disney planners seriously underestimated the number of cars the Disney-MGM parking lot would have to accommodate. During the summer of 1991 it was almost routine for the lot to fill by 10:30 or 11 A.M. Monday through Thursday, with thousands of late arriving guests being turned away. In 1992, however, the parking facility was greatly enlarged and it is more rare nowadays for the lot to fill to capacity.

Moving Your Car from Lot to Lot on the Same Day

Once you have paid to park in any of the major theme park lots, hang on to your receipt. If you decide to visit another theme park later in the same day, you will be admitted to that park's parking complex without additional charge upon showing your receipt. Walt Disney World lodging guests are not charged to park in any of the theme park lots.

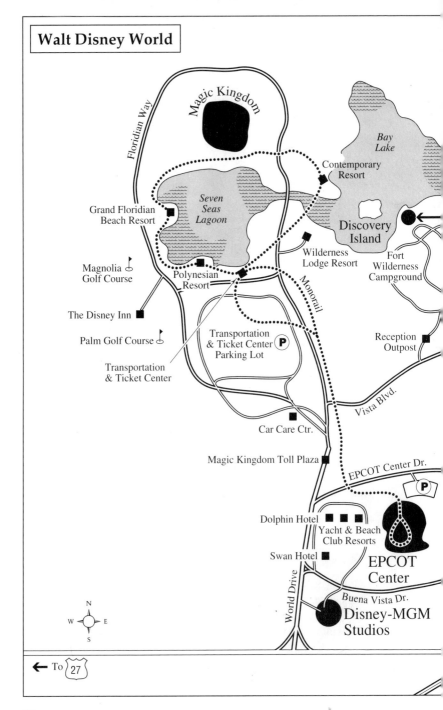

Walt Disney World

Magic Kingdom

Floridian Way

Bay Lake

Contemporary Resort

Seven Seas Lagoon

Grand Floridian Beach Resort

Discovery Island

Magnolia Golf Course

Wilderness Lodge Resort

Fort Wilderness Campground

Polynesian Resort

The Disney Inn

Palm Golf Course

Monorail

Transportation & Ticket Center Parking Lot

Reception Outpost

Transportation & Ticket Center

Car Care Ctr.

Vista Blvd.

Magic Kingdom Toll Plaza

EPCOT Center Dr.

Dolphin Hotel

Yacht & Beach Club Resorts

Swan Hotel

EPCOT Center

World Drive

Buena Vista Dr.

Disney-MGM Studios

N
W E
S

← To 27

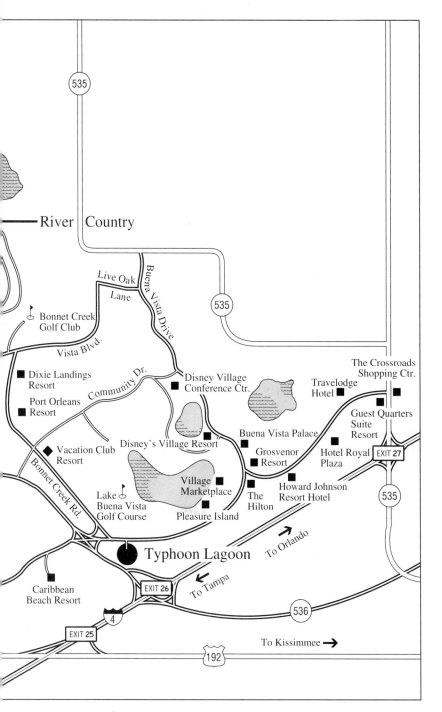

River Country

535

Live Oak Lane

Buena Vista Drive

535

Bonnet Creek Golf Club

Vista Blvd.

Dixie Landings Resort

Port Orleans Resort

Community Dr.

Disney Village Conference Ctr.

The Crossroads Shopping Ctr.

Travelodge Hotel

Guest Quarters Suite Resort

Vacation Club Resort

Disney's Village Resort

Buena Vista Palace

Grosvenor Resort

Hotel Royal Plaza

EXIT 27

Bonnet Creek Rd.

Lake Buena Vista Golf Course

Village Marketplace

Pleasure Island

The Hilton

Howard Johnson Resort Hotel

535

Typhoon Lagoon

To Orlando

Caribbean Beach Resort

EXIT 26

To Tampa

536

4

EXIT 25

To Kissimmee →

192

Taking a Tram or Shuttle Bus from Your Hotel

Trams and shuttle buses are provided by many hotels and motels in the vicinity of Walt Disney World. They represent a fairly carefree alternative for getting to and from the theme parks, letting you off right at the entrance and saving you the cost of parking. The rub is that they might not get you there as early as you desire (a critical point if you take our touring advice) or be available at the time you wish to return to your lodging. Also, some shuttles go directly to Walt Disney World while others make stops at other motels and hotels in the vicinity. Each shuttle service is a little bit different so check out the particulars when you arrive at your hotel.

Be forewarned that most hotel shuttle services do not add additional vehicles at park opening or closing times. In the mornings, your biggest problem is you might not get a seat. However, at closing time or following a hard rain, you can expect a mass exodus from the park. The worst case scenario is that more people will be waiting for the shuttle to your hotel than the bus will hold and that some will be left. While most (but not all) hotel shuttles return for stranded guests, you may suffer a wait of 20 minutes to an hour or more. Our suggestion, if you are depending on hotel shuttles, is to leave the park at least 45 minutes before closing. If you stay in the park until closing and lack the energy to hassle with the shuttle, catch a bus or monorail to the nearest Disney hotel and take a cab from there.

If there is a hard rain during the day and you want to return to your hotel, we suggest taking a Disney bus or the monorail to the nearest resort hotel and catching a cab from there.

Making the Most of
Your Time and Money

Allocating Time

During Walt Disney World's first decade, a family with a week's vacation could enjoy the Magic Kingdom and River Country and still have several days for the beach or other area attractions. Since the opening of EPCOT Center in 1982, however, Walt Disney World has steadily been enlarging to monopolize the same family's entire week. Today, with the additions of Typhoon Lagoon, the Disney-MGM Studios, and Pleasure Island, you had best allocate five days for a whirlwind tour (or seven days if you're old-fashioned and insist on a little relaxation during your vacation). If you do not have five or seven days, or think you might want to venture beyond the edge of "The World," be prepared to make some hard choices.

The theme parks, studios, and swimming attractions are **huge,** require a lot of walking, and sometimes a lot of waiting in lines. Moving in and among typically large crowds all day is exhausting. Oftentimes, the unrelenting central Florida sun zaps the most hearty traveler, making tempers short. In our many visits to Walt Disney World we observed, particularly on hot summer days, a dramatic transition from happy enthusiastic tourists upon arrival to zombies plodding along later in the day. Visitors who began their day enjoying the wonders of Disney imagination lapsed into an exhausted, production-line mentality ("We've got two more rides in Fantasyland, then we can go back to the hotel").

We recommend that you approach Walt Disney World the same way you would approach an eight-course Italian dinner: with plenty of time between courses. The best way not to have fun is to attempt to cram too much into too little time.

Prices Subject to Change Without Notice

Book reviewers who complain that prices quoted in guidebooks are out of date should note that Walt Disney World ticket prices seem to change about as often as the prime rate. If we were publishing a daily newspaper, maybe we could keep up. But since we are covering Walt Disney World in a book, we've decided to throw in the towel; no more listing admission prices. We will tell you this much: expect to pay about $36 for an adult One-Park/One-Day Ticket, about $132 for a 4-Day all three parks Super Pass, about $163 for a 4-Day Super Duper Pass (includes both major and minor parks), and about $180 for a 5-Day Super Duper Pass. Annual Passports cost about $201, and Florida Four-Season Passes run around $105. All of the above admission cost estimates include tax. Incidentally, price increases on the various Walt Disney World admission options ranged from 3–7% during the past year.

Walt Disney World Admission Options

There are basically seven Walt Disney World admission options (several with silly names):

1. One-Park/One-Day Ticket (1-Day Ticket)
2. 4-Day Super Pass
3. 4-Day Super Duper Pass (introduced in the spring of 1993)
4. 5-Day Super Duper Pass
5. Be Our Guest Pass
6. Annual Passport
7. Florida Four-Season Pass

The **One-Day Ticket** is good for admission and unlimited use of "attractions and experiences" at the Magic Kingdom *or* EPCOT Center *or* the Disney-MGM Studios, but does *not* provide same day admission to more than one of the three.

The **4-Day Super Pass** "allows you to come and go as you please at the Magic Kingdom, EPCOT Center, and the Disney-MGM Studios, and includes unlimited use of the transportation systems linking the parks." *Remember to get your hand stamped for reentry, if you leave a park but plan to return later.*

The **4-Day Super Duper Pass** provides same-day admission to the three major parks, unlimited use of the transportation systems, plus admission to the minor parks (Pleasure Island, Typhoon Lagoon, River

Country, and Discovery Island). Admission to the minor parks is unlimited for a seven-day period beginning the day the pass is first used at one of the three major parks.

The **5-Day Super Duper Pass** provides same day admission to all three parks, unlimited use of the transportation systems, plus admission to Pleasure Island, Typhoon Lagoon, River Country, and Discovery Island. Admission to these last is unlimited for a seven-day period beginning the day the pass is first used at one of the three major parks.

The **Be Our Guest Pass** is an admissions program for Walt Disney World lodging and campground guests. It provides the same benefits as the Super Duper Passes (described above), but can be purchased for *any* length of stay from one night to two days or longer. The Be Our Guest program is the first time Walt Disney World has offered a comprehensive admission option (all major and minor parks) for stays shorter than four days. Be Our Guest Passes additionally provide a cost savings of about 7% compared to the Super Duper Passes. On the negative side, Be Our Guest Passes are good only for the guest's inclusive length of stay, while unused days on the Super Pass and the Super Duper Passes are good forever.

The **Annual Passport** is good for unlimited use of the major theme parks for one year. An add-on option can be purchased that also provides unlimited use of the minor theme parks. In addition to theme park admission, Annual Pass holders are accorded a number of perks, including complimentary parking and the privilege of making advance reservations at Walt Disney World restaurants.

The **Florida Four-Season Pass** is a cut-rate pass that allows the holder to enjoy unlimited use of the three major theme parks during specific, quieter times of the year. While applicants must prove Florida residency to be eligible, it is not necessary to have a Florida driver's license or live in Florida year-round. Proof of ownership of property in Florida, or even a Florida phone bill, is considered adequate documentation for the issuance of the Four-Season Pass.

With any of the multi-day passes, you can tour the Disney-MGM Studios in the morning, stop by the Magic Kingdom for an afternoon parade, and eat dinner at one of EPCOT Center's ethnic restaurants that evening. The four- and five-day Super and Super Duper Passes do not have to be used on consecutive days and are, in fact, good forever. Four-day passes can be upgraded to five-day passes as long as they have at least one day's admission remaining by paying the difference between the four-day and five-day pass price.

If you only have one day to spend, select the park that most interests you and buy the 1-Day Ticket. If you have two days and do not plan on returning to Florida for a couple of years, buy two 1-Day Tickets (or a Be Our Guest Pass if you are Disney lodging guest). If you think you might be passing through the area again in the next year or two, go ahead and spring for a four- or five-day pass. Use two days of admission to see as much of all three parks as you can, and save the remaining days for another trip. Remember that with the Super Duper Passes, admission to Pleasure Island, Typhoon Lagoon, River Country, and Discovery Island expires within seven days of the first time you use your pass at the Magic Kingdom, EPCOT Center, or the Disney-MGM Studios. If you plan to spend three or more days at Walt Disney World, buy the four- or five-day pass. If you live in Florida or plan to spend seven or more days in the major theme parks, the Annual Passport at about $201 is a good buy. If you live in Florida and do not mind being restricted to visiting Walt Disney World at designated off-peak times of year, the Florida Four-Season Pass at about $105 should be considered.

Many readers write asking if they can use remaining admissions on partially redeemed four- and five-day Super and Super Duper Passes brought home by relatives. The facts are as follows:

1. The pass is sold to the purchaser on a non-transferable basis. The pass states on the back, "To be valid this Pass must be used by the same person for all days."

2. There is nothing on the pass that in any way identifies the purchaser.

3. Disney admission attendants do not request to see a receipt or any other proof-of-purchase documentation for admission passes.

Where to Buy Your Admission in Advance

You can buy your admission before you leave home at a Disney Store or, if you're driving, at Disney's Ocala Information Center at exit 68 on I-75. If you plan to fly to Walt Disney World, you will be able to purchase tickets at the airport Disney Store.

Tickets are also available through the mail from the Walt Disney World Ticket Mail Order Service (see page 27). In addition, you can purchase tickets at most of the Walt Disney World hotels.

Where Not to Buy Your Admission in Advance

Because admission passes to Walt Disney World are not discounted, any offers of free or cut-rate tickets should trigger warning signals. Anyone offering free tickets to any attraction in the Orlando/Kissimmee area is probably selling real estate or time-share condominiums. You may actually receive a free ticket, but you will have to subject yourself to a lengthy site inspection and/or high-pressure sales pitch.

Many hotels outside of Walt Disney World make tickets to area attractions available through independent travelbrokers who maintain a kiosk or desk in the hotel's lobby. While these brokers are legitimate operators, the only advantage to buying from them is convenience. In the case of Disney admission passes, expect to pay 5–10 percent more for your tickets if you purchase them from an independent.

How Much Does It Cost to Go to Walt Disney World for a Day?

Let's say we have a family of four, Mom and Dad, Tim (age 12), and Sandy (age 8), driving their own car and staying outside of Walt Disney World. Since they plan to be in the area for a week they intend to buy 4-Day All Three Parks Passports. Here is how much a typical day would cost, excluding lodging and transportation:

Breakfast for four at Denny's with tax & tip	$18.75
EPCOT Center parking fee	5.00
One day's admission on a 4-Day All Three Parks Passport	
Dad: Adult 4-Day with tax = $132 divided by four (days)	33.00
Mom: Adult 4-Day with tax = $132 divided by four (days)	33.00
Tim: Adult 4-Day with tax = $132 divided by four (days)	33.00
Sandy: Child 4-Day with tax = $104 divided by four (days)	26.00
Morning break (soda or coffee)	8.50
Fast-food lunch (sandwich or burger, fries, soda), no tip	23.00
Afternoon break (soda and popcorn)	11.50
Dinner at Italy (no alcoholic beverages), with tax and tip	86.00
Souvenirs (Mickey T-shirts for Tim and Sandy) with tax *	33.50
One-day Total (does not include lodging or transportation)	$311.25

*Cheer up, you won't have to buy souvenirs every day.

Which Park to See First?

This question is less academic than it appears at first glance, especially if there are children or teenagers in your party. Children who see the Magic Kingdom first expect more of the same type of entertainment at EPCOT Center and the Disney-MGM Studios. At EPCOT Center they are often disappointed by the educational orientation and more serious tone (many adults react the same way). Disney-MGM offers some pretty wild action, but here too the general presentation is educational and more adult.

For first-time visitors especially, see EPCOT Center first; you will be able to enjoy it fully without having been preconditioned to think of Disney entertainment as solely in the fantasy/adventure genre. Parties which include children should definitely see EPCOT Center first. Children will be more likely to judge and enjoy EPCOT Center according to its own merits if they see it first, as well as being more relaxed and patient in their touring.

Next, see the Disney-MGM Studios. The Studios help both young and old make a fluid transition from the imposing EPCOT Center to the fanciful Magic Kingdom. Also, because the Studios are smaller, you will not have to walk as much or stay as long. Save the Magic Kingdom for last.

—— Optimum Touring Situation ——

An optimum touring situation at Walt Disney World requires a good itinerary, a minimum of five days on site (i.e., not including travel time), and a fair amount of money. It also requires a fairly prodigious appetite for Disney-type entertainment. We will provide the itinerary; the rest is up to you.

The essence of an Optimum Touring Situation is to see the various attractions of Walt Disney World in a series of shorter, less exhausting visits during the cooler, less crowded parts of the day, with plenty of rest and relaxation between visits.

Since an Optimum Touring Situation calls for leaving and returning to the theme parks on most days, it obviously makes for easier logistics if you are staying in one of the Walt Disney World resort hotels connected by the monorail. Also, if you stay in Walt Disney World you are accorded early entry privileges at the Magic Kingdom four days each week, as well as the option of making advance reservations for the *Hoop Dee Doo Revue* and the various dinner shows performed nightly at the resort hotels. In-World guests also have freer use of the bus, boat, and monorail transportation system, and have more alternatives for baby-sitting and children's programs. Sound good? It is, but be prepared to pay.

If you do not plan to stay at a Walt Disney World property, you can still use the day-by-day plan listed below. The plan will not be as efficient owing to increased commuting time, but it will be a whole lot less expensive.

Buy a 5-Day Super Duper Pass or, if you are staying in a Disney hotel, a Be Our Guest Pass. This will allow you to come and go as you desire at all of the major and minor theme parks.

If you visit Walt Disney World during a busy period (see page 32), you need to get up early to beat the crowds. Short lines and stress-free touring are basically incompatible with sleeping in. If you want to sleep late *and* enjoy your touring experience, visit Walt Disney World during a time of year when attendance is lighter.

We do not believe that there is one ideal itinerary. Tastes, levels of energy, and basic perspectives on what constitutes entertainment and relaxation vary. This understood, what follows is our personal version of an optimum Walt Disney World vacation week. It is the itinerary we use when asked to host a tour or guide a dignitary.

Before You Go

1. Make reservations as far in advance as possible for the Grand Floridian Beach Resort. If you cannot afford the Grand Floridian, go for the Contemporary Resort, Polynesian Resort, or The Disney Inn in that order (if your party is all adult, make The Disney Inn your second choice). The Disney Inn is serviced by the Disney bus system. The other three hotels are located along the monorail line. If all of the hotels mentioned above are too expensive, try Port Orleans or the Dixie Landings.

2. When you book your accommodations, try to make reservations for the *Hoop Dee Doo Revue*, a dinner show performed nightly in Pioneer Hall at the Fort Wilderness Campground. Try to obtain reservations for one of the days on which you do not visit EPCOT Center or the Magic Kingdom.

3. Reserve a rental car if you want to try local (off-World) restaurants or other attractions such as Universal Studios Florida, Sea World, or the Kennedy Space Center.

On Site

Day 0—Travel Day

1. Arrive and get settled. Explore the features and amenities of your hotel.

2. If you get checked in by 3 P.M. or earlier, and the Magic Kingdom is open until 9 P.M. or later, go ahead and run the itinerary for Day 4. If you arrive later in the day and are looking for something to do, this would be a perfect night for the *Hoop Dee Doo Revue*.

3. Before 9 P.M. call 56 (campground guests 45) and make next-day reservations for the EPCOT restaurants of your choice (Walt Disney World resort guests can make one- to three-day advance reservations for any Disney-MGM, EPCOT Center, or Magic Kingdom full-service restaurant). Try for a 1 P.M. lunch seating and a 7 or 8 P.M. dinner seating.

Day 1

1. Tour EPCOT Center using the Touring Plans provided in this guide. Break off the plan after lunch and return to the hotel for a nap and some beach time.

2. Return to EPCOT Center between 4 and 5 P.M., visiting any attractions in the Future World section of the park that you missed during the morning. Tour until dinner time.

3. After dinner, tour the World Showcase section of EPCOT Center until dark. Then find a good vantage point for watching IllumiNations, a fireworks, music, and laser spectacular performed nightly on the World Showcase Lagoon.

Day 2

1. Tour the Disney-MGM Studios according to the Touring Plans in this guide. You should be able to see everything by mid-afternoon.

2. Return to your hotel for rest and rejuvenation.

3. Try a quiet dinner in or out of Walt Disney World and then enjoy a performance of the Electrical Water Pageant at the waterfront of the Polynesian Resort. This is another good night for the *Hoop Dee Doo Revue* or one of the other Walt Disney World or local dinner shows. Early to bed.

Day 3

1. Visit Typhoon Lagoon utilizing the Touring Plan provided in this guide. Once again, be on hand when the park opens.

2. Return to the hotel sometime after lunch for campers' quiet time.

3. Eat a relatively early dinner in or out of the World and then visit Pleasure Island for a night of Disney family-style nightclubbing. If you have children with you, there are several baby-sitting/children's program alternatives available to choose from (see pages 171–72).

Day 4

1. Sleep late after your big night out. Eat lunch at the hotel and then take the monorail to the Magic Kingdom. If your party includes young children, use the Magic Kingdom Touring Plan for Parents with Small Children, starting at Step 13. If your group consists of adults and children over eight, use Day 2 of the Magic Kingdom Two-Day Touring Plan A.

2. Between 6 and 7 P.M., catch the monorail to one of the resort hotels for dinner. Before or after dinner, call 56 (campground guests 45) and make next-day dinner reservations for the EPCOT Center restaurant of your choice. Go for a 7 or 8 P.M. seating.

3. Return to the Magic Kingdom after dinner. Continue touring according to the Touring Plan, taking breaks to watch the evening parade and Fantasy in the Sky fireworks.

Day 5

1. Get up early and return to the Magic Kingdom, arriving early. If your party includes young children, use the Magic Kingdom One-Day Touring Plan for Parents with Small Children starting

with Step 1 and continue until you have seen everything. If your group is made up of adults and children over eight, use Day 1 of the Magic Kingdom Two-Day Touring Plan A.

2. Have a late lunch and get some rest at your hotel. In the late afternoon take the monorail to EPCOT Center. Visit any of the attractions you missed on Day 1 and have dinner.

—— Seeing Walt Disney World on a Tight Schedule ——

Many visitors do not have five days to devote to Disney attractions. Some are en route to other destinations or may wish to spend time sampling the attractions of Orlando and central Florida. For these visitors, efficient, time-effective touring is a must. They cannot afford long waits in line for rides, shows, or meals.

Even the most efficient touring plan will not allow the visitor to cover two or more of the major theme parks in one day, so plan on allocating at least an entire day to each park (an exception to this rule is when the theme parks close at different times, allowing the visitor to tour one park until closing time and then proceed to another park). If your schedule permits only one day of touring overall, we recommend concentrating your efforts on only one of the theme parks and saving the others for a subsequent visit.

One-Day Touring

A comprehensive tour of the Magic Kingdom, EPCOT Center, or the Disney-MGM Studios in one day is possible but requires a knowledge of the park, good planning, and no small reserve of energy and endurance. One-day touring does not leave much time for leisurely meals in sit-down restaurants, prolonged browsing in the many shops, or lengthy rest periods. Even so, one-day touring can be a fun, rewarding experience.

Successful one-day touring of either the Magic Kingdom or EPCOT Center, or of the Disney-MGM Studios, hinges on **three cardinal rules**:

1. Determine in Advance What You Really Want to See

What are the rides and attractions that appeal to you most? Which additional rides and attractions would you like to experience if you have any time left? What are you willing to forgo?

2. Arrive Early! Arrive Early! Arrive Early!

This is the single most important key to efficient touring and avoiding long lines. First thing in the morning there are no lines and relatively few people. The same four rides which you can experience in one hour in the early morning can take as long as three hours to see after 11:30 A.M. Have breakfast before you arrive so you will not have to waste your prime touring time sitting in a restaurant.

Always call the park, (407) 824-4321, the day before you visit to inquire at what time the park will open and close.

For the Magic Kingdom: Four days each week (usually on Tuesday, Thursday, Saturday, and Sunday) Walt Disney World hotel and campground guests (excluding guests at the Walt Disney World Village Hotels) are invited to enter the Magic Kingdom one hour before the general public is admitted. During this hour, the early entrants can enjoy all of the attractions in Fantasyland, as well as Space Mountain and the Grand Prix Raceway in Tomorrowland.

If you stay at a Walt Disney World hotel or campground, you definitely want to tour the Magic Kingdom on a morning when the program is in effect. Plan to arrive a half hour before the early entry opening time. If the official opening time is 9 A.M., for example, then the official early entry time for Disney hotel guests is 8 A.M. You should arrive at the park 30–40 minutes before that, at about 7:30 A.M.

On the other hand, if you are not eligible for early entry privileges, you want to avoid the Magic Kingdom on Tuesday, Thursday, Saturday, and Sunday, using these days to visit the other theme parks. On a Friday, Monday, or Wednesday, arrive at the Magic Kingdom parking lot an hour before the park's stated opening time (the parking lot and Transportation and Ticket Center open two hours early).

Those lodging outside of Walt Disney World must balance the least crowded days of the week (see pages 37–38) with an estimation of the impact of early entry. As a rule of thumb, however, we recommend that off-property patrons not tour the Magic Kingdom on early entry days. It is far better to arrive early and stay ahead of the crowd on non-early-entry days, than to enter the Magic Kingdom on an early entry day when a hoard of Disney lodging guests have been allowed into the park ahead of you. The ultimate key to efficient touring in any of the parks is to be one of the first guests through the turnstiles.

As an aside, those not eligible for early entry should not attempt sneaking in with the early entry guests. All Disney hotel and campground guests, including children, are issued dated identification cards on check-in at their hotel. These Disney I.D.'s must be presented along with a valid admission pass in order to enter the Magic Kingdom on an early entry morning.

Because the Disney people are always changing things, we suggest you call Walt Disney World Information at (407) 824-4321 before you leave home to verify which days of the week will be early entry days during your stay.

For EPCOT Center: Arrive at the main parking lot 45–50 minutes before the stated opening time. Buy your admission pass and line up at the turnstile to be admitted as soon as the park opens. EPCOT Center almost always opens a half hour earlier than the stated opening time.

For Disney-MGM Studios: Arrive at the Studios parking lot 40 minutes before the stated opening time. Have your admission and be ready to go.

Taking our advice about arriving early will work in your favor most of the time, particularly if you are vacationing at Walt Disney World over any holiday period (including National Education Association breaks or spring break) or during the summer. Because Disney opening procedures are flexible, however, you may occasionally suffer a few extra minutes waiting to be admitted. Rest assured that this investment in time is well spent.

The Disney folks vary opening procedures according to the number of visitors they anticipate on a given day. Simply stated, they open up as early as required to avoid crowds overwhelming the parking facilities, ticket sellers, and transportation systems. On busier days this almost always translates into admitting visitors a half hour to an hour before the officially stated opening time.

3. Avoid Bottlenecks

Helping you avoid bottlenecks is what this guide is all about. Bottlenecks occur as a result of crowd concentrations and/or less than optimal crowd management. Concentrations of hungry people create bottlenecks at restaurants during the lunch and dinner hours; concentrations of people moving towards the exit near closing time create bottlenecks in the gift shops en route to the gate; concentrations of visitors at new and unusually popular rides create bottlenecks and long waiting lines; rides which are slow in boarding and disembarking passengers create bottlenecks and long waiting lines. Avoiding bottlenecks involves being able to predict where, when, and why they occur. To this end we provide **Touring Plans** for the Magic Kingdom, EPCOT Center, and the Disney-MGM Studios, as well as for Typhoon Lagoon and Pleasure Island, to assist you in avoiding bottlenecks. In addition we provide detailed information on all rides and performances which allows you to estimate how long you may have to wait in line, and which also allows you to compare rides in terms of their capacity to accommodate large crowds. Touring Plans for the Magic Kingdom begin on page 271, Touring Plans for EPCOT Center begin on page 368, and the Touring Plan for Disney-MGM Studios begins on page 425. The Touring Plan for Typhoon Lagoon begins on page 465, and the Pleasure Island Touring Plan may be found on pages 491–94. For your convenience we have also included One-Day Touring Plans for Universal Studios Florida on pages 453–55.

In response to many reader requests, we have also added clip-out versions of the touring plans at the end of this book.

—— *Touring Plans: What They Are and How They Work* ——

When we interviewed Walt Disney World visitors who toured the theme parks on slow days, say in early December, they invariably waxed eloquent about the sheer delight of their experience. When we questioned visitors who toured on a moderate or busy day, however, they spent much of the interview telling us about the jostling crowds and how much time they stood in line. What a shame, they said, that you should devote so much time and energy to fighting the crowds in a place as special as Walt Disney World.

Given this complaint, we descended on Walt Disney World with a team of researchers to determine whether a touring plan could be devised that would move visitors counter to the flow of traffic and allow them to see any of the theme parks in one day with only minimal waits in line. On some of the busiest days of the year, our team monitored traffic flow into and through the theme parks, noting how the parks filled and how the patrons were distributed among the various attractions. Likewise, we observed which rides and attractions were most popular and where bottlenecks were most likely to form.

After many long days of collecting data, we devised a number of preliminary touring plans which we tested during one of the busiest weeks of the entire year. Each day individual members of our research team would tour the park according to one of the preliminary plans, noting how long it took to walk from place to place and how long the wait in line was for each ride or show. Combining the knowledge gained through these trial runs, we devised a master plan which we retested and fine-tuned. This plan, with very little variance from day to day, allowed us to experience all of the major rides and attractions, and most of the lesser ones, in one day, with an average wait in line at each ride or show of less than five minutes.

From this master plan we developed a number of alternative plans that take into account the varying tastes and personal requirements of different Walt Disney World patrons. Each plan operates with the same efficiency as the master plan but addresses the special needs and preferences of its intended users.

Finally, after all of the plans were tested by our staff, we selected (using convenience sampling) a number of everyday Walt Disney World patrons to test the plans. The only prerequisite for being chosen for the test group (the visitors who would test the touring plans) was that the guest must be visiting a Disney park for the first time. A second group of ordinary patrons was chosen for a "control group," first-time visitors who would tour the park according to their own plans but who would make notes of what they did and how much time they spent waiting in lines.

When the two groups were compared, the results proved no less than amazing. On days when EPCOT Center's and the Magic Kingdom's attendance exceeded 48,000, visitors touring on their own (without the plan) **averaged** 3⅔ hours more waiting in line per day than the patrons touring according to our plan, and they experienced 37 percent fewer rides and attractions.

Will the Plans Continue to Work Once the Secret Is Out?

Yes! First, all of the plans require that a patron be on hand when the theme parks open. Many vacationers simply refuse to make the sacrifice of rising early, but could see more in the one hour just after the parks open than in several hours once the parks begin to fill. Second, it is anticipated that less than one percent of any given day's attendance will have been exposed to the plans, not enough to bias the results. Last, most groups will interpret the plans somewhat, skipping certain rides or shows as a matter of personal taste.

How Frequently Are the Touring Plans Revised?

Because the Disney folks are always adding new attractions or changing operational procedures, we revise the Touring Plans every year. Most of the complaints we receive concerning the Touring Plans come from readers who are using older, out-of-date editions of the *Unofficial Guide*.

Touring Plans and the Obsessive/Compulsive Reader

We suggest that you follow the Touring Plans religiously, especially in the mornings, if you are visiting Walt Disney World during busier, more crowded times of year. The consequence of touring spontaneity in peak season is literally hours of otherwise avoidable standing in line.

During the quieter times of year, as our readers point out, there is no need to be compulsive about following the Touring Plans.

From a mom in Atlanta, Georgia:

Emphasize perhaps *not* following [the Touring Plans] in off-season. There is no reason to criss-cross the park when there are no lines.

From a Marlboro, New Jersey, father:

The time we went in November, the longest line was about a five minute wait. [At this time of year], your readers do not have to be so neurotic about running into the park and then to various attractions.

From a mother in Minneapolis:

I feel you should let your readers know to stop along the way to various attractions to appreciate what else may be going on around them. We encountered many families using the *Unofficial Guide* [who] became too serious about getting from one place to the next, missing the fun in between.

Finally, even on days when the parks are crowded, we realize that the Touring Plans can contribute to some stress and fatigue. A mother wrote us from Stillwater, Maine, saying:

> We were thankful for the Touring Plan and were able to get through the most popular rides early before the lines got long. One drawback was all the bouncing around we did backtracking through different parts of the Magic Kingdom in order to follow the Touring Plan. It was tiring and a bit hectic at times.

What can we say? It's one of those *lesser of two evils* situations. If you choose to visit Walt Disney World at a busy time of year, you can either get up early and hustle around, or you can sleep in and take it easy, consequently seeing less and spending a lot of time standing in lines.

Tour Groups from Hell

We have discovered that tour groups of up to 100 people are using our touring plans. A lady from Memphis writes:

> When we arrived at The Land [pavilion at EPCOT], a tour guide was holding your book and shouting into a bullhorn, "Step 7. Proceed to Journey into Imagination." With this, about 65 Japanese tourists in red T-shirts ran out the door.

Unless your party is as large as the above tour group, this development should not cause you undue stress. Because there are so many in a touring group, they move slowly and have to stop periodically to collect stragglers. The tour guide also has to accommodate the unpredictable needs of five dozen or so individual bladders. In short you should have no problem passing a group after the initial encounter.

Variables That Will Affect the Success of the Touring Plans

How quickly you move from one ride to another; when and how many refreshment and rest room breaks you take; when, where, and how you eat meals; and your ability (or lack thereof) to find your way around will all have an impact on the success of the plans. Smaller groups almost always move faster than larger groups, and parties of adults can generally cover more ground than families with young children. Regardless of the composition of your group, we recommend continuous, expeditious touring until around 11:30 A.M. After that hour, breaks and so on will not affect the plans significantly.

Some variables that can have a profound effect on the touring plans are beyond your control. Chief among these are the manner and timing of bringing a particular ride to full capacity. For example, Big Thunder Mountain Railroad, a roller coaster in the Magic Kingdom, has five trains. On a given morning it may begin operation with two of the five, and then add the other three if and when needed. If the waiting line builds rapidly before the Disney operators decide to go to full capacity, you could have a long wait, even early in the morning. This often happens at 20,000 Leagues Under the Sea, also in the Magic Kingdom, causing our team to label the ride as the biggest bottleneck in "the World."

Another variable relates to the time that you arrive for a Disney theater performance. Usually, your wait will be the length of time from your arrival to the end of the presentation then in progress. Thus, if *Country Bear Jamboree* is 15 minutes long, and you arrive one minute after a show has begun, your wait for the next show will be 14 minutes. Conversely, if you happen to arrive just as the ongoing show is wrapping up, your wait will be only a minute or two. It's luck of the draw.

General Overview

The Walt Disney World Touring Plans are step-by-step plans for seeing as much as possible with a minimum of time wasted standing in line. They are designed to assist you in avoiding crowds and bottlenecks on days of moderate to heavy attendance. On days of lighter attendance (see "Selecting the Time of Year for Your Visit," page 32), the plans will still save you time but will not be as critical to successful touring.

Touring Plan Clip-out Pocket Outlines

For your convenience, we have prepared outline versions of all the Touring Plans presented in this guide. The Pocket Outline versions present the same touring itineraries as the detailed Touring Plans, but with vastly abbreviated directions. First, select the Touring Plan which is most appropriate for your party, then familiarize yourself with the detailed version of the Touring Plan. Once you understand how the Touring Plan works, clip out the Pocket Outline version of your selected Touring Plan from the back of this guide, and carry it with you as a quick reference when you visit the theme park.

A Chicken in Every Pot, a Car in Every Garage, a Touring Plan in Every Pocket

We are inundated with mail from readers requesting that we develop additional Touring Plans. Plans we have been asked to create include: a plan for ninth and tenth graders, a plan for rainy days, a senior's plan, a plan for folks who sleep late, a plan that omits rides that "bump, jerk, and clonk," a plan for gardening enthusiasts, and a plan for single women.

The Touring Plans presented in this book are intended to be flexible. The idea is to adapt them to the preferences of your group. If you do not want to go on rides that bump and jerk, simply skip any such attractions when they come up in a Touring Plan. If you wish to sleep in and not go to the park until noon or so, use the afternoon part of a Plan. If you are a ninth grader and want to ride Space Mountain three times in a row, go ahead and ride. Will it decrease the effectiveness of the Touring Plan? Sure, but the Plan was only created to help you have fun. Don't let the tail wag the dog. It's your day.

PART TWO: Tips and Warnings

Everyday Matters

— Credit Cards —

- MasterCard, VISA, and American Express are accepted for theme park admission.
- No credit cards are accepted in the theme parks at fast-food restaurants.
- Walt Disney World shops, sit-down restaurants, and theme resort hotels will accept MasterCard, VISA, and American Express credit cards only.

— Rain —

If it rains, go anyway; the bad weather will serve to diminish the crowds. Additionally, most of the rides and attractions are under cover. Likewise, all but a few of the waiting areas are protected from inclement weather.

— Closed for Repairs —

It is always a good idea to check in advance with Walt Disney World to see which, if any, rides and attractions may be closed for maintenance or repair during your visit. If you are particularly interested in a certain attraction, this precaution could save you a lot of disappointment. A mother from Dover, Massachusetts, wrote, lamenting:

> We were disappointed to find Space Mountain, Swiss Family Treehouse, and the Liberty Square Riverboat closed for repairs. We felt that a large chunk of the Magic Kingdom was not working, yet the tickets were still full price and expensive!

— Going from Park to Park —

If you have a pass that allows you to visit the Magic Kingdom, EPCOT Center, and Disney-MGM Studios in the same day, the pass will be marked with the day's date when you enter your first park. Later if you decide to go to one of the other parks, you must get a reentry stamp on your hand before departing. If you start the day at the Magic Kingdom, for instance, and then want to go to EPCOT Center for dinner, you must get a reentry stamp when you leave the Magic Kingdom. When you arrive at EPCOT Center, use the entrance gate marked "Same Day Reentry" and show your handstamp. The handstamp, which is only visible under ultraviolet light, will not come off if you wash your hands or go swimming (usually).

— A License to Print Money —

One of Disney's more sublime ploys for separating you from your money is the printing and issuing of Disney Dollars. Available in denominations of $1 (Mickey Moolah), $5 (Goofy Greenbacks), and $10 (Minnie Money), the colorful cash can be used for purchases at Walt Disney World, Disneyland, and at Disney Stores nationwide. Disney Dollars can also be exchanged one-for-one for U.S. currency. Disney money can be acquired all over Walt Disney World and is sometimes included as a perk (for which you are charged dollar-for-dollar) in Walt Disney Travel Company packages.

While the idea of Disney Dollars sounds fun and innocent, it is one of the better moneymakers in the Disney bag of tricks. Some guests take the money home as souvenirs. Others forget to spend or exchange it before they leave Walt Disney World. Once home, it is rare that a tourist will go to the effort of finding a Disney Store or trying to get the money exchanged through the mail. Usually the weird dollars end up forgotten in a drawer, which is exactly what the Disney folks hoped would happen.

— Visitors with Special Needs —

Disabled visitors will find rental wheelchairs available if needed. Most rides, shows, attractions, restrooms, and restaurants at the theme parks are designed to accommodate the disabled. For specific inquiries or problems call (407) 824-4321. If you are in the Magic Kingdom and need some special assistance go to City Hall on Main Street. At EPCOT Center, inquire at the Guest Relations booth in Earth Station at the base of Spaceship Earth. At Disney-MGM Studios, assistance can be obtained at Guest Services to the left of the main entrance on Hollywood Boulevard.

In addition to ordinary wheelchairs, a limited number of self-propelled, electric "motorized convenience vehicles" are available for rent at the Magic Kingdom and EPCOT Center. Easy to operate and fun to drive, these vehicles afford nonambulatory guests a tremendous degree of freedom and mobility. For some unknown reason, the vehicles at the Magic Kingdom are much faster than those at EPCOT Center.

Close-in parking is available for disabled visitors at all Walt Disney World parking complexes. Simply request directions when you pay your parking fee upon entering. All monorails and most rides, shows, restrooms, and restaurants can accommodate wheelchairs. One major exception is the Contemporary Resort Hotel monorail station, where passengers must enter or exit via escalators.

A special information booklet for disabled guests is available at wheelchair rental locations throughout Walt Disney World. Maps of the respective theme parks issued to each guest on admission are symbol-coded to inform nonambulatory guests which attractions accommodate wheelchairs.

Nonambulatory guests are welcome to ride almost all of the attractions at Walt Disney World. As mentioned above, many attractions are engineered to allow a guest to board the attraction in a wheelchair. For attractions that do not accommodate wheelchairs, nonambulatory guests may still ride if they can transfer from the wheelchair to the vehicle of the ride in question. Disney attraction staff, however, are not trained or permitted to assist nonambulatory guests in transfering from their wheelchair to the ride. Guests must be able to get on the ride alone or, alternatively, have a member of their own party assist them. In either case, members of the nonambulatory guest's party will be permitted to go along on the ride.

Because the queuing areas of most rides and shows will not accommodate wheelchairs, nonambulatory guests and their party should request special boarding instructions from a Disney attendant as soon as they arrive at an attraction. Almost always, the whole group will receive priority treatment and can board without a lengthy wait.

Telephones accessible to guests in wheelchairs are located throughout all three major theme parks.

Visitors with Dietary Restrictions. Visitors on special or restricted diets, including those requiring kosher meals, can make arrangements for assistance at the theme parks by going to City Hall in the Magic Kingdom, Spaceship Earth at EPCOT Center, or the Guest Services Building at the Disney-MGM Studios. For Walt Disney World restaurants located outside the theme parks, call the restaurant one day in advance for assistance.

Sight- and/or Hearing-Impaired Guests. The Magic Kingdom, EP-COT Center, and the Disney-MGM Studios each provide complimentary tape cassettes and portable tape players to assist sight-impaired guests. They are available at City Hall in the Magic Kingdom, Earth Station at EPCOT Center, and the Guest Services Building at the Disney-MGM Studios. A deposit is required. At the same locations, a Telecommunication Device for the Deaf (TDD) is available for hearing-impaired guests.

In addition to TDDs, many of the pay phones in the major theme parks are equipped with amplified headsets. See your Disney handout of the park map for phone locations.

Foreign Language Assistance is available throughout Walt Disney World. Inquire by calling (407) 824-4321 or by stopping at City Hall in the Magic Kingdom, Earth Station Guest Relations at EPCOT Center, or at Hollywood Boulevard Guest Services at the Disney-MGM Studios.

Messages can be left at City Hall in the Magic Kingdom, Earth Station Guest Relations at EPCOT Center, or at Hollywood Boulevard Guest Services at the Disney-MGM Studios.

Car Trouble. If you decide to lock your keys in your car to prevent losing them, or leave your headlights on to make the car easier to find at the end of the day, you may have a little problem leaving the theme park. Fortunately, with such simple problems, one of the security or tow truck patrols continually on duty can put you back in business.

If your car seriously goes on the fritz, the Disney Car Care Center will come to the rescue. Arrangements can be made for transportation to your Walt Disney World destination and for a lift to the Car Care Center. You can phone the Car Care Center by calling (407) 824-4813.

Lost and Found.   If you lose (or find) something in the Magic Kingdom, City Hall (once again) is the place to go. At EPCOT Center the Lost and Found is located in the Entrance Plaza, and at Disney-MGM Studios it is located at Hollywood Boulevard Guest Services. If you do not discover your loss until you have left the park(s), call (407) 824-4245 (for all parks). See page 26 for the number to call in each park if you *do* discover something is missing while still in the park(s).

—— *Excuse Me, but Where Can I Find . . .* ——

Someplace to Put All These Packages?   Lockers are available on the ground floor of the Main Street Railroad Station in the Magic Kingdom, to the right of Earth Station in EPCOT Center, and on both the east and west ends of the Ticket and Transportation Center. At Disney-MGM Studios, lockers are to the right of the entrance on Hollywood Boulevard at Oscar's Super Service.

A Package Pick-up service is available at EPCOT Center. Simply request the salesperson to send your purchases to Package Pick-up. When you leave the park they will be waiting for you at either the main entrance or the International Gateway. Be sure you specify the exit.

Disney Souvenirs?   Though Disney souvenirs can be found in any Walt Disney World structure large enough to hold a cash register, we get a lot of mail from readers asking where to find the greatest variety and the best deals. Starting with variety, these shops have the greatest selection of Disney trademark stuff (Mickey T-shirts, Goofy hats, etc.):

Magic Kingdom

Main Street	Emporium (largest selection at Magic Kingdom)
	Disneyana Collectibles
Fantasyland	The Mad Hatter
	The AristoCats
Tomorrowland	Mickey's Star Traders

EPCOT Center

Future World	Gateway Gifts
	Centorium (largest selection at EPCOT Center)
World Showcase	Disney Traders (on the left side of Showcase Plaza)

Disney-MGM Studios

Hollywood Boulevard	Mickey's of Hollywood
Studio Courtyard	Animation Gallery

There are stuffed toys of the Disney characters, Disney books and records, character hats, and a number of other items which are hard if not impossible to find outside the Disney shops. T-shirts, however, are another story. The most popular souvenir item of all, Disney T-shirts, can be found in stores all over the area.

The shirts sold at Walt Disney World are expensive ($14–21), but are high quality, 100% cotton. Shirts sold outside the world are usually of lesser quality, 50% cotton and 50% polyester, and sell for $7–15. Both inside and outside Walt Disney World, you can find many of the same designs of Mickey, Minnie, and Goofy. The only difference is that shirts sold in Disney shops will say "Walt Disney World" or, possibly, "EPCOT Center" or "Disney-MGM Studios." Shirts sold outside the world will usually say "Florida" next to the imprint of the character.

If you are a member of the Magic Kingdom Club, you are eligible for a 10% discount on merchandise puchased at Pleasure Island and the Disney Village Marketplace. There is no discount for Magic Kingdom card holders at the theme parks or the hotels. If you are a club member and are planning an expensive purchase (watches, Disney art, etc.), you will realize significant savings by shopping at the Disney Village Marketplace.

The only retailer that sells discounted items *from* Walt Disney World is the Character Warehouse, located in Mall Two of the Belz Factory Outlet World at the north end of International Drive. The store is open from 10 A.M. to 9 P.M. Monday through Saturday, and 10 A.M. to 6 P.M. on Sunday.

Bargain World, with locations at 6454 International Drive (next to Shell World) and on US 192 west of the entrance to Walt Disney World, offers a good selection of the 50% and 50% shirts as well as Disney beach towels and other character merchandise.

A Mixed Drink or a Beer?   If you are in the Magic Kingdom you are out of luck. You will have to exit the park and proceed to one of the resort hotels. In EPCOT Center you can have a drink, but you may need a reservation. Alcoholic beverages are served primarily in full-service eateries, although beer is available at the Cantina de San Angel opposite the Mexican pavilion; at Le Cellier, a cafeteria on the lower right side of the Canadian pavilion; and at the pub section of the Rose & Crown Pub & Dining Room in the United Kingdom complex. The latter is popular not only because of the beer, but because of its unparalleled view of the World Showcase Lagoon. Finally, beer is also available at Yakatori House, the fast-food eatery in the Japanese pavilion. At Disney-MGM Studios, beer and wine are available at the Soundstage and Backlot restaurants, at the Catwalk Bar and the Tune In Lounge, the full-service Hollywood Brown Derby, the 50's Prime Time Cafe, and at Mama Melrose's Ristorante Italiano.

Some Chewing Gum?   Sorry, chewing gum is not sold in any of the theme parks. B.Y.O.

Some Rain Gear?   If you get caught in a central Florida monsoon, here's where you can find something to cover up with:

Magic Kingdom

Main Street:	The Emporium
Tomorrowland:	Mickey's Mart
Fantasyland:	Mad Hatter
	AristoCats
Frontierland:	Frontier Trading Post
Adventureland:	Bwana Bob's

EPCOT Center:	Almost all retail shops

Disney-MGM Studios:	Almost all retail shops

At the theme park shops, rain gear is available but not always displayed. As the Disney people say, it is sold "under the counter." In other words, you have to ask for it. If you are caught without protection on a rainy day, do not slog around dripping. Rain gear is one of the few shopping bargains at Walt Disney World. Ponchos can be had for less than $5 and umbrellas go for about $7.

A Cure for This Headache? Aspirin and various other sundries can be purchased on Main Street in the Magic Kingdom at the Emporium (they keep them behind the counter so you have to ask), at most retail outlets in EPCOT Center Future World, and in many of the World Showcase shops. Likewise at the Disney-MGM Studios, aspirin is available at almost all retail shops.

A Prescription Filled? The closest pharmacy is located in the Goodings Supermarket on FL 535 in Lake Buena Vista, (407) 827-1200.

Suntan Lotion? Suntan lotion and various other sundries can be purchased on Main Street in the Magic Kingdom at the Emporium (they keep them behind the counter so you have to ask), at most retail outlets in EPCOT Center Future World, and in many of the World Showcase shops. At the Disney-MGM Studios, suntan lotion is sold at almost all retail shops.

A Smoke? Cigarettes are readily available throughout the Magic Kingdom, EPCOT Center, and the Disney-MGM Studios. For the record, smoking is prohibited on all attractions, in all attraction waiting areas, and in all shops.

Feminine Hygiene Products? Feminine hygiene products are available in women's restrooms throughout Walt Disney World.

Cash? Branches of the Sun Bank are located respectively on Main Street in the Magic Kingdom, on Hollywood Boulevard at the Disney-MGM Studios, and to the left of the turnstiles as you enter EPCOT Center. Service at the Disney-MGM Studios is limited to an automatic teller machine. At the Magic Kingdom and EPCOT Center the following services are available:

— *Provide cash advances* on MasterCard, VISA, and American Express credit cards ($50 minimum with a maximum equaling the patron's credit limit).

— *Cash personal checks* of $25 and less drawn on U.S. banks upon presentation of a valid driver's license and a major credit card.

— *Cash and sell traveler's checks*. The bank cashes the first check without charge, but levies a $2 service fee for each additional check cashed.

— *Facilitate the wiring of money* from the visitor's bank to the Sun Bank.

— *Exchange foreign currency* for dollars.

If you want to use an automatic teller machine in Walt Disney World to obtain cash, your credit card must be compatible with the Cirrus network. All American Express cards will work, but you will need to check the back of other credit cards for the Cirrus logo. If you do not have a Cirrus system card, but are at the Magic Kingdom or EPCOT Center, a bank teller will be able to process your transaction at the teller window. If, however, you are at the Disney-MGM Studios or anyplace else where service is limited to an automatic teller, you will be out of luck.

A Place to Exchange My Foreign Currency?　The currency of most countries can be exchanged for dollars before you enter the theme parks, at the Guest Services window of the Ticket and Transportation Center, the Guest Services window in the ticketing area of the Disney-MGM Studios, and at the Guest Services window to the right of the entrance turnstiles at EPCOT Center.

A Place to Leave My Pet?　Cooping up an animal in a hot car while you tour can lead to disastrous results. Additionally, pets are not allowed in the major or minor theme parks. Kennels and holding facilities are provided for the temporary care of your pets, and are located adjacent to the Transportation and Ticket Center, to the left of the EPCOT Center entrance plaza, and to the left of the Disney-MGM Studios entrance plaza. If you are adamant, the folks at the kennels will accept custody of just about any type of animal, though owners of exotic and/or potentially vicious pets must place their charges in the assigned cage. Small pets (mice, hamsters, birds, snakes, turtles, alligators, etc.) must arrive in their own escape-proof quarters.

In addition to the above, there are several other details that you may need to know:

— When traveling with your pet in Florida, bring your certificate of vaccination and immunization.

— It is against the law in the state of Florida to leave a pet in a closed vehicle.

— Advance reservations for animals are not accepted.

— Kennels open one hour before the theme parks open and close one hour after the theme parks close.

— Only Walt Disney World Resort guests may board a pet over-night. Guests who board their pets should be advised that the kennels are not really set up for multi-day boarding. Only the most elementary and essential services are provided; the kennels are not manned overnight, and Disney personnel will not exercise pets.

— Guests leaving exotic pets should supply food for their pet.

Cameras and Film?   If you do not have a camera, Disney will rent you a 35mm Kodak. The rental fee is $5 per day, with a $100 deposit. Also available for rent are VHS video camcorders at $40 for the first day, decreasing by $5 each succeeding day down to a minimum daily charge of $20. The deposit required on the camcorder is $600. You can use either cash or credit card to cover the deposit, and you must present a picture I.D. when you rent. Equipment is available at the Camera Centers of the Magic Kingdom, EPCOT Center, and Disney-MGM Studios. Equipment rented at one theme park can be returned to the Camera Center in another park. Film is available throughout Walt Disney World.

Film developing services are provided by most Disney hotel gift shops and the Camera Centers. For two-hour developing service look for the Photo Express sign at various locations around the theme parks. Simply drop your film in the container and pick up your pictures at the Camera Center as you leave the park. If you use the Express service and intend to stay in the park until closing, drop by and get your pictures sometime earlier in the evening to avoid the last minute rush.

Finally, photo tips as well as recommendations for settings and exposures are detailed in the respective theme park maps provided free when you enter the park.

Walt Disney World for Seniors, Couples, and Singles

—— Walt Disney World For Seniors ——

Most seniors' problems and concerns are common to Walt Disney World visitors of all ages. Even so, seniors often find themselves in predicaments attributable to touring with persons a few or many years their junior. Run ragged, and pressured by the grandchildren to endure a frantic pace, many seniors concentrate more on surviving their visit to Walt Disney World than enjoying it. The Disney parks have as much to offer the mature visitor as the youngster, and seniors must either insist on setting the pace or dispatch the young folks to tour on their own.

We received this letter from an older reader in Alabaster, Alabama:

The main thing I want to say is that being a senior is not for wussies. At Disney World particularly, it requires courage and pluck. Things that used to be easy take a lot of effort, and some-times your brain has to wait for your body to catch up. Half the time your grandchildren treat you like a crumbling ruin, and then turn around and trick you into getting on a roller coaster in the dark. What you need to tell seniors is that they have to be alert and not trust anyone. Not their children or even the Disney people, and especially not their grandchildren. When your grandchildren want you to go on a ride, don't follow along blindly like a lamb to the slaughter. Make sure you know what the ride is all about. Stand your ground and do not waffle. He who hesitates is launched!

Most seniors we interview enjoy Walt Disney World more (much more) when they tour with folks their own age, without any kids along. If you are contemplating a Walt Disney World visit with your grand-children, however, we recommend a preliminary visit without them to

119

get oriented. If you know first-hand what to expect, it is much easier to establish limits, maintain control, and set a comfortable pace when you visit with the youngsters.

If you are determined to bring the grandkids, we recommend that you read carefully those sections of this book that discuss family touring. (Hint: The Dumbo-or-Die-in-a-Day Touring Plan has been known to bring grown-ups of any age to their knees.)

In our experience, because seniors are a varied and willing lot, there are not any Walt Disney World attractions that we would categorically suggest they avoid. For seniors, as with other Walt Disney World patrons, personal taste is more important than age. We hate to see mature visitors pass up an exceptional attraction like Splash Mountain because some younger visitors classify it as a "thrill ride." Splash Mountain is a full-blown Disney adventure which derives its appeal more from its music and visual effects than from the thrill of the ride. As you must pick from many attractions those which might interest you, we have provided as much information as we can to help you make informed choices.

That having been said, we acknowledge that it's easy to get caught up in the spectacle and wonder of Walt Disney World—so much so that before you know it, you've followed the crowd onto something you haven't thought much about. After all, they make these rides for kids: How bad can they be?

We believe that forewarned is forearmed, so below we discuss some of the rides offered in the name of "fun."

Magic Kingdom

Space Mountain. If you thought the roller coaster at Coney Island was a thrill, this won't be far behind, with dips and pops that pull you through curves and over humps. This ride vibrates quite a bit, so take your glasses off and store them safely in your fanny pack. I can't guarantee they'll stay in your pocket.

Big Thunder Mountain Railroad. Although rather sedate and constrained if compared with Space Mountain, this ride is very jarring. The cars jerk back and forth along the track, and though there are a few drops, it is the side-to-side shaking that gets to most people.

Splash Mountain. This ride combines the whimsy of Disney with the thrill of a log flume. There is one big drop near the end and a bit of a splash (engineered by spray guns and a water cannon, not the drop itself). The enchantment of the Brer Rabbit story makes it worth getting a little wet.

The Swiss Family Treehouse. This is by no means a thrill ride, but it does involve a lot of stair climbing and a very unsteady pontoon bridge.

Mad Tea Party. An adaptation of the standard carnival midway ride where you spin around in big tea cups until you are nauseated. If you approach this instrument of the devil while it is sitting still, your cunning grandchildren may try to pass it off as an *al fresco* dining patio.

EPCOT Center

Body Wars. This ride is more jolting than Star Tours (at the Disney-MGM Studios) and more prone to cause motion sickness than the Mad Hatter's tea cups. It combines the visual shock of a graphic anatomy lesson with the trauma of being chauffeured by a teenager driving his first stick-shift.

MGM

Star Tours. Using the plot and characters from *Star Wars*, this flight-simulation ride is a real Disney masterpiece. If you are extremely prone to motion sickness, this ride will affect you. Otherwise, we suspect it might be the highlight of your Walt Disney World vacation.

Getting Around

For many seniors, walking is a prefered form of exercise. Be advised, however, that you will normally walk between four and eight miles in the course of a seven-hour visit to one of the major theme parks. If you are not up for that much hiking, don't be reluctant to allow a more athletic member of your party to push you around in a rented wheelchair. EPCOT Center and the Magic Kingdom also offer electric carts (convenience vehicles) which, in addition to saving shoe leather, are fun to drive. The main thing is to not let your pride get in the way of having a good time. Sure, you could march ten miles if you had to, but the point is *you don't have to!* Pamper yourself; go for the good time instead of the Purple Heart.

A big advantage to renting a wheelchair is the special boarding privilege granted to guests (and their immediate parties) who use the special entrances for wheelchairs at most attractions. Waiting times at these special boarding areas will vary depending on the attraction and the crowd, but you will almost always get to ride sooner than if you had waited in the regular queue. You must check in with a host or hostess before you board.

Your wheelchair rental deposit slip is good for a replacement wheelchair in any park during the same day. So keep your ticket. You can rent a chair at the Magic Kingdom in the morning, turn it back in, go to EPCOT Center, present your deposit slip, and get another chair without paying twice.

Timing your Visit

Retired seniors are in an ideal position to take advantage of the "off-season" for visiting Walt Disney World. Make use of your flexible schedule—plan your trip for times when the weather is the nicest, and the crowds the thinnest, namely the fall and the spring, holiday weeks excluded. The crowds are also sparse from the end of January through the beginning of February, but the weather is unpredictable at this time of year. If you choose to see Walt Disney World in the winter, you will need to bring coats and sweaters as well as more moderate dress; be prepared for anything from near-freezing rain to afternoon temperatures in the 80s.

Visiting during the off-season also allows you more flexibility in choosing which days to go to the park. Normally, Monday, Tuesday, and Wednesday are the most crowded days. The best possible option is to arrive on a Wednesday in order to start touring on a Thursday. However, the day of the week you choose to begin your touring is less crucial than it would be if you were visiting the park during peak season.

The Price of Admission

Walt Disney World never offers discount tickets for admission to its theme parks (see page 93) and senior discounts are no exception. The best deal for senior touring we've found takes advantage of the off-season by offering an annual, cut-rate ticket for unlimited use of the parks to Florida residents. The Florida Four-Season Pass is good only for the following dates: April 30–June 6; August 29–September

30; November 28–December 19; and January 3–February 6. Another good option is the Annual Pass. For additional information, see the section in this guide on admission options.

The only other special ticket worth mentioning is a group rate on a two-day pass offered to Florida residents through AAA. This ticket is about $10 cheaper than the standard two-day pass. Contact AAA for more information.

Lodging

Like all sojourners to a strange place, seniors are concerned with their lodging options in the Orlando/Kissimmee area. Our first recommendation is to stay in Walt Disney World if economically feasible. If you are concerned about the quality of your accommodations or the availability of transportation, staying inside the Disney complex will do much to put your mind at ease. The rooms are some of the nicest in the area, always clean and well-kept. And transportation is always available, at no extra cost, to any destination in Walt Disney World.

At the Disney hotels, rooms closer to restaurants and transportation are kept available for guests of any age who cannot tolerate a lot of walking. The hotels provide fancy golf carts to pick up and deliver guests to and from their rooms. Pick-up times for the golf cart service can vary dramatically depending on the time of day and number of guests requesting service. For example, at check-in time (around 3 P.M.), the wait for a ride could be as long as 40 minutes.

While there are many quality hotels in the area that we could recommend, there are several reasons we think staying in Walt Disney World is a good idea for seniors:

1. The quality of the properties is consistently above average.
2. The transportation companies that operate buses for "outside" hotels run only every hour or so. Disney buses run continuously. By staying in Walt Disney World, you guarantee your ability to get transportation whenever you need it.
3. You will be able to make dinner reservations over the phone and in advance—"outside" guests have to wait until they arrive at the park to make reservations. Similarly, you can alert Disney restaurants in advance of any special dietary needs or restrictions.
4. You may be eligible for special discounts to shows and early entrance to the parks.

5. Boarding pets at the kennels overnight is available only to guests staying in Walt Disney World.
6. You are guaranteed admission to the theme parks during peak season.
7. You are eligible for free parking in the major theme parks' lots.
8. You are accorded preferential tee times on resort golf courses.

Our first choice for seniors who prefer quiet and elegant surroundings is The Disney Inn. The Grand Floridian, also elegant, though more expensive and spread out, runs a close second. The main advantage of staying at the Grand Floridian is its location on the monorail. Buses are available to take guests at The Disney Inn to the parks.

The Contemporary Resort is a good choice for mobile seniors (wheelchairs cannot access the monorail platform) who want to be on the monorail system, as is the Polynesian Resort, though the Polynesian is spread out over many acres and may entail more walking.

Finally, the RV crowd will find pleasant surroundings at Walt Disney World's Fort Wilderness Campground. In addition to Fort Wilderness, there are several KOA campgrounds within 20 minutes of Walt Disney World. None of the KOA sites, however, offer the wilderness setting or amenities of the Disney campground. On the other hand, they don't charge nearly as much either.

Elderhostels

Recently we were introduced to Elderhostel by friends active in the program. It is an educational travel and study program for seniors who are looking for something a little different. The one-week sessions are hosted, for the most part, by educational institutions, though some programs use private resort or hotel facilities.

The Elderhostel program offers classes on subjects ranging from anthropology to zoology, from French to cabinet making. These classes take about an hour and a half each day. Most programs do not assign homework, so there is a lot of time left for visiting, making friends, or even taking an afternoon trip to Walt Disney World.

Elderhostel encourages its participants to be "students-in-residence," and advises them to arrange their sight-seeing before or after their stay with the Elderhostel system. However, several of the programs in the central Florida area advertise their proximity to Walt Disney World. These include:

- Camp Challenge in Sorrento, 20 miles north of Orlando
- Canterbury Retreat and Conference Center in Oviedo, 5 miles northeast of Orlando
- Thunderbird Outdoor Center at Wekiva Springs, 20 minutes northwest of Orlando
- Stetson University/Off Campus, in De Land, 35 miles north of Orlando
- Deerhaven Camp and Conference Center in the Ocala National Forest, 16 miles west of De Land and about an hour and 40 minutes from Orlando
- University of Florida/Cerveny Conference Center, two hours northwest of Orlando

For information on the Elderhostel program, do not contact the camps listed above. Instead, write or call Elderhostel:

Elderhostel
P.O. Box 1959
Dept. TN
Wakefield, MA 01880-5959
Phone: (615) 426-8056

Transportation

The roads throughout Walt Disney World can be daunting to the uninitiated. Armed with a moderate sense of direction and an above-average sense of humor, even the most timid driver can learn to get around in the World. If you are intimidated easily, pick a hotel on the monorail and stay off the road.

If you drive, or seek to limit your walking, parking is not a problem. Parking lots are serviced by a tram system that runs between the parking area and the front gate of the theme park. For guests who are marginally or wholly nonambulatory, parking spaces are reserved adjacent to the entrance complex at each park. The parking attendant at the pay booth will give you a special ticket for your dashboard as well as direct you to the special lot. Though Walt Disney World stipulates that you be recognized as officially handicapped to utilize this parking, in practice the temporarily disabled or injured are also permitted access.

Senior Dining

Our advice is to either eat breakfast at your hotel restaurant or save money by having juice and rolls in your room. Although you are not allowed to bring any food into the parks, fruit, fruit juice, and soft drink vendors are located throughout Walt Disney World. We recommend you make your lunch reservations for early in the day, before noon, say, and avoid the lunch crowds altogether. This way, you'll be ready for an early dinner and will be out of the restaurants, rested and ready for evening touring and fireworks, long before the main crowd even begins to think about dinner.

Part of our senior touring plan is to fit dining and rest times into the day. Remember the Dad on the Dumbo-or-Die-in-a-Day Touring Plan? He will be scarfing down fast food as he hauls his toddlers around the park at breakneck speed. Reserve a window table for your early lunch, and wave to him as he goes by. Lunch is your break in the day, so sit back, relax, and enjoy. After lunch, return to your hotel for a nap.

Have a Plan

Our maxim for touring Walt Disney World ("Have a plan or get a frontal lobotomy") is easily adapted to senior touring. From planning the time of year to visit to the first rule of touring ("Arrive early! Arrive early! Arrive early!"), seniors are, in general, the perfect *Unofficial Guide* patrons. If you are a person who can get by on less sleep, enjoy the stress-free pleasure of touring the theme parks in the early morning. If you enjoy sleeping late, make sure you visit Walt Disney World during the less crowded, off-peak times of year.

Select the Touring Plan you want to follow. Pick what you want to see or skip ahead of time, so that you will be able to efficiently follow the plan. Check out the ride and show descriptions before you go. Arrive at the entrance gates at least a half hour before the official opening time. Move as fast as you can early in the day, so you will be able to slow down and relax after an hour or so, knowing the most strenuous part of the plan (as well as potential bottlenecks) is behind you.

We think at least one of the Behind-the-Scenes tours should be part of any senior's visit. These tours, offering an in-depth look at the operations of Walt Disney World, are primarily at EPCOT Center. Especially worth seeing are Hidden Treasures and Gardens of the World. If you don't have the time for these lengthy tours, a "must-see" is the shorter Harvest Tour at The Land pavilion, also in EPCOT Center.

Finally, do not forget to include camper's quiet time in your itinerary. We recommend Disney patrons of all ages return to the hotel during the hot, crowded part of the day for lunch, a nap, and even a swim.

When You Need to Contact the Outside World

Pay telephones are located throughout Walt Disney World. If your hearing is not what it used to be, special, amplified handsets are available in all three major theme parks. Handset locations are marked on each park's map, provided free when you enter. In addition, TDDs are available at City Hall in the Magic Kingdom, Earth Station in EPCOT Center, and Guest Services at the Disney-MGM Studios.

Telephones that guests in wheelchairs can reach are scattered all over the parks, except for in the Magic Kingdom where they are all under the Walt Disney World Railroad Station.

Walt Disney World for Couples

So many couples wed or honeymoon at Walt Disney World that Disney has organized an entire department to take care of their needs. *Disney's Fairy Tale Weddings & Honeymoons* department offers a full range of wedding venues and services, as well as honeymoon packages.

Weddings

The primary requisite for getting married at Walt Disney World is big bucks. A tiny wedding with all local guests (i.e., no hotel rooms) runs a minimum of $3,500 and does not include floral arrangements, decorations, entertainment, wedding officiant, or music. If you are willing to drop a bundle, however, you can arrive at your wedding in Cinderella's glass coach, have Goofy for an usher, Minnie as maid of honor, and drive off after the ceremony in a limo chauffeured by Mickey. If you don't have many friends, you can rent additional Disney characters to attend your wedding. Volume discounts are available; characters run: one for $395, two for $525, three for $775, and so on. If the character prices sound a little steep, be comforted that they don't eat or drink.

A number of indoor and outdoor locations are available for wedding ceremonies at the Grand Floridian, Yacht Club, Beach Club, Contemporary, Polynesian, Disney Village, and Disney Inn resorts. You can have a nautical wedding aboard the Kingdom Queen stern wheeler on Bay Lake or the Empress Lilly Riverboat at the Walt Disney World Village. For the nocturnal, wedding sites are available at Pleasure Island nightclubs. The theme parks are supposedly not available for weddings, but, hey, this is *Walt Disney World* . . . money talks.

One of the most improbable services the wedding department offers is arranging bachelor parties. I'm not sure what goes on at a Disney bachelor party. Maybe stag cartoons or a private showing of *The Making of Me*. Get down!

If you wish to be married at Walt Disney World, you can obtain a marriage license at any county courthouse in Florida. Currently blood tests are not required, but you must present proper identification in the form of a driver's license, passport, or birth certificate. If you were divorced within the last year, you must also produce a copy of your divorce decree. Marriage licenses cost about $64, statewide. Cash or money orders only, please. There is no waiting period in Florida; your license is issued at the time of application. The marriage license must be used within 60 days.

Honeymoons

The honeymoon packages are basically adaptations of the regular Disney Travel Company vacation packages. No special rooms or honeymoon suites are included in the packages unless you upgrade. In fact, the only specific honeymoon feature (in two of the packages) is room service.

If you are interested in either a Disney wedding or honeymoon, contact:

> Disney's Fairy Tale Weddings & Honeymoons
> P.O. Box 10,020
> Lake Buena Vista, Florida 32830-0020
> Phone (407) 363-6333

Romantic Getaways

Many people consider the Utopian Disney environment very romantic. Consequently, Walt Disney World is a favorite getaway spot for honeymooners and other couples. Needless to say, you do not have to purchase a Disney honeymoon package to enjoy a romantic interlude at Walt Disney World.

Not all the Disney hotels are equally romantic. Some are too family oriented, others are aswarm with convention-goers. We recommend the following Disney lodging for the romantically inclined:

1. Polynesian Resort
2. Grand Floridian Beach Resort
3. Disney's Wilderness Lodge Resort
4. Disney's Yacht and Beach Clubs
5. The Disney Inn

All of the properties listed are expensive. Of the five, The Disney Inn is the most adult. There are also some nice secluded villas at Disney's Village Resort.

Quiet, Romantic Places to Eat

If you are looking for a quiet, romantic setting and good food in the theme parks, your choices are extremely limited. Only the Coral Reef and the San Angel Inn at EPCOT Center satisfy both requirements. At the hotels, however, there is a wider selection. Victoria & Albert's at the Grand Floridian offers waterfront dining, as do the three restaurants on the Empress Lilly Riverboat at the Walt Disney World Village, and Cap'n Jack's Oyster Bar at the Disney Village Marketplace. Ariel's at the Beach Club is a good spot for seafood and the Yachtsman Steakhouse at the Yacht Club serves a pretty decent steak. Sum Chows and Ristorante Carnevale at the Swan and Dolphin resorts offer good food and a quiet atmosphere. Though the setting is romantic, avoid restaurants at the Polynesian Resort. For more information about the restaurants mentioned, see the chapter on "Dining In and Around Walt Disney World."

Romantic Stuff to Do

Couples, like everyone else, have their own agenda at Walt Disney World. That having been said, here are a few romantic diversions you might not have on your list:

1. There is a nice (albeit pricey) lounge on the top floor of the Contemporary Resort. This is a great place to watch a sunset or, later in the evening, view the fireworks at the nearby Magic Kingdom. If you just want to go for the view (and not drink), you can access an outside promenade through a set of glass doors at the end of the lounge.

2. The Floating Electrical Pageant is one of Disney's most romantic entertainments. It consists of a train of barges, each with a spectacular light display depicting sea creatures. The show starts after dark to music by Handel played on synthesizers. All you can see are the lights. The best place to watch is from the pier or beach at the Polynesian Resort.

3. Take a launch to Fort Wilderness. At the Fort Wilderness dock you can rent various types of boats for exploring Bay Lake and the Seven Seas Lagoon. The Fort Wilderness Campground is honeycombed with footpaths and makes a lovely setting for an early morning or early evening walk. If you really enjoy hiking

and boating, take a day and visit the Juniper Springs Recreation Area in the Ocala National Forest. About an hour and a half north of Walt Disney World, the forest is extraordinarily beautiful. Trails are well marked and canoes are available for rent (shuttle included). Paddling down Juniper Springs is like floating through a natural version of the Jungle Cruise.

4. During the more temperate months of the year, enjoy a picnic on the beaches of Bay Lake and the Seven Seas Lagoon. Room service at the resort hotels will prepare your lunch to order. Drinks, including wine and beer, are available at less cost from the hotel convenience shops. Fort Wilderness Campground is also a good place to picnic.

5. Small boats shuttle guests to and from the Grand Floridian, Polynesian Resort, Magic Kingdom, and Fort Wilderness Campground well into the night. On a summer night, cap your day with a tranquil cruise around Bay Lake and the Seven Seas Lagoon.

Some Things to Bring with You

Once ensconced in your Walt Disney World hideaway, it can be inconvenient to go out after something you've forgotten. Many couples have written us and listed things they wish they'd remembered to bring. Here are a few of the items most often mentioned.

1. Wine (wine can be purchased by the bottle at Walt Disney World, but the selection is pretty dismal)
2. Corkscrew (wine glasses are available from room service)
3. Liquor, appertifs, cordials
4. Mixers for fancy drinks like Margaritas, olives for Martinis, lemons and limes
5. Portable tape or disc player and your favorite music
6. Bicycles
7. Picnic basket and blanket or tablecloth
8. Candles and holders
9. Cooler
10. Special snacks such as caviar, chocolates, cheeses (with knife), fruit

Walt Disney World for Singles

Most of the singles at Walt Disney World work there. If you are looking to hook up with someone new and exciting for a little romance, heaven knows there are better places than Walt Disney World. Even at Pleasure Island, the nighttime entertainment complex, you need to check your dancing partner's wristband to determine whether he or she is old enough to buy a drink.

A simple demographic truth is that single men, by and large, do not vacation at Walt Disney World while single women, including single parents, do. Generally speaking, therefore, for women there are precious few *qualified* prospects. There are men, of course, both single for real and single for the moment, attending meetings and conventions at the resort hotels, but these guys are rarely on a schedule that permits the development of anything meaningful. Filling the void, consequently, are local single (and married) men who realize all too well that single women on vacation (and looking for a little romance) are frequently vulnerable. As a rule, it's probably a good idea to avoid the locals.

For singles of both sexes, the rules at Walt Disney World are the same as at home. Take it slow and easy and make sure you know who you are dealing with. The easiest and safest way to meet anyone at Walt Disney World is at the theme parks, including the water theme parks. (Most locals "on the make" are not going to shell out the price of admission and hang around the park all day.) The theme parks give all guests something in common to talk about. There is no easier place on earth to strike up a conversation than waiting in line for an attraction. A more organized way to meet people at Walt Disney World is to take one of the several tours available especially for adults. These are listed and described on pages 267 and 365.

How to Travel Around The World
(or the Real Mr. Toad's Wild Ride)

The multi-day passes allow a guest to visit more than one of the major Walt Disney World theme parks in a day, coming and going at the guest's convenience. A guest can travel to and fro in his car, or take the monorail, the bus, or sometimes even a boat. Unfortunately for the guest, there is precious little convenience.

When considering the much-vaunted monorail, picture three loops. Loop A is an express route which runs counterclockwise connecting the Magic Kingdom with the Transportation and Ticket Center (TTC). A second loop, B, runs clockwise alongside Loop A. Loop B makes all stops, with service to (in this order) the TTC, the Polynesian Resort, the Grand Floridian Beach Resort, the Magic Kingdom, and the Contemporary Resort (then around again). A third long loop, C, dips like a tail to the southeast connecting the TTC with EPCOT Center. The hub for all three loops is the TTC (where you usually park when visiting the Magic Kingdom).

While your multi-day pass suggests that you can flit from park to park at will, actually getting there is somewhat more complex. You cannot go directly from the Magic Kingdom to EPCOT Center by monorail, for example. You must catch the express monorail (Loop A) to the TTC and there transfer to the Loop C monorail over to EPCOT Center. If you do not have to wait in a long line to board either monorail, you can usually make it over to EPCOT Center in about 25–35 minutes. But should you want to go to EPCOT Center for dinner (as many people do) and you are departing the Magic Kingdom in the late afternoon, you might have to wait a half hour or more just to get on the express Loop A monorail. Adding this wait pops your commuting time up to about 45–55 minutes.

Once, when asking directions to the town of Louisa in the eastern Kentucky mountains, I was told in so many words, "You can't get there from here." Sometimes trying to commute around Walt Disney World gives rise to a similar frustration. "What you can do is this,"

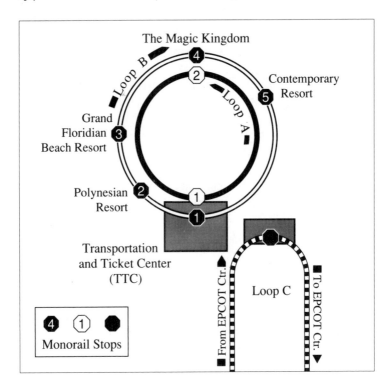

a Magic Kingdom street vendor proposed: "You can take the ferry or the monorail to the Transportation and Ticket Center. Then you can get another monorail, or you can catch the bus, or you can take a tram out to your car and drive over there yourself." What the vendor did not say was that any conceivable combination from this transportation smorgasbord would take longer than riding over to EPCOT Center on a mule. This must be what Toffler meant by "future shock."

Now having alerted you that there is no efficient way to travel around Walt Disney World, we will endeavor to help you choose the *least* inefficient way. Just don't wait until ten minutes before your seating at Alfredo's to get moving.

—— *Transportation System Trade Offs for Guests Lodging Outside Walt Disney World* ——

Walt Disney World day guests (those not staying in Walt Disney World) can use the monorail system, most of the bus system, and some of the boat system. If you go to the Disney-MGM Studios in the morning and decide to go over to EPCOT Center for lunch, for instance, you can take a direct bus. The most important advice we can give to day guests is that you end up with your car parked in the lot of the theme park (or other Walt Disney World destination) where you plan to finish your day. This is particularly critical if you stay at one of the parks until closing time.

Going to the Magic Kingdom

To get to the Magic Kingdom from the TTC in the morning, you can take a ferry or the monorail. If the line for the monorail extends down the ramp from the loading platform, go with the ferry. Remember, one ferry holds almost as many passengers as three monorail trains. The trip takes the monorail about three-and-a-half to five minutes. Crossing time on the ferry is six-and-a-half minutes. To get to the Magic Kingdom from the TTC any other time of day, the monorail is usually your best bet unless you just happen to catch a ferry loading.

Leaving the Magic Kingdom at the End of the Day

If you close out the day at the Magic Kingdom and need to get back to the TTC, try the ferry first. If the ferry is mobbed (which usually happens only at closing), take the monorail to the Polynesian Resort. Having disembarked, there is a short walkway connecting the hotel to the TTC.

Concerning this last tactic, be forewarned that monorail attendants sometimes demand hotel guest identification before allowing you to board the resort Loop B train. We think this is heavy-handed and totally out of line. Guests lodging outside the World are encouraged to shop, eat, and patronize dinner theaters in the resort hotels, but if it is the end of the day (i.e., not much opportunity remaining to spend more money), then it's "Sorry Charlie, go stand in another line."

Obviously, Disney's intent is to make things easier for its resort lodging guests, but there is a basic inconsistency in the policy. As long as the resort hotels are open to all, be it for a room, a banquet, a business meeting, or just a meal, access to the hotels—by whatever means—should likewise be open. In point of fact, the essence of the problem has nothing to do with whether a visitor is lodging at a resort hotel or what special privileges should accrue to that guest. The bottom line is that Disney cannot handle the traffic to the TTC at closing time and that it chooses to visit the inconvenience of this shortcoming on those not staying at the monorail-connected hotels. A guest at the Magic Kingdom pays for the use of the monorail as part of his admission. We believe a sensible policy would be to allow a Magic Kingdom guest to board either the express (Loop A) or the resort local (Loop B) at his discretion. Differentiating trains as express versus local has presented riders on every mass transit system in the country with clear and fair commuting alternatives. Why not then at Walt Disney World?

Sometimes when you reach the TTC, you will find a throng of people at the boarding area for the parking lot trams. Rather than wait with the crowd, walk to the closest section of the parking lot (Chip 'n Dale) and wait for a tram to come along. When the tram stops and a few people get off, hop on and ride to wherever your car is parked.

Going to EPCOT Center from the Magic Kingdom

If you are trying to get to EPCOT Center from the Magic Kingdom in the morning, take the monorail to the TTC and transfer to the EPCOT Center monorail. If you are commuting in the afternoon, take the ferry to the TTC. If you plan to spend the remainder of the day at EPCOT Center and your car is in the TTC lot, go ahead and drive your car over. But if you plan to return to the Magic Kingdom or you do not have a car at the TTC, catch the EPCOT Center monorail.

Going to the Magic Kingdom from EPCOT Center

To go from EPCOT Center to the Magic Kingdom, take the monorail to the TTC and then transfer to the Magic Kingdom express monorail. If you do not plan to return to EPCOT Center and you have a car in the EPCOT Center lot, drive to the TTC and then take the ferry or monorail as crowd conditions suggest.

Going to the Disney-MGM Studios

Getting to and from the Disney-MGM Studios is pretty cut and dried: by car or bus. Either way, it's best if you can take take your own car, especially if you want to leave the Studios for one of the other parks. Your parking fee covers all Disney pay lots for the entire day.

—— *Transportation System Trade Offs for Guests Staying in Walt Disney World* ——

Readers who plan to stay in Walt Disney World frequently ask about needing a car. If your vacation plans do not include restaurants, attractions, or other destinations outside of Walt Disney World, the answer is a very qualified no. You will not need a car, but, after you read the following, you might want one.

While the Walt Disney World transportation system is large, diversified, and generally efficient, it is sometimes overwhelmed during peak traffic periods, most particularly at park opening and closing times. If you could be assured of getting on a bus or a launch or a monorail at these critical times, we would simply advise you to leave your car at home. The reality, however, is that when everyone wants to go somewhere at the same time, delays are unavoidable. In addition, while some destinations are served directly, many others require one or more transfers. Finally, it is rather difficult to figure out how the bus, boat, and monorail systems interconnect.

If a resort hotel offers boat or monorail service, its bus service will be limited. What this means, essentially, is you will have to transfer at the Transportation and Ticket Center (TTC) for many Walt Disney World destinations. If you are staying at one of the Magic Kingdom resort hotels serviced by monorail (Polynesian, Contemporary, Grand Floridian), you will be able to commute efficiently to the Magic Kingdom on the monorail. If, however, you want to visit EPCOT Center or the Disney-MGM Studios, you must take the monorail to the TTC and there transfer to a bus for the Studios, or to the EPCOT loop monorail for EPCOT Center. While guests at the Polynesian Resort would be best served by taking the monorail to the Magic Kingdom, they would be much better off driving cars to EPCOT Center or the Disney-MGM Studios.

If you are staying at one of the EPCOT resort hotels (Swan, Dolphin, Yacht and Beach Clubs) you can walk or commute via tram to the International Gateway (back door) entrance of EPCOT Center. This is great for returning to your hotel in the evening, but is the wrong end of EPCOT Center to begin your morning touring. Although bus service is available directly from the EPCOT resorts to the Magic Kingdom, there is no direct bus service to the main entrance of EPCOT Center or to the Disney-MGM Studios. To get to the Studios from the EPCOT resorts you must take a rather slow boat. Once again, except in the cases of commuting to the Magic Kingdom and returning *from* EPCOT Center, you would be better off driving your own car.

The Caribbean Beach, Dixie Landings, and Port Orleans Resorts; the Disney Vacation Club; and Disney's Village Resort offer the most efficient transportation with direct buses to all three theme parks. The rub here is that guests must walk a long way to the bus stops at Dixie Landings and Port Orleans; or at the Caribbean Beach Resort, sit through almost a dozen pick-up stops before actually getting underway to the park(s). Commuting to the parks in the mornings from these resorts is generally no sweat (though you may have to ride standing up). Returning in the evening, however, can be a different story. If you plan to stay at one of the parks until closing, we suggest driving your own car.

It should be noted that the Buena Vista Palace and The Hilton in the Village Hotel Plaza terminated their guest transportation contract with Disney Transportation Operations and initiated service with another carrier. The substitute service, which in our opinion does not measure up, constitutes a real problem for guests at these hotels. At the time of this revision, there were rumblings to the effect that other independently owned hotels in the Village Hotel Plaza were considering scrapping the Disney bus service. Before booking a hotel at the Hotel Plaza Village, we suggest you check to make sure the hotel is serviced by Disney Transportation.

Fort Wilderness guests must use the internal Fort Wilderness bus system to reach the boat landings or the Pioneer Hall bus stop. From these departure points, respectively, guests can travel directly by boat to the Magic Kingdom or by bus to the Disney-MGM Studios, or to other destinations via transfer at the TTC. With the exception of commuting to the Magic Kingdom, the best way to get around for Fort Wilderness guests is to drive.

An important footnote to this discussion is that Walt Disney World lodging guests do not have to pay to park in any of the theme park pay lots.

Finally, if you are staying at Walt Disney World and there are teens in your party, familiarize yourself with the Walt Disney World bus system. Safe, clean, and operating until 1 A.M. on most nights, the buses are a great way for the young folks to get around the World. Buses from all over Walt Disney World stop at the TTC, from whence passengers can transfer to such destinations as Fort Wilderness/River Country, Disney-MGM Studios, Typhoon Lagoon, Pleasure Island, Walt Disney World Village, EPCOT Center, and the golf courses.

Walt Disney World Bus Service

All Walt Disney World buses have a color-coded pennant painted on the sides and rear of the coach. Each pennant is identified on a bus route chart that gives you all locations a particular bus serves. The bus route chart will be given to you when you check in, or can be obtained in your hotel at the guest services desk. The person at guest services can also answer any questions you have about reaching a particular Walt Disney World destination. Day guests using the bus system usually can find pennant coding explained on a placard at each bus stop.

Buses initiate service to the theme parks at about 7:15 A.M. on days when the park's official opening time is 9 A.M. In general the buses run once every 15–20 minutes. Buses to Disney-MGM or EPCOT deliver you to the entrance of the park. Buses to the Magic Kingdom, however, deliver you to the Transportation and Ticket Center (TTC) before 8:15 A.M. (where you must transfer to the monorail or the ferry), and only directly to the entrance of the Magic Kingdom at 8:15 A.M. or later. To be on hand for the *real* opening time (when the official opening time is 9 A.M.), catch direct buses to EPCOT Center and the Disney-MGM Studios between 7:30 and 8 A.M. Catch direct buses to the Magic Kingdom between 8 and 8:15 A.M. If you must transfer to reach the park of your choice, leave 15–20 minutes earlier. On days when the official opening time is 8 A.M., move up your departure time accordingly. If you are commuting to the Magic Kingdom on an early entry morning, you can count on the park opening an hour and a half before the official opening time for the general public. Buses to the Magic Kingdom on early entry mornings start running about two hours before the stated opening time. Believe it or not, on an early entry day when the Magic Kingdom's official opening time for the general public is 8 A.M., Disney lodging guests can catch a bus to the park as early as 6 A.M., and can enter the park by 6:30 A.M.

For your return bus trip in the evening, try to get out of the park 40 minutes to an hour before closing to avoid the rush. If you get caught in the mass exodus at closing, don't worry. You may be inconvenienced, but you will not be stranded. Buses, boats, and monorails continue to operate for two hours after the parks close.

Walt Disney World Monorail Service

The monorail system serving the Magic Kingdom resort hotels usually cranks up two hours before the official opening time on early entry days, and an hour and a half before official opening time on other days. If you are staying at a Magic Kingdom resort hotel and wish to be among the first in the Magic Kingdom on a non–early entry morning when the official opening time is 9 A.M., board the monorail at the times indicated below. On an early entry morning (when the official opening time is 9 A.M.), get moving 45–60 minutes earlier. If the official opening time is 8 A.M., bounce everything up yet another hour.

What's that? You don't possess the circadian rhythms of a farmer or a morning paper boy? Get with the program, Bubba, this is a *Disney* vacation. Haul your lazy behind out of bed and go have some fun!

From the Contemporary Resort	7:45–8 A.M.
From the Polynesian Resort	7:50–8:05 A.M.
From the Grand Floridian	8:00–8:10 A.M.

If you are a day guest (no early entry privileges), you will be allowed on the monorail at the TTC between 8:15–8:30 A.M. on a day when the official opening time is 9 A.M. If you want to board earlier, take the walkway from the TTC to the Polynesian Resort and board there.

The monorail loop connecting EPCOT Center with the TTC opens at 7:30 A.M. on days when EPCOT Center's official opening time is 9 A.M. To be at EPCOT Center when the park opens, catch the EPCOT monorail (at the TTC) no later than 8:05 A.M.

The monorails usually run for two hours after closing to insure that everyone is accommodated. If the monorail is too crowded, or you need transportation after the monorails have stopped running, catch a bus.

Dining In and Around Walt Disney World

Dining in Walt Disney World

Veteran readers of the *Unofficial Guide* are well aware that we are somewhat disparaging of the quality of food in many Walt Disney World restaurants. While in the main we find the fare disappointing and the prices exorbitant, there are several Walt Disney World full-service restaurants that are worthy of note.

To assist you in your selection, we have developed summary profiles of the Walt Disney World full-service restaurants. Each profile allows you, in just a second, to check out the restaurant's name, cuisine, location, star rating, cost range, quality rating, and value rating.

Star Rating. The star rating represents the entire dining experience: style, service, and ambience in addition to taste, presentation, and quality of food. Five stars is the highest possible rating and indicates the restaurant offers the best of everything. Four-star restaurants are above average, and three-star restaurants offer good, though not memorable meals. Two-star restaurants serve essentially mediocre fare, and one-star restaurants are below average. Our star ratings do not correspond to ratings awarded by AAA, Mobil, Zagat, or other restaurant reviewers.

Cost. The next rating gives a general description of how much a complete meal will cost. For our purposes, a complete meal consists of a main dish with vegetable or side dish and a choice of soup or salad. Appetizers, desserts, drinks, and tips are excluded. We've rated the cost as inexpensive, moderate, or expensive.

Inexpensive = $14 and less per person
Moderate = $15–30 per person
Expensive = Over $30 per person

Quality Rating. If you are a person who wants the best food available, and cost is not an issue, you need look no further than the quality ratings. The quality rating is based on a scale of 0–100, with 100 as the best possible, and zero (0) as the worst. The quality rating is based solely on the preparation, presentation, taste, freshness of ingredients, and creativity of the food served. There is no consideration of price, service, or atmosphere—just the food.

Value Rating. If, on the other hand, you are looking for both quality and a good deal, then you should check the value rating. The value ratings range from A to E, as follows:

> A = Exceptional value, a real bargain
> B = Good value
> C = Fair value, you get exactly what you pay for
> D = Somewhat overpriced
> F = Extremely overpriced

Theme Park Full-Service Restaurant Profiles (in alphabetical order)

Name	Cuisine	Location	Star Rating	Cost Range	Quality Rating	Value Rating
Akershus	Norwegian Buffet	EPCOT	★★★½	Moderate	89	B
Biergarten	German	EPCOT	★★★	Moderate	81	C
Bistro de Paris	French	EPCOT	★★★½	Expensive	89	C
Chefs de France	French	EPCOT	★★★	Expensive	84	D
Coral Reef	Seafood	EPCOT	★★★★	Expensive	90	D
50's Prime Time Cafe	American	Disney-MGM	★★	Moderate	64	D
Hollywood Brown Derby	American	Disney-MGM	★★★	Expensive	82	D
King Stefan's	American	Magic Kingdom	★	Expensive	51	F
Land Grille Room	American	EPCOT	★★★	Moderate	82	C
Liberty Tree Tavern	American	Magic Kingdom	★★★	Moderate	77	C

Theme Park Full-Service Restaurant Profiles (in alphabetical order) (continued)

Name	Cuisine	Location	Star Rating	Cost Range	Quality Rating	Value Rating
L'Originale Alfredo di Roma	Italian	EPCOT	★★★½	Expensive	86	D
Mama Melrose's	Italian	Disney-MGM	★★★	Moderate	82	C
Marrakesh	Moroccan	EPCOT	★★★	Moderate	81	C
Nine Dragons	Chinese	EPCOT	★★½	Expensive	74	F
Rose & Crown	English	EPCOT	★★★	Moderate	83	C
San Angel Inn	Mexican	EPCOT	★★★½	Moderate	87	D
Sci-Fi Dine-In	American	Disney-MGM	★½	Moderate	59	D
Tempura Kiku	Japanese	EPCOT	★★★	Moderate	83	C
Teppanyaki	Japanese	EPCOT	★★★½	Expensive	88	C
Tony's Town Square	Italian	Magic Kingdom	★★	Moderate	68	D

Walt Disney World Hotel Restaurant Profiles (in alphabetical order)

Name	Cuisine	Location	Star Rating	Cost Range	Quality Rating	Value Rating
American Vineyards	American	Hilton at WDW Village	★★★	Moderate	78	D
Ariel's	Seafood	Beach Club	★★★★	Expensive	92	C
Arthur's 27	American	Buena Vista Palace	★★★½	Expensive	87	D
Baskervilles	American	Grosvenor Resort	★★★	Moderate	82	C
Benihana	Japanese steakhouse	Hilton at WDW Village	★★½	Moderate	75	C
Boatwright's	American/ Cajun	Dixie Landings	★★	Moderate	69	D

Walt Disney World Hotel Restaurant Profiles (in alphabetical order) (continued)

Name	Cuisine	Location	Star Rating	Cost Range	Quality Rating	Value Rating
Bonfamille's Cafe	Seafood	Port Orleans	★★★	Moderate	80	C
Cape May Cafe	Seafood buffet	Beach Club	★★★	Moderate	82	B
Chef Mickey's	American	Village Marketplace	★★★	Moderate	82	C
Contemporary Cafe	American buffet	Contemporary	★★★	Moderate	81	B
Crockett's Tavern	American	Fort Wilderness	★★	Moderate	63	D
Empress Room	Continental	Empress Lilly Riverboat	★★★★	Expensive	91	C
Fireworks Factory	Barbeque	Pleasure Island	★★★	Moderate	79	D
Fisherman's Deck	Seafood	Empress Lilly Riverboat	★★★	Expensive	77	C
Flagler's	Italian	Grand Floridian	★★★	Moderate	79	D
Garden Gallery	American	Disney Inn	★★★★	Moderate	91	B
Garden Grove Cafe	American	Swan	★★★	Moderate	80	C
Grand Floridian Cafe	American	Grand Floridian	★★	Moderate	68	D
Harry's Safari	Steak & seafood	Dolphin	★★★	Expensive	81	D
Minnie Mia's	Italian	Disney Village	★★★★	Inexpensive	90	B
Narcoossee's	Steak & seafood	Grand Floridian	★★★★	Expensive	90	C
Olivia's Cafe	American	Vacation Club	★★★	Moderate	80	C
Outback (The)	Steak	Buena Vista Palace	★★	Expensive	67	D
Palio	Italian	Swan	★★★	Expensive	84	D

Walt Disney World Hotel Restaurant Profiles *(in alphabetical order)* *(continued)*

Name	Cuisine	Location	Star Rating	Cost Range	Quality Rating	Value Rating
Papeete Bay Verandah	Oriental	Polynesian	★½	Moderate	62	D
Plaza Diner	American	Hotel Royal Plaza	★★★	Inexpensive	81	C
Pompano Grill	American	Disney's Village Resort	★★★	Moderate	80	C
Portobello Yacht Club	Italian	Pleasure Island	★★★½	Expensive	85	D
Ristorante Carnevale	Italian	Dolphin	★★★★	Expensive	92	D
Steerman's Quarters	Steak	Empress Lilly Riverboat	★★½	Expensive	75	D
Sum Chows	Chinese	Dolphin	★★★★	Expensive	93	C
Victoria and Albert's	Continental	Grand Floridian	★★★★½	Expensive	95	D
Yachtsman Steakhouse	Steak	Yacht Club	★★★	Expensive	80	D

A Few Caveats

Before you commence eating your way through Walt Disney World there are a few things you need to know:

1. In many Walt Disney World restaurants, particularly full-service restaurants in the Magic Kingdom and the Disney-MGM Studios, the subtlety and creativity of the dishes described on the menu is often vastly beyond the kitchen's ability to deliver. Expressed differently, stay away from fancy food. Try to order dishes that would be really hard to screw up.

2. Be forewarned that the quality of beef has declined in many of the Disney-owned kitchens during the past two years. The best of the Disney steak houses is the Yachtsman Steakhouse at Disney's

Yacht Club. Even the Yachtsman Steakhouse, however, has been affected by the recent glut of tough, gristly cuts.

3. Do not order baked, broiled, poached, or grilled seafood unless the restaurant specializes in seafood or, alternatively, rates at least 3½ stars on our restaurant profile.

4. There seems to be a concerted effort in the theme park restaurants to rush you through your meal in order to clear the table for the next contingent of diners. This mach 2 food ingestion may have appeal to a family with small, restless children; for anyone wanting to relax, it feels more like *Beat the Clock* than fine dining.

    If you want to relax and linger over your expensive meal, do not, repeat, do not, order your entire dinner at once. Place drink orders while you study the menu. If you would like a second drink, request it before you order. Order appetizers, but tell the waiter you need more time to choose your main course. Order your entree only after the appetizers have been served. Feel free to dawdle over coffee and dessert.

5. If you are dining in one of the theme parks, and expense is an issue, have your main meal at lunch. The entrees are much the same as on the dinner menu, but the prices are significantly lower.

Getting a Handle on Restaurant Reservations

Getting a reservation for a particular theme park restaurant depends on its popularity and seating capacity, and the size of the crowd on the day of your visit. Each restaurant has seatings for both lunch and dinner.

Guests staying at Walt Disney World lodgings may make reservations at hotel or theme park restaurants one to three days in advance by dialing 56 (45 for campground guests). If you wish to make dining reservations before you arrive at Walt Disney World (one to three days in advance), call (407) 824-3737. Guests who are lodging out of the World can make reservations at Disney hotel restaurants by phoning the restaurant directly. To make reservations at theme park restaurants, however, guests not staying at Disney hotels or campgrounds must do so the same day they would like a table.

Off-World guests who are making same-day reservations (during the busier times of the year) should arrive at the entrance turnstiles at least 30 minutes before the official opening time, admission passes in hand. Make your reservation as follows:

1. At the Magic Kingdom, make reservations for the *Diamond Horseshoe Jamboree* at the Hospitality House, located opposite Town Hall at the end of Main Street. For other Magic Kingdom full-service restaurants, make reservations at the door of the restaurant.

2. At EPCOT Center, go to Earth Station (the building at the base of the dome). Lunch and dinner reservations for all EPCOT Center full-service restaurants can be made here. Be prepared with alternatives for both restaurants and seating times in case your first choices are filled.

3. At the Disney-MGM Studios, reservations can be made at the door of the restaurant or, on some days, a reservations desk set up on the sidewalk near the Hollywood Brown Derby restaurant on Hollywood Boulevard.

Where the Author and Research Team Eat

Since we are very critical of the food served at Walt Disney World, it is only fair that we share our personal preferences for dining in the parks and hotels.

We try to avoid eating at the Magic Kingdom altogether. When we have no choice we usually go for fast food (the simpler the better) or eat at the Liberty Tree Tavern. The Liberty Tree is the best full-service restaurant in the Magic Kingdom, offering some excellent soups, sandwiches, and a pretty fair turkey dinner.

At EPCOT Center we enjoy chicken mole and quesadillas at the San Angel Inn Restaurant in Mexico, and the buffet and draft Ringnes beer at Restaurant Akershus in Norway. We also like most of the dishes at Restaurant Marrakesh in Morocco, though the bastila tends to be a little leathery. The Biergarten is also pretty decent; our only complaint is that the sauerbraten is never marinated long enough. Teppan dining at Japan is some of the best we have had anywhere, and the Bistro de Paris (France) and the Rose & Crown (United Kingdom) can always be counted on for a well prepared meal. Finally, for good seafood in a knock-out underwater setting, you can't beat the Coral Reef at the Living Seas pavilion.

At the Disney-MGM Studios, the most fun restaurants (Sci-Fi Dine-

In and 50's Prime Time Cafe) serve lackluster food. We eat at the Hollywood Brown Derby or Mama Melrose's and then go to the Sci-Fi or Prime Time for dessert.

The best deals in Walt Disney World are the buffets at the Contemporary Cafe in the Contemporary Resort and the clambake at the Cape May Cafe at Disney's Beach Club. The Contemporary dinner buffet includes such unlikely selections as pizza and peel-and-eat boiled shrimp. The clambake includes tasty (albeit extremely chewy) littleneck clams, mussels, superb New England clam chowder, barbequed pork ribs, corn on the cob, Caesar salad, and a great desert selection.

Other restaurants we patronize when left to our own devices are the Fireworks Factory (avoid all appetizers) on Pleasure Island and The Garden Gallery at the Disney Inn. Ariel's at the Beach Club and Ristorante Carnevale and Sum Chows at the Walt Disney World Dolphin are expensive, but good.

Dining Outside of Walt Disney World

Unfortunately, we are not able to eat many meals outside of Walt Disney World, and a couple of our favorite off-World spots have dropped in quality lately. Restaurants we can recommend include Numero Uno for Cuban food (cheap), Siam Orchid for Thai food (expensive), and Ming Court for Chinese (moderate to expensive). Another great favorite of ours on International Drive is Passage to India, an outstanding and affordable Indian restaurant.

Scott Joseph, wine and food critic of the *Orlando Sentinel*, has published a guide to the Orlando area dining in which he recommends the following restaurants:

American	Chatham's Place; 7575 Dr. Phillips Blvd., Orlando; Moderate to expensive
	Pebbles; 12551 State Road 535, Crossroads Shopping Center, Lake Buena Vista; Moderate to expensive
Beef	Butcher Shop Steakhouse; Mercado Mediterranean Village, 8445 International Drive, Orlando; Moderate
Chinese	Ming Court; 9188 International Drive, Orlando; Expensive
Cuban	Numero Uno; 2499 S. Orange Avenue, Orlando; Inexpensive

Indian	Passage to India; 5532 International Drive, Orlando; Moderate
Italian	Capriccio; 9801 International Drive, Orlando; Moderate to expensive
	Rosario's; 4838 W. Irlo Bronson; Kissimmee; Moderate
Middle Eastern	Phoenician; 7600 Dr. Phillips Blvd., Orlando; Inexpensive
Seafood	Banana Bay Grille; 2948 Vineland Road, Kissimmee; Moderate
	Hemingway's; 1 Grand Cypress Blvd., Hyatt Regency Grand Cypress Resort, Orlando; Expensive
Thai	Siam Orchid; 7575 Republic Drive, Orlando; Moderate to expensive

To order a copy of *The Orlando Sentinel Restaurant Guide*, by Scott Joseph, send $9.95 to Sentinel Books, P.O. Box 1100, Orlando, FL 32802. Or call 1-800-347-6868, extension 5521, for credit card orders.

Walt Disney World Attractions

Walt Disney World's primary appeal is in its rides and shows. Understanding how these rides and shows are engineered to accommodate guests provides some information which, aside from being interesting, is invaluable in developing an efficient itinerary.

All the attractions at Walt Disney World, regardless of the theme park in which they are located, are affected by two overriding elements: capacity and popularity. Capacity is simply how many guests the attraction can serve at one time, in an hour, or in a day. Popularity is a comparative term describing how well visitors like a particular attraction.

Capacity can be adjusted for some attractions. It is possible, for instance, to add additional trams at the Disney-MGM Backstage Studios Tour, or to put a couple of extra boats on the water at the Jungle Cruise in the Magic Kingdom. For the most part, however, capacity remains relatively fixed.

From a designer's perspective, the idea is to match capacity and popularity as closely as possible. A big high-capacity ride which is not very popular is a failure of sorts. Lots of money, space, and equipment have been poured into the attraction, yet there are always empty seats. Dreamflight, a newer ride in the Magic Kingdom, comes closest to fitting this profile.

While it is extremely unusual for a new Disney attraction such as Dreamflight not to measure up, it is fairly common for an older ride to lose its appeal. Many, if not most, of the original rides at Disneyland in California have been replaced. At Walt Disney World, the Magic Kingdom's *Mission to Mars* often plays to half-full audiences, as does *Tropical Serenade*.

In general Disney attractions are immensely popular when they are new. Some, like Space Mountain (Magic Kingdom), have sustained great appeal years beyond their debut while others, like EPCOT Center's The Living Seas, have declined in popularity after just a year or two of operation. Most attractions, however, work through the honeymoon and then settle down to handle the level of demand for which they were designed. When this happens, there are enough interested guests during peak hours to fill almost every seat, but not so many as to develop a prohibitively long line.

Sometimes Disney properly estimates an attraction's popularity but then fouls up the equation by mixing in a third variable such as location. Spaceship Earth, the ride inside the huge geosphere at EPCOT Center, is a good example. Placing the ride squarely in the path of every tourist entering the park assures that it will be inundated and overwhelmed during the morning hours when the park is filling up. On the other side of the coin, *The American Adventure*, located at the extreme opposite end of EPCOT Center, has a huge capacity but plays to a partially filled theater until about noon, when guests finally work their way into that part of the park.

If demand is high and capacity is low, large lines will materialize. Dumbo, the Flying Elephant in the Magic Kingdom has the smallest capacity of almost any Walt Disney World attraction, yet it is probably the most popular ride among young children. The result of this mismatch is that children and parents must often suffer long, long waits for a one-and-a-half-minute ride. Dumbo is a simple yet visually appealing midway ride. Its capacity (and that of many other attractions, including Space Mountain) is limited by the very characteristics which contribute to its popularity.

Capacity design is always predicated on averages: the average number of people in the park, the normal distribution of traffic to specific areas within the park, and the average number of staff required to operate the ride. On a holiday weekend when all the averages are exceeded, all but a few attractions operate at maximum capacity, and even then are overwhelmed by the huge crowds. On low-attendance fall days full capacity is often not even approximated and guests can literally walk onto most rides without any wait whatsoever.

The Magic Kingdom offers the greatest variety in both capacity and popularity, offering rides and shows of vastly differing sorts. Only the Magic Kingdom offers low-capacity midway rides, spook house genre rides, and roller coasters. Technologically, its product mix ranges from state of the art to the antiquated. This diversity makes efficient touring of the Magic Kingdom much more challenging. If guests do not understand the capacity/popularity relationship and plan accordingly, they might spend most of the day waiting in line.

While EPCOT Center and the Disney-MGM Studios have fewer rides and shows than the Magic Kingdom, almost all of their attractions are major features and rank on a par with the Magic Kingdom's Pirates of the Caribbean and Jungle Cruise in scope, detail, imagination, and spectacle. All but one or two of the EPCOT Center and Disney-MGM rides are fast-loading, and most have large carrying capacities. Because EPCOT Center and Disney-MGM attractions are on average well-engineered and very efficient, lines may appear longer than those in the Magic Kingdom, but usually move more quickly. There are no amusement park rides at EPCOT Center or the Disney-MGM Studios and few attractions which are specifically intended for children.

In the Magic Kingdom, crowded conditions are more a function of the popularity and engineering of individual attractions. At EPCOT Center, traffic flow and crowding is much more affected by the park layout. For touring efficiency, it is important to understand how the Magic Kingdom rides and shows operate. At EPCOT Center this knowledge is decidedly less important.

Crowds at the Disney-MGM Studios have been larger than anticipated since it opened in 1989. Greater-than-expected attendance coupled with a relatively small number of attractions has resulted in long lines, long waits, and frustrated guests. Disney plans to double the size of the theme park, but in the meantime a well-considered touring plan is essential.

It is necessary to understand how the rides and shows are designed and how they function to develop an efficient touring plan. We will examine both.

— Cutting Down Your Time in Line by Understanding the Rides —

There are many different types of rides at Walt Disney World. Some rides, like The Great Movie Ride at the Disney-MGM Studios, are engineered to carry more than 3,000 people every hour. At the other extreme, such rides as Dumbo, the Flying Elephant can only accommodate around 400 persons in an hour. Most rides fall somewhere in between. Lots of factors figure into how long you will have to wait to experience a particular ride: the popularity of the ride; how it loads and unloads; how many persons can ride at one time; how many units (cars, rockets, boats, flying elephants, Skyway gondolas, etc.) are in service at a given time; and how many staff personnel are available to operate the ride. Let's take them one by one:

1. *How popular is the ride?*

Newer rides like Splash Mountain at the Magic Kingdom attract a lot of people, as do longtime favorites such as the Jungle Cruise. If you know a ride is popular, you need to learn a little more about how it operates to determine when might be the best time to ride. But a ride need not be especially popular to form long lines; the lines can be the result of less than desirable traffic engineering (i.e., it takes so long to load and unload that a line builds up anyway). This is the situation at the Mad Tea Party and Cinderella's Golden Carrousel in Fantasyland. Since mostly children and teens ride the Mad Tea Party, it only serves a small percentage of any day's attendance at the Magic Kingdom. Yet, because it takes so long to load and unload this comparatively less popular ride, long waiting lines form.

2. *How does the ride load and unload?*

Some rides never stop. They are like a circular conveyor belt that goes around and around. We call these "continuous loaders." The Haunted Mansion in the Magic Kingdom is a continuous loader, as is Spaceship Earth at EPCOT Center. The number of people that can be moved through in an hour depends on how many cars, "doom buggies," or whatever are on the conveyor. The Haunted Mansion and Spaceship Earth have lots of cars on the conveyor belt and consequently can move more than 2,000 people an hour.

Still other rides are "interval loaders." This means that cars are unloaded, loaded, and dispatched at certain set intervals (sometimes controlled manually and sometimes by a computer). Space Mountain in Tomorrowland is an interval loader. It has two separate tracks (in other words the ride has been duplicated in the same facility). Each track can run up to 14 space capsules, released at 36-second, 26-second, or 21-second intervals. (The bigger the crowd, the shorter the interval.)

In one kind of interval loader, like Space Mountain, empty cars (space capsules) are returned to the starting point where they line up for reloading. In a second type of interval loader, one group of riders enters the vehicle while the last group of riders departs. We call these "in-and-out" interval loaders. Splash Mountain is a good example of an in-and-out interval loader. As a boat pulls up to the dock, those who have just completed their ride exit to the left. At almost the same time, those waiting to ride enter the boat from the right. The boat is released to the dispatch point a few yards down the line where it is launched according to whatever time interval is being used.

Interval loaders of both types can be very efficient at moving people if (1) the dispatch (launch) interval is relatively short and (2) the ride can accommodate a large number of vehicles in the system at one time. Since many boats can be floating through Pirates of the Caribbean at a given time, and since the dispatch interval is short, almost 3,000 people an hour can see this attraction. 20,000 Leagues Under the Sea is an in-and-out interval loader which can only run a maximum of nine submarines at a time with a fairly long dispatch interval. Thus 20,000 Leagues can only handle up to 1,600 people an hour.

A third group of rides are "cycle rides." Another name for these rides is "stop-and-go" rides. Here those waiting to ride exchange places with those who have just ridden. The main difference between in-and-out interval rides and cycle rides is that with a cycle ride the whole system shuts down when loading and unloading is in progress. While one boat is loading and unloading in It's a Small World (an interval loader), many other boats are advancing through the ride. But when Dumbo, the Flying Elephant touches down, the whole ride is at a standstill until the next flight is launched. Likewise, with Cinderella's Golden Carrousel, all riders dismount and the Carrousel stands stationary until the next group is mounted and ready to ride. In discussing a cycle ride, the amount of time the ride is in motion is called "ride time." The amount of time that the ride is idle while loading and unloading is called "load time." Load time added to ride time equals "cycle time," or the time expended from the start of one run of the ride until the start of the succeeding run.

Cycle rides are the least efficient of all rides in terms of traffic engineering. The only cycle rides at Walt Disney World are in the Magic Kingdom.

3. *How many persons can ride at one time?*

This figure is defined in terms of "per ride capacity" or "system capacity." Either way the figures allude to the number of people who can be riding at the same time. Our discussion above illustrates that the greater the carrying capacity of a ride (all other things being equal) the more visitors it can accommodate in an hour. Also, as mentioned previously, some rides can add extra units (cars, boats, etc.) as crowds build to increase carrying capacity, while others like the StarJets in Tomorrowland have a fixed capacity (it being impossible to add additional rockets).

4. *How many "units" are in service at a given time?*

A "unit" is simply our term for the vehicle you sit in during your ride. At the Mad Tea Party the unit is a tea cup, at 20,000 Leagues it's a submarine, and at the Grand Prix Raceway it's a race car. On some rides (mostly cycle rides), the number of units in operation at a given time is fixed. Thus, there are always 16 flying elephant units operating on the Dumbo ride, 90 horses on Cinderella's Golden Carrousel, and so on. What this fixed number of units means to you is that there is no way to increase the carrying capacity of the ride by adding more units. On a busy day, therefore, the only way to carry more people each hour on a fixed-unit cycle ride is to shorten the loading time (which, as we will discuss next, is sometimes impossible) or by decreasing the riding time, the actual time the ride is in motion. The bottom line on a busy day for a cycle ride is that you will wait longer and possibly be rewarded for your wait with a shorter ride. This is why we try to steer you clear of the cycle rides unless you are willing to ride them early in the morning or late at night. The following are cycle rides, all located in the Magic Kingdom:

Fantasyland:	Dumbo, the Flying Elephant
	Cinderella's Golden Carrousel
	Mad Tea Party
Tomorrowland:	StarJets

Many other rides throughout Walt Disney World can increase their carrying capacity by adding more units as the crowds build. Big Thunder Mountain Railroad in Frontierland is a good example. If attendance is very light, Big Thunder can start the day by only running one of their five available mine trains from one of two available loading platforms. If lines start to build, the other loading platform is opened and more mine trains placed into operation. At full capacity a total of five trains can carry about 2,400 persons an hour. Likewise Star Tours at Disney-MGM Studios can increase its capacity by adding more simulators, and the Maelstrom boat ride at EPCOT Center can add more Viking ships. Sometimes a long queue will disappear almost instantly when new units are brought on line. When an interval-loading ride places more units into operation, it usually shortens the dispatch intervals, so more units are being dispatched more often.

5. *How many staff personnel are available
to operate the ride?*

Allocation of additional staff to a given ride can allow extra units to be placed in operation, or additional loading areas or holding areas to be opened. In the Magic Kingdom, Pirates of the Caribbean and It's a Small World can run two separate waiting lines and loading zones. The Haunted Mansion has a one-and-a-half-minute preshow which is staged in a "stretch room." On busy days a second stretch room can be activated, thus permitting a more continuous flow of visitors to the actual loading area.

Additional staff make a world of difference in some cycle rides. Often there is only a single attendant operating the Mad Tea Party. This one person must clear visitors from the ride just completed, admit and seat visitors for the upcoming ride, check that all tea cups are properly secured (which entails an inspection of each tea cup), return to the control panel, issue instructions to the riders, and finally activate the ride (whew!). A second attendant allows for the division of these responsibilities and has the effect of cutting loading time by 25 to 50 percent.

By knowing the way a ride loads, its approximate hourly capacity, and its relative popularity, we can anticipate which rides are likely to develop long lines, and more importantly how long we will have to wait to ride at any given time of day.

—— Cutting Down Your Time in Line by Understanding the Shows ——

Many of the featured attractions at Walt Disney World are theater presentations. While not as complex as rides from a traffic engineering viewpoint, a little enlightenment concerning their operation may save some touring time.

Most of the theater attractions at Walt Disney World operate in three distinct phases:

1. There are the guests who are in the theater viewing the presentation.
2. There are the guests who have passed through the turnstile into a holding area or waiting lobby. These people will be admitted to the theater as soon as the presentation in progress is concluded. Several attractions offer a preshow in their waiting lobby to enter-

tain guests until they are admitted to the main show. Among these are *Tropical Serenade* (*Enchanted Tiki Birds*) and *Mission to Mars* in the Magic Kingdom, *Captain EO* and Universe of Energy at EPCOT Center, and *The Monster Sound Show* and *MuppetVision 3-D* at the Disney-MGM Studios.

3. There is the outside line. Those waiting here will enter the waiting lobby when there is room, and will ultimately move from the waiting lobby to the theater.

The theater capacity and the popularity of the presentation, along with the level of attendance in the park, determine how long the lines will be at a given theater attraction. Except for holidays and other days of especially heavy attendance, the longest wait for a show usually does not exceed the length of one complete performance.

Since almost all Walt Disney World theater attractions run continuously, only stopping long enough for the previous audience to leave and the waiting audience to enter, a performance will be in progress when you arrive. If a showing of *Impressions de France* in the French pavilion at EPCOT Center is 18 minutes in duration, the longest wait under normal circumstances should be about 18 minutes if you were to arrive just after the show had begun.

All Walt Disney World theaters (except the Main Street Cinema in the Magic Kingdom and various amphitheater productions) are very strict when it comes to controlling access. Unlike a movie theater at home, you cannot just walk in during the middle of a performance. This being the case, you will always have at least a short wait.

Most of the theaters at Walt Disney World hold a lot of people. When a new audience is admitted, the outside line (if there is one) will usually disappear. Exceptions are *Country Bear Jamboree* in the Magic Kingdom, *The Making of Me* in the Wonders of Life pavilion at EPCOT Center, and *The Voyage of the Little Mermaid* at the Disney-MGM Studios. Because these shows are so popular (or have a small seating capacity like *The Making of Me*), you may have to wait through two or more shows before you are admitted (unless you go early in the morning).

— *How to Deal with Obnoxious People* —

At every theater presentation at Walt Disney World, visitors in the preshow area elbow, nudge, and crowd one another in order to

make sure that they are admitted to the performance. Not necessary—
if you are admitted through the turnstile into the preshow area a seat
has automatically been allocated for you in the theater. When it is time
to proceed into the theater don't rush; just relax and let other people
jam the doorways. When the congestion has been relieved simply stroll
in and take a seat.

Attendants at many theaters will instruct you to enter a row of seats
and move completely to the far side, filling every seat so that each row
can be completely filled. And invariably some inconsiderate, thick-
skulled yahoo will plop down right in the middle of the row, stopping
traffic or forcing other visitors to climb over him. Take our word for
it—there is no such thing as a bad seat. All of the Disney theaters
have been designed to provide a near-perfect view from every seat
in the house. Our recommendation is to follow instructions and move
to the far end of the row, and if you encounter some dummy blocking
the middle of the row, have every person in your party step very hard
on his toes as you move past him.

The Disney people also ask that visitors not use flash photography in
the theaters (the theaters are too dark for the pictures to turn out, *plus*
the flash is disruptive to other viewers). Needless to say, this admoni-
tion is routinely ignored. Flashers are more difficult to deal with than
row-blockers. You can threaten to turn the offenders over to Disney
Security, or better yet, simply hold your hand over the lens (you have
to be quick) when they raise their cameras.

Tami Knight

PART THREE: *Walt Disney World with Kids*

The Agony and the Ecstasy

The national media and advertising presence of Disney is so overwhelming that any child who watches TV or shops with Mom is likely to get all revved up about going to Walt Disney World. Parents, if anything, are even more susceptible. Almost every parent has brightened with anticipation at the prospect of guiding their children through the wonders of this special place. "Imagine little Tammy's expression when she first sees Mickey Mouse. Think of her excitement and awe as she crosses the moat to Cinderella Castle. Imagine her small arms around me when Dumbo takes off." Are these not the treasured moments we long to share with our children?

While dreams of visiting Disney World are tantamount to Nirvana for a three-year-old, and dear enough to melt the heart of any parent, the reality of actually taking that three-year-old (particularly during the summer) is usually a lot closer to "the agony" than to "the ecstasy."

A mother from Dayton, Ohio, describes taking her five-year-old to Walt Disney World in July:

> I felt so happy and excited before we went. I guess it was all worth it, but when I look back I think I should have had my head examined. The first day we went to Disney World [the Magic Kingdom] and it was packed. By 11 in the morning we had walked so far and stood in so many lines that we were all exhausted. Kristy cried about going on anything that looked or even sounded scary, and was frightened by all of the Disney characters (*they are so big!*) except Minnie and Snow White.
>
> We got hungry about the same time as everyone else but the lines for food were too long and my husband said we would have to wait. By one in the afternoon we were just plugging along, not seeing anything we were really interested in, but picking rides because the lines were short, or because whatever it was was air-conditioned. We rode Small World three times in a row and I'll never get that song out of my head (Ha!). At around 2:30 we finally got something to eat, but by then we were so hot and tired

that it felt like we had worked in the yard all day. Kristy insisted on being carried and we had fifty fights about not going on rides where the lines were too long. At the end, we were so P.O.'d and uncomfortable that we weren't having any fun. Mostly by this time we were just trying to get our money's worth.

Before you stiffen in denial, let me assure you that the Ohio family's experience is fairly typical. Most small children are as picky about the rides as they are about what they eat, and more than 50% of preschoolers are intimidated by the friendly Disney characters. Few humans (of any age), moreover, are mentally or physically equipped to march all day in a throng of 50,000 people, not to mention the unrelenting Florida sun. Finally, would you be surprised to learn that almost 60% of preschoolers said the thing they liked best about their Walt Disney World Vacation was the hotel swimming pool?

Reality Testing—Whose Dream Is It?

Remember when you were little and you got that nifty electric train for Christmas, the one your Dad wouldn't let you play with? Did you ever wonder who that train was really for? Ask yourself the same question about your vacation to Walt Disney World. Whose dream are you trying to make come true, yours or your child's?

Small children are very adept at reading their parents' emotions. When you ask, "Honey, how would you like to go to Disney World?" your child will be responding more to your smile and excitement and the idea of doing something with Mom and Dad than to any notion of what Disney World is all about. The younger the child in question, the more this is true. For many preschoolers you could elicit the same enthusiastic response by asking, "Honey, how would you like to go to Cambodia on a dogsled?"

So, is your warm, fuzzy fantasy of introducing your child to the magic of Disney a pipe dream? Not necessarily, but you will have to be practical and open to a little reality testing. For instance, would you increase the probability of a happy, successful visit by holding off a couple of years? Is your child spunky and adventuresome enough to willingly sample the variety of Disney World? Will your child have sufficient endurance and patience to cope with long waits in line and large crowds?

—— *Recommendations for Making the Dream Come True* ——

When contemplating a Disney World vacation with small children, anticipation is the name of the game. Here are some of the things you need to consider:

Age. Although the color and festivity of Walt Disney World excite children of all ages, and while there are specific attractions which delight toddlers and preschoolers, the Disney entertainment mix is generally oriented to older kids and adults. We believe that children should be a fairly mature seven years old to *appreciate* the Magic Kingdom, and a year or two older to get much out of EPCOT Center or the Disney-MGM Studios.

Time of Year to Visit. If there is any way you can swing it, avoid the hot, crowded summer months. Try to go in October, November (except Thanksgiving), early December, March, and April (except Easter). If your kids are preschoolers, don't even think about going during the summer. If you have children of varying ages and your school-age kids are good students, take the older ones out of school so you can visit during the cooler, less congested off-season. Arrange special study assignments relating to the many educational aspects of Walt Disney World. If your school-age children are not great students and cannot afford to miss any school, take your vacation as soon as the school year ends in late May or early June. Nothing, repeat, nothing will enhance your Walt Disney World vacation as much as avoiding summer months and holiday periods.

Building Naps and Rest into Your Itinerary. The Disney theme parks are huge, so don't try to see everything in one day. Tour in the early morning and return to your hotel around 11:30 A.M. for lunch, a swim, and a nice nap. Even during the off-season when the crowds are smaller and the temperature more pleasant, the sheer size of the major theme parks will exhaust most children under eight by lunchtime. Go back to the park in the late afternoon or early evening and continue your touring.

Where to Stay. The time and hassle involved in commuting to and from the theme parks will be somewhat lessened if you can afford to stay in Walt Disney World. But even if, for financial or other reasons, you lodge outside of the World, it remains imperative that you get small children out of the parks each day for a few hours to rest and recuperate. Neglecting to relax and unwind is the best way we know to get the whole family in a snit and ruin the day (or the entire vacation).

With small children, there is simply no excuse for not planning ahead. Make sure you get a hotel, in or out of Walt Disney World, within a 20 minute one-way commute of the theme parks. Naps and relief from the frenetic pace of the theme parks, even during the off-season, are indispensable. While it's true that you can gain some measure of peace by retreating to one of the Disney resort hotels for lunch or by finding a quiet spot or restaurant in the theme parks, there is no substitute for returning to the familiarity and security of your own hotel. Regardless of what you have heard or read, children too large to sleep in a stroller will not relax and revive unless you get them back to your hotel.

Thousands of new rooms have been built in and around Walt Disney World, many of them very affordable. With sufficient lead time you should have no difficulty finding accommodations that fulfill your requirements.

Be in Touch with Your Feelings. While we acknowledge that a Walt Disney World vacation seems like a major capital investment, remember that having fun is not necessarily the same as seeing everything. When you or your children start getting tired and irritable, call timeout and regroup. Trust your instincts. What would really feel best right now? Another ride, a rest break with some ice cream, going back to the room for a nap? *The way to protect your investment is to stay happy and have a good time, whatever that takes.* You do not have to meet a quota for experiencing a certain number of attractions or watching parades or anything else. It's your vacation; you can do what you want.

Least Common Denominators. Remember the old saying about a chain being only as strong as its weakest link? The same logic applies to a family touring the Disney theme parks. Somebody is going to run out of steam first; when they do the whole family will be affected. Sometimes a cold Coke and a rest break will get the flagging member back into gear. Sometimes, however, as Marshall Dillon would say, "You just need to get out of Dodge." Pushing the tired or discontented beyond their capacity is like driving on a flat tire: it may get you a few more miles down the road but you will further damage your car in the process. Accept that energy levels vary among individuals and be prepared to respond to small children or other members of your group who poop out. Hint: "We've driven a thousand miles to take you to Walt Disney World and now you're going to ruin everything!" is not an appropriate response.

Setting Limits and Making Plans.   The best way to avoid arguments and disappointment is to develop a game plan before you go. Establish some general guidelines for the day and get everybody committed in advance. Be sure to include:

1. Wake-up time and breakfast plans.
2. What time you need to depart for the park.
3. What you need to take with you.
4. A policy for splitting the group up or for staying together.
5. A plan for what to do if the group gets separated or someone is lost.
6. How long you intend to tour in the morning and what you want to see, including fall-back plans in the event an attraction is closed or too crowded.
7. A policy on what you can afford for snacks and refreshments.
8. A target time for returning to the hotel to rest.
9. What time you will return to the park and how late you will stay.
10. Plans for dinner.
11. A policy for shopping and buying souvenirs, including who pays: Mom and Dad or the kids.

Be Flexible.   Having a game plan does not mean forgoing spontaneity or sticking rigidly to the itinerary. Once again, listen to your intuition. Alter the plan if the situation warrants. Any day at Walt Disney World includes some surprises, so be prepared to roll with the punches.

Overheating, Sunburn, and Dehydration.   The most common problems of smaller children at Walt Disney World are overheating, sunburn, and dehydration. A small bottle of sunscreen carried in a pocket or fanny pack will help you take precautions against overexposure to the sun. Be sure to put some on children in strollers, even if the stroller has a canopy. Some of the worst cases of sunburn we have seen were on the exposed foreheads and feet of toddlers and infants in strollers. To avoid overheating, rest at regular intervals in the shade or in an air-conditioned restaurant or show.

Do not count on keeping small children properly hydrated with soft drinks and water fountain stops. Long lines often make buying refreshments problematic and water fountains are not always handy. What's more, excited children may not realize or inform you that they're thirsty or overheated. We recommend renting a stroller for children six years old and under and carrying plastic water bottles. If you forget to bring your own water containers, plastic squeeze bottles with caps are sold in all three parks for about three dollars.

Blisters and sore feet are common for visitors of all ages, so wear comfortable, well broken-in shoes and two pairs of thin socks (preferable to one pair of thick socks). If you or your children are unusually susceptible to blisters, carry some precut "Moleskin" bandages; they offer the best possible protection, stick great, and won't sweat off. When you feel a hot spot, stop, air out your foot, and place a Moleskin bandage over the area before a blister forms. Moleskin is available by name at all drugstores. Sometimes small children won't tell their parents about a developing blister until it's too late. We recommend inspecting the feet of preschoolers two or more times a day.

First Aid.   There is a First Aid Center in each of the theme parks. In the Magic Kingdom it is next to the Crystal Palace at the end of Main Street near Adventureland. At EPCOT Center it is on the World Showcase side of the Odyssey Restaurant, and at Disney-MGM it is in the Guest Services Building just inside the main entrance. If you or your children have a medical problem, do not hesitate to use the First Aid Centers. The Disney First Aid Centers are warmer and friendlier than most doctor's offices and are accustomed to treating everything from paper cuts to allergic reactions.

Children on Medication.   For various reasons, some parents of hyperactive children on medication elect to discontinue or decrease the child's normal dosage at the close of the school year. Be forewarned that Walt Disney World might stimulate such a child to the point of system overload. Consult your physician before altering your child's medication regimen.

Sunglasses.   If you want your smaller children to wear sunglasses, it's a good idea to affix a strap or string to the frames so the glasses will stay on during rides and can hang from the child's neck while indoors.

Things You Forgot or Things You Ran Out of. Rain gear, diapers, diaper pins, formula, film, aspirin, topical sunburn treatments, and other sundries are available for sale at all the major theme parks and at Typhoon Lagoon, River Country, and Pleasure Island. For some reason rain gear is a bargain, but most other items are pretty high. Ask for goods you do not see displayed; some are stored behind the counter.

Strollers are available for a modest rental fee at all three major theme parks. The rental covers the entire day. If you rent a stroller at the Magic Kingdom and later decide to go to EPCOT Center or Disney-MGM Studios, turn in your Magic Kingdom stroller and hang on to your rental receipt. When you arrive at the next park present your receipt. You will be issued another stroller without additional charge.

Strollers at the Magic Kingdom and EPCOT Center are large, sturdy models with sun canopies and cargo baskets. We have seen families load as many as three children on one of these strollers at the same time. The strollers available at the Disney-MGM Studios are the light collapsible type. Strollers can be obtained to the right of the entrance at the Magic Kingdom, on the left side of the Entrance Plaza at EPCOT Center, and at Oscar's Super Service just inside the entrance of the Disney-MGM Studios. The rental procedure at all parks is fast and efficient and returning the stroller is a breeze. Even at EPCOT Center, where up to 900 strollers are turned in following the evening fireworks show, there is no wait and no hassle.

When you enter a show or board a ride, you will have to park your stroller, usually in an open, unprotected area. If it rains before you return, you will need a cloth, towel, or spare diaper to dry off the stroller.

For infants and toddlers the strollers are a must, but we have observed many sharp parents renting strollers for somewhat older children (up to five or six years old). The stroller prevents parents from having to carry children when they run out of steam and provides an easy, convenient way to carry water, snacks, diaper bags, etc.

If you would like to bring your own stroller from home, it is perfectly permissible to do so. You should not have to worry about your stroller being stolen provided it is marked with your name. Be advised, however, that only collapsible strollers are permitted on the Disney monorails and buses.

Stroller Wars. Sometimes strollers disappear while you are enjoying a ride or a show. Do not be alarmed. You won't have to buy the missing stroller and you will be issued a new stroller for your continued use. In the Magic Kingdom, replacement centers are located at the Trading Post in Frontierland, the Tinkerbell Toy Shop in Fantasyland, and at Spaceport in Tomorrowland, as well as at the main rental facility near the park entrance. At EPCOT Center, in addition to the Entrance Plaza rental headquarters, strollers can be replaced at the International Gateway (in the World Showcase between the United Kingdom and France) and at the German pavilion. At present, strollers at Disney-MGM can only be replaced at Oscar's Super Service.

While replacing a ripped-off stroller is no big deal, it is an inconvenience. A family from Minnesota complained that their stroller had been taken six times in one day at EPCOT Center and five times in a single day at the Disney-MGM Studios. Even with free replacements, larceny on this scale represents a lot of wasted time. Through our own experiments, and suggestions from our readers, we have developed several techniques for hanging on to your rented stroller:

1. At EPCOT Center and the Magic Kingdom, write your name in magic marker on a 6 by 9 inch card, put the card in a transparent freezer bag, and secure the bag to the canopy of the stroller with masking or duct tape.

2. Affix something personal (but expendable) to the handle of the stroller. Evidently most strollers are pirated by mistake (since they all look the same) or because it's easier to swipe someone else's stroller (when yours disappears) than to troop off to the replacement center. Since most stroller theft is a function of confusion, laziness, or revenge, the average pram pincher will balk at hauling off a stroller bearing another person's property. After trying several items, we concluded that a bright, inexpensive scarf or bandanna tied to the handle works well, or a sock partially stuffed with rags or paper works even better (the weirder and more personal the object, the greater the deterrent). Best of all is a dead mackerel dangling from the handle, though in truth, the kids who must ride in the stroller prefer the other methods.

Bound and determined not to have her stroller ripped-off, an Ann Arbor, Michigan, mother describes her stroller security plan as follows:

> We used a variation on your stroller identification theme. We tied a clear plastic bag with a diaper in it on the stroller. Jon even poured a little root beer on the diaper for effect. Needless to say, no one took our stroller and it was easy to identify.

Finally, be aware that Disney cast members will often rearrange strollers parked outside of an attraction. Sometimes this is done simply to "tidy up." At other times the strollers are moved to make additional room along a walkway. In any event, do not assume your stroller has been stolen because it is not exactly where you left it. Check around. Chances are it will be "neatly arranged" just a few feet away.

— Baby-Sitting —

Childcare Centers. Childcare services are not available within the theme parks, but each of the Magic Kingdom resorts (hotels connected by the monorail) and EPCOT resorts (Swan and Dolphin hotels, Yacht and Beach Club Resorts) offer a childcare service for potty-trained children over three. Services vary somewhat, but in general children can be left between 4 P.M. and midnight. Milk and cookies are provided at all of the childcare centers, as are blankets and pillows. Play is supervised but not organized, and toys, videos, and games are on hand in quantity. Guests at any Walt Disney resort hotel (or campground) may use the childcare service.

The most elaborate of the childcare centers (variously called "clubs" or "camps") is the Neverland Club at the Polynesian Resort. This is the only center which includes a buffet dinner at the club, though at the other locations you can arrange for hotel room service to bring your children's meals. At Camp Dolphin in the Walt Disney World Dolphin, there is the option of having children eat at the Coral Cafe or the Soda Shop next door.

We get a lot of mail from readers concerning the Neverland Club, invariably complimentary. A dad from Houston wrote:

> There were two outstanding surprises during our visit. The first was the babysitting club at the Polynesian Hotel, the Neverland Club. I can tell you that our children enjoyed the Neverland Club as much as anything at WDW. It is somewhat expensive ($7 per child per hour, three hour minimum), but that includes dinner, free video games, Disney movies, group games and activities, and a visit by an expert from Discovery Island with several birds and animals. A woman registering her child told my wife that her daughter had stayed at the Neverland Club on a visit two years ago, and considered it her favorite attraction at WDW!

In addition to the above, a Disney character (usually Goofy) visits the children each night. What was the reader's second outstanding surprise? Pleasure Island.

The following childcare clubs operate afternoons and evenings. Reservations are required by all.

Hotel	Name of Program	Ages	Phone
Buena Vista Palace	All About Kids	3–12	(407) 827-2727
Contemporary Resort	Mouseketeer Clubhouse	3–9	(407) 824-1000, ext. 3038
Grand Floridian	Mouseketeer Club	3–9	(407) 824-3000, ext. 2985
The Hilton	Youth Hotel	4–12	(407) 827-4000
Polynesian Resort	Neverland Club	3–12	(407) 824-2170
WDW Dolphin	Camp Dolphin	3–12	(407) 934-4241
WDW Swan	Camp Swan	3–12	(407) 934-1621
Yacht and Beach Clubs	Sandcastle Club	3–12	(407) 934-7000

Kinder-Care Learning Centers also operate childcare facilities at Walt Disney World. Originally developed for the use of Disney employees, the Kinder-Care Centers will also take children of guests on a space available basis. Kinder-Care provides basically the same services as a hotel club, except that the daytime *Learning While Playing Development Program* is more structured and educational. For childcare service in the morning and early afternoon, Kinder-Care is the only game in town. They accept children who are toilet trained through age 12, and reservations can be made by calling (407) 827-5437.

In-Room Baby-Sitting. For those staying in the World, in-room baby-sitting is available through Kinder-Care (407-827-5444) or through the Fairy Godmother service (no joke) described below.

Outside of Walt Disney World, childcare services and in-room sitting can be arranged through most of the larger hotels and motels, or by calling the Fairy Godmothers. On call 24 hours a day, you will never get an answering machine when you call the Fairy Godmothers. Though not cheap (the Godmothers can turn your billfold into a pumpkin), they offer the most flexible and diversified service in town. They will come to any hotel at any hour of the day or night. If you pay, they will take your children to the theme parks. No child is too young or too old for a Fairy Godmother (they also care for the elderly), and they will even take care of your pets. Base rates are $6 an hour for up to three children (in the same family), with a four-hour minimum and a $5 travel fee. Godmothers will also sit a group of children from different families for $5 an hour per family. Wishing won't get it with these Fairy Godmothers; you've got to call them on the phone at (407) 277-3724 or 275-7326.

Caring for Infants at the Theme Parks

The Magic Kingdom, EPCOT Center, and Disney-MGM Studios have special centralized facilities for the care of infants and toddlers. Everything necessary for changing diapers, preparing formulas, warming bottles and food, etc., is available in ample quantity. A broad selection of baby supplies is on hand for sale, and there are even rockers and special chairs for nursing mothers. In the Magic Kingdom the Baby Center is located next to the Crystal Palace at the end of Main Street. At EPCOT Center, Baby Services is located near the Odyssey Restaurant, to the right of the World of Motion in Future World. At Disney-MGM Studios, Baby Care is located in the Guest Services Building to the left of the entrance. Dads in charge of little ones are welcome at the Baby Centers and can avail themselves of most services offered. In addition, changing tables have been placed in several men's rooms in the major theme parks.

—— *Walt Disney World Learning Programs for Children* ——

Developed in coordination with leading educators, four special learning programs are available for persons 15 years and younger at Walt Disney World. The well-presented and enjoyable programs include admission to any theme park visited, classroom materials, and lunch. All of the courses are limited in class size, so make your reservation as soon as possible.

While the courses are expensive, they provide an interesting and educational glimpse of Walt Disney World behind the scenes. They also offer (as if you hadn't thought of it) some time for parents to be alone. If you are considering taking your children out of school to visit Walt Disney World, participation in one of the educational programs sometimes helps secure teacher approval for the absence.

Kidventure Program

This four-hour program held at the Discovery Island zoological park focuses on identifying plants and wildlife. Offered daily during the summer and only on Wednesdays during off-season months, the course costs $30 per person ($25 for Walt Disney World lodging and campground guests) and is restricted to students 8–14 years old. Boat transportation to the island is included. For reservations call (407) 824-3784.

Wonders of Walt Disney World

Exploring Nature: A True-Life Adventure. This program explores the interrelation of mankind and the natural environment. Students visit Discovery Island and the Disney World conservation area. Highlights include seeing several rare and endangered species. Six hours long, the course is limited to students 10–15 years old and costs $75. For reservations and information, call (407) 354-1855.

Art Magic: Bringing Illusion to Life. In this program, students are offered an introduction to animation, as well as a look at how costuming, set design, and landscaping are used in movies, stage shows, and theme parks. Tuition for the six-hour program, open to students 10–15 years old, is $75. Reservations can be made by calling (407) 354-1855.

The Walt Disney World of Entertainment takes a look at what goes into a Disney stage show. Students meet performers and technicians and observe how timing, music, lighting, and costumes combine to create a show. The six-hour course is for 10–15 year olds. Tuition is $75. For information, or to register, call (407) 354-1855.

—— Lost Children ——

Lost children do not usually pose much of a problem. All Disney employees are schooled to handle the situation should it be encountered. If you lose a child in the Magic Kingdom, report the situation to a Disney employee, and then check in at the Baby Center and at City Hall where lost-children "logs" are maintained. At EPCOT Center the procedure is the same; report the child lost and then check at Baby Services near the Odyssey Restaurant. At Disney-MGM Studios, report the child lost at the Guest Services Building at the entrance end of Hollywood Boulevard. Paging systems are not used in any of the parks, but in an emergency, an "all points bulletin" can be issued throughout the park(s) via internal communications.

It is amazingly easy to lose a child (or two) at the theme parks. We suggest that children under eight be color-coded by dressing them in purple T-shirts or equally distinctive attire. It is also a good idea to sew a label into each child's shirt that states his or her name, your name, and the name of your hotel. The same thing can be accomplished less elegantly by writing the information on a strip of masking tape: hotel security professionals suggest that the information be printed in small letters and that the tape be affixed to the outside of the child's shirt five inches or so below the armpit. Finally, special name tags can be obtained at all three major theme parks.

How Kids Get Lost.   Children get separated from their parents every day at the Disney theme parks under circumstances which are remarkably similar (and predictable).

1. *Preoccupied Solo Parent.*   In this scenario the only adult in the party is preoccupied with something like buying refreshments, loading the camera, or using the rest room. Junior is there one second and gone the next.

2. *The Hidden Exit.*   Sometimes parents wait on the sidelines while allowing two or more young children to experience a ride together. As it usually happens, the parents expect the kids to exit the attraction in one place and, lo and behold, the young ones pop out somewhere else. The exits of some Disney attractions are considerably distant from the entrances. Make sure you know exactly where your children will emerge before letting them ride by themselves.

3. *After the Show.*   At the completion of many shows and rides, a Disney staffer will announce, "Check for personal belongings and take small children by the hand." When dozens, if not hundreds, of people leave an attraction at the same time it is easy for parents to temporarily lose contact with their children unless they have them directly in tow.

4. *Rest Room Problems.*   Mom tells six-year-old Tommy, "I'll be sitting on this bench when you come out of the rest room." Three situations: One, Tommy exits through a different door and becomes disoriented (Mom may not know there *is* another door). Two, Mom decides belatedly that she will also use the rest room, and Tommy emerges to find her absent. Three, Mom

pokes around in a shop while keeping an eye on the bench, but misses Tommy when he comes out.

If you cannot be with your child in the rest room, make sure there is only one exit. For disorienting visitors, the rest room situated along a passageway between Frontierland and Adventureland in the Magic Kingdom is the all-time champ. Children and adults alike have walked in from the Adventureland side and walked out on the Frontierland side (and vice versa). Adults making this mistake intuit pretty quickly that something is wrong. Young children, however, sometimes fail to get the message. Designate a meeting spot more distinctive than a bench, and be specific and thorough in your instructions: "I'll meet you by this flagpole. If you get out first, stay right here." Have your child repeat the directions back to you.

5. *Parades.* There are many special parades and shows at the theme parks during which the audience stands. Children, because they are small, tend to jockey around for a better view. By moving a little this way and a little that way, it is amazing how much distance kids can put between you and them before anyone notices.

6. *Mass Movements.* Another situation to guard against is when huge crowds disburse after fireworks, a parade, or at park closing. With 20,000 to 40,000 people suddenly moving at once, it is very easy to get separated from a small child or others in your party. Extra caution is recommended following the evening parade and fireworks in the Magic Kingdom or IllumiNations at EPCOT Center. Families should develop specific plans for what to do and where to meet in the event they are separated.

7. *Character Greetings.* A fair amount of activity and confusion is commonplace when the Disney characters are on the scene. See the section on meeting the Disney characters (pages 193–96).

—— Disney, Kids, and Scary Stuff ——

Disney rides and shows are adventures. They focus on the substance and themes of all adventure, and indeed of life itself: good and evil, quest, death, beauty and the grotesque, fellowship and enmity. As you sample the variety of attractions at Walt Disney World, you transcend the mundane spinning and bouncing of midway rides to a more thought-provoking and emotionally powerful entertainment experience. Though the endings are all happy, the impact of the adventures, with Disney's gift for special effects, is often intimidating and occasionally frightening to small children.

There are rides with menacing witches, rides with burning towns, and rides with ghouls popping out of their graves, all done tongue-in-cheek and with a sense of humor, providing you are old enough to understand the joke. And bones, lots of bones: human bones, cattle bones, dinosaur bones, and whole skeletons everywhere you look. There have to be more bones at Walt Disney World than at the Smithsonian Institution and Tulane Medical School combined. There is a stack of skulls at the headhunter's camp on the Jungle Cruise; a veritable platoon of skeletons sailing ghost ships in Pirates of the Caribbean; a haunting assemblage of skulls and skeletons in The Haunted Mansion; and more skulls, skeletons, and bones punctuating Snow White's Adventures, Peter Pan's Flight, and Big Thunder Mountain Railroad, to name a few.

It should be mentioned that the monsters and special effects at the Disney-MGM Studios are more real and sinister than those of the other theme parks. If your child is having difficulty coping with the witch in Snow White's Adventures, think twice about exposing him to machine-gun battles, earthquakes, and the creature from *Alien* at the Studios.

One reader wrote us the following after taking his preschool children on Star Tours:

> We took a four-year-old and a five-year-old and they had the shit scared out of them at Star Tours. We did this first thing in the morning and it took hours of Tom Sawyer Island and Small World to get back to normal.
>
> Our kids were the youngest by far in Star Tours. I assume that

177

either other adults had more sense or were not such avid readers of your book.

Preschoolers should start with Dumbo and work up to the Jungle Cruise in the late morning, after being revved up and before getting hungry, thirsty, or tired. Pirates of the Caribbean is out for preschoolers. You get the idea.

The reaction of young children to the inevitable system-overload of Walt Disney World should be anticipated. Be sensitive, alert, and prepared for almost anything, even behavior which is out of character for your child at home. Most small children take Disney's variety of macabre trappings in stride, and others are quickly comforted by an arm around the shoulder or a little squeeze of the hand. For parents who have observed in their kids a tendency to become upset, we recommend taking it slow and easy by sampling more benign adventures like the Jungle Cruise, gauging reactions, and discussing with the children how they felt about the things they saw.

Sometimes small children will rise above their anxiety in an effort to please their parents or siblings. This behavior, however, does not necessarily indicate a mastery of fear, much less enjoyment. If children come off a ride in ostensibly good shape, we recommend asking if they would like to go on the ride again (not necessarily right now, but sometime). The response to this question will usually give you a clue as to how much they actually enjoyed the experience. There is a lot of difference between having a good time and mustering the courage to get through something.

Evaluating a child's capacity to handle the visual and tactile effects of Walt Disney World requires patience, understanding, and experimentation. Each of us, after all, has our own demons. If a child balks at or is frightened by a ride, respond constructively. Let your children know that lots of people, adults as well as children, are scared by what they see and feel. Help them understand that it is okay with you if they get frightened, and that their fear does not lessen your love or respect. Take pains not to compound the discomfort by making a child feel inadequate; try not to undermine self-esteem, impugn courage, or subject a child to ridicule. Most of all, do not induce guilt, as if your child's trepidation might be ruining the family's fun. When older siblings are present, it is sometimes necessary to restrain their taunting and teasing.

A visit to Walt Disney World is more than an outing or an adventure for a small child. It is a testing experience, a sort of controlled rite of passage. If you help your little one work through the challenges, the time can be immeasurably rewarding, and a bonding experience for both of you.

The Fright Factor

While each youngster is different, there are essentially seven attraction elements, which alone or combined punch a child's buttons:

1. *The name of the attraction.* Small children will naturally be apprehensive about something called "The Haunted Mansion" or "Mr. Toad's Wild Ride."

2. *The visual impact of the attraction from outside.* Splash Mountain and the Big Thunder Mountain Railroad look scary enough to give adults second thoughts. To many small children these rides are visually terrifying.

3. *The visual impact of the indoor queuing area.* Pirates of the Caribbean with its caves and dungeons, and The Haunted Mansion with its "stretch rooms" have the capability of frightening small children before they even board the ride.

4. *The intensity of the attraction.* Some attractions are so intense as to be overwhelming; they inundate the senses with sights, sounds, movement, and even smell. *Captain EO* at EPCOT Center, for instance, combines loud music, laser effects, lights, and 3-D cinematography to create a total sensory experience. For some preschoolers, this is two or three senses too many.

5. *The visual impact of the attraction itself.* As discussed previously, the sights in various attractions range from falling boulders to lurking buzzards, from grazing dinosaurs to attacking white blood cells. What one child calmly absorbs may scare the bejabbers out of another child the same age.

6. *Dark.* Many Disneyland attractions are "dark" rides, i.e., they operate indoors in the dark. For some children, this alone triggers a lot of apprehension. A child who is frightened on one dark ride, for example, Snow White's Adventures, may be unwilling to try other indoor rides.

7. *The ride itself; the tactile experience.* Some Disney rides are downright wild—wild enough to induce motion sickness, wrench backs, and generally discombobulate patrons of any age.

Small Child Fright Potential Chart

As a quick reference, we have provided a "Fright Potential Chart" to warn you which attractions to be wary of, and why. Remember that the chart represents a generalization and that all kids are different. The chart relates specifically to kids 3–7 years of age. On average, as you would expect, children at the younger end of the age range are more likely to be frightened than children in their sixth or seventh year.

MAGIC KINGDOM

Main Street, U.S.A.

Walt Disney World Railroad: Not frightening in any respect
Main Street Cinema: Not frightening in any respect.
Main Street Vehicles: Not frightening in any respect.

Adventureland

Swiss Family Treehouse: Not frightening in any respect.
Jungle Cruise: Moderately intense, some macabre sights; a good test attraction for little ones.
Tropical Serenade: A small thunderstorm momentarily surprises very small children.
Pirates of the Caribbean: Slightly intimidating queuing area; intense boat ride with gruesome (though humorously presented) sights, and a short, unexpected slide down a flume.

Frontierland

Splash Mountain: Visually intimidating from the outside with moderately intense visual effects. The ride itself is somewhat hair-raising for all ages, culminating in a 52-foot plunge down a steep chute. Switching-off option provided (see page 187).
Big Thunder Mountain Railroad: Visually intimidating from the outside with moderately intense visual effects. The roller coaster is wild enough to frighten many adults, particularly seniors. Switching-off option provided (see page 187)
Tom Sawyer Island: Some very small children are intimidated by dark, walk-through tunnels that can be easily avoided.
Country Bear Jamboree: Not frightening in any respect.
Frontierland Shootin' Gallery: Not frightening in any respect.
The Diamond Horseshoe Jamboree: Not frightening in any respect.

Liberty Square

The Hall of Presidents: Not frightening, but boring for small ones.
Liberty Square Riverboat: Not frightening in any respect.
Mike Fink Keelboats: Not frightening in any respect.
The Haunted Mansion: Name of attraction raises anxiety, as do the
    sounds and sights of waiting area. An intense attraction with humor-
    ously presented macabre sights.The ride itself is gentle.

Fantasyland

Mad Tea Party: Midway-type ride can induce motion sickness in all
    ages.
20,000 Leagues Under the Sea: Not frightening in any respect.
Mr. Toad's Wild Ride: Name of ride intimidates some. Moderately
    intense spook-house genre attraction with jerky ride. Only frightens a
    small percentage of preschoolers.
Snow White's Adventures: Moderately intense spook-house genre
    attraction with some grim characters. Absolutely terrifying to many
    preschoolers.
Magic Journeys: Certain special effects and a wicked witch frighten
    some small children.
Dumbo, the Flying Elephant: A tame midway ride; a great favorite of
    most small children.
Cinderella's Golden Carrousel: Not frightening in any respect.
It's a Small World: Not frightening in any respect.
Peter Pan's Flight: Not frightening in any respect.
Skyway to Tomorrowland: Not frightening except for those afraid of
    heights.

Mickey's Starland

Mickey's House and Starland Show: Not frightening in any respect.
Mickey's Hollywood Theater: Not frightening in any respect.
Grandma Duck's Petting Farm: Not frightening in any respect.

Tomorrowland

Mission to Mars: Vibrations and other effects are marginally frightening
    to a small percentage of preschoolers.
American Journeys: Not frightening in any respect, but audience must
    stand.
Dreamflight: Not frightening in any respect.
WEDway PeopleMover: Not frightening in any respect.
Skyway to Fantasyland: Not frightening in any respect.

Space Mountain: Very intense roller coaster in the dark; the Magic Kingdom's wildest ride and a scary roller coaster by anyone's standards; switching-off option provided (see page 187).

StarJets: Visually intimidating from the waiting area. The ride is actually tame. See safety warning on page 190.

Carousel of Progress: Not frightening in any respect.

Grand Prix Raceway: Noise of waiting area slightly intimidating to preschoolers; otherwise, not frightening.

EPCOT CENTER

Future World

Spaceship Earth: Dark and imposing presentation intimidates a small percentage of preschoolers.

CommuniCores East and West: Not frightening in any respect.

Universe of Energy: Dinosaur segment frightens some preschoolers; visually intense with intimidating effects in parts.

Wonders of Life – Body Wars: Very intense with frightening visual effects. Ride induces motion sickness in susceptible riders of all ages. Switching-off option provided (see page 187).

Wonders of Life – Cranium Command: Not frightening in any respect.

Wonders of Life – The Making of Me: Not frightening in any respect.

Horizons: Not frightening in any respect.

World of Motion – It's Fun to Be Free: Not frightening in any respect.

Journey into Imagination Ride: Contains a few sights that frighten an extremely small percentage of preschoolers.

Captain EO: Extremely intense visual effects and loud volume frighten some preschoolers.

The Land – Listen to the Land: Not frightening in any respect.

The Land – Harvest Theater: Not frightening in any respect.

The Land – Kabaret Theater: Not frightening in any respect.

World Showcase

Mexico – El Rio del Tiempo: Not frightening in any respect.

Norway – Maelstrom: Visually intense in parts. Ride ends with a plunge down a 20-foot flume. A few preschoolers are frightened.

China – Wonders of China: Not frightening in any respect, but audience must stand.

Germany: Not frightening in any respect.
Italy: Not frightening in any respect.
The American Adventure: Not frightening in any respect.
Japan: Not frightening in any respect.
Morocco: Not frightening in any respect.
France–Impressions de France: Not frightening in any respect.
United Kingdom: Not frightening in any respect.
Canada – O Canada!: Not frightening in any respect, but audience must stand.

DISNEY-MGM STUDIOS

The Twilight Zone Tower of Terror: Visually intimidating to small children; contains intense and realistic special effects. Be forewarned that plummeting elevator at end of ride frightens many adults.
The Great Movie Ride: Intense in parts with very realistic special effects and some visually intimidating sights.
SuperStar Television: Not frightening in any respect.
The Monster Sound Show: Name of show causes some apprehension; the actual production is not frightening.
Indiana Jones Epic Stunt Spectacular: An intense show with powerful special effects including explosions, but presented in an educational context that small children generally handle well.
Star Tours: Extremely intense visually for all ages; the ride itself is one of the wildest in the Disney repertoire. Not as likely to cause motion sickness as Body Wars at EPCOT Center. Switching-off option is provided (see page 187).
Backstage Shuttle Tour: Sedate and nonintimidating except for "Catastrophe Canyon," where an earthquake and a flash flood are simulated. Smaller children should be prepared for this part of the tour.
Backstage Walking Tour (Inside the Magic): Not frightening in any respect.
MuppetVision 3-D: Intense and loud, but not frightening.
Honey, I Shrunk the Kids Movie Set Adventure Playground: Everything is oversized, but nothing is scary.
The Voyage of the Little Mermaid: Not frightening in any respect.
Animation Tour: Not frightening in any respect.

— *Attractions That Eat Adults* —

You may spend so much energy worrying about Junior's welfare that you forget to take care of yourself. If the ride component of the attraction (i.e., the actual motion and movement of the conveyance itself) is potentially disturbing, persons of any age may be adversely affected. The attractions most likely to cause motion sickness or other problems for older children and adults are:

Magic Kingdom:	Tomorrowland – Space Mountain
	Fantasyland – Mad Tea Party
	Frontierland – Big Thunder Mountain Railroad
	Frontierland – Splash Mountain
EPCOT Center:	Future World – Body Wars
Disney-MGM Studios:	Star Tours

Waiting Line Strategies for Adults with Small Children

Children hold up better through the day if you minimize the time they have to spend in lines. Arriving early and using the Touring Plans in this guide will reduce waiting time immensely. There are, however, additional measures you can employ to reduce stress on little ones.

1. Line Games. It is a smart parent who anticipates how restless children get waiting in line, and how a little structured activity can relieve the stress and boredom. In the morning kids handle the inactivity of waiting in line by discussing what they want to see and do during the course of the day. Later, however, as events wear on, they need a little help. Watching for, and counting, Disney characters is a good diversion. Simple guessing games like "20 Questions" also work well. Lines for rides move so continuously that games which require pen and paper are cumbersome and impractical. Waiting in the holding area of a theater attraction, however, is a different story. Here tic-tac-toe, hangman, drawing, and coloring can really make the time go by.

2. Last Minute Entry. If a ride or show can accommodate an unusually large number of people at one time, it is often unnecessary to stand in line. The Liberty Square Riverboat in the Magic Kingdom is a good example. The boat holds about 450 people, usually more than are waiting in line to ride. Instead of standing uncomfortably in a throng with dozens of other guests, grab a snack and sit relaxed in the shade until the boat arrives and loading is well under way. After the line has all but disappeared, go ahead and board.

At large capacity theaters like *The American Adventure* in EPCOT Center, ask the entrance greeter how long it will be until guests are admitted to the theater for the next show. If the answer is fifteen minutes or more, use the time for a rest room break or to get a snack, returning to the attraction just a few minutes before the show starts. You will not be permitted to carry any food or drink into the attraction, so make sure you have time to finish your snack before entering.

The following is a list of attractions that you can usually enter at the last minute:

Magic Kingdom

Main Street	*The Walt Disney Story*
Liberty Square	*The Hall of Presidents*
	Liberty Square Riverboat
Fantasyland	*Magic Journeys*
Mickey's Starland	*Mickey's Starland Show*
Tomorrowland	*American Journeys*

EPCOT Center

Future World	Harvest Theater
World Showcase	*Wonders of China*
	The American Adventure
	O Canada!

Disney-MGM Studios

	SuperStar Television
	MuppetVision 3-D

3. The Hail-Mary Pass.   When waiting, certain lines are configured in such a way as to allow you and your smaller children to pass under the rail to join your partner just before actual boarding or entry. This technique allows the kids and one adult to rest, snack, cool off, or tinkle, while another adult or older sibling does the waiting. Other guests are very understanding when it comes to using this strategy to keep small children content. You are likely to meet hostile opposition, however, if you try to pass older children or more than one adult under the rail. Attractions where it is usually possible to complete a Hail-Mary Pass include:

Magic Kingdom

Adventureland	Swiss Family Treehouse
	Jungle Cruise
Frontierland	*Country Bear Jamboree*
Fantasyland	Mad Tea Party
	Mr. Toad's Wild Ride
	Snow White's Adventures
	Dumbo, the Flying Elephant
	Cinderella's Golden Carrousel
	Peter Pan's Flight
Tomorrowland	Grand Prix Raceway

EPCOT Center

Future World	Spaceship Earth
The Land	Listen to The Land
World of Motion	It's Fun to Be Free
Disney-MGM Studios	*The Monster Sound Show*

4. Switching Off (also known as The Baby Swap): Several attractions have minimum height and/or age requirements, usually 3'8" tall to ride with an adult, or seven years of age *and* 3'8" tall to ride alone. Some couples with children too small or too young forgo these attractions, while others split up and take turns riding separately. Missing out on some of Disney's best rides is an unnecessary sacrifice and waiting in line twice for the same ride is a tremendous waste of time.

A better way to approach the problem is to take advantage of an option known as "switching off" or "The Baby Swap." To switch off there must be at least two adults. Everybody waits in line together, both adults and children. When you reach a Disney attendant (known as a "greeter"), say you want to switch off. The greeter will allow everyone, including the small children, to enter the attraction. When you reach the loading area, one adult will ride while the other stays with the kids. The riding adult disembarks and takes responsibility for the children while the other adult rides. A third adult in the party can ride twice, once with each of the switching off adults, so they do not have to experience the attraction alone.

Most rides with minimum age and height requirements load and unload in the same area, thus facilitating switching off. An exception is Space Mountain where the first adult (at the conclusion of the ride) must inform the unloading attendant that he or she is engaged in switching off. The unloading attendant will admit the first adult to an internal stairway that goes back to the loading area.

Altogether, there are five attractions where switching off is routinely practiced:

Magic Kingdom

Tomorrowland	Space Mountain
Frontierland	Splash Mountain
	Big Thunder Mountain Railroad

EPCOT Center

Future World	Wonders of Life pavilion: Body Wars
Disney-MGM Studios	Star Tours

Tami Knight

5. *How to Ride Twice in a Row without Waiting.* Many small children like to ride a favorite attraction two or more times in succession. Riding the second time often gives the child a feeling of mastery and accomplishment. Unfortunately, even in the early morning, repeat rides can be time consuming. If you ride Dumbo as soon as the Magic Kingdom opens, for instance, you will only have a minute or two wait for your first ride. When you come back for your second ride your wait will be about 12 minutes. If you want to ride a third time count on a 20 minute or longer wait.

The best way for getting your child on the ride twice (or more) without blowing your whole morning is by using the "Chuck Bubba Relay" (named in honor of a reader from Kentucky):

- a. Mom and little Bubba enter the waiting line.
- b. Dad lets a certain number of people go in front of him (24 in the case of Dumbo) and then gets in line.
- c. As soon as the ride stops, Mom exits with little Bubba and passes him to Dad to ride the second time.
- d. If everybody is really getting into this, Mom can hop in line again, no less than 24 people behind Dad.

The Chuck Bubba Relay will not work on every ride because of differences in the way the waiting areas are configured (i.e., it is impossible in some cases to exit the ride and make the pass). For those rides (all in Fantasyland) where the Bubba Relay does work, however, here are the number of people to count off:

Mad Tea Party: 53 people
Mr. Toad's Wild Ride: 22 people
Snow White's Adventures: 52 people
Dumbo, the Flying Elephant: 24 people
Cinderella's Golden Carrousel: 75 people
Peter Pan's Flight: 64 people

If you are the second adult in line, you will reach a point in the waiting area which is obviously the easiest place to make the handoff. Sometimes this point is where those exiting the ride pass closest to those waiting to board. In any event, you will know it when you see it. Once there, if the first parent has not arrived with little Bubba, just let those behind you slip past until they show up.

6. *Last-Minute Cold Feet.* If your small child gets cold feet at the last minute after waiting for a ride (where there is no age or height requirement), you can usually arrange with the loading attendant for a switch off. This situation arises frequently at Pirates of the Caribbean where small children lose their courage while winding through the forbidding, dungeon-like waiting area.

There is no law that says you have to ride. If you get to the boarding area and someone is unhappy, just tell a Disney attendant you have changed your mind and you will be shown the way out.

7. Elevator Shoes for the Short and the Brave.   If you have a child who is crazy to go on the rides with height requirements, but who is just a little too short, slip heel lifts into his Nikes before he gets to the measuring point. Be sure to leave the heel lifts in because he may get measured again at the boarding area.

8. Throw Yourself on the Grenade, Mildred!   For by-the-book, do-the-right-thing parents determined to sacrifice themselves on behalf of their children, we provide a new Magic Kingdom One-Day Touring Plan called the "Dumbo-or-Die-in-a-Day Touring Plan, for Parents with Small Children." This Touring Plan, detailed on pages 291–94, will ensure that you run yourself ragged. Designed to help you forfeit everything of personal interest for the sake of your children's pleasure, the Plan is guaranteed to send you home battered and exhausted with extraordinary stories of devotion and heroic perseverance. By the way, the plan really works. Anyone under eight years old will love it.

9. Catch-22 at the Grand Prix Raceway.   Though the Grand Prix Raceway is a great treat for small children, they are required to be 4' 4" tall in order to drive. In that very few children six and under top this height, the ride is essentially withheld from the very age group which would most enjoy it. To resolve this Catch-22, go on the ride with your small child. The attendants will assume that you will drive. After getting into the car, however, shift your child over behind the steering wheel. From your position you will still be able to easily control the foot pedals. To your child it will feel like really driving. Because the car travels on a self-guiding track, there is no way your child can make a mistake while steering.

10. Tomorrowland StarJets—a Safety Warning.   Sometimes parents get into the seat of the StarJet prior to lifting their child on board from the loading platform. Because the attendant cannot see small children on the side of the ride opposite his control station, the ride can be activated before a child is safely placed in the cockpit. If you take a small child on this attraction, place the child in the StarJet *first* and then get in.

11. *20,000 Leagues Under the Sea.* This attraction is a lot better at night, but don't expect short lines unless you ride during the evening parade or fireworks.

—— *The Disney Characters* ——

For many years the costumed, walking versions of Mickey, Minnie, Donald, Goofy, and others have been a colorful supporting cast at Disneyland and Walt Disney World. Known unpretentiously as the "Disney characters," these large and friendly figures help provide a link between Disney animated films and the Disney theme parks.

Audiences, it has been observed, cry during the sad parts of Disney animated films and cheer when the villain is vanquished. To the emotionally invested, the characters in these features are as real as next-door neighbors, never mind that they are drawings on plastic. In recent years, the theme park personifications of Disney characters have likewise become real to us. For thousands of visitors, it is not just some person in a mouse costume they see, it is really Mickey. Similarly, running into Goofy or Snow White in Fantasyland is a memory to be treasured, an encounter with a real celebrity.

While there are literally hundreds of Disney animated film characters, only about 250 have been brought to life in costume. Of these, a relatively small number (less than a fifth) are "greeters" (the Disney term for characters who mix with the patrons). The remaining characters are relegated exclusively to performing in shows or participating in parades. Originally confined to the Magic Kingdom, the characters can now be found in all three major theme parks and in the resort hotels.

Character Watching. Character watching has developed into a pastime. Where families were once content to stumble across a character occasionally, they now pursue them relentlessly, armed with autograph books and cameras. For those who pay attention, some characters are much more frequently encountered than others. Mickey, Minnie, and Goofy, for example, are seemingly everywhere, while Winnie the Pooh comes out only on rare occasions. Other characters are around regularly but limit themselves to a specific location. Cinderella, not unexpectedly, hangs out at Cinderella Castle in Fantasyland.

The very fact that some characters are seldom seen has turned character watching into character collecting. Mickey Mouse may be the best known and most loved character, but from a collector's perspective he is also the most common. To get an autograph from Mickey is no big deal, but Daisy Duck's signature is a real coup. To commercially tap into the character collecting movement, Disney sells autograph books throughout Walt Disney World.

Preparing Your Children to Meet the Characters. Since most small children are not expecting Minnie Mouse to be the size of a forklift, it's best to discuss the characters with your kids before you go. Almost all of the characters are quite large, and several, like Brer Bear, are huge! All of them can be extremely intimidating to a preschooler.

On first encounter, it is important not to thrust your child on the character. Allow the little one to come to terms with this big thing from whatever distance the child feels safe. If there are two adults present, one should stay close to the youngster while the other approaches the character and demonstrates that the character is safe and friendly. Some kids warm to the characters immediately, while some never do. Most take a little time and often several different encounters.

The characters do not talk or make noises of any kind. Because the cast members could not possibly imitate the distinctive cinema voice of the character, the Disney folks have determined that it is more effective to keep them silent. Lack of speech notwithstanding, the characters are extremely warm and responsive and communicate very effectively with gestures. As with the characters' size, children need to be forewarned that the characters do not talk.

Parents need to understand that some of the character costumes are very cumbersome and that cast members often suffer from very poor visibility. You have to look close, but the eye holes are frequently in the mouth of the costume or even down on the neck. What this means in practical terms is that the characters are sort of clumsy and have a limited field of vision. Children who approach the character from the back or the side may not be noticed, even if the child is touching the character. It is perfectly possible in this situation for the character to accidently step on the child or knock him down. The best way for a child to approach a character is from the front, and occasionally not even this works. For example, the various duck characters (Donald, Daisy, Uncle Scrooge, etc.) have to peer around their bills. If it appears that the character is ignoring your child, pick your child up and hold her in front of the character until the character responds.

It is okay to touch, pat, or hug the character if your child is so inclined. Understanding the unpredictability of children, the character will keep his feet very still, particularly refraining from moving backwards or to the side. Most of the characters will sign autographs or pose for pictures. Once again be sure to approach from the front so the character will understand your intentions. If your child collects autographs, it is a good idea to carry a big, fat pen the size of a magic marker. The costumes make it exceedingly difficult for the characters to wield a pen, so the bigger the better.

The Big Hurt. Many children expect to bump into Mickey the minute they enter the park and are disappointed when he is not around. If your children are unable to settle down and enjoy things until they see Mickey, simply ask a Disney cast member where to find him. If the cast member does not know Mickey's whereabouts, he or she can find out for you in short order.

"Then Some Confusion Happened." Be forewarned that character encounters give rise to a situation during which small children sometimes get lost. Usually there is a lot of activity around a character, with both adults and children touching the character or posing for pictures. In the most common scenario, Mom and Dad stay in the crowd while Junior marches up to get acquainted with the character. With the excitement of the encounter, all of the milling people, and the character moving around, Junior gets lost and heads off in the wrong direction looking for Mom and Dad. In the words of a Salt Lake City mom: "Milo was shaking hands with Dopey one minute, then some confusion happened and he [Milo] was gone." Families with several small children and parents who are busy fooling around with cameras can lose track of a youngster in a heartbeat. Our recommendation for parents of preschoolers is to stay with the kids when meeting the characters, stepping back only long enough to take a picture, if necessary.

Meeting Characters for Free. You can *see* the Disney characters in live shows at all three theme parks and in parades at the Magic Kingdom and the Disney-MGM Studios. For times consult your daily entertainment schedule. If you have the time and money, you can share a meal with the characters at the theme parks and at most of the resort hotels (more about this later). But if you want to *meet* the characters, get autographs, and take photos, it's helpful to know where the characters hang out.

At the Magic Kingdom. Characters are encountered more frequently at the Magic Kingdom than anywhere else in Walt Disney World. There will almost always be a character next to City Hall on Main Street, and usually one or more in Town Square or around the railroad station. If it's rainy, look for characters on the veranda connecting Tony's Restaurant and *The Walt Disney Story*. Characters make appearances in all the "lands," but are particularly thick in Fantasyland and Mickey's Starland. At Mickey's Hollywood Theater in Mickey's Starland, you can meet Mickey backstage in his dressing room. See page 238 for touring tips. Cinderella regularly greets diners at King Stefan's Banquet Hall on the second floor of the Castle (reservation required). Also look for characters in the Central Hub, by the Tomorrowland Theater, and by Splash Mountain in Frontierland.

Characters are featured in the afternoon and evening parades, and in *Mickey's Starland Show* performed more than 20 times daily. Characters also play a major role in Castle Forecourt shows (at the entrance to the castle on the moat side) and at the Tomorrowland Theater. Performance times for all shows and parades are listed in the Magic Kingdom daily entertainment schedule. Sometimes after the shows, characters will stick around to greet the audience.

At EPCOT Center. At first Disney management did not think that characters would be appropriate for the more serious, educational style of EPCOT Center. Later, however, in response to criticism that EPCOT lacked warmth and humor, the characters were imported. In an effort to integrate them thematically, new and often bizarre costumes were created. Goofy roams Future World in a metallic silver cape reminiscent of Buck Rogers. Mickey greets guests in front of *The American Adventure* decked out like Ben Franklin.

It is unclear whether there are fewer characters at EPCOT or if it just seems that way because the place is so big. In any event, don't expect to encounter either the number or variety of characters at EPCOT that you would in the Magic Kingdom. Characters gather at the Stargate Restaurant in CommuniCore East each day between 9 and 10 A.M., and appear several times a day at the Odyssey Restaurant, to the left of Mexico. At the Odyssey there is a short show after which the characters join the audience for photos and autographs. Show times are posted on the door of the restaurant. At both the Stargate and the Odyssey, the arrangement is informal and you do not have to buy anything. Two EPCOT original characters, Dreamfinder and Figment, lurk around the Journey to Imagination pavilion in Future World, and characters are commonly on hand at the American Adventure pavilion in the World Showcase. While characters are not featured in parades at EPCOT Center, character shows are performed daily at the Showcase Plaza and at the American Gardens Theater in the World Showcase; check the park's daily entertainment schedule.

In the World Showcase, look for the following characters in these countries:

- Mexico: Donald Duck, Jose, Panchito, Baloo
- China: Chip 'n Dale
- Norway: Daisy Duck
- Germany: Pinocchio, Foulfellow, Gideon
- American Adventure: Mickey Mouse, Roger Rabbit
- Morocco: Pooh, Tigger, Eeyore
- France: Minnie Mouse, Pluto
- United Kingdom: Goofy

Characters may not be as plentiful at EPCOT Center, but they are often easier to meet. According to a father from Effingham, Illinois:

> Trying to get autographs and pictures with Disney characters in the Magic Kingdom was a nightmare. Every character we saw was mobbed by kids *and adults*. Our kids had no chance. But at EPCOT and Disney-MGM things were much better. We got autographs, pictures, and more involvement. Our kids danced with several characters and received a lot of personal attention.

At the Disney-MGM Studios. At the Studios, characters are likely to turn up anywhere but are most frequently found in front of the Animation Building, along Mickey Avenue (leading to the sound stages), and at the end of New York Street on the back lot. Characters figure prominently in shows, with *The Voyage of the Little Mermaid* running almost continuously, and the Teenage Mutant Ninja Turtles doing street shows about a dozen times daily. Characters are also frequently featured in presentations staged at the Backlot Theater, near the end of New York Street.

Character Dining

Fraternizing with the characters has become so popular that the Disney folks offer character breakfasts, brunches, and dinners where families can eat a meal in the presence of Mickey, Minnie, Goofy, and the costumed versions of other animated celebrities. Besides grabbing some market share from Denny's and Hardees, the character meals provide a familiar, controlled setting in which small children can warm to the characters in an unhurried way. Though we mention only the featured character(s) in our descriptions, all meals are attended by several different characters. Adult prices apply to anyone 12 or older, kids 3 to 11 are charged the children's price, and little ones under 3 eat free. Obtain additional information on character dining by calling (407) 824-4500.

Character Breakfasts

Though a number of character breakfasts are offered around Walt Disney World, attending them will usually prevent you from arriving at the theme parks in time for opening. If you want to try a character breakfast, go some morning when your touring objectives are pretty modest, such as the morning you check out or a day when you do not plan to go to the parks until late afternoon. If your kids are picky eaters, or simply do not like eggs, choose a breakfast which offers a buffet or general menu selection.

EPCOT Center: Stargate Restaurant. This counter-service eatery in CommuniCore East (Future World) offers an informal character breakfast with no reservations required, no set menu, and no obligation to actually purchase anything. The characters are just there to socialize with whoever drops in for a bite. Characters in attendance vary, but usually include Goofy, Mickey, Minnie, and Chip and Dale. Breakfast is served from the time the park opens until about 11 A.M. The characters come and go, but are generally present until 10 A.M.

Disney Beach Club: Cape May Cafe. This breakfast is held daily from 8–11 A.M. The C.I.C. (Character in Charge) is Goofy. It costs $13 for adults (over 12) and $8 for ages 3 to 11. No reservations are required.

Contemporary Resort: Contemporary Cafe. Goofy hosts this buffet daily from 8–11 A.M. The cost is $11 for adults and $8 for children. No reservations are required.

Polynesian Resort: Papeete Bay Verandah. This breakfast is called Minnie's Menehune (difficult to pronounce at any time, much less first thing in the morning) and is served from 7:30–10:30 A.M. It costs $10 and $7 for adults and children respectively. Reservations are required; call (407) 824-1391. The C.I.C., obviously, is Minnie; the theme is tropical.

Grand Floridian Beach Resort: 1900 Park Fare. This breakfast features a buffet hosted by Mary Poppins, and runs daily from 7:30 to noon. The price is $15 for adults and $10 for children. Reservations can be made by calling (407) 824-2383.

Pleasure Island: Empress Lilly Riverboat. This breakfast offers a set menu with eggs as the main dish. The C.I.C. is Mickey. There are 8:30 A.M. and 10 A.M. seatings. The tab is $11 for adults and $8 for children. Reservations can be made by calling (407) 828-3900.

Walt Disney World Swan: Garden Grove Cafe. Held only on Wednesdays and Saturdays from 8–11 A.M., the Garden Grove character breakfast offers you a choice of buffet or menu selection. Different characters appear. The cost is around $11 for adults and $7 for children. No reservations are required. For additional information call (407) 934-1281.

Character Brunches

Walt Disney World Dolphin: Ristorante Carnevale. This brunch features Chip and Dale, Pluto, and Goofy, and offers a buffet at $16 for adults and $8 for kids. Available only on Sundays from 8:30 A.M.– 12:30 P.M. Reservations are required for parties of ten or more; call (407) 934-4085.

Character Dinners

Grand Floridian Beach Resort: 1900 Park Fare. Mickey and Minnie host a dinner buffet daily from 5–9 P.M. It costs $18 for adults and $10 for children. For reservations call (407) 824-2383.

Polynesian Resort: Mickey's Tropical Revue. This is actually a dinner show featuring Pacific Island dancing and the Disney characters. Staged outdoors at 4:30 P.M., the show is fun if: (1) you are hungry that early, and (2) you go during one of the cooler months of the year. Regardless of when you go, be prepared for the lackluster food. The cost is $27 for adults, $21 for juniors (12 to 20), and $12 for children (3 to 11).

Walt Disney World Village: Chef Mickey's Village Restaurant. Chef Mickey appears among the diners. Selection is from the menu and prices vary. Open for dinner 5:30–10 P.M. daily. A decent restaurant, most folks go to Chef Mickey's for the food. Getting to meet Mickey is a nice extra. For reservations call (407) 828-3900.

Character Campfire

There is a campfire and sing-along each night at 8 P.M. near the Meadow Trading Post at the Fort Wilderness Campground. Chip and Dale lead the songs, and afterwards, a full-length Disney feature film is shown. The program is open to resort guests, and is complimentary.

PART FOUR:
The Magic Kingdom

Arriving and Getting Oriented

The ferryboat, monorail, and Walt Disney World buses discharge passengers at the entrance to the Magic Kingdom—the Train Station at the foot of Main Street. Stroller and wheelchair rentals are to the right, lockers for your use are on the ground floor of the Train Station. Entering Main Street, City Hall is to your left, serving as the center for information, lost and found, some reservations, and entertainment.

If you haven't been given a guide to the Magic Kingdom by now, City Hall is the place to pick one up. The guide contains maps, gives tips for good photos, lists all the attractions, shops, and eating places, and provides helpful information about first aid, baby care, assistance for the handicapped, and more.

While at City Hall inquire about special events, live entertainment, Disney character parades, concerts, and other activities scheduled for that day. Usually City Hall will have a printed schedule of the day's events.

Notice from your map that Main Street ends at a central hub, from which branch the entrances to five other sections of the Magic Kingdom: Adventureland, Frontierland, Liberty Square, Fantasyland, and Tomorrowland. Mickey's Starland is wedged like a dimple between the cheeks of Fantasyland and Tomorrowland, and does not connect to the central hub.

Cinderella Castle serves as the entrance to Fantasyland and is the focal landmark and visual center of the Magic Kingdom. If you start in Adventureland and go clockwise around the Magic Kingdom, the castle spires will always be roughly on your right; if you start in Tomorrowland and go counterclockwise through the park, the spires will always be roughly on your left. Cinderella Castle is a great place to meet if your group decides to split up for any reason during the day, or as an emergency meeting place if you are accidentally separated.

Starting the Tour

Everyone will soon find his own favorite and not-so-favorite attractions in the Magic Kingdom. Be open-minded and adventure-

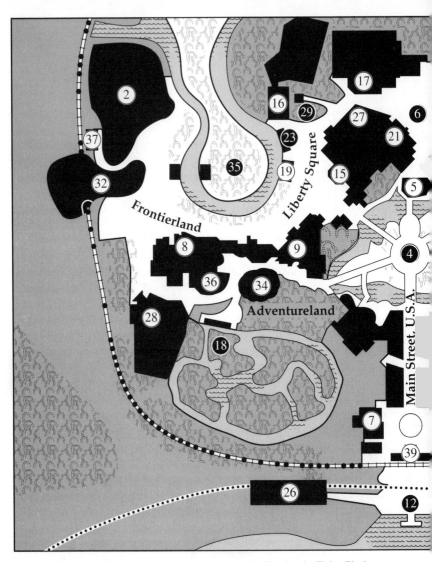

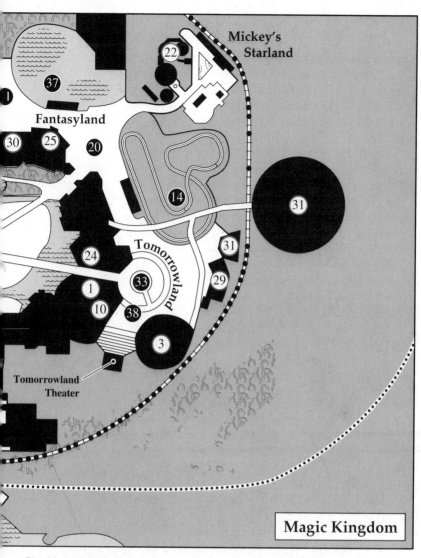

Fantasyland

Mickey's
Starland

Tomorrowland

Tomorrowland
Theater

Magic Kingdom

some. Don't dismiss a particular ride or show as being not for you until **after** you have tried it. Our personal experience as well as our research indicates that each visitor is different in terms of which Disney offerings he most enjoys. So don't miss seeing an attraction because a friend from home didn't like it; that attraction may turn out to be your favorite.

We do recommend that you take advantage of what Disney does best—the fantasy adventures like the Jungle Cruise and The Haunted Mansion, and the AudioAnimatronics (talking robots, so to speak) attractions such as *The Hall of Presidents* and Pirates of the Caribbean. Unless you have almost unlimited time, don't burn a lot of daylight browsing through the shops. Except for some special Disney souvenirs, you can find most of the same merchandise elsewhere. Try to minimize the time you spend on carnival-type rides; you've probably got an amusement park, carnival, or state fair closer to your hometown. (Don't, however, mistake rides like Space Mountain and the Big Thunder Mountain Railroad as being amusement park rides. They may be of the roller coaster genre, but they represent pure Disney genius.) Similarly, do not devote a lot of time to waiting in lines for meals. Food at most Magic Kingdom eateries is mediocre and uninspiring at best. Eat a good early breakfast before you come and snack on vendor-sold foods during the touring day.

Main Street, U.S.A.

Main Street opens a half hour to an hour before, and closes a half hour to an hour after, the rest of the park. This is where you'll begin and end your visit to the Magic Kingdom. We have already mentioned that assistance and information are available at City Hall. The Walt Disney World Railroad stops at the Main Street Station: you can board here for a grand tour of the Magic Kingdom, or you can get off the train in Frontierland or Mickey's Starland.

Main Street is a re-creation of a turn-of-the-century American small town street. Many visitors are surprised to discover that all the buildings are real and not elaborate props. Attention to detail here is exceptional—all the interiors, furnishings, and fixtures are true to the period. As with any Main Street, the Disney version is a collection of shops and eating places, a city hall, and a fire station, with an old-time cinema thrown in for good measure. Horse-drawn trolleys, double-decker buses, fire engines, and horseless carriages offer rides along Main Street and transport visitors to the central hub.

—— Main Street Services ——

Most of the park's service facilities are centered in the Main Street section, including the following:

Wheelchair & Stroller Rental	To the right of the main entrance before passing under the Railroad Station
Banking Services/ Currency Exchange	To the left of City Hall at the Railroad Station end of Main Street
Storage Lockers	On the ground floor of the Railroad Station at the end of Main Street. All lockers are cleaned out each night.
Lost & Found	City Hall Building at the Railroad Station end of Main Street

Live Entertainment and Parade Information	City Hall Building at the Railroad Station end of Main Street
Lost Persons	City Hall Building
The Diamond Horseshoe Jamboree Reservations	At Hospitality House, to your right in Town Square
Walt Disney World & Local Attraction Information	City Hall Building
First Aid	Next to the Crystal Palace around the central hub to the left (toward Adventureland)
Baby Center/Baby Care Needs	Next to the Crystal Palace around the central hub to the left (toward Adventureland)

—— *Main Street Attractions* ——

Walt Disney World Railroad

Type of Attraction: Scenic railroad ride around perimeter of the Magic Kingdom; also transportation to Frontierland and Mickey's Starland.

When to Go: After 11 A.M. or when you need transportation

Special Comments: Main Street is usually the least congested station

Author's Rating: Plenty to see; ★★★½ [Critical ratings are based on a scale of zero to five stars. Five stars is the best possible rating.]

Overall Appeal by Age Group:

Pre- school	Grade School	Teens	Young Adults	Over 30	Senior Citizens
★★★★	★★★	★★½	★★★	★★★½	★★★½

Duration of Ride: About 19 minutes for a complete circuit

Average Wait in Line per 100 People Ahead of You: 8 minutes

Assumes: 2 or more trains operating

Loading Speed: Fast

DESCRIPTION AND COMMENTS   A transportation ride that blends an unusual variety of sights and experiences with an energy-saving way of getting around the park. The train provides a glimpse of all the lands except Adventureland.

TOURING TIPS   Save the train ride until after you have seen the featured attractions, or use when you need transportation. On busy days, lines form at the Frontierland Station, but rarely at the Main Street and Mickey's Starland Stations.

Main Street Cinema

Type of Attraction: Old-time movies and vintage Disney cartoons
When to Go: Whenever you want
Author's Rating: Wonderful selection of flicks; ★★★
Overall Appeal by Age Group:

Pre-school	Grade School	Teens	Young Adults	Over 30	Senior Citizens
★★½	★★★	★★½	★★★	★★★	★★★

Duration of Presentation: Runs continuously
Preshow Entertainment: None
Probable Waiting Time: No waiting

DESCRIPTION AND COMMENTS   Excellent old-time movies including some vintage Disney cartoons. Since the movies are silent, six are shown simultaneously. No seats; viewers stand.

TOURING TIPS   Good place to get out of the sun or rain, or to kill time while others in your group shop on Main Street. Not something you can't afford to miss.

—— *Main Street Minor Attractions* ——

Transportation Rides

DESCRIPTION AND COMMENTS   Trolleys, buses, etc., which add color to Main Street.

TOURING TIPS   Will save you a walk to the central hub. Not worth waiting in line.

Penny Arcade

DESCRIPTION AND COMMENTS   The Penny Arcade features some vintage arcade machines which can actually be played for a penny or a nickel. Located toward the central hub end of Main Street on the left as you face the Castle.

TOURING TIPS   If you arrive early when Main Street is the only part of the park open, you might want to spend a few minutes here.

Main Street Eateries and Shops

DESCRIPTION AND COMMENTS   Some of the Magic Kingdom's better food and specialty/souvenir shopping in a nostalgic, happy setting. The Emporium offers the best selection of Disney trademark souvenir items in the Magic Kingdom.

TOURING TIPS   The shops are fun but the merchandise can be had elsewhere (except for certain Disney trademark souvenirs). If seeing the park attractions is your objective, save the Main Street eateries and shops until the end of the day. If shopping is your objective, you will find the shops most crowded during the noon hour and near closing time. Remember, Main Street opens at least a half hour earlier, and closes a half hour to an hour later than the rest of the Magic Kingdom.

The Crystal Palace, at the central hub end of Main Street (towards Adventureland) provides good cafeteria service and is often overlooked by the lunch-hour (but not dinner-hour) masses. Give it a try if you are nearby at the noon hour.

Adventureland

Adventureland is the first land to the left of Main Street and combines an African safari theme with an old New Orleans/Caribbean atmosphere.

Swiss Family Treehouse

Type of Attraction: Walk-through exhibit
When to Go: Before 11:30 A.M. and after 5 P.M.
Special Comments: Requires climbing a lot of stairs
Author's Rating: A very creative exhibit; ★★★½
Overall Appeal by Age Group:

Pre-school	Grade School	Teens	Young Adults	Over 30	Senior Citizens
★★★★	★★★★	★★★★	★★★★	★★★★	★★★★

Duration of Tour: 10–15 minutes
Average Wait in Line per 100 People Ahead of You: 7 minutes
Assumes: Normal staffing
Loading Speed: Does not apply

DESCRIPTION AND COMMENTS   A fantastic replication of the shipwrecked family's home will fire the imagination of the inventive and the adventurous.

TOURING TIPS   A self-guided walk-through tour which involves a lot of climbing up and down stairs, but no ropes or ladders or anything fancy. People stopping during the walk-through to look extra long or to rest sometimes create bottlenecks which slow crowd flow. We recommend visiting this attraction in the late afternoon or early evening if you are on a one-day tour schedule, or first thing in the morning of your second day.

Jungle Cruise

Type of Ride: A Disney boat ride adventure
When to Go: Before 11 A.M. or two hours before closing
Author's Rating: A long-enduring Disney masterpiece; ★★★★
Overall Appeal by Age Group:

Pre-school	Grade School	Teens	Young Adults	Over 30	Senior Citizens
★★★★½	★★★★½	★★★★	★★★★	★★★★	★★★★

Duration of Ride: 8–9 minutes
Average Wait in Line per 100 People Ahead of You: 3½ minutes
Assumes: 10 boats operating
Loading Speed: Moderate to fast

DESCRIPTION AND COMMENTS   A boat ride through jungle waterways. Passengers encounter elephants, lions, hostile natives, and a menacing hippo. A long-enduring Disney favorite, with the boatman's spiel adding measurably to the fun.

TOURING TIPS   One of the park's "not to be missed" attractions. A good staff and an improved management plan have speeded up the lines for this ride. On the negative side, it is very difficult to estimate the length of the wait for the Jungle Cruise. A mother from the Bronx, New York, wrote complaining:

> The line for this ride is extremely deceiving. We got on line towards the early evening; it was long but we really wanted to take this ride. Every time the winding line brought us near the loading dock and we thought we were going to get on, we'd discover a whole new section of winding lanes to go through. It was extremely frustrating. We must have waited a good 20–30 minutes before the two of us finally gave up and got out.

Pirates of the Caribbean

Type of Ride: A Disney adventure boat ride
When to Go: Before noon or after 5 P.M.
Special Comments: Frightens some small children
Author's Rating: Disney AudioAnimatronics at its best; ★★★★★

Overall Appeal by Age Group:

Pre-school	Grade School	Teens	Young Adults	Over 30	Senior Citizens
★★★	★★★★★	★★★★★	★★★★★	★★★★★	★★★★★

Duration of Ride: Approximately 7½ minutes
Average Wait in Line per 100 People Ahead of You: 1½ minutes
Assumes: Both waiting lines operating
Loading Speed: Fast

DESCRIPTION AND COMMENTS   Another boat ride, this time indoors, through a series of sets depicting a pirate raid on an island settlement, from the bombardment of the fortress to the debauchery that follows the victory. All in good, clean fun.

TOURING TIPS   Another "not to be missed" attraction. Undoubtedly one of the most elaborate and imaginative attractions in the Magic Kingdom. Engineered to move large crowds in a hurry, Pirates is a good attraction to see during the later part of the afternoon. It has two waiting lines, both under cover.

Tropical Serenade (Enchanted Tiki Birds)

Type of Attraction: AudioAnimatronic Pacific Island musical show
When to Go: Before 11 A.M. and after 3:30 P.M.
Author's Rating: Very, very unusual; ★★★
Overall Appeal by Age Group:

Pre-school	Grade School	Teens	Young Adults	Over 30	Senior Citizens
★★½	★★★	★★	★★★	★★★	★★★

Duration of Presentation: 15½ minutes
Preshow Entertainment: Talking birds
Probable Waiting Time: 15 minutes

DESCRIPTION AND COMMENTS   An unusual sit-down theater performance where more than two hundred birds, flowers, and Tiki-god statues sing and whistle through a musical program.

TOURING TIPS   One of the more bizarre of the Magic Kingdom's entertainments, but usually not too crowded. We like it in the late afternoon when we can especially appreciate sitting for a bit in an air-conditioned theater.

A reader from Cookeville, Tennessee, took exception to our rating for preschoolers, writing:

> I know that visitor reactions vary widely, but the Tropical Serenade was our toddler's favorite Magic Kingdom attraction (we nearly omitted it because of the rating for preschoolers).

Adventureland Eateries and Shops

DESCRIPTION AND COMMENTS   You will find more specialty shopping a la Banana Republic in Adventureland. There are also several restaurants, which tend to be less crowded during lunch than other Magic Kingdom eateries.

TOURING TIPS   The Adventureland Veranda Restaurant is a good bet for less congestion and speedier service between 11:30 A.M. and 1:30 P.M. Try the stir-fried teriyaki steak sandwich (with onions and peppers). It may be the best lunch in the Magic Kingdom.

Frontierland

Frontierland adjoins Adventureland as you move clockwise around the Magic Kingdom. The focus here is on the Old West with stockade-type structures and pioneer trappings.

Splash Mountain

Type of Ride: Water-flume ride

When to Go: As soon as the park opens

Special Comments: Children must be 3'8" tall to ride; those under 7 years must ride with an adult. Switching-off option provided (see page 187).

Author's Rating: A wet winner, not to be missed; ★★★★★

Overall Appeal by Age Group: *

Pre-school	Grade School	Teens	Young Adults	Over 30	Senior Citizens
†	★★★★★	★★★★★	★★★★★	★★★★★	★★★½

† Many preschoolers are too short to meet the height requirement and others are visually intimidated by watching the ride from standing in line. Of those preschoolers who actually ride, most give the attraction high marks (3–5 stars).

Duration of Ride: About 10 minutes

Average Wait in Line per 100 People Ahead of You: 3½ minutes

Assumes: Operation at full capacity

Loading Speed: Moderate

DESCRIPTION AND COMMENTS   Splash Mountain is an amusement park flume ride Disney style, bigger than life and more imaginative than anyone thought possible. The ride combines steep chutes with a variety of Disney's best special effects. Covering over half a mile, the ride splashes through swamps, caves, and backwood bayous before climaxing in a five-story plunge and Brer Rabbit's triumphant return home. The entire ride is populated by more than 100 AudioAnimatronic char-

WARNING!

For Bouffants, Rug Wearers, and Elvis Impersonators

This Ride Will Muss Your 'Do

acters, including Brer Rabbit, Brer Bear, and Brer Fox, all regaling riders with songs, including "Zip-A-Dee-Doo-Dah."

TOURING TIPS   This ride, happy, exciting, and adventuresome all at once, vies with Space Mountain as the most popular ride in the Magic Kingdom. Even as the park opens, hundreds are poised to move as rapidly as their feet will carry them to Splash Mountain. Crowds will build fast in the morning and waits of more than two hours can be expected once the Magic Kingdom fills on a busy day. Get in line first thing, and certainly no later than 45 minutes after the park opens. Long lines will persist throughout the day. If you miss Splash Mountain in the morning, your best shot at a shorter wait is to ride during the afternoon or evening parade(s), or just before the Magic Kingdom closes.

As with Space Mountain in Tomorrowland, literally hundreds crowd the starting gate to race to Splash Mountain when the park opens. The best strategy for this sprint (which we call the Rapid Rampage) is to go to the end of Main Street and turn left to the Crystal Palace restaurant. In front of the Crystal Palace you will find a bridge that provides a shortcut to Adventureland. Stake out a position at the barrier rope, and wait until the park opens and the rope is dropped. While we do not advocate running, we will tell you candidly that all the folks around you aren't down in a four-point stance to inspect the pavement.

When the rope drops, move as fast as feels comfortable (understanding the pandemonium just unleashed behind you is comparable to a buffalo stampede) and cross the bridge to Adventureland. Okay, now pay attention, here's another shortcut. Just past the first group of buildings on your right, roughly across from the Swiss Family Treehouse, there is a small passageway where rest rooms and phones are located.

This passageway, which is easy to overlook, connects Adventureland to Frontierland. Go through the passageway into Frontierland and take a hard left. As you emerge along the waterfront you will see Splash Mountain ahead. If you miss the passageway and the shortcut, don't fool around looking for it. You can also reach Splash Mountain by continuing straight on through Adventureland.

A less exhausting way to reach Splash Mountain first thing in the morning is to board the Walt Disney World Railroad as soon as you enter the park. Take a seat on the train at Main Street Station and wait for the rest of the park to open. The train will pull out of the station at the same time the rope drops at the central hub end of Main Street. Ride to the Frontierland Station (the first stop) and disembark. As you come down the stairs at the station, the entrance to Splash Mountain will be on your right. Because of the time required to unload at the station, train passengers will not arrive at Splash Mountain ahead of those who sprint from the central hub. You will, however, arrive well in advance of most other guests.

It is almost a certainty that you will get wet, and possibly drenched, riding Splash Mountain. If you visit on a cool day, you may want to carry a plastic garbage bag. By tearing holes in the bottom and sides, you can fashion a sack dress of sorts to keep you dry (oops, make that drier). Be sure to tuck the bag in under your bottom. By the way, it doesn't matter whether you ride in front or in back. You will get wet regardless. If you have a camera, either leave it with a nonriding member of your party or wrap it in a plastic bag.

One final word: This is not just a fancy flume ride, it is a full-blown Disney adventure. The scariest part, by far, is the steep chute you see when standing in line, and even this drop looks worse than it really is.

Big Thunder Mountain Railroad

Type of Ride: Tame roller coaster with exciting special effects

When to Go: Before 11 A.M. or after 5:30 P.M.

Special Comments: Children must be 3′4″ tall to ride. Those under 7 years must ride with an adult. Switching-off option provided (see page 187).

Author's Rating: Great effects/relatively tame ride; ★★★★½

Overall Appeal by Age Group:

Pre-school	Grade School	Teens	Young Adults	Over 30	Senior Citizens
★★★	★★★★	★★★★	★★★★	★★★★	★★★

Duration of Ride: Almost 3½ minutes
Average Wait in Line per 100 People Ahead of You: 2½ minutes
Assumes: 5 trains operating
Loading Speed: Moderate to fast

WARNING!

For Bouffants, Rug Wearers, and Elvis Impersonators

This Ride Will Muss Your 'Do

DESCRIPTION AND COMMENTS   A roller coaster ride through and around a Disney "mountain." The time is Gold Rush days, and the idea is that you are on a runaway mine train. Along with the usual thrills of a roller coaster ride (about a 5 on a "scary scale" of 10), the ride showcases some first-rate examples of Disney creativity; lifelike scenes depicting a mining town, falling rocks, and an earthquake, all humorously animated.

TOURING TIPS   A superb Disney experience, but not too wild of a roller coaster. The emphasis here is much more on the sights than on the thrill of the ride itself. Regardless, it's a "not to be missed" attraction. The best bet for riding Big Thunder without a long wait in line is to ride early in the morning or between 10:00–11:00 when the ride has been brought up to peak carrying capacity.

The opening of nearby Splash Mountain in the fall of 1992 has changed forever the traffic patterns to Big Thunder Mountain Railroad. More adventuresome guests ride Splash Mountain first and then go next door to ride Big Thunder. This means much larger crowds in Frontierland all day and longer waits for Big Thunder Mountain. The best way to experience the Magic Kingdom's "mountains" is to ride Space Mountain first thing when the park opens and then go directly to Big Thunder Mountain, and from there to Splash Mountain. If you miss Big Thunder in the morning, try again during one of the parades or just before the park closes.

As an example of how differently guests experience Disney attractions, consider this letter we received from a lady in Brookline, Massachusetts:

> Being in the senior citizens' category and having limited time, my friend and I confined our activities to those attractions rated as four or five stars for seniors.
>
> Because of your recommendation and because you listed it as "not to be missed," we waited for one hour to board the Big Thunder Mountain Railroad, (which you) rated a "5" on a scary scale of "10." After living through three-and-a-half minutes of pure terror, I will rate that attraction a "15" on a scary scale of "10." We were so busy holding on and screaming and even praying for our safety that we did not see any falling rocks, a mining town, or an earthquake. In our opinion the Big Thunder Mountain Railroad should not be recommended for seniors or preschool children.

Along similar lines, another woman from New England writes,

> My husband, who is 41, found Big Thunder Mountain too intense for his enjoyment, and feels that anyone who does not like roller coasters would not enjoy this ride.

The Diamond Horseshoe Jamboree

Type of Attraction: Live song/dance/comedy stage show

When to Go: As per your reservations

Special Comments: Seating by reservation only, made on the day of the show, at the Hospitality House on Main Street. No reservations taken at the Saloon itself. Lunch is available.

Author's Rating: Absolutely superb, not to be missed; ★★★★

Overall Appeal by Age Group:

Pre- school	Grade School	Teens	Young Adults	Over 30	Senior Citizens
★★★½	★★★★	★★★★	★★★★★	★★★★★	★★★★★

Duration of Presentation: About 30 minutes

Preshow Entertainment: None

Probable Waiting Time: See Touring Tips

DESCRIPTION AND COMMENTS   A half-hour, G-rated re-creation of an Old West dance hall show, with dancing, singing, and lots of corny comedy. Visitors are seated at tables where sandwiches and beverages (nonalcoholic) can be ordered before the show. This is a clever, wonderfully cast, uproariously funny show that you should try to work into your schedule.

TOURING TIPS   Though an excellent show (ranked as "not to be missed"), it is a real hassle to see, particularly if you have only one day at the Magic Kingdom. Here's why: Seating is by reservation only, made in person on the day you want to see the show. To obtain a reservation you have to go to the Hospitality House on Main Street. Reservation lines move very slowly because every visitor needs to ask questions and receive instructions. If you are able to obtain a reservation for one of the several shows you will be required to appear for seating one half hour before showtime when you will wait in line again (this time to be admitted to the theater). Once allowed inside you will wait for another fifteen minutes for food orders to be taken and processed before the show finally begins. By observation and experimentation we have determined that a Magic Kingdom visitor spends an average of 15 minutes making his reservation, and 45 minutes waiting for the show to begin, plus changing his other touring plans to get back to Frontierland in time to be seated. Thus, counting the show itself: a 1½-hour investment of valuable time to see a 30-minute song-and-dance show. We recommend that you see the *Jamboree* on your second day, if you have one. For those with only one day, we have incorporated the *Diamond Horseshoe* into our One-Day Touring Plans as an option that combines the show with lunch and eliminates as much wasted time as possible. See "Magic Kingdom Touring Plans," pages 271–75. One last thing: the sandwiches at the Diamond Horseshoe are pretty big. If your children are small, have them split a sandwich.

Country Bear Jamboree

Type of Attraction: AudioAnimatronic country hoedown stage show

When to Go: Before 11:30 A.M. and during the two hours before closing

Special Comments: Changes shows at Christmas and during the summer

Author's Rating: A Disney classic, not to be missed; ★★★★½

Overall Appeal by Age Group:

Pre-school	Grade School	Teens	Young Adults	Over 30	Senior Citizens
★★★★	★★★★	★★★★	★★★★½	★★★★½	★★★★½

Duration of Presentation: 15 minutes

Preshow Entertainment: None

Probable Waiting Time: This is a very popular attraction with a comparatively small seating capacity. An average waiting time on a busy day between the hours of noon and 5:30 P.M. would be from 30 to 50 minutes.

DESCRIPTION AND COMMENTS   A cast of charming AudioAnimatronic (robotic) bears sing and stomp their way through a Western-style hoedown. Though one of the Magic Kingdom's most humorous and upbeat shows, *Country Bear Jamboree* has not been revised for many moons, much to the consternation of repeat visitors.

TOURING TIPS   Yet another "not to be missed" attraction, the Jamboree is extremely popular and draws large crowds even early in the day. We recommend seeing this one before 11:30 A.M.

Tom Sawyer Island and Fort Sam Clemens

Type of Attraction: Walk-through exhibit/rustic playground

When to Go: Mid-morning through late afternoon

Special Comments: Closes at dusk

Author's Rating: The place for rambunctious kids; ★★★★

Overall Appeal by Age Group:

Pre-school	Grade School	Teens	Young Adults	Over 30	Senior Citizens
★★★★★	★★★★★	★★★½	★★★	★★★	★★★

DESCRIPTION AND COMMENTS   Tom Sawyer Island manages to impart something of a sense of isolation from the rest of the park. It has hills to climb, a cave and a windmill to explore, a tipsy barrel bridge to cross, and paths to follow. It's a delight for adults and a godsend for children who have been in tow all day. They love the freedom of the exploration and the excitement of firing air guns from the walls of Ft. Sam Clemens. There's even a "secret" escape tunnel.

TOURING TIPS   Tom Sawyer Island is not one of the Magic Kingdom's more celebrated attractions, but it's certainly one of the better done. Attention to detail is excellent and kids particularly revel in its adventuresome frontier atmosphere. We think it's a must for families with children five through fifteen. If your party is adult, visit the island on your second day or stop by on your first day if you have seen the attractions you most wanted to see.

We like Tom Sawyer Island from about noon until the island closes at dusk. Access is by raft from Frontierland and you will have to stand in line to board both coming and going. Two rafts operate simultaneously, however, and the round trip is usually pretty efficient. Tom Sawyer Island takes about 25 minutes or so to see; many children could spend a whole day visiting.

Davy Crockett's Explorer Canoes

Type of Ride: Scenic canoe ride

When to Go: Before noon or after 5 P.M.

Special Comments: Skip if the lines are long; closes at dusk

Author's Rating: The most fun way of seeing the Rivers of America; ★★★½

Overall Appeal by Age Group:

Pre-school	Grade School	Teens	Young Adults	Over 30	Senior Citizens
★★★★	★★★★	★★★★	★★★★	★★★★	★★★★

Duration of Ride: 9–15 minutes depending how fast you paddle

Average Wait in Line per 100 People Ahead of You: 28 minutes

Assumes: 3 canoes operating

Loading Speed: Slow

DESCRIPTION AND COMMENTS Paddle-powered ride (your power) around Tom Sawyer Island and Ft. Sam Clemens. Runs the same route with the same sights as the Liberty Square Riverboat and the Mike Fink Keelboats. The canoes only operate during the busy times of the year. The sights are fun and the ride is a little different in that the tourists paddle the canoe.

TOURING TIPS The canoes represent one of three ways to see the same territory. Since the canoes and keelboats are slower loading, we usually opt for the large riverboat. If you are not up for a boat ride, a different view of the same sights can be had hoofing around Tom Sawyer Island and Ft. Sam Clemens.

Frontierland Shootin' Gallery

Type of Attraction: Electronic shooting gallery
When to Go: Whenever convenient
Special Comments: Costs 25 cents per play
Author's Rating: A very nifty shooting gallery; ★★½
Overall Appeal by Age Group:

Pre-school	Grade School	Teens	Young Adults	Over 30	Senior Citizens
★★★½	★★★½	★★★½	★★★	★★½	★★★

DESCRIPTION AND COMMENTS   A very elaborate shooting gallery, this is one of the few attractions not included in the Magic Kingdom admission.

TOURING TIPS   Good fun for them "what likes to shoot," but definitely not a place to be blowing your time if you are on a tight schedule. Try it on your second day if time allows.

Walt Disney World Railroad

DESCRIPTION AND COMMENTS   The Walt Disney World Railroad stops in Frontierland on its circle-tour around the park. See the description of the Walt Disney World Railroad under Main Street for additional details regarding the sights along the route.

TOURING TIPS   A pleasant and feet-saving way to commute to Main Street and Mickey's Starland. Be advised, however, that the Frontierland Station is usually more congested than its two counterparts.

Frontierland Eateries and Shops

DESCRIPTION AND COMMENTS   Coonskin caps and western-theme specialty shopping, along with fast-food eateries that are usually very crowded between 11:30 A.M. and 2 P.M.

TOURING TIPS   Don't waste time browsing shops or standing in line for food unless you have a very relaxed schedule or came specifically to shop.

Liberty Square

Liberty Square recreates the atmosphere of Colonial America at the time of the American Revolution. Architecture is Federal or Colonial, with a real 130-year-old live oak (dubbed the "Liberty Tree") lending dignity and grace to the setting.

The Hall of Presidents

Type of Show: AudioAnimatronic historical presentation
When to Go: Any time
Author's Rating: Impressive and moving; ★★★½
Overall Appeal by Age Group:

Pre-school	Grade School	Teens	Young Adults	Over 30	Senior Citizens
★	★★½	★★★	★★★½	★★★★	★★★★

Duration of Presentation: Almost 23 minutes
Preshow Entertainment: None
Probable Waiting Time: Lines for this attraction LOOK awesome but are usually swallowed up as the theater turns over. Your wait will probably be the remaining time of the show that's in progress when you arrive. Even during the busiest times of the day, waits rarely exceed 40 minutes.

DESCRIPTION AND COMMENTS   A 20-minute strongly inspirational and patriotic program highlighting milestones in American history. The performance climaxes with a roll call of presidents from Washington through the present, with a few words of encouragement from President Lincoln. A very moving show coupled with one of Disney's best and most ambitious AudioAnimatronics (robotic) efforts.

Our high opinion notwithstanding, we have received a lot of mail from readers who get more than entertainment from *The Hall of Presidents*. A lady in St. Louis, wrote: "We always go to the Hall of Presidents when my husband gets cranky so he can take a nice nap."

And, from a young mother in Marion, Ohio: "The Hall of Presidents and Magic Journeys [Fantasyland] are great places to breast feed."

TOURING TIPS   The detail and costume of the chief executives is incredible, and if your children tend to fidget during the show, take notice of the fact that the Presidents do, too. This attraction is one of the most popular, particularly among older visitors, and draws large crowds from 11 A.M. through about 5 P.M. Do not be dismayed by the lines, however. The theater holds more than 700 people, thus swallowing up large lines at a single gulp when visitors are admitted. One show is always in progress while the lobby is being filled for the next show. At less than busy times you will probably be admitted directly to the lobby without waiting in line. When the waiting lobby fills, those remaining in line outside are held in place until those in the lobby move into the theater just prior to the next show, at which time another 700 people from the outside line are admitted to the lobby.

Liberty Square Riverboat

Type of Ride: Scenic boat ride

When to Go: Any time

Author's Rating: Provides an excellent vantage point; ★★★

Overall Appeal by Age Group:

Pre-school	Grade School	Teens	Young Adults	Over 30	Senior Citizens
★★★	★★★	★★½	★★★	★★★	★★★

Duration of Ride: About 16 minutes

Average Wait to Board: 10–14 minutes

Assumes: Normal operations

DESCRIPTION AND COMMENTS   Large-capacity paddle wheel riverboat that navigates the waters around Tom Sawyer Island and Ft. Sam Clemens. A beautiful craft, the riverboat provides a lofty perspective of Frontierland and Liberty Square.

TOURING TIPS   One of three boat rides that survey the same real estate. Since Davy Crockett's Explorer Canoes and the Mike Fink Keelboats are slower loading, we think the riverboat is the best bet. If you are not in the mood for a boat ride, much of the same sights can be seen by hiking around the island.

The Haunted Mansion

Type of Ride: A Disney one-of-its-kind
When to Go: Any time
Special Comments: Frightens some very small children
Author's Rating: Some of Walt Disney World's best special
effects; ★★★★★

Overall Appeal by Age Group:

Pre- school	Grade School	Teens	Young Adults	Over 30	Senior Citizens
Varies	★★★★★	★★★★½	★★★★½	★★★★½	★★★★ ½

Duration of Ride: 7-minute ride plus a 1½-minute preshow
Average Wait in Line per 100 People Ahead of You: 2½ minutes
Assumes: Both "stretch rooms" operating
Loading Speed: Fast

DESCRIPTION AND COMMENTS A fun attraction more than a scary one
with some of the best special effects in the Magic Kingdom. In their
guidebook the Disney people say, "Come face to face with 999 happy
ghosts, ghouls, and goblins in a 'frightfully funny' adventure." That
pretty well sums it up. Be warned that some youngsters become overly
anxious concerning what they think they will see. The actual attraction
scares almost nobody.

TOURING TIPS This attraction would be more at home in Fantasyland, but no matter, it's Disney at its best; another "not to be missed"
feature. Lines at The Haunted Mansion ebb and flow more than do
the lines of most other Magic Kingdom high spots. This is due to the
Mansion's proximity to *The Hall of Presidents* and the Liberty Square
Riverboat. These two attractions disgorge 750 and 450 people respectively at the completion of each show or ride. Many of these folks head
right over and hop in line at The Haunted Mansion. Try this attraction
before noon and after 4:30 P.M. and make an effort to slip in between
crowds.

Mike Fink Keelboats

Type of Ride: Scenic boat ride
When to Go: Before 11:30 A.M. or after 5 P.M.
Special Comments: Don't ride if the lines are long; closes at dusk

Author's Rating: ★★★

Overall Appeal by Age Group:

Pre-school	Grade School	Teens	Young Adults	Over 30	Senior Citizens
★★★½	★★★	★★★	★★★	★★★	★★★

Duration of Ride: 9½ minutes

Average Wait in Line per 100 People Ahead of You: 15 minutes

Assumes: 2 boats operating

Loading Speed: Slow

DESCRIPTION AND COMMENTS   Small river keelboats which circle Tom Sawyer Island and Ft. Sam Clemens, taking the same route as Davy Crockett's Explorer Canoes and the Liberty Square Riverboat. The top deck of the keelboat is exposed to the elements.

TOURING TIPS   This trip covers the same circle traveled by Davy Crockett's Explorer Canoes and the Liberty Square Riverboat. Since the keelboats and the canoes load slowly we prefer the riverboat. Another way to see much of the area covered by the respective boat tours is to explore Tom Sawyer Island and Ft. Sam Clemens on foot.

Liberty Square Eateries and Shops

DESCRIPTION AND COMMENTS   American crafts and souvenir shopping, along with one restaurant, the Liberty Tree Tavern, which is often overlooked by the crowds at lunch.

TOURING TIPS   Even though the Liberty Tree Tavern is the most improved restaurant in the Magic Kingdom, our suggestion is to stick with sandwiches. Reservations are recommended.

Fantasyland

Truly an enchanting place, spread gracefully like a miniature Alpine village beneath the lofty towers of Cinderella Castle, Fantasyland is the heart of the Magic Kingdom.

It's a Small World

Type of Ride: Scenic boat ride

When to Go: Between 11 A.M. and 5 P.M.

Author's Rating: A pleasant change of pace; ★★★½

Overall Appeal by Age Group:

Pre-school	Grade School	Teens	Young Adults	Over 30	Senior Citizens
★★★★	★★★½	★★½	★★★	★★★	★★★½

Duration of Ride: Approximately 11 minutes

Average Wait in Line per 100 People Ahead of You: 1¾ minutes

Assumes: Busy conditions with 30 or more boats operating

Loading Speed: Fast

DESCRIPTION AND COMMENTS   A happy, upbeat attraction with a world brotherhood theme and a catchy tune that will roll around in your head for weeks. Small boats convey visitors on a tour around the world, with singing and dancing dolls showcasing the dress and culture of each nation. Almost everyone enjoys It's a Small World, but it stands, along with the *Enchanted Tiki Birds*, as an attraction that some could take or leave while others think it is one of the real masterpieces of the Magic Kingdom. Try it and form your own opinion.

TOURING TIPS   A good place to cool off during the heat of the day, It's a Small World is a fast-loading ride with two waiting lines and is usually a good bet between 11 A.M. and 5 P.M.

Skyway to Tomorrowland

Type of Ride: Scenic transportation to Tomorrowland

When to Go: Before noon or during special events

Special Comments: If there's a line, it will probably be quicker to walk

Author's Rating: Nice view; ★★★

Overall Appeal by Age Group:

Pre-school	Grade School	Teens	Young Adults	Over 30	Senior Citizens
★★★★	★★★★	★★★½	★★★½	★★★½	★★★½

Duration of Ride: Approximately 5 minutes one way

Average Wait in Line per 100 People Ahead of You: 10 minutes

Assumes: 45 or more cars operating

Loading Speed: Moderate to slow

DESCRIPTION AND COMMENTS   Part of the Magic Kingdom internal transportation system, the Skyway is a chairlift that conveys tourists high above the park to Tomorrowland. The view is great, and sometimes the Skyway can even save a little shoe leather. Usually, however, you could arrive in Tomorrowland much faster by walking.

TOURING TIPS   We enjoy this scenic trip in the morning, during the afternoon character parade, during an evening parade, or just before closing (this ride opens later and closes earlier than other rides in Fantasyland). In short, before the crowds fill the park, when they are otherwise occupied or when they are on the decline. These times also provide the most dramatic and beautiful vistas.

Peter Pan's Flight

Type of Ride: A Disney fantasy adventure

When to Go: Before 11 A.M. or after 6 P.M.

Author's Rating: Happy, mellow and well done; ★★★★

Overall Appeal by Age Group:

Pre-school	Grade School	Teens	Young Adults	Over 30	Senior Citizens
★★★★	★★★★	★★★½	★★★★	★★★★	★★★★

Duration of Ride: A little over 3 minutes

Average Wait in Line per 100 People Ahead of You: 5½ minutes
Assumes: Normal operation
Loading Speed: Moderate to slow

DESCRIPTION AND COMMENTS   Though not considered to be one of the major attractions, Peter Pan's Flight is superbly designed and absolutely delightful with a happy theme, a reunion with some unforgettable Disney characters, beautiful effects, and charming music.

TOURING TIPS   Though not a major feature of the Magic Kingdom, we nevertheless classify it as "not to be missed." Try to ride before 11 A.M. or after 6 P.M., or during the afternoon character parade.

Magic Journeys

Type of Show: 3-D fantasy film
When to Go: Between noon and 4 P.M.
Special Comments: Some small children frightened by the film
Author's Rating: Solid production; ★★★½
Overall Appeal by Age Group:

Pre-school	Grade School	Teens	Young Adults	Over 30	Senior Citizens
★★★★	★★★★	★★★½	★★★★	★★★★	★★★★

Duration of Presentation: Approximately 17 minutes
Preshow Entertainment: 3-D cartoons
Probable Waiting Time: 12 minutes

DESCRIPTION AND COMMENTS   This delightful film was exported to Fantasyland from EPCOT Center when *Captain EO* arrived. A longtime favorite, *Magic Journeys* appeals to all ages. The production is solid, the theme happy and upbeat, and the 3-D effects incredible. All over the theater, children (and many adults) reach out involuntarily to grab objects which seem to be floating out from the screen. The story is about a group of children and their flights of imagination.

TOURING TIPS   We recommend seeing this film during the heat of the day when 20 minutes of relaxing in an air-conditioned theater might improve your attitude. There is almost never a line for this attraction.

Cinderella's Golden Carrousel

Type of Ride: Merry-go-round

When to Go: Before 11 A.M. or after 6 P.M.

Special Comments: Adults enjoy the beauty and nostalgia of this ride

Author's Rating: A beautiful children's ride; ★★★

Overall Appeal by Age Group:

Pre-school	Grade School	Teens	Young Adults	Over 30	Senior Citizens
★★★★	★★½	★	★★½	★★★	★★★

Duration of Ride: Approximately 2 minutes

Average Wait in Line per 100 People Ahead of You: 5 minutes

Assumes: Normal staffing

Loading Speed: Slow

DESCRIPTION AND COMMENTS   A merry-go-round to be sure, but certainly one of the most elaborate and beautiful you will ever see, especially when the lights are on.

TOURING TIPS   Unless there are small children in your party we suggest you appreciate this ride from the sidelines. If your children insist on riding, try to get on before 11 A.M. or after 6 P.M. While nice to look at, the Carrousel loads and unloads very slowly.

Mr. Toad's Wild Ride

Type of Ride: Disney version of a spook house track ride

When to Go: Before 11 A.M. or after 6 P.M.

Author's Rating: Just O.K.; ★★½

Overall Appeal by Age Group:

Pre-school	Grade School	Teens	Young Adults	Over 30	Senior Citizens
★★★½	★★★½	★★★	★★½	★★½	★★½

Duration of Ride: About 2¼ minutes

Average Wait in Line per 100 People Ahead of You: 5½ minutes

Assumes: Both tracks operating

Loading Speed: Slow

DESCRIPTION AND COMMENTS   This is an amusement park spook house that does not live up to many visitors' expectations or to the

Disney reputation for high quality. The facade is intriguing; the size of the building which houses the attraction suggests an elaborate ride. As it happens, the building is cut in half with similar, though not exactly identical, versions of the same ride in both halves. There is, of course, a separate line for each half.

TOURING TIPS   We receive a lot of mail disagreeing with our critical appraisal of this ride. Clearly, Mr. Toad has his advocates. If you are on a tight schedule, we do not suggest waiting very long for Mr. Toad. If you have two days allotted for the Magic Kingdom, or just want to add your opinion to the controversy, go ahead and ride. If you want to be a supertoad, be sure to try both sides.

Snow White's Adventures

Type of Ride: Disney version of a spook-house track ride
When to Go: Before 11 A.M. and after 6 P.M.
Special Comments: Terrifying to many small children
Author's Rating: Worth seeing if the wait is not long; ★★★
Overall Appeal by Age Group:

Pre-school	Grade School	Teens	Young Adults	Over 30	Senior Citizens
★★★	★★★	★★½	★★★	★★★	★★★

Duration of Ride: Almost 2½ minutes
Average Wait in Line per 100 People Ahead of You: 6¼ minutes
Assumes: Normal operation
Loading Speed: Moderate to slow

DESCRIPTION AND COMMENTS   You ride in a mining car through a spook house featuring Snow White as she narrowly escapes harm at the hands of the wicked witch. The action and effects are a cut above Mr. Toad's Wild Ride, but not as good as Peter Pan's Flight.

TOURING TIPS   We get more mail from our readers about this ride than any other Disney attraction. In short, it terrifies a lot of kids six and under. The witch is both relentless and ubiquitous, while Snow White is conspicuously absent. Many readers inform us that their small children will not ride *any* attraction that operates in the dark after experiencing Snow White's Adventures. A mother from Knoxville, Tennessee, commented:

The outside looks cute and fluffy, but inside, the evil witch just keeps coming at you. My five year old, who rode Space Mountain three times and took the Great Movie Ride's monster from *Alien* right in stride, was near panic when our car stopped unexpectedly twice during Snow White. [After Snow White] my six-year-old niece spent a lot of time asking "if a witch will jump out at you" before other rides. So I suggest that you explain a little more what this ride is about. It's tough on preschoolers who are expecting forest animals and dwarfs. This ride is not great, but it is good.

Experience Snow White if the lines are not too long or on a second day at the park. Ride before 11 A.M. or after 6 P.M., if possible.

20,000 Leagues Under the Sea

Type of Ride: Adventure/scenic boat ride
When to Go: Before 9:30 A.M., during parades, or just before closing
Special Comments: This ride is better if experienced after dark
Author's Rating: Interesting and fun; ★★★
Overall Appeal by Age Group:

Pre-school	Grade School	Teens	Young Adults	Over 30	Senior Citizens
★★★★	★★★	★★★	★★★	★★★	★★★½

Duration of Ride: Approximately 8½ minutes
Average Wait in Line per 100 People Ahead of You: 8 minutes
Assumes: 9 submarines operating
Loading Speed: Slow

DESCRIPTION AND COMMENTS   This attraction is based on the Disney movie of the same title. One of several rides that have been successful at both Disneyland (California) and the Magic Kingdom, the ride consists of a submarine voyage which encounters ocean-floor farming, various marine life (robotic), sunken ships, giant squid attacks, and other sights and adventures. An older ride, it struggles to maintain its image along with such marvels as Pirates of the Caribbean or Splash Mountain. A reader from Hawthorne Woods, Illinois, writes:

The only ride that I would not rate as highly as you was 20,000 Leagues Under the Sea. The lines were really slow moving and the ride was not nearly as imaginative as some of the others. I almost felt like we were riding through a concrete ditch with plastic fish on strings and coral stuck around the ditch for effect.

Another reader from Pittsburgh made this comment:

> At 20,000 Leagues Under the Sea, lines were long all day, and Grandma (who loves Disney World) said it was stupid.

TOURING TIPS This ride could be renamed "20,000 Bottlenecks Under the Sun." It is the traffic engineering nightmare of the Magic Kingdom. Even 15 minutes after opening, there are long lines and 20- to 30-minute waits. The problem is mainly due to the fact that this slow-loading boat ride is brought up to maximum carrying capacity (nine subs) very tardily. Ride operators fall behind almost as soon as the park opens and never seem to clear the backlog. If you do not want to ride Splash Mountain or Space Mountain, ride 20,000 Leagues first thing in the morning when the park opens.

Dumbo, the Flying Elephant

Type of Ride: Disneyfied midway ride

When to Go: Before 10 A.M. and after 5 P.M.

Author's Rating: An attractive children's ride; ★★★

Overall Appeal by Age Group:

Pre-school	Grade School	Teens	Young Adults	Over 30	Senior Citizens
★★★★★	★★★★	★★	★½	★½	★½

Duration of Ride: 1½ minutes

Average Wait in Line per 100 People Ahead of You: 20 minutes

Assumes: Normal staffing

Loading Speed: Slow

DESCRIPTION AND COMMENTS A nice, tame, happy children's ride based on the lovable Disney flying elephant, Dumbo. An upgraded rendition of a ride that can be found at state fairs and amusement parks across the country. This notwithstanding, Dumbo is the favorite Magic Kingdom attraction of many younger children.

A lot of readers take us to task for lumping Dumbo in with carnival midway rides. These comments from a reader in Armdale, Nova Scotia, are representative:

I think you have acquired a jaded attitude. I know [Dumbo] is not for everybody, but when we took our oldest child (then just four), the sign at the end of the line said there would be a ninety-minute wait. He knew and he didn't care, and he and I stood in the hot afternoon sun for 90 blissful minutes waiting for his 90-second flight. Anything that a four-year-old would wait for that long and that patiently must be pretty special.

TOURING TIPS This is a slow-loading ride that we recommend you bypass unless you are on a very relaxed touring schedule. If your kids are excited about Dumbo, try to get them on the ride before 10 A.M. or just before the park closes.

Mad Tea Party

Type of Ride: Midway-type spinning ride

When to Go: Before 11:30 A.M. and after 5 P.M.

Special Comments: You can make the tea cups spin faster by turning the wheel in the center of the cup.

Author's Rating: Fun, but not worth the wait; ★★½

Overall Appeal by Age Group:

Pre-school	Grade School	Teens	Young Adults	Over 30	Senior Citizens
★★★★	★★★★	★★★★	★★★	★★	★★

Duration of Ride: 1½ minutes

Average Wait in Line per 100 People Ahead of You: 7½ minutes

Assumes: Normal staffing

Loading Speed: Slow

DESCRIPTION AND COMMENTS An amusement park ride, though well done in the Disney style. *Alice in Wonderland*'s Mad Hatter provides the theme, and riders whirl around feverishly in big tea cups. A rendition of this ride, sans Disney characters, can be found at every local carnival and fair.

TOURING TIPS This ride, aside from not being particularly unique, is notoriously slow to load. Skip it on a busy schedule if the kids will let you. Ride in the morning of your second day if your schedule is more relaxed. A warning for parents who have not given this ride much thought: Teenagers like nothing better than to lure an adult onto the tea cups and then turn the wheel in the middle (which makes the cup spin faster) until the adults are plastered against the side of the cup and are on the verge of throwing up. Unless your life's ambition is to be the test subject in a human centrifuge, do not even consider getting on this ride with anyone younger than 21.

Fantasyland Eateries and Shops

DESCRIPTION AND COMMENTS   If you prefer atmosphere with your dining, you can (with reservations) eat in Cinderella Castle at King Stefan's Banquet Hall. Many of the Magic Kingdom visitors we surveyed wanted to know "What is in the castle?" or "Can we go up into the castle?" Well, Virginia, you can't see the whole thing, but if you eat at King Stefan's you can inspect a fair-sized chunk. Be forewarned, however, that our dining experiences at King Stefan's have been unqualified disasters. We eat there at least once each year and anticipate it with dread. This past year we were served soup containing an "unidentifiable wad." After we sent said wad back to the kitchen for analysis, we were duly informed that the wad was "beef." Fantasyland beef perhaps, but certainly not from any cow or steer on this planet. If your kids are really hot to see the inside of the castle, we recommend making a reservation at King Stefan's for a time convenient to you. However, order only dessert. Eat your main meal someplace else.

Shops in Fantasyland present more specialty and souvenir shopping opportunities. Mickey's Christmas Carol offers an exceptional selection of Christmas decorations and ornaments.

TOURING TIPS   To eat at King Stefan's in the castle you must have reservations. If you are lodging in Walt Disney World you can call 56 (campground guests 45) one to three days in advance to make reservations. If not, make reservations first thing in the morning at the door of the restaurant. We do not recommend a meal at King Stefan's if you are on a tight schedule or if you are sensitive about paying fancy prices for ho-hum (or worse) food. If you plan to spend two days in the Magic Kingdom and are curious about the inside of the castle, you might give it a try on your second day. If there are small children in your party, ask when Cinderella will be present before making your reservation. Another Fantasyland lunch option is Gurgi's Munchies & Crunchies where parents can obtain hot box lunches for children. Don't waste time in the shops unless you have a relaxed schedule or shopping is a big priority.

Mickey's Starland

Mickey's Starland is the first new "land" to be added to the Magic Kingdom since its opening, and the only land that does not connect to the central hub. Attractions include a live musical stage show featuring the Disney characters, a chance to meet Mickey Mouse, Mickey Mouse's house, a town of miniature buildings (Duckburg), a petting farm, and a young children's play area.

All in all, as Whoopi Goldberg might say, Mickey's Starland is a strange piece of work. To begin with, it is sandwiched between Fantasyland and Tomorrowland, like an afterthought, on about three acres that were formerly part of the Grand Prix Raceway. It is by far the smallest of the "lands" and seems more like an attraction than a section of the park. Though you can wander in on a somewhat obscure path from Fantasyland, Mickey's Starland is basically set up to receive guests arriving by the Walt Disney World Railroad.

Once you arrive at Mickey's Starland (which is located in the town of Duckburg), there is no indication of where or when the character show takes place. What you see as you leave the train station is a children's play area on your left, and a street of miniature buildings on your right. There is one normally sized house (Mickey's) among the little buildings, with a cluster of what looks like circus tents puffing up colorfully behind. To see the show, go through Mickey's house and watch cartoons in the waiting area until showtime.

Mickey's House and Mickey's Starland Show

Type of Show: Live musical comedy featuring the Disney characters

When to Go: Between 11 A.M. and 5 P.M.

Special Comments: After the show, guests can meet Mickey backstage at Mickey's Hollywood Theater

Author's Rating: Warm, happy, funny and all Disney; ★★★

Overall Appeal by Age Group:

Pre-school	Grade School	Teens	Young Adults	Over 30	Senior Citizens
★★★★½	★★★★	★★★½	★★★	★★★½	★★★½

Duration of Presentation: Approximately 14 minutes
Preshow Entertainment: Mickey Mouse cartoons
Probable Waiting Time: About 10 minutes

DESCRIPTION AND COMMENTS *Mickey's Starland Show*, the feature attraction of Mickey's Starland, is reached by walking through Mickey's House (which is full of Mickey Mouse and Walt Disney memorabilia), through Mickey's backyard, and into an air-conditioned, preshow tent where Mickey Mouse cartoons are viewed on TV monitors. Many patrons who find their way this far have no idea that there is anything more to see. They watch cartoons for a few minutes and then turn around and walk out. Had they stayed, they would have been treated to a funny, happy, and energetic live stage show featuring the Disney characters.

After the show, guests pass through a gift shop and photo opportunity area. As you exit outside, Mickey's Hollywood Theater is on the right. Here Mickey receives visitors in his dressing room to pose for photographs. This is a nice touch, but as with the stage show, this business of meeting Mickey in person backstage is never made very clear. For the most part, folks just walk into Mickey's Hollywood Theater and line up, not knowing what the line is for.

TOURING TIPS There is no problem catching a performance of *Mickey's Starland Show* once you know it's there and how to get to it. We recommend seeing the show during the hot, early afternoon hours when a few minutes in a nice, air-conditioned theater is relaxing. If you want to meet Mickey backstage without a lot of waiting, try one of the following:

1. In the waiting area for the character show (a tentlike structure with Mickey Mouse cartoons on T.V.), position yourself in front of the farthest left of several doors leading to the theater. When admitted you will proceed down a long passageway to another set of doors. Again try to be in front and on the left. When finally admitted to the actual theater, you will enter a row of seats and move all the way to the far end. At this point you should be positioned perfectly to duck out of the theater as soon as the curtain

falls. When the time comes, hustle out the door to your immediate left, pass quickly through the post-show area, and go outside. Mickey's Hollywood Theater will be on your right and several hundred other guests will be 30 steps behind you and headed for the same place. Or;

2. Enjoy the petting farm or walk around Duckburg for about 15 minutes after exiting the show. Line up to see Mickey just before the show following yours concludes; this is when the line will be shortest. A lady from Pittsburgh wrote suggesting:

> You might want to mention that only a few people are let into Mickey's dressing room at a time—maybe four small family groups. When they are done, the next batch comes in. So it's more intimate than, say, seeing Santa at the mall. By the way, Mickey autographed our *Unofficial Guide*, shaking his head sadly, and underlining "unofficial" several times, both on the cover and on the frontispiece.

—— *Other Mickey's Starland Attractions* ——

Grandma Duck's Petting Farm

Type of Attraction: Walk-through petting farm
When to Go: Anytime
Special Comments: Animals are real
Author's Rating: Improved; ★★½
Overall Appeal by Age Group:

Pre-school	Grade School	Teens	Young Adults	Over 30	Senior Citizens
★★★	★★★	★½	★½	★½	★½

DESCRIPTION AND COMMENTS   A modest barn and farm with a dozen or so animals. Unlike most petting farms, this one does not let you walk among the animals (goats, pigs, ducks, chickens, calves, etc.). You must pet them when possible through fences. The featured animal is Minnie Moo, a cow with a marking shaped like Mickey's head on her flank. Much of the attraction is along gravel paths, which make walking very difficult.

TOURING TIPS   Visit the animals any time. You will not encounter large crowds here, as a rule.

Small Children's Play Area

DESCRIPTION AND COMMENTS   This area is designed for small children and features slides, tunnels, ladders, and a variety of other creative playground structures. Children enjoy the chance to let off steam while adults enjoy the tour intermission. The big shortcoming is the lack of shade; attending adults must swelter in the hot Florida sun.

TOURING TIPS   If you are on a tight schedule, skip the playground.

Tomorrowland

Tomorrowland is a futuristic mix of rides and experiences that relate to the technological development of man and what life will be like in the years to come. If this sounds a little bit like the EPCOT Center theme, it's because Tomorrowland was very much a breeding ground for the ideas that resulted in EPCOT Center. Yet Tomorrowland and EPCOT Center are very different. Aside from differences in scale, Tomorrowland is more "just for fun." While EPCOT Center educates in its own delightful style, Tomorrowland allows you to hop in and try the future on for size.

Tomorrowland is 22 years old, and many of its buildings and attractions are past their prime. *Mission to Mars* (formerly *Spaceflight to the Moon*) draws only Disney first-timers and folks trying to get out of the hot sun. The *Carousel of Progress* and *American Journeys* are great attractions, but are more reflective than forward-looking. The Grand Prix Raceway, StarJets, and the Skyway to Fantasyland are straight out of the sixties. Only Space Mountain continues to offer a taste of the future. A renovation of Tomorrowland is planned but don't hold your breath. Most of the new attractions are not scheduled to come on line until 1996.

Space Mountain

Type of Ride: Roller coaster in the dark

When to Go: First thing when the park opens or during the hour before closing or between 6 and 7 P.M.

Special Comments: Great fun and action, much wilder than Big Thunder Mountain. Children must be 3'8" tall to ride, and if under seven years old, must be accompanied by an adult. Switching-off option provided (see page 243).

Author's Rating: A great roller coaster with excellent special effects; ★★★★★

Overall Appeal by Age Group:

Pre-school	Grade School	Teens	Young Adults	Over 30	Senior Citizens
†	★★★★★	★★★★★	★★★★½	★★★★	†

† Some preschoolers loved Space Mountain, others were frightened. The sample size of senior citizens who experienced this ride was too small to develop an accurate rating.

Duration of Ride: Almost 3 minutes

Average Wait in Line per 100 People Ahead of You: 3 minutes

Assumes: Two tracks operating at 21-second dispatch intervals

Loading Speed: Moderate to fast

WARNING!

For Bouffants, Rug Wearers, and Elvis Impersonators

This Ride Will Muss Your 'Do

DESCRIPTION AND COMMENTS Space Mountain is a roller coaster in the dark. Totally enclosed in a mammoth futuristic structure, the attraction is a marvel of creativity and engineering. The theme of the ride is a spaceflight through the dark recesses of the galaxy. The effects are superb and the ride is the fastest and wildest in the Disney repertoire. As a roller coaster, Space Mountain is a lulu, much zippier than the Big Thunder Mountain ride.

TOURING TIPS Space Mountain is a "not to be missed" feature (if you can handle a fairly wild roller coaster ride). People who are not timid about going on roller coasters will take Space Mountain in stride. What sets Space Mountain apart is that the cars plummet through the dark with only occasional lighting effects piercing the gloom.

Space Mountain is the favorite attraction of many Magic Kingdom visitors between seven and fifty years of age. Each morning prior to opening, particularly during the summer and holiday periods, several hundred S.M. "junkies" crowd the rope barriers at the central hub awaiting the signal to sprint (literally) the 250 yards to the ride's entrance. As our research team called it, the "Space Mountain Morning Mini Marathon" pits tubby, out-of-shape dads and moms against their svelte, speedy offspring, brother against sister, blossoming co-eds against truck drivers, nuns against beauticians. If you want to ride Space Mountain without a long wait you had better do well in the "Mini Marathon," because at five minutes after opening, Space Mountain has more guests in line waiting to ride than any other attraction in the Magic Kingdom.

There was a time when Disney personnel tried to keep guests from running (they still tell you not to run) to Space Mountain, but even in the Magic Kingdom reality is a force to be reckoned with. The reality in this case is that a dozen Disney security personnel cannot control several hundred stampeding, flipped-out, early-morning space cadets. So here you are, a nice normal dental hygienist from Toledo, and you are thinking you'd like to ride Space Mountain. Well, Virginia, you're in the big league now; tie up them Reeboks and get ready to run.

But first, a word from the coach. There are a couple of things you can do to get a leg up on the competition. First, arrive early; be one of the first in the park. Proceed to the end of Main Street and cut right past the Plaza Restaurant, and stop under an archway that says:

The Plaza Pavilion Terrace Dining

where a Disney worker will be standing behind a rope barrier. From this point, you are approximately 100 yards closer to Space Mountain, on a route through the Plaza Pavilion, than your competition waiting to take off from the central hub. From this point of departure, middle-aged folks walking fast can beat most of the teens sprinting from the central hub. And if you are up to some modest jogging, well. . . . Another advantage of starting from the Plaza Pavilion entrance is that your wait until opening will be cool, comfortable, and in the shade.

Couples touring with children too small to ride Space Mountain can both ride without waiting in line twice by taking advantage of a procedure called "switching off." Here is how it works. When you enter the Space Mountain line alert the first Disney attendant (known as Greeter One) that you want to switch off. The attendant will allow you, your spouse, and your small child (or children) to continue together, phoning ahead to Greeter Two to expect you. When you reach Greeter

Two (at the turnstile near the boarding area), you will be given specific directions. One of you will go ahead and ride while the other stays with the kids. Whoever rides will be admitted by the unloading attendant to stairs leading back up to the boarding area. Here you switch off; the second parent rides, and the first parent takes the kids down the stairs to the unloading area where everybody joins up and exits. Switching off is also available as an option on the Big Thunder Mountain Railroad and on Splash Mountain.

For parents whose children meet the minimum height and age requirements to ride Space Mountain, be advised that all riders have their own seat. You cannot sit next to your child.

If you do not catch Space Mountain early in the morning, try again during the hour before closing. Often at this time of day, Space Mountain visitors are held in line outside the entrance until all those previously in line have ridden, thus emptying the attraction inside. The appearance from the outside is that the waiting line is enormous when, in reality, the only people waiting are those visible in front of the entrance. This crowd-control technique, known as "stacking," has the effect of discouraging visitors from riding because they perceive the wait to be too long. Stacking is used in several Walt Disney World rides and attractions during the hour before closing to insure that the ride will be able to close on schedule. For those who do not let the long-appearing line run them off, the waiting period is usually short.

Splash Mountain, which opened in 1992, siphons off a number of guests who previously would have made Space Mountain their first stop. Even so, you can still depend on a mob rushing to Space Mountain as soon as the park opens. If you especially like the thrill rides, ride Space Mountain first thing in the morning, followed by Big Thunder Mountain Railroad, and then Splash Mountain.

If you are a Disney resort hotel or campground guest and are eligible for early admission, you can enjoy Space Mountain to your heart's content for an hour before the general public is admitted on Tuesdays, Thursdays, Saturdays, and Sundays. Though Disney staff may insist that only Fantasyland is "officially" open for early entrants, Space Mountain and, sometimes, the Grand Prix Raceway (both in Tomorrowland) are often open as well. To determine whether Space Mountain is open early, simply head for Tomorrowland. If you are permitted to enter Tomorrowland, Space Mountain will be operating (Disney security will not allow early entry guests into any part of the park not yet open). If you are not allowed to enter Tomorowland from its main entrance at the central hub, try again about 20 minutes later using the walkway between Fantasyland and Tomorrowland.

If you are an early morning entrant and Big Thunder Mountain and Splash Mountain are also high on your priority list, ride Space Mountain (as well as Fantasyland attractions) until about 10–15 minutes before the hour the general public is admitted. At this time, go to the boundary of Fantasyland and Liberty Square and wait for the rest of the park to open. When it does, enter Liberty Square and move quickly along the Liberty Square and Frontierland waterfronts to Big Thunder Mountain and Splash Mountain.

If you are not eligible for early entry, try to visit the Magic Kingdom on a Monday, Wednesday, or Friday, and make Space Mountain your first attraction of the day. If your schedule requires you visit on an early entry day, ride Splash Mountain and Big Thunder Railroad first, then head to Space Mountain.

Grand Prix Raceway

Type of Ride: Drive-'em-yourself miniature cars
When to Go: Before 11 A.M. and after 5 P.M.
Special Comments: Must be 4'4" tall to drive
Author's Rating: Boring for adults (★); great for preschoolers
Overall Appeal by Age Group:

Pre-school	Grade School	Teens	Young Adults	Over 30	Senior Citizens
★★★½	★★★	★	½	½	½

Duration of Ride: Approximately 4¼ minutes
Average Wait in Line per 100 People Ahead of You: 4½ minutes
Assumes: 285-car turnover every 20 minutes
Loading Speed: Slow

DESCRIPTION AND COMMENTS An elaborate miniature raceway with gasoline-powered cars that will travel at speeds of up to seven miles an hour. The raceway design with its sleek cars, racing noises, and Grand Prix billboards is quite alluring. Unfortunately, however, the cars poke along on a track leaving the driver with little to do. Pretty ho-hum for most adults and teenagers. Of those children who would enjoy the ride, many are excluded by the requirement that drivers be 4'4" tall.

TOURING TIPS   This ride is appealing to the eye but definitely expendable to the schedule of adults. Preschoolers, however, love it. If your preschooler is too short to drive, ride along and allow your child to steer (the car runs on a guide rail) while you work the foot pedal.

A mom from North Billerica, Massachusetts, writes:

> I was truly amazed by the number of adults in the line. Please emphasize to your readers that these cars travel on a guided path and are not a whole lot of fun. The only reason I could think of for adults to be in the line would be an insane desire to go on absolutely every ride at Disney World. The other feature about the cars is that they tend to pile up at the end, so it takes almost as long to get off as it did to get on. Parents riding with their preschoolers should keep the car going as slow as [possible] without stalling. This prolongs the preschooler's joy and decreases the time you will have to wait at the end.

Skyway to Fantasyland

Type of Ride: Scenic transportation to Fantasyland
When to Go: Before noon and during special events
Special Comments: If a line, probably quicker to walk
Author's Rating: Nice view; ★★★
Overall Appeal by Age Group:

Pre-school	Grade School	Teens	Young Adults	Over 30	Senior Citizens
★★★★	★★★★	★★★½	★★★½	★★★½	★★★½

Duration of Ride: Approximately 5 minutes one way
Average Wait in Line per 100 People Ahead of You: 10 minutes
Assumes: 45 or more cars operating
Loading Speed: Moderate

DESCRIPTION AND COMMENTS   A skylift that will transport you from Tomorrowland to the far corner of Fantasyland near the border it shares with Liberty Square. The view is one of the best in the Magic Kingdom, but walking is usually faster if you just want to get there.

TOURING TIPS   Unless the lines are short, the Skyway will not save you any time as a mode of transportation. As a ride, however, it affords some incredible views. Ride in the morning, during the two hours before the park closes, or during one of the daily parades (this ride sometimes opens later and closes earlier than other rides in Tomorrowland).

StarJets

Type of Ride: Very mild midway-type thrill ride
When to Go: Before 11 A.M. or after 5 P.M.
Author's Rating: Not worth the wait; ★★
Overall Appeal by Age Group:

Pre-school	Grade School	Teens	Young Adults	Over 30	Senior Citizens
★★★★	★★★	★★½	★½	★	★

Duration of Ride: 1½ minutes
Average Wait in Line per 100 People Ahead of You: 13½ minutes
Assumes: Normal staffing
Loading Speed: Slow

DESCRIPTION AND COMMENTS   A carnival-type ride involving small rockets which rotate on arms around a central axis.

TOURING TIPS   Slow loading and expendable on any schedule. If you take preschoolers on this ride, place them in the seat first, then situate yourself.

WEDway PeopleMover

Type of Ride: Scenic
When to Go: During the hot, crowded period of the day (11:30 A.M.–4:30 P.M.)
Special Comments: A good way to check out the crowd at Space Mountain
Author's Rating: Scenic, relaxing, informative; ★★★
Overall Appeal by Age Group:

Pre-school	Grade School	Teens	Young Adults	Over 30	Senior Citizens
★★★	★★★	★★½	★★½	★★★	★★★

Duration of Ride: 10 minutes
Average Wait in Line per 100 People Ahead of You: 1½ minutes

Assumes: 39 trains operating

Loading Speed: Fast

DESCRIPTION AND COMMENTS   A once unique prototype of a linear induction powered system of mass transportation. Tram-like cars take you on a leisurely tour of Tomorrowland, including a peek at the inside of Space Mountain.

TOURING TIPS   A nice, pleasant, relaxing ride where the lines move quickly and you seldom have to wait. A good ride to take during the busier times of the day.

Carousel of Progress

Type of Show: AudioAnimatronic theater production
When to Go: Between 11:30 A.M. and 4 P.M.
Author's Rating: Nostalgic, warm and happy; ★★★½
Overall Appeal by Age Group:

Pre-school	Grade School	Teens	Young Adults	Over 30	Senior Citizens
★★★	★★★½	★★★½	★★★½	★★★★	★★★★½

Duration of Presentation: 18 minutes
Preshow Entertainment: None
Probable Waiting Time: Less than 10 minutes

DESCRIPTION AND COMMENTS   This is a warm and nostalgic look at the way technology and electricity have changed the lives of an Audio-Animatronics family over several generations. Though not rated "not to be missed," *Carousel of Progress* is thoroughly delightful. The family depicted is easy to identify with, and a happy, sentimental tune (which you will find yourself humming all day) serves to bridge the gap between generations.

TOURING TIPS   While not on our "not to be missed" list, this attraction is a great favorite of Magic Kingdom repeat visitors. A great favorite of ours as well, it is included on all of our One-Day Touring Plans. *Carousel of Progress* handles big crowds effectively and is a good choice for touring during the busier times of the day.

Dreamflight

Type of Ride: Special-effects travel ride
When to go: Between 11:30 A.M. and 4:30 P.M.
Author's Rating: Pleasant; ★★★
Projected Overall Appeal by Age Group:

Pre-school	Grade School	Teens	Young Adults	Over 30	Senior Citizens
★★★½	★★★½	★★★½	★★★½	★★★½	★★★½

Duration of Ride: About 6 minutes
Average Wait in Line per 100 People Ahead of You: 3 minutes
Assumes: Normal operation
Loading Speed: Fast

DESCRIPTION AND COMMENTS: Presented by Delta Airlines, Dream-flight is a somewhat fanciful depiction of the history of flight. Pleasant but not particularly compelling, this new addition to the Tomorrow-land lineup could have been a lot more interesting. Having a bit of the feel of Peter Pan's Flight mixed with a very EPCOT Center style of presentation, Dreamflight is best characterized as "nice."

TOURING TIPS   Very seldom is there a line at Dreamflight. See it during the heat of the day or whenever the mood strikes.

World Premier Circle-Vision: **American Journeys**

Type of Show: Patriotic travelog projected onto multiple screens
When to Go: During the hot, crowded period of the day (11:30 A.M.–4 P.M.)
Special Comments: Audience must stand throughout presentation
Author's Rating: Wonderful; not to be missed; ★★★½
Overall Appeal by Age Group:

Pre-school	Grade School	Teens	Young Adults	Over 30	Senior Citizens
★★	★★★	★★★	★★★½	★★★½	★★★★

Duration of Presentation: About 20 minutes
Preshow Entertainment: About 10 minutes
Probable Waiting Time: Less than 10 minutes

DESCRIPTION AND COMMENTS   Here the visitor stands in the center of a huge theater where multiple projectors make a 360° screen come alive. It's another trip around the world, but this time you not only see where you are going, but what's on either side, and what's behind you. The movie, which demonstrates this cinematic marvel, is fast paced, well produced, and very much deserving of your attention. More than a travelog, *American Journeys* takes you down the awesome rapids of the Colorado River, on a surfing expedition in Hawaii, and in close for a space-shuttle blast-off.

TOURING TIPS   An excellent film and an exciting motion picture technique make this an attraction you will want to see. The theater has the largest single-room capacity of any theater in the Magic Kingdom, making it a perfect show to see during peak attendance hours.

Mission to Mars

Type of Show: Theater-in-the-round simulation of space journey
When to Go: During the hot, crowded period of the day (11 A.M.– 4:30 P.M.)
Special Comments: Special effects sometimes frighten toddlers
Author's Rating: ★★½
Overall Appeal by Age Group:

Pre-school	Grade School	Teens	Young Adults	Over 30	Senior Citizens
★★	★★½	★★	★★	★★	★★

Duration of Presentation: About 12 minutes
Preshow Entertainment: About 6 minutes
Probable Waiting Time: Less than 10 minutes

DESCRIPTION AND COMMENTS   Here the visitor takes a simulated space shuttle flight from earth to Mars. The voyage is dramatic, marginally educational, and features realistic special effects.

TOURING TIPS   Somewhat dated, and expendable to anyone on a tight schedule, *Mission to Mars* is best enjoyed during the hot, crowded part of the day.

Tomorrowland Eateries and Shops

DESCRIPTION AND COMMENTS   The Tomorrowland Terrace is the largest and most efficient of the Magic Kingdom's numerous fast-food restaurants. The Plaza Pavilion, however, serves the best food. Try the Italian hoagie.

Several shops provide yet additional opportunities for buying souvenirs and curiosities.

TOURING TIPS   Forget browsing the shops until your second day unless shopping is your top priority.

Not to Be Missed at the Magic Kingdom

Adventureland	Jungle Cruise
	Pirates of the Caribbean
Frontierland	Big Thunder Mountain Railroad
	Country Bear Jamboree
	The Diamond Horseshoe Jamboree
	Splash Mountain
Liberty Square	The Haunted Mansion
Fantasyland	Peter Pan's Flight
Tomorrowland	Space Mountain
Special events	Evening Parade

Live Entertainment in the Magic Kingdom

Live entertainment in the form of bands, Disney character appearances, parades, singing and dancing, and ceremonies further enliven and add color to the Magic Kingdom on a daily basis. For specific information about what's going on the day you visit, stop by City Hall as you enter the park. Be forewarned, however, that if you are on a tight schedule, it is impossible to see both the Magic Kingdom's featured attractions **and** take in the numerous and varied live performances offered. In our one-day Touring Plans we exclude the live performances in favor of seeing as much of the park as time permits. This is a considered, tactical decision based on the fact that some of the parades and other performances siphon crowds away from the more popular rides, thus shortening waiting lines.

But the color and pageantry of live happenings around the park are an integral part of the Magic Kingdom entertainment mix and a persuasive argument for second-day touring. The following is an incomplete list and description of those performances and events that are scheduled with some regularity and for which no reservations are required.

Fantasy Faire Stage	Site of various concerts in Fantasyland.
Steel Drum Bands	Steel drum bands perform daily at the Caribbean Plaza in Adventureland.
Frontierland Stuntmen	Stuntmen stage shootouts in Frontierland according to the daily live entertainment schedule.
Kids of the Kingdom	A youthful song and dance group which performs popular music daily in the Castle Forecourt. Disney characters usually join in the fun.
Flag Retreat	Daily at 5 P.M. at Town Square (the railroad station end of Main Street). Sometimes done

with great fanfare and college marching bands, sometimes with a smaller Disney band.

Sword in the Stone Ceremony	A ceremony with audience participation based on the Disney animated feature of the same name. Merlin the Magician selects youngsters from among the guests to test their courage and strength by removing the sword, Excalibur, from the stone. Staged several times each day behind Cinderella Castle; check the daily entertainment schedule.
Bay Lake and Seven Seas Lagoon Floating Electrical Pageant	This is one of our favorites of all the Disney extras, but you have to leave the Magic Kingdom to see it. The Floating Electrical Pageant is a stunning electric light show afloat on small barges and set to nifty electronic music. The Pageant is performed at nightfall on the Seven Seas Lagoon and on Bay Lake. Exit the Magic Kingdom and take the monorail to the Polynesian Resort. Get yourself a drink and walk out to the end of the pier. The show will begin shortly (about 9 P.M. during the summer).
Fantasy in the Sky	A stellar fireworks display unleashed after dark on those nights the park is open late.
Tomorrowland Terrace Stage & Tomorrowland Theater	These stages in Tomorrowland feature top-40 rock music, rap, and jazz, as well as Disney characters and the Kids of the Kingdom.
Disney Character Shows & Appearances	On busy days, a character *du jour* is on duty for photo posing 9 A.M. until 10 P.M. next to City Hall. Disney character shows run back-to-back at Mickey's Starland from 9:40 A.M. until 9:30 P.M. (when the park is open late). Shows at the Castle Forecourt Stage (front of the castle) feature the Disney characters several times a day according to the daily entertainment schedule, as do shows in the Tomorrowland Theater. Finally, characters roam the park throughout the day, but can almost always be found in Fantasyland and Mickey's Starland.
Magic Kingdom Bands	Various banjo, dixieland, steel drum, marching, and fife and drum bands roam the Magic Kingdom daily.

Tinkerbell's Flight   A nice special effect in the sky above Cinderella Castle at 10 P.M. to herald the beginning of Fantasy in the Sky fireworks (when the park is open late).

—— Parades ——

Parades are a big deal at the Magic Kingdom, full-fledged spectaculars with dozens of Disney characters and some amazing special effects. In late 1991, the beloved Main Street Electrical Parade was unplugged and sent abroad, and the afternoon parade was replaced by an eye-popping celebration of carnivals around the world. The new parades are larger, more colorful, and more elaborate than any Disney street production to date. We rate the afternoon parade as outstanding and the evening parade as "not to be missed."

In addition to providing great entertainment, the parades also serve to lure guests away from the attractions. If getting on rides is more appealing than watching a parade, you will find the wait for all attractions substantially diminished just before and during parades. Because the parade route does not pass through Adventureland, Tomorrowland, or Fantasyland, attractions in these lands are particularly good bets.

Afternoon Parade

Usually staged at 3 P.M., the parade features bands, floats, marching Disney characters, as well as huge inflated Disney characters towering 55 feet above Main Street. New Orleans's Mardi Gras, Brazil's Carnivale de Rio, and Europe's Carnival in Venice are represented in music, dance, and costume.

Evening Parade(s)

The evening parade goes high-tech with a whole new production featuring giant holographs, electro-luminescent and fiber-optic technologies, light-spreading thermoplastics (do not try this at home), and clouds of underlit liquid nitrogen smoke. In spite of how appealing this sounds, don't worry. You won't need a gas mask or an asbestos suit, nor will your hair fall out in three weeks. For those who flunked chemistry and physics, the parade also features music, Mickey Mouse, and twinkle lights. Depending on closing time, the evening parade is staged once at 9 P.M., or twice when the park is open late at 9 and 11 P.M.

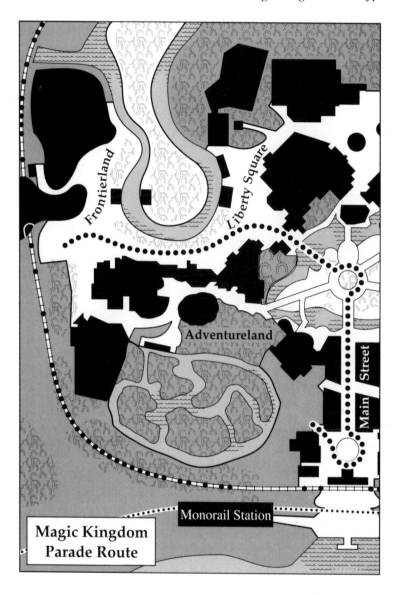

Frontierland

Liberty Square

Adventureland

Main Street

Monorail Station

Magic Kingdom Parade Route

Parade Route and Vantage Points

Magic Kingdom parades circle Town Square, head down Main Street, go around the central hub, and then cross over the bridge to Liberty Square. In Liberty Square the parade progresses along the waterfront and ends in Frontierland. Sometimes parades begin in Frontierland and run the same route in the opposite direction, terminating in Town Square.

Most guests tend to watch from the central hub or from Main Street. One of the best vantage points, and certainly one of the most popular, is the upper platform of the Walt Disney Railroad Station at the Town Square end of Main Street. This is also a particularly good place for watching the Fantasy in the Sky fireworks. A big problem with the train platform, however, is that you literally have to stake out your position 30–45 minutes before the parade begins.

Because the majority of spectators pack Main Street and the central hub, we recommend watching the parades from Liberty Square or Frontierland. There are several great vantage points which are frequently overlooked:

1. The Sleepy Hollow sandwich shop, on your immediate right as you cross the bridge into Liberty Square, is a good spot. If you arrive early you can buy refreshments and get a table by the rail. You will have a perfect view of the parade as it passes over the Liberty Square bridge.

2. A pathway runs along the Liberty Square side of the moat from the Sleepy Hollow sandwich shop to Cinderella's Castle. Any point along this path offers a clear and unobstructed view of the parade as it passes over the Liberty Square bridge.

3. There is a covered walkway connecting the Liberty Tree Tavern and *The Diamond Horseshoe Jamboree*. This elevated vantage point is perfect for watching parades (particularly on rainy days) and usually goes unnoticed until just before the parade starts.

4. There are elevated wooden platforms in front of the Frontierland Shootin' Gallery, the Frontier Trading Post, and in front of the building with the sign reading "Frontier Merchandise." These select spots usually get picked off 10–12 minutes before parade time.

5. Along the outside perimeter of the central hub, between the entrances to Liberty Square and Adventureland, are several benches. Usually not occupied until after the parade begins, the

benches offer a comfortable resting place and an unobstructed (though somewhat removed) view of the parade as it crosses the Liberty Square bridge. What you lose in proximity, however, you make up in comfort.

6. There are also some good viewing places along the Liberty Square and Frontierland dockside areas, but these spots are usually grabbed early.

Eating in the Magic Kingdom

The Magic Kingdom is a wonder and a marvel, a testimony to the creative genius of man. But for all of the beauty, imagination, and wholesomeness of this incredible place, it is almost impossible to get a really good meal. Simply put, what is available is that same computerized, homogenized fare that languishes beneath the heat lamps of every fast-food chain restaurant in America. Logistically we are sympathetic; it is overwhelming to contemplate preparing and serving 130,000-or-so meals each day. But our understanding, unfortunately, does not make the food any more palatable. Do not misunderstand, the food at the Magic Kingdom is not awful. It is merely mediocre in a place that has set the standard in virtually every other area for quality in tourism and entertainment. Given the challenge of feeding so many people each day, we might be more accepting of the bland fare if (1) we didn't believe the Disney people could do better, and if (2) obtaining food didn't require such an investment of time and effort. The variety found on the numerous menus indicates that somebody once had the right idea.

—— Alternatives and Suggestions for Eating in the Magic Kingdom ——

Remember, this discussion is about the Magic Kingdom. EPCOT Center and the Disney-MGM Studios are treated separately under a similar heading beginning on pages 352 and 420.

1. Eat a good breakfast before arriving at the Magic Kingdom. You do not want to waste touring time eating breakfast at the park. Besides, there are some truly outstanding breakfast specials at restaurants outside of Walt Disney World.

2. Having eaten a good breakfast, keep your tummy happy as you

tour by purchasing snacks from the many vendors stationed throughout the Magic Kingdom. This is especially important if you have a tight schedule; you cannot afford to spend a lot of time waiting in line for food.

3. Correctly assuming that we don't take off for Orlando every time we get hungry, readers frequently ask where we eat when working in the Magic Kingdom. Fair enough; here's where:

Adventureland	*Adventureland Veranda.* We like the stir-fried steak sandwich, the noodles, and the teriyaki chicken sandwich.
	El Pirata Y el Perico. We eat here sometimes as it is frequently overlooked. Nothing fancy. We usually have hot dogs.
Liberty Square	*Columbia Harbour House.* The Monte Cristo sandwich is pretty good.
	Sleepy Hollow. If we get hungry between 2 and 3 P.M., we head for Sleepy Hollow. The food is decent, but more importantly, we can settle comfortably at a table along the rail to watch the 3 P.M. parade.
	Liberty Tree Tavern. Our favorite full-service restaurant in the Magic Kingdom, particularly for sandwiches. Reservations required.
Tomorrowland	*Plaza Pavilion.* The Italian hoagies are good here.
Contemporary Resort	*Contemporary Cafe.* Our absolute favorite, if we have the time, is this restaurant's buffet on the main level of the Contemporary Resort. Good for lunch or dinner.
Favorite Snacks	We love churros, a Mexican pastry sold by vendor wagons. Magic Kingdom popcorn is also good.

4. If you are on a tight schedule and the park closes early, stay until closing and eat dinner outside of Walt Disney World be-

fore returning to your hotel. If the Magic Kingdom stays open late, eat an early dinner at about 4 P.M. or 4:30 P.M. in the Magic Kingdom eatery of your choice. You should have missed the last wave of lunch diners and sneaked in just ahead of the dinner crowd.

5. Take the monorail to one of the resort hotels for lunch. The trip over and back takes very little time, and because most guests have left the hotels for the parks, the resort hotels' restaurants are often slack. The food is better than in the Magic Kingdom, the service is faster, the atmosphere more relaxed, and beer, wine, and mixed drinks are available. Of the resort hotels connected directly to the Magic Kingdom by monorail, we prefer the fare at the Contemporary Resort. The restaurants at the Grand Floridian are good, but pricey.

6. If you decide to eat in the Magic Kingdom during the midday rush (11 A.M.–2 P.M.) or the evening rush (5 P.M.–8 P.M.), try The Crystal Palace towards Adventureland at the central hub end of Main Street, the Adventureland Veranda to the right of the Adventureland entrance bridge, or El Pirata Y el Perico in Adventureland around the corner from Frontierland's Pecos Bill Cafe. All three of these eateries serve decent food and usually are not crowded. As another alternative, a lunch-hour reservation for *The Diamond Horseshoe Jamboree* combines a good show with an easy meal.

7. Many of the Magic Kingdom restaurants serve a cold sandwich of one sort or another. It is possible to buy a cold lunch (except for the drinks) before 11 A.M. and then carry your food until you are ready to eat. We met a family which does this routinely, with Mom always remembering to bring several small plastic bags in which to pack the food. Drinks are purchased at an appropriate time from any convenient drink vendor.

8. Most fast-food eateries in the Magic Kingdom have more than one service window. Regardless of time of day, check out the lines at *all* of the windows before queuing. Sometimes a manned, but out of the way, window will have a much shorter line or no line at all.

9. Restaurants which accept reservations for lunch and/or dinner

fill their respective meal seatings quickly. To obtain reservations you must hot-foot it over to the restaurant in question (King Stefan's Banquet Hall, etc.) as soon as you enter the park or blow your most effective touring time waiting in line to make your meal reservation. Often you are asked to return well in advance of your seating time, and even then, on many occasions, will have to wait well past your scheduled time for a table. Guests staying at one of the Walt Disney World lodging properties can avoid some of this hassle by making reservations by phone up to three days in advance of their visit.

10. Of the three Magic Kingdom full-service restaurants, the Liberty Tree Tavern in Liberty Square is the best. Tony's Town Square Restaurant on Main Street serves nice salads, but is otherwise hit or miss. We don't recommend King Stefan's Banquet Hall in Cinderella Castle for anything except dessert. A good rule of thumb at any Magic Kingdom full-service eatery is to keep it simple. Go for sandwiches and other basic dishes (roast turkey and mashed potatoes, etc.) that are hard to mess up. Stay away from roast beef or steak whether offered as a main dish or in sandwich form.

11. Just so you know, the Disney people have a rule against bringing your own food and drink into the park. We interviewed one woman who, ignoring the rule, brought a huge picnic lunch for her family of five packed in a large diaper/baby paraphernalia bag. She secured the bag in a locker under the Main Street Station and retrieved it later when the family was hungry. A Texas family returned to their camper in the parking lot for lunch, where they had a cooler, lawn chairs, and plenty of food in the college football tailgating tradition.

We receive many letters from readers relating how they approached eating at the Magic Kingdom. Here is one from a family in Pennsylvania:

Despite the warning against bringing food into the park, we packed a double picnic lunch in a backpack and a small shoulder bag. Even with a small discount, it cost $195 for the seven of us to tour the park for a day, and I felt that spending another $150 or so on two meals was not in the cards. We froze juice boxes to keep the meat sandwiches cool (it worked fine), and had an

extra round of juice boxes and peanut butter sandwiches for a
late afternoon snack. We took raisins and a pack of fig bars for
sweets, but didn't carry any other cookies or candy to avoid a
"sugar-low" during the day. Fruit would have been nice, but it
would have been squashed.

Shopping in the Magic Kingdom

Shops in the Magic Kingdom add realism and atmosphere to the various theme settings and make available an extensive inventory of souvenirs, clothing, novelties, decorator items, and more. Much of the merchandise displayed (with the exception of Disney trademark souvenir items) is available back home and elsewhere at a lower price. In our opinion, shopping is not one of the main reasons for visiting the Magic Kingdom. We recommend bypassing the shops on a one-day visit. If you have two or more days to spend in the Magic Kingdom, browse the shops during the early afternoon when many of the attractions are crowded. Remember that Main Street, with its multitude of shops, opens earlier and closes later than the rest of the park. Lockers in the Main Street Train Station allow you to stash your purchases safely as opposed to dragging them around the park with you. The Parcel Pick-up service, offered for a year or two, has been discontinued.

Our recommendations notwithstanding, we realize that for many guests Disney souvenirs and memorabilia are irresistible. If you have decided that you would look good in a Goofy hat with shoulder-length floppy ears, you are in the right place. What's more, you have plenty of company. Writes one of our readers,

> I've discovered that people have a compelling need to buy Disney stuff when they are at WDW. When you get home you wonder why you ever got a cashmere sweater with Mickey Mouse embroidered on the breast, or a tie with tiny Goofys all over it. Maybe it's something they put in the food.

Disney trademark merchandise tends to be more expensive at the Disney shops than in independent stores out of the World. Quality, however, is better at the Disney shops. The best place for quality and value is the Character Warehouse in Mall 2 of the Belz Factory Outlet World on International Drive off I-4. Unfortunately, the selection at the outlet store is rather limited.

If you remember on your flight home that you forgot to buy mouse ears for your nephew, you can order most of the Disney trademark merchadise sold at Walt Disney World by calling the Walt Disney Attractions Mail Order Department at (407) 363-6200.

Behind the Scenes in the Magic Kingdom

Innovations in Action provides an opportunity for groups of no fewer than 15 adults (17 years and over) to tour the Magic Kingdom behind the scenes. This fascinating guided program provides an informative and detailed look at the logistical, technical, and operational side of the Magic Kingdom, including the tree farm, the waste treatment plant, and the tunnel system (under the theme park). For additional information, call (407) 824-7997. The program, which costs $50 per person, is available only to Walt Disney World resort guests. Groups must be formed and arrangements made prior to arrival.

Traffic Patterns in the Magic Kingdom

When we began our research on the Magic Kingdom we were very interested in traffic patterns throughout the park, specifically:

1. *Which sections of the park and what attractions do visitors head for when they first arrive?* When visitors are admitted to the various lands during the summer and holiday periods, traffic to Tomorrowland and Frontierland is heaviest, followed by Fantasyland, Adventureland, Liberty Square, and Mickey's Starland. During the school year when there are fewer young people in the park, early-morning traffic is more evenly distributed, but is still heaviest in Tomorrowland, Frontierland, and Fantasyland. In our research we tested the claim, often heard, that most people turn right into Tomorrowland and tour the Magic Kingdom in an orderly counterclockwise fashion. We found it without basis. As the park fills, visitors seem to head for the top attractions, which they wish to ride before the lines get long. This more than any other factor determines traffic patterns in the morning. Attractions which receive considerable patronage in the early morning are:

Tomorrowland:	Space Mountain
Frontierland:	Splash Mountain
	Big Thunder Mountain Railroad
Fantasyland:	Dumbo, the Flying Elephant
	20,000 Leagues Under the Sea
Adventureland:	Jungle Cruise

2. *How long does it take for the park to reach peak capacity for a given day? How are the visitors dispersed throughout the park?* There is a surge of "early birds" who arrive before or around opening time, but are quickly dispersed throughout the empty park. After the initial onslaught is absorbed, there is a lull that lasts roughly an hour after opening. Then the park is inundated with arriving guests for

about two hours, peaking between 10 and 11 A.M. Guests continue to arrive in a steady, but diminishing stream until around 2 P.M. The lines we sampled were longest between 1 and 2 P.M., indicating more arrivals than departures into the early afternoon. For general touring purposes, most attractions develop long lines between 10:30 and 11:30 A.M. Through the middle of the morning and the early hours of the afternoon, attendance is equally distributed through all of the lands. In late afternoon, however, we noted a concentration of visitors in Fantasyland, Liberty Square, and Frontierland, with a slight decrease of visitors in Adventureland, and a marked decrease of visitors in Tomorrowland (except for Space Mountain). This pattern did not occur consistently day to day, but did happen often enough for us to suggest Tomorrowland as the least crowded land for late afternoon touring.

3. *How do most visitors go about touring the park? Is there a difference in the touring behavior of first-time visitors versus repeat visitors?* Many first-time visitors are accompanied by friends or relatives familiar with the Magic Kingdom, who guide their tour. The tours sometimes do and sometimes do not proceed in an orderly touring sequence. First-time visitors without personal touring guides tend to be more orderly in their touring. Many first-time visitors, however, are drawn to Cinderella Castle upon entering the park and thus commence their rotation from Fantasyland. Repeat visitors usually proceed directly to their favorite attractions.

4. *What effect do special events, such as the parades and live shows, have on traffic patterns?* The parades pull huge numbers of guests away from an attraction's line and provides a window of opportunity for experiencing more popular attractions with less of a wait. Castle Forecourt shows also attract a lot of people but have only a slight effect on lines.

5. *What are the traffic patterns near to and at closing time?* On our sample days, in season and out of season, park departures outnumbered arrivals beginning mid-afternoon. Many visitors left during the late afternoon as the dinner hour approached. When the park closed early, there were steady departures during the two hours before closing time, with a huge exodus of remaining visitors at closing time. When the park closed late, the exodus immediately followed the early evening

parade and fireworks. Mass departures at closing time mainly affect conditions on Main Street and at the monorail and ferry stops, due to the crowds generated when the other six lands close. In the other six lands, touring conditions are normally uncrowded just before closing time.

6. *I have heard that when there are two or more lines, the shortest wait is always the left line. Is this true?*   We do not recommend the "left-line strategy" because, with the occasional exception of food lines, it simply does not hold up. The Disney people have a number of techniques for both internal and external crowd control which distribute line traffic nearly equally. Placing research team members at the same time in each available line, we could discern no consistent pattern as to who would be served first. Further, staffers entering the same attraction via different lines would almost always exit the attraction within 30 to 90 seconds of each other.

What does occasionally occur, however, is that guests will ignore a second line that has just been opened and persist in standing in the established line. As a rule, if you encounter a waiting area with two lines and no barrier to entry for either, and one line is empty or conspicuously less populated than the other, get in it.

Magic Kingdom Touring Plans

The Magic Kingdom Touring Plans are field-tested, step-by-step plans for seeing as much as possible in one day with a minimum of time wasted standing in line. They are designed to assist you in avoiding crowds and bottlenecks on days of moderate to heavy attendance. On days of lighter attendance (see "Selecting the Time of Year for Your Visit," page 32), the plans will still save you time, but will not be as critical to successful touring as on busier days. Do not be concerned that other people will be following the same touring strategy, thus rendering it useless. Fewer than 1 in every 500 people in the park will have been exposed to this information.

Choosing the Right Touring Plan

We present these six different Magic Kingdom Touring Plans:

- Magic Kingdom One-Day Touring Plan, for Adults

- Author's Selective Magic Kingdom One-Day Touring Plan, for Adults

- Magic Kingdom One-Day Touring Plan, for Parents with Small Children

- Magic Kingdom Dumbo-or-Die-in-a-Day Touring Plan, for Parents with Small Children

- Magic Kingdom Two-Day Touring Plan A, for When the Park Is Open Late

- Magic Kingdom Two-Day Touring Plan B, for Morning Touring and for When the Park Closes Early

If you have two days to spend at the Magic Kingdom, the two-day touring plans are by far the most relaxed and efficient. Two-Day Touring Plan B takes advantage of early morning touring when lines are short and the park has not yet filled with guests. This plan works well year-round, and is particularly recommended for days when the Magic Kingdom closes before 9 P.M. On the other hand, Two-Day Touring Plan A combines the efficiency of early morning touring on the first day with the splendor of the Magic Kingdom at night on the second day. The plan is perfect for guests who wish to sample both the attractions and the special atmosphere of the Magic Kingdom after dark, including parades and fireworks.

If you only have one day, but wish to see as much as possible, use the One-Day Touring Plan, for Adults. This plan packs as much into a single day as is humanly possible, but is pretty exhausting. If you prefer a more relaxed visit, try the Author's Selective One-Day Touring Plan. This plan features the best the Magic Kingdom has to offer (in the author's opinion), eliminating some of the less impressive attractions.

If you have children under eight years of age, you may want to use the One-Day Touring Plan, for Adults with Small Children. This plan represents a compromise, integrating the preferences of smaller children with those of older siblings and adults. The plan includes many of the children's rides in Fantasyland, but omits roller coaster rides and other attractions that are frightening, or that little ones cannot ride because of Disney height requirements. An alternative would be to use the One-Day Touring Plan, for Adults or the Author's Selective One-Day Touring Plan, and take advantage of switching off, a technique where children accompany adults to the loading area of a ride with age and height requirements but do not actually ride (see page 187). Switching off allows adults to enjoy the more adventuresome attractions while keeping the whole group together.

Finally, there is the Dumbo-or-Die-in-a-Day Touring Plan, for Parents with Small Children. This plan is designed for the peace of mind of parents who want to insure that no effort and sacrifice has been spared on behalf of the children. On the Dumbo-or-Die plan, adults pretty much just stand around, sweat, wipe noses, pay for stuff, and watch the children enjoy themselves. It's great.

Touring Plan Clip-out Pocket Outlines

For your convenience, we have prepared outline versions of all the Touring Plans presented in this guide. The Pocket Outline versions present the same touring itineraries as the detailed Touring Plans, but with vastly abbreviated directions. First, select the Touring Plan which is most appropriate for your party, then familiarize yourself with the detailed version of the Touring Plan. Once you understand how the Touring Plan works, clip out the Pocket Outline version of your selected Touring Plan from the back of this guide, and carry it with you as a quick reference when you visit the theme park.

The Single-Day Touring Conundrum

Touring the Magic Kingdom in a single day is complicated by the fact that the Magic Kingdom's two premier attractions, Splash Mountain and Space Mountain, are almost at opposite ends of the park, making it virtually impossible to ride both without encountering a line at one or the other. If you ride Space Mountain right after the park opens, you will ride without much, if any, wait. By the time you exit Space Mountain and hustle over to Frontierland, however, the line for Splash Mountain will have grown to substantial proportions. The same situation prevails if you ride Splash Mountain first: Splash Mountain, no problem; Space Mountain, a fair-sized line. From ten minutes after opening until just before closing, you can expect long waits at these headliner attractions.

The only effective way to ride both without waiting is to tour the Magic Kingdom in two days: ride Space Mountain first thing one morning and Splash Moutain first thing on the other. If you have only one day and are basically unwilling to suffer a lengthy wait (45 minutes to 2 hours) for these rides, you can do one of two things. Your first option is to ride one ride when the park opens and the other just before closing. Many guests who attempt this strategy fail, because they become too worn out to stay until near closing time.

The second option, which we recommend in the one-day touring plans, requires a lot of hustle and still involves one wait of 15–30 minutes. It is sort of a "bite the bullet" strategy, but all things considered, probably works best. Make sure you arrive early and rush straight to Space Mountain and ride. After Space Mountain, speed over to Frontierland and ride the Big Thunder Mountain Railroad (the park's third most popular thrill ride). When you leave Big Thunder, exit to your right and ride Splash Mountain, next door. If your group travels fast, your wait should be less than 5 minutes at Space Mountain, about 10 minutes at Big Thunder Mountain, and about 15–30 minutes at Splash Mountain. After riding Splash Mountain, you can be comforted by the knowledge that you have the most popular attractions and longest lines behind you.

This strategy takes advantage of what we call the morning lull, a period of about 30–45 minutes after the park opens, when those on hand at opening have been absorbed and new arrivals are comparatively few. While you are riding Space Mountain and Big Thunder Mountain, Splash Mountain is accommodating the crowd of early birds who rushed to that ride as soon as the Magic Kingdom opened. By the time you finish riding Space Mountain and Big Thunder Mountain, most of this first wave will have finished riding Splash Mountain. Because of the morning lull, the line at Splash Mountain will not have built up again and your wait will be comparatively brief.

Magic Kingdom Early Entry for Walt Disney World Resort Guests

Walt Disney World hotel and campground guests have the opportunity to enter the Magic Kingdom one hour before the general public on selected days of the week. Early entry guests can enjoy all the attractions in Fantasyland, as well as Space Mountain and, sometimes, the Grand Prix Raceway in Tomorrowland (the rest of the park remains closed until the general public is admitted). Disney resort guests have a huge advantage over the general public who must wait at the turnstiles for the park to open. Specifically, Disney resort guests can ride Space Mountain and all the attractions in Fantasyland to their hearts' content and hustle over to Splash Mountain when the other lands open. The head start puts them in a position to sail through the entire day without much waiting. Conversely, a guest who does not have early entry privileges will be at a considerable disadvantage. When admitted to the park, this guest will find Fantasyland and Tomorrowland already full of people and a large number of the early entry folks already spreading out into the other lands.

Take advantage of the early entry program if you are a Walt Disney World hotel or campground guest. Ride Space Mountain and all the Fantasyland attractions that interest you. If you have small children in your group, let them get their fill of Dumbo.

If you are not eligible for early entry, avoid morning touring at the Magic Kingdom on days when the program is in effect. If your schedule will not permit you to avoid these days, go immediately to Frontierland and ride Splash Mountain and Big Thunder Mountain as soon as the park opens. During the summer and holiday periods, be prepared to write off Space Mountain and Peter Pan. Lines for these attractions will already be quite long by the time you are admitted to the park, and will only continue to grow as the day progresses. If you are not eligible for early entry and will be spending two days at the Magic Kingdom, use our Two-Day Touring Plan A. Choose a non–early entry morning for the day that calls for morning touring.

—— Preliminary Instructions for All Magic Kingdom Touring Plans ——

On days of moderate to heavy attendance follow the Touring Plan of your choice exactly, deviating only:

1. *When you are not interested in an attraction called for on the Touring Plan.* For instance, the Touring Plan may indicate that you go next to Tomorrowland and ride Space Mountain, a roller coaster ride. If you do not enjoy roller coasters, simply skip this step of the plan and proceed to the next step.

2. *When you encounter a very long line at an attraction called for by the Touring Plan.* Crowds ebb and flow at the Magic Kingdom, and by chance an unusually large line may have gathered at an attraction to which you are directed. For example, upon arrival at The Haunted Mansion, you find the waiting lines to be extremely long. It is possible that this is a temporary situation occasioned by several hundred people arriving en masse from a recently concluded performance of *The Hall of Presidents* nearby. If this is the case, simply skip The Haunted Mansion and move to the next step, returning later in the day to try The Haunted Mansion once again.

Park Opening Procedures

Your success during your first hour of touring will be affected somewhat by the particular opening procedure the Disney people use that day.

A. Sometimes all guests are held at the turnstiles until the entire park opens (which may or may not be at the official opening time). If this is the case on the day you visit, blow right past Main Street and head for the first attraction on whatever Touring Plan you are following.

B. Sometimes guests are admitted to Main Street a half hour to an hour before the remaining lands open. Access to the other lands will be blocked by a rope barrier at the central hub end of Main

Street. Once admitted, move to the rope barrier and stake out a position as follows:

If you are going to Splash Mountain first, take up a position in front of the Crystal Palace restaurant, on the left at the central hub end of Main Street. Wait next to the rope barrier blocking the walkway to Adventureland. When the rope is dropped, move quickly to Frontierland (and Splash Mountain) by way of Adventureland.

If you are going to Space Mountain first, turn right at the end of Main Street and wait at the entrance of the Plaza Pavilion restaurant. When the rope drops at opening time, run *through* the Plaza Pavilion into Tomorrowland and then bear right to Space Mountain.

If you are going to Fantasyland or Liberty Square, proceed to the end of Main Street and line up left of center at the rope.

If you are going to Mickey's Starland first, go to the Main Street Station of the Walt Disney World Railroad and board the first train of the day. Get off at the second stop. The train pulls out of the Main Street Station at the same time the rope is dropped at the central hub end of Main Street.

C. If you are admitted on the early entry program for Disney hotel and campground guests, you will encounter little to no congestion at the entrance turnstiles. Be prepared to show your Disney guest I.D. as well as a valid admission pass. Once inside the park, you will be directed down Main Street (everything on Main Street will be closed) to the central hub, and from there to Fantasyland. With early entry, you will rarely experience the crush associated with opening the park to the general public. Proceed leisurely to Fantasyland and from there (if you want to ride Space Mountain) to Tomorrowland.

Before You Go

1. Call (407) 824-4321 the day before you go for the official opening time. At the same time, determine whether the early entry program for Walt Disney World resort guests will be in effect the day you plan to visit.
2. Purchase admission prior to your arrival. You can either order tickets through the mail before you leave home or buy them at the Disney Store in your local mall, the Walt Disney World Information Center off I-75 near Ocala (north of Orlando), the Disney

Store in the Orlando airport, or at Walt Disney World lodging properties.

3. Become familiar with the park opening procedures (described above) and read over the Touring Plan you've chosen so that you will have an understanding of what you are likely to encounter.

NOTE: The renovation of Tomorrowland is scheduled to begin sometime during the next 18 months. One plan under discussion is to close all of Tomorrowland for the duration of the construction. If this happens during your visit, simply omit those steps in the Touring Plan which pertain to Tomorrowland.

—— *Magic Kingdom One-Day Touring Plan, for Adults* ——

FOR: **Adults without small children.**

ASSUMES: Willingness to experience all major rides (including roller coasters) and shows.

Be forewarned that this plan requires a lot of walking and some backtracking; this is necessary to avoid some long waits in line. A little extra walking coupled with some hustle in the morning will save you from two to three hours of standing in line. Note also that you might not complete the tour. How far you get will depend on how quickly you move from ride to ride, how many times you pause for rest or food, how quickly the park fills, and what time the park closes. With a little zip and some luck, it is possible to complete the Touring Plan even on a busy day when the park closes early.

1. Arrive at the Magic Kingdom's parking lot 50 minutes before the park's stated opening time. This will give you time to park and catch the tram to the Transportation and Ticket Center (TTC). Arrive an hour earlier than opening time if it is a holiday period or you must purchase your admission.

2. If the line for the monorail is short, take the monorail; otherwise catch the ferry.

3. When you arrive at the Magic Kingdom, proceed through the entry turnstiles. Split your party up. Have one person go to the Hospitality House (across the square from City Hall) to make reservations for the 12:15 P.M. (or there about) seating of *The Diamond Horseshoe Jamboree* (show and lunch). Have another person stop at City Hall for park maps and a copy of the daily entertainment schedule.

4. Regroup and move as fast as you can down Main Street to the central hub. Because the Magic Kingdom uses two basic procedures when opening the park to the general public, you will probably encounter one of the following:

a. The entire park will be open. If this is the case, proceed quickly to Space Mountain in Tomorrowland.

b. Only Main Street will be open. In this case, turn right at the end of Main Street (before you reach the central hub), past the Plaza Ice Cream Parlor and the Plaza Restaurant, and stake out a place for your group at the entrance of the Plaza Pavilion. When the rope barrier is dropped at opening time, jog through the Plaza Pavilion and on to Space Mountain. Starting at the entrance to the Plaza Pavilion will give you about a 100-yard head start over anyone coming from the central hub. Ride Space Mountain.

NOTE: If you are a Walt Disney World resort guest and enter the park on an early entry day, ride Space Mountain and see as much of Fantasyland as possible. As the time approaches for the park to open to the public, position yourself at the boundary of Fantasyland and Liberty Square. When the other lands open, head for Frontierland via the Liberty Square waterfront. Pick up the Touring Plan at Big Thunder Mountain, skipping past any steps that direct you to attractions experienced during your early entry hour.

5. Leave Tomorrowland via the central hub and enter Liberty Square. Turn left and proceed along the waterfront to Big Thunder Mountain. Ride.
6. Exit Big Thunder to the right and go next door to Splash Mountain.
7. Exit Splash Mountain to the right and enter Adventureland. Ride the Jungle Cruise.
8. Leave Adventureland and go to Fantasyland via the central hub. Ride Snow White's Adventures.
9. While in Fantasyland, ride Peter Pan's Flight.
10. Exit Peter Pan to the left and return to Liberty Square. Bear right at the waterfront and go to The Haunted Mansion.
11. Leave The Haunted Mansion and follow the waterfront back around to Frontierland. While in Frontierland, see *Country Bear Jamboree*.
12. Head in the direction of Splash Mountain and return to Adventureland to ride Pirates of the Caribbean.

NOTE: This is about as far as you can go on a busy day before the crowds catch up with you, but you will have experienced nine of the more popular rides and shows and cleared almost all of the Magic Kingdom's traffic bottlenecks. Note also that you are doing a considerable amount of walking and some back-tracking. Do not be dismayed; the extra walking will save you as much as two hours of standing in line. Remember, during the morning (through Step 12) keep moving. In the afternoon, adjust the pace to your liking.

13. Unless you ran into some bad luck, you should be within a half hour or so of your 12:15 P.M. seating at *The Diamond Horseshoe Jamboree* in Frontierland. If you have completed the touring plan through Step 12 before noon, and have a half hour or more to kill, go ahead and ride the Liberty Square Riverboat before you head for the *Jamboree*. If, however, you did not make it to Step 12 before *Diamond Horseshoe* time, simply pick up the Touring Plan wherever you left off following the show.

14. If you did not make reservations for *The Diamond Horseshoe Jamboree*, go ahead and eat lunch at El Pirata Y el Perico, a decent but often overlooked eatery, in Adventureland around the corner from Frontierland's Pecos Bill Cafe.

15. After lunch go next door to Liberty Square and check out *The Hall of Presidents* and the Liberty Square Riverboat. If either is within ten minutes of getting underway, choose the one with the shortest wait. If the wait for both exceeds ten minutes, and you missed The Haunted Mansion before lunch, try to see it now. When you have experienced all three of these attractions, proceed to Step 16.

16. Leave Liberty Square and return to Frontierland. Pass into Adventureland using the passage which runs between the Frontierland Shootin' Gallery and the wood carving shop. See *Tropical Serenade (Enchanted Tiki Birds)*.

17. While in Adventureland, explore the Swiss Family Treehouse.

18. Turn left on exiting the Treehouse, pass by the Pirates of the Caribbean, and head for the Frontierland Station of the Walt Disney World Railroad. Take the train one stop to Mickey's Starland.

19. In Mickey's Starland, walk through Mickey's House to see a performance of *Mickey's Starland Show*.

20. After the show, go to Mickey's Hollywood Theater to meet and photograph Mickey. If this is something you want to do, read the Touring Tips for *Mickey's Starland Show* to help you avoid a long wait.

21. Exit Mickey's Starland along the path to Fantasyland. In Fantasyland, see *Magic Journeys*.

22. While in Fantasyland, ride It's a Small World.

23. Go to Tomorrowland via the Skyway from Fantasyland (if the line is not long) or on foot. In Tomorrowland, ride the WEDway PeopleMover.

24. While in Tomorrowland, see the *Carousel of Progress*.

25. Try Dreamflight, also in Tomorrowland.

26. Proceed toward the central hub entrance to Tomorrowland and experience the *Mission to Mars*. If the wait for this attraction exceeds 15 minutes, skip it.

27. Walk across the street and see *American Journeys*.

28. If you have some time left before closing, backtrack to pick up attractions you may have missed or bypassed because the lines were too long. Check out any parades, fireworks, or live performances that interest you. Grab a bite to eat. Save Main Street until last since it remains open after the rest of the park closes.

29. Continue to tour until everything closes except Main Street. Finish your day by browsing along Main Street.

30. If you leave the park at closing time, the monorail to the TTC will be mobbed. Either take the ferry or board a monorail to the Polynesian Resort and from there take the short walkway to the TTC.

NOTE: Sometimes Walt Disney World monorail personnel ask for proof that you are a guest at one of the monorail-connected hotels before allowing you to board. As restaurants, bars, shows, and shops in the hotels are open to the public this request for guest documentation is inconsistent and, in our opinion, totally out of line. Until the hotel shops and restaurants are declared off-limits to all but guests in residence, you have a perfect right to ride the hotel monorail. Stand your ground.

Author's Selective Magic Kingdom One-Day Touring Plan, for Adults

FOR: **Adults touring without small children.**

ASSUMES: Willingness to experience all major rides (including roller coasters) and shows.

This Touring Plan is selective and includes only those attractions which, in the author's opinion, represent the best the Magic Kingdom has to offer. Be forewarned that this plan requires a lot of walking and some backtracking; this is necessary to avoid some long waits in line. A little extra walking coupled with some hustle in the morning will save you from two to three hours of standing in line. Note also that you might not complete the tour. How far you get will depend on how quickly you move from ride to ride, how many times you pause for rest or food, how quickly the park fills, and what time the park closes. With a little zip and some luck, it is possible to complete the Touring Plan even on a busy day when the park closes early.

1. Arrive at the Magic Kingdom's parking lot 50 minutes before the park's stated opening time. This will give you time to park and catch the tram to the Transportation and Ticket Center (TTC). Arrive an hour earlier than opening time if it is a holiday period or you must purchase your admission.

2. If the line for the monorail is short, take the monorail; otherwise catch the ferry.

3. When you arrive at the Magic Kingdom, proceed through the entry turnstiles. Split your party up. Have one person go to the Hospitality House (across the square from City Hall) to make reservations for the 12:15 P.M. seating of *The Diamond Horseshoe Jamboree* (show and lunch). Have another person stop at City Hall for park maps and a copy of the daily entertainment schedule.

4. Regroup and move as fast as you can down Main Street to the central hub. Because the Magic Kingdom uses two basic procedures when opening the park to the general public, you will probably encounter one of the following:

a. The entire park will be open. If this is the case, proceed quickly to Space Mountain in Tomorrowland.

b. Only Main Street will be open. In this case, turn right at the end of Main Street (before you reach the central hub), past the Plaza Ice Cream Parlor and the Plaza Restaurant, and stake out a place for your group at the entrance of the Plaza Pavilion. When the rope barrier is dropped at opening time, jog through the Plaza Pavilion and on to Space Mountain. Starting at the entrance to the Plaza Pavilion will give you about a 100-yard head start and an advantage over anyone coming from the central hub. Ride Space Mountain.

NOTE: If you are a Walt Disney World resort guest and enter the park on an early entry day, ride Space Mountain and see as much of Fantasyland as possible. As the time approaches for the park to open to the public, position yourself at the boundary of Fantasyland and Liberty Square. When the other lands open, head for Frontierland via the Liberty Square waterfront. Pick up the Touring Plan at Big Thunder Mountain, skipping steps that direct you to attractions experienced during your early entry hour.

5. Leave Tomorrowland via the central hub and enter Liberty Square. Turn left and proceed along the waterfront to Big Thunder Mountain. Ride.

6. Exit Big Thunder to the right and go next door to Splash Mountain.

7. Exit Splash Mountain to the right and enter Adventureland. Ride the Jungle Cruise.

8. Leave Adventureland and go to Fantasyland via the central hub. Ride Peter Pan's Flight.

9. Exit Peter Pan to the left and return to Liberty Square. Bear right at the waterfront and go to The Haunted Mansion.

10. Leave The Haunted Mansion and follow the waterfront back around to Frontierland. While in Frontierland, see *Country Bear Jamboree*.

11. Head in the direction of Splash Mountain and return to Adventureland to ride Pirates of the Caribbean.

NOTE: This is about as far as you can go on a busy day before the crowds catch up with you, but you will have experienced eight of the more popular rides and shows and cleared almost all of the Magic Kingdom's traffic bottlenecks. Note also that you are doing a considerable amount of walking and some backtracking. Do not be dismayed; the extra walking will save you as much as two hours of standing in line. Remember, during the morning (through Step 11) keep moving. In the afternoon, adjust the pace to your liking.

12. Unless you ran into some bad luck, you should be within a half hour or so of your 12:15 P.M. seating at *The Diamond Horseshoe Jamboree* in Frontierland. If you have completed the touring plan through Step 11 before noon, and have a half hour or more to kill, go ahead and ride the Liberty Square Riverboat before you head for the *Jamboree*. If, however, you did not make it to Step 11 before *Diamond Horseshoe* time, simply pick up the Touring Plan wherever you left off following the show.

13. If you did not make reservations for *The Diamond Horseshoe Jamboree*, go ahead and eat lunch at El Pirata Y el Perico, a decent but often overlooked eatery, in Adventureland around the corner from Frontierland's Pecos Bill Cafe.

14. After lunch go next door to Liberty Square and check out *The Hall of Presidents* and the Liberty Square Riverboat. If either is within ten minutes of getting underway, choose the one with the shortest wait. If the wait for both exceeds ten minutes, and you missed The Haunted Mansion before lunch, try to see it now. When you have experienced all three of these attractions, proceed to Step 15.

15. Return to Frontierland. Take the Walt Disney Railroad to Mickey's Starland.

16. In Mickey's Starland, walk through Mickey's House to see a performance of *Mickey's Starland Show*.

NOTE: Check your daily entertainment schedule to see if there are any parades, live performances, fireworks, or other events you would like to integrate into your schedule. If so, simply interrupt the Touring Plan and pick up where you left off after the event is over.

17. Exit Mickey's Starland along the path to Fantasyland. In Fantasyland, see *Magic Journeys*.
18. Exit *Magic Journeys* to the left and cross the courtyard. Ride It's a Small World.
19. Go to Tomorrowland via the Skyway from Fantasyland (if the line is not long) or on foot.
20. While in Tomorrowland, see the *Carousel of Progress*.
21. Ride Dreamflight, also in Tomorrowland.
22. Go next door and see *American Journeys*.
23. Leave Tomorrowland via the central hub and proceed to Adventureland. See *Tropical Serenade (Enchanted Tiki Birds)*.
24. Turn left after *Tropical Serenade* and proceed to the Swiss Family Treehouse.
25. If you have some time left before closing, backtrack to pick up attractions you may have missed or bypassed because the lines were too long. Check out any parades, fireworks, or live performances that interest you. Grab a bite to eat. Save Main Street until last since it remains open after the rest of the park closes.
26. Continue to tour until everything closes except Main Street. Finish your day by browsing along Main Street.
27. If you leave the park at closing time, the monorail to the TTC will be mobbed. Either take the ferry or board a monorail to the Polynesian Resort and from there take the short walkway to the TTC. See note on page 282.

Magic Kingdom One-Day Touring Plan, for Parents with Small Children

FOR: **Parents with children under 8 years of age.**

ASSUMES: Periodic stops for rest, rest rooms, and refreshment.

This Touring Plan represents a compromise between the observed tastes of adults and the observed tastes of younger children. Included in this Touring Plan are many amusement park rides which children may have the opportunity to experience (although in less exotic surroundings) at local fairs and amusement parks. Though these rides are included in the Touring Plan, we suggest, nevertheless, that they be omitted if possible. The following cycle-loading rides often require long waits in line, consuming valuable touring time:

Mad Tea Party	Dumbo, the Flying Elephant
Cinderella's Golden Carrousel	StarJets

This time could be better spent experiencing the many attractions which best demonstrate the Disney creative genius and are only found in the Magic Kingdom. As an alternative to this Touring Plan, we suggest trying either of the One-Day Plans for Adults and taking advantage of "switching off." This allows parents and small children to enter the ride together. At the boarding area, the parents take turns watching the children while the other rides.

The big decision you need to make before going to the Magic Kingdom is whether you will come back to your hotel for a rest in the middle of the day. We strongly recommend that you break off your tour and return to your hotel for a swim and a nap (even if you are not lodging in Walt Disney World). True, you will not see as much, but what's more important: keeping everyone relaxed, fresh, and happy, or trying to see everything?

Be forewarned that this Touring Plan requires a lot of walking and some backtracking; this is necessary to avoid long waits in line. A little extra walking will save you from two to three hours of standing in line. Note also that you may not complete the tour. How far you get will depend on how quickly you move from ride to ride, how many times

287

you pause for rest or food, how quickly the park fills, and what time the park closes. With a little hustle and some luck, it is possible to complete the Touring Plan even on a busy day when the park closes early.

1. Arrive at the Magic Kingdom's parking lot at least 50 minutes before the stated opening time. Arrive an hour earlier than opening time if it is a holiday period or you must purchase your admission.

2. Take the monorail to the Magic Kingdom. When the gates open, enter the park.

3. If you intend to leave the park in the middle of the day for a rest break, rent strollers, if necessary; pick up a daily entertainment schedule; and proceed to Step 4. If you plan to remain in the park for the day, the most relaxing way to have lunch is to attend *The Diamond Horseshoe Jamboree*. Have one person in your party make reservations at the Hospitality House (through the Main Street Station and to your immediate right) for the 12:15 P.M. seating of the *Jamboree* while the rest of the family goes to rent a stroller, if necessary. Regroup at the Hospitality House and pick up a daily entertainment schedule.

4. Move quickly to the end of Main Street. If the entire park is open, proceed quickly to Fantasyland. Otherwise, take a position by the rope barrier at the central hub. When the barrier is dropped, go through the main door of the castle and ride Dumbo, the Flying Elephant.

   NOTE: If you are a Walt Disney World resort guest and are admitted to the park early, ride Peter Pan's Flight; 20,000 Leagues Under the Sea; Cinderella's Golden Carrousel; Mr. Toad's Wild Ride; the Mad Tea Party; and, if operating, the Grand Prix Raceway in Tomorrowland. As the time approaches for the park to open to the public, position yourself at the boundary of Fantasyland and Liberty Square. When the other lands open, head for Liberty Square. Pick up the Touring Plan at (step 8), skipping past steps that direct you to attractions you experienced during your early entry hour.

5. While in Fantasyland, ride 20,000 Leagues Under the Sea.
6. While in Fantasyland, ride Mr. Toad's Wild Ride.
7. While in Fantasyland, also ride Peter Pan's Flight.

8. Exit left out of Peter Pan and head toward Liberty Square. In Liberty Square, turn right at the waterfront and go to The Haunted Mansion.

9. Leave Liberty Square and enter Frontierland. Move on to Adventureland via the passageway between the Frontierland Shootin' Gallery and Frontierland Wood Carving. In Adventureland, ride the Jungle Cruise.

10. Exit left from the Jungle Cruise, and ride Pirates of the Caribbean.

11. Turn left out of Pirates of the Caribbean and then turn right into Frontierland.

12. Unless you ran into some bad luck, you should be within a half-hour or so of your 12:15 P.M. seating at *The Diamond Horseshoe Jamboree*. If you have 35 minutes or more remaining before seating time, go ahead and enjoy the *Country Bear Jamboree*. Do not, however, risk your *Diamond Horseshoe* reservations by arriving late. Your seats will be given to someone else. If you do not have time for the *Country Bear Jamboree* before your seating, go right after lunch and the *Diamond Horseshoe* show.

    If you did not make reservations at the *Diamond Horseshoe,* go ahead and see the *Country Bear Jamboree*. After the show, return to Main Street (you can walk or take the railroad) and leave the park for lunch and an afternoon rest break at your hotel. Be sure to have your hand stamped for reentry as you leave. Also hang onto your parking receipt so you won't have to pay for parking again when you come back. Return refreshed to the Magic Kingdom at about 3:30 or 4 P.M.; once inside the park, walk or take the train to Frontierland and proceed to Step 13.

13. In Frontierland, take the raft to Tom Sawyer Island. Children will play here all day, so set some limits based on the park's closing time, your energy level, and how many more attractions you wish to experience.

14. Return via raft from Tom Sawyer Island and go to the Frontierland Railroad Station. Catch the Walt Disney World Railroad to Mickey's Starland.

15. Get off the train at Mickey's Starland. Go see *Mickey's Starland Show* (enter through Mickey's House). After the show, visit Mickey in his dressing room at Mickey's Hollywood Theater (see pages 238–39 for instructions on avoiding a long wait).

Next enjoy the playground and Grandma Duck's Petting Farm.

16. Exit Mickey's Starland via the path to Fantasyland. In Fantasyland, see *Magic Journeys*.

17. While in Fantasyland, ride It's a Small World.

18. Exit Fantasyland via the Skyway (if not too crowded) or on foot by way of the Castle and central hub and go to Tomorrowland. Ride Dreamflight.

19. While in Tomorrowland, ride the WEDway PeopleMover.

20. Enjoy *Carousel of Progress*, also in Tomorrowland.

21. Head back toward the entrance of Tomorrowland and try *Mission to Mars*. Skip this attraction if the wait exceeds 15 minutes.

22. Cross the street and see *American Journeys*.

23. If you have any time or energy left, catch a live performance, grab a bite, or try any attractions you might have missed using the Touring Plan.

24. Save touring Main Street until last, since it stays open later than the rest of the park.

25. If you are parked at the Transportation and Ticket Center (TTC), catch the ferry or ride the monorail to the Polynesian Resort and then proceed to the TTC via the short connecting walkway (see note on page 282).

Magic Kingdom Dumbo-or-Die-in-a-Day Touring Plan, for Parents with Small Children

FOR: Adults who feel compelled to devote every waking moment to the pleasure and entertainment of their small children, or rich people who are paying someone else to take their children to the theme park.

PREREQUISITE: This Touring Plan is designed for days when the Magic Kingdom does not close until 9 P.M. or later.

ASSUMES: Frequent stops for rest, rest rooms, and refreshment.

NOTE: The name of the Touring Plan notwithstanding, this itinerary is not a joke. Regardless of whether you are loving, guilty, masochistic, truly selfless, insane, or saintly, this Touring Plan will provide a small child with about as perfect a day as is possible at the Magic Kingdom.

This Touring Plan is a concession to those adults who are determined, even if it kills them, to give their small children the ultimate Magic Kingdom experience. The Touring Plan addresses the preferences, needs, and desires of small children to the virtual exclusion of those of adults or older siblings. If you left the kids with a sitter yesterday or wouldn't let little Marvin eat barbeque for breakfast, this is the perfect plan for expiating your guilt. This is also a wonderful Touring Plan if you are paying a sitter, nanny, or chauffeur to take your children to the Magic Kingdom.

1. Arrive at the Magic Kingdom's parking lot at least 50 minutes before the park's stated opening time. Arrive an hour earlier than opening time if you must purchase your ticket.
2. Take the monorail to the Magic Kingdom.
3. Enter the park and rent a stroller, if needed.
4. Move quickly to the end of Main Street. If the entire park is open, proceed quickly to Fantasyland. Otherwise, take a position by the rope barrier at the central hub. When the barrier is dropped, go through the main door of the castle to King Stefan's Banquet Hall (see Step 5).

NOTE: If you are a Walt Disney World resort guest and are admitted to the park early, ride Peter Pan's Flight; 20,000 Leagues Under the Sea; Cinderella's Golden Carrousel; Mr. Toad's Wild Ride; the Mad Tea Party; and, if operating, the Grand Prix Raceway in Tomorrowland. As the time approaches for the park to open to the public, position yourself at the boundary of Fantasyland and Liberty Square. When the other lands open, remain in Tomorrowland and pick up the Touring Plan at Step 14. Skip any subsequent steps that direct you to attractions experienced during your early entry hour.

5. At King Stefan's (on your right as you enter Cinderella Castle), make dinner reservations for 7 P.M. This will give your kids a chance to see the inside of the castle and to meet Cinderella. If you are a guest at a Walt Disney World hotel or campground, you can make your reservation one to three days in advance by dialing 56 (45 for campground guests).

6. Go next to Dumbo, the Flying Elephant and ride.

7. Hey, you're on vacation! Ride again (using the Bubba Relay if there are two adults in your party; see page 189).

8. While in Fantasyland, ride 20,000 Leagues Under the Sea.

9. Next, ride Mr. Toad's Wild Ride, also in Fantasyland (back toward Dumbo).

10. Ride Peter Pan's Flight, also in Fantasyland.

11. Ride Cinderella's Golden Carrousel, also in Fantasyland.

12. Bearing left toward Liberty Square, go to the Skyway. Ride to Tomorrowland.

13. In Tomorrowland, ride the Grand Prix Raceway. Let your child control the steering wheel (cars run on a guide rail) while you work the foot pedal.

14. Also in Tomorrowland, ride StarJets. Safety note: Seat your children in the plane before you get in.

15. While in Tomorrowland, ride Dreamflight (near StarJets).

16. Exit Tomorrowland via the central hub and return to Main Street. Leave the park and return to your hotel for lunch, a nice nap, and even a swim. Have your hand stamped for reentry when you leave the Magic Kingdom, and make sure (if you have a car) that you hang onto your parking receipt so you will not be charged for parking when you return.

17. Return to the Magic Kingdom refreshed at about 4 or 4:30 P.M. Take the Walt Disney World Railroad to Frontierland.

18. In Frontierland, take the raft to Tom Sawyer Island. Stay as long as the kids want.
19. After you return from the island, see the *Country Bear Jamboree,* also in Frontierland.
20. Return to Frontierland Station. Take the train to Mickey's Starland.
21. Walk through Mickey's House and see *Mickey's Starland Show.* If you want to meet Mickey after the show, follow the Touring Tips for *Mickey's Starland Show* on pages 238–39.
22. After you see the show and meet Mickey, go pet some animals at Grandma Duck's Petting Farm, also in Mickey's Starland.
23. Right next to the farm is a nice playground. Try it out.
24. Check your watch. You should be within an hour or less of your dinner reservations at King Stefan's. Proceed to Fantasyland. If you have 20 minutes before your seating, ride It's a Small World (don't forget to sing). If you are way too early for your reservation, see *Magic Journeys* before you ride It's a Small World.

    NOTE: In our opinion the main dishes at King Stefan's are average at best, totally unappetizing at worst, and expensive regardless. Try to get by with a salad for yourself and a hot dog and alphabet fries for the kids. Or better yet, just order dessert. If you plan to make an early night of it, let the kids eat while you have coffee. Later, back at your hotel, you can order a pizza.

25. After dinner, enjoy *Magic Journeys* and/or It's a Small World if you missed them earlier.
26. Leave Fantasyland and go to Liberty Square. If your children are up to it, try The Haunted Mansion. If not, skip to the next step.
27. The evening parade is quite worthwhile. If you are interested, adjust the remainder of the Touring Plan to allow you to take up a viewing position about ten minutes before the parade starts (usually 9 P.M.). See our recommendations for good vantage points on page 258. If the parade doesn't excite you, enjoy the attractions in Adventureland while the parade is in progress. The lines will be vastly diminished.
28. Either via Liberty Square and Frontierland or by way of the central hub, go to Adventureland. Take the Jungle Cruise if the wait is not prohibitive. If the line for the Jungle Cruise is too intimidating, try the *Tropical Serenade* and/or the Swiss Family

Treehouse. If you think your children can stand a few skeletons, Pirates of the Caribbean is also in Adventureland.

29. If you have time or energy left, repeat any attractions the kids especially liked or try ones you might have missed using the Touring Plan. Buy some Goofy hats if that cranks your tractor.

30. This concludes the Touring Plan. If you are parked at the Transportation and Ticket Center (a.k.a. the main parking lot) catch the ferry; or ride the monorail to the Polynesian Resort and hoof it over to the TTC via the short connecting walkway (see note on page 282 and diagram on page 134).

FOR: **Parties who want to enjoy the Magic Kingdom at different times of day,** including evenings and early mornings.

ASSUMES: Willingness to experience all major rides (including roller coasters) and shows.

TIMING: This two-day Touring Plan is for those visiting the Magic Kingdom on days when the park is open late (after 8 P.M.). The plan offers morning touring on one day and late afternoon and evening touring on the other day. If the park closes early, or if you prefer to do all your touring during the morning and early afternoon, use the Magic Kingdom Two-Day Touring Plan B on page 300. If you do not have early entry privileges, schedule Day-One of this Touring Plan for a day when early entry is *not* in effect.

Day One

1. Arrive at the Magic Kingdom's parking lot 50 minutes before the park's stated opening time. This will give you time to park and catch the tram to the Transportation and Ticket Center (TTC). Arrive an hour earlier than opening time if it is a holiday period or you must purchase your admission.

2. If the line for the monorail is short, take the monorail; otherwise catch the ferry.

3. When you arrive at the Magic Kingdom, proceed through the entry turnstiles. Split your party up. Have one person go to the Hospitality House (across the square from City Hall) to make reservations for the 12:15 P.M. seating of *The Diamond Horseshoe Jamboree* (show and lunch). Have another person stop at City Hall for park maps and a copy of the daily entertainment schedule.

4. Regroup and move as fast as you can down Main Street to the central hub. Because the Magic Kingdom uses two basic procedures when opening the park to the general public, you will probably encounter one of the following:

a. The entire park will be open. If this is the case, proceed quickly to Space Mountain in Tomorrowland.

b. Only Main Street will be open. In this case, turn right at the end of Main Street (before you reach the central hub), past the Plaza Ice Cream Parlor and the Plaza Restaurant, and stake out a place for your group at the entrance of the Plaza Pavilion. When the rope barrier is dropped at opening time, jog through the Plaza Pavilion and on to Space Mountain. Starting at the entrance to the Plaza Pavilion will give you about a 100-yard head start and an advantage over anyone coming from the central hub. Ride Space Mountain.

NOTE: If you are a Walt Disney World resort guest and enter the park on an early entry day, ride Space Mountain and see as much of Fantasyland as possible. As the time approaches for the park to open to the public, position yourself at the boundary of Fantasyland and Liberty Square. When the other lands open, head for Frontierland via the Liberty Square waterfront. Pick up the Touring Plan at Big Thunder Mountain, skipping steps that direct you to attractions experienced during your early entry hour.

5. Leave Tomorrowland via the central hub and enter Liberty Square. Turn left and proceed along the waterfront to Big Thunder Mountain. Ride.

6. Exit Big Thunder to the right and go next door to Splash Mountain.

7. Exit Splash Mountain to the right and enter Adventureland. Ride the Jungle Cruise.

8. Leave Adventureland and go to Fantasyland via the central hub. Ride Peter Pan's Flight.

9. Exit Peter Pan to the left and return to Liberty Square. Bear right at the waterfront and go to The Haunted Mansion.

10. Leave The Haunted Mansion and follow the waterfront back around to Frontierland. While in Frontierland, see *Country Bear Jamboree*.

11. Head in the direction of Splash Mountain and return to Adventureland to ride Pirates of the Caribbean.

NOTE: This is about as far as you can go on a busy day before the crowds catch up with you, but you will have experienced eight of the more popular rides and shows and cleared almost all of the Magic Kingdom's traffic bottlenecks. Note also that you are doing a considerable amount of walking and some backtracking. Do not be dismayed; the extra walking will save you as much as two hours of standing in line. Remember, during the morning (through Step 11) keep moving. In the afternoon, adjust the pace to your liking.

12. Unless you ran into some bad luck, you should be within a half hour or so of your 12:15 P.M. seating at *The Diamond Horseshoe Jamboree* in Frontierland. If you have completed the touring plan through Step 11 before noon, and have a half hour or more to kill, go ahead and ride the Liberty Square Riverboat before you head for the *Jamboree*. If, however, you did not make it to Step 11 before *Diamond Horseshoe* time, simply pick up the Touring Plan wherever you left off following the show.

13. If you did not make reservations for *The Diamond Horseshoe Jamboree*, go ahead and eat lunch at El Pirata Y el Perico, a decent but often overlooked eatery in Adventureland around the corner from Frontierland's Pecos Bill Cafe.

14. After lunch go next door to Liberty Square and check out *The Hall of Presidents* and the Liberty Square Riverboat. If either is within ten minutes of getting underway, choose the one with the shortest wait. When you have experienced both of these attractions, proceed to Step 15.

15. At the Frontierland waterfront, take a raft to Tom Sawyer Island.

16. After exploring the island, return to the mainland and proceed to Frontierland Station.

17. Take the train to Mickey's Starland.

18. In Mickey's Starland, walk through Mickey's House to see a performance of *Mickey's Starland Show*.

19. After the show you can visit Mickey's Hollywood Theater to meet and photograph Mickey. If this is something you want to do, read the Touring Tips for *Mickey's Starland Show* to help you avoid a long wait (pages 238–39).

20. Return to the Mickey's Starland Station and ride the train to Main Street.

21. Before you leave the Magic Kingdom, browse along Main Street.

22. If for some reason (shopping, eating, parades, etc.) you think you might return to the Magic Kingdom that evening or you plan to visit EPCOT Center or the Disney-MGM Studios, have your hand stamped as you exit.

Day Two

1. If you want to see the afternoon parade, arrive at the TTC at about 2 P.M. If the afternoon parade does not interest you, arrive at the TTC at about 4:30 P.M. and skip Step 3.
2. Take the ferry to the Magic Kingdom if it is in port, otherwise catch the monorail.
3. Enter the Magic Kingdom and pick a good spot to watch the afternoon parade. The earlier you arrive, the better your vantage point will be (see parade suggestions on page 258).
4. After the parade, make dinner reservations at the Liberty Tree Tavern in Liberty Square if you want to have a full-service dinner in the park. For other dining options, see Step 13.
5. Next, head for Fantasyland. See *Magic Journeys*.
6. Turn left after *Magic Journeys* and ride It's a Small World.
7. Turn right after exiting, proceed to the Skyway, and ride to Tomorrowland. If the wait for the Skyway is too long, walk to Tomorrowland.
8. While in Tomorrowland, ride the WEDway PeopleMover.
9. Try the *Carousel of Progress*, also in Tomorrowland.
10. In Tomorrowland, also ride Dreamflight.
11. Proceed toward the central hub entrance to Tomorrowland and experience the *Mission to Mars*.
12. Walk across the street and view *American Journeys*.
13. If you are hungry, leave Tomorrowland and proceed via the central hub to The Crystal Palace in Main Street for dinner. The best choice for a full-service meal in the park is the Liberty Tree Tavern in Liberty Square. For a more leisurely meal, leave the park (get your hand stamped for reentry) and take the monorail to one of the Magic Kingdom resort hotels for dinner. If you wish to limit your time outside the park to a minimum, try the buffet at the Contemporary Cafe in the Contemporary Resort.

    NOTE: At this point check your daily entertainment schedule to see if there are any parades, fireworks, or live performances which interest you. Make note of the times and alter the Touring

Plan accordingly. Since you have already seen all the attractions that cause bottlenecks and have big lines, an interruption of the Touring Plan here will not cause you any problems. Simply pick up where you left off before the parade or show. The evening parade and the Fantasy in the Sky fireworks are particularly worthwhile.

14. After dinner, proceed to Adventureland and tour the Swiss Family Treehouse.
15. While in Adventureland, see the *Tropical Serenade (Enchanted Tiki Birds)*.
16. If you have some time left before closing, backtrack to any attractions you may have missed, such as 20,000 Leagues Under the Sea in Fantasyland, or bypassed because the lines were too long. Explore the shops, but save Main Street until last since it remains open after the rest of the park closes.
17. In the hour just before closing, lines range from short to non-existent for almost all attractions. If you have a favorite ride you would enjoy experiencing one more time, try it now.
18. Continue touring until everything closes except Main Street. Finish your day by browsing along Main Street.
19. If you leave the park at closing time, the monorail to the TTC will be mobbed. Either take the ferry or board a monorail to the Polynesian Resort and from there take the short walkway to the TTC. See note on page 282.

— Magic Kingdom Two-Day Touring Plan B, for Morning Touring and for When the Park Closes Early —

FOR: **Parties wishing to spread their Magic Kingdom visit over two days and parties preferring to tour in the morning.**

ASSUMES: Willingness to experience all major rides (including roller coasters) and shows.

TIMING: The following two-day Touring Plan takes advantage of early morning touring. On each day you should complete the structured part of the plan by about 3 P.M. or so. If you are visiting the Magic Kingdom during a period of the year when the park is open late (after 8 P.M.), you might prefer our alternate two-day Touring Plan which offers morning touring on one day and late afternoon and evening touring on the other day. If you are not a Walt Disney World resort or campground guest, schedule both days of this Touring Plan for mornings when the early entry program (for resort guests) in not in effect.

Day One

1. Arrive at the Magic Kingdom's parking lot 50 minutes before the park's stated opening time. This will give you time to park and catch the tram to the Transportation and Ticket Center (TTC). Arrive an hour earlier than opening time if it is a holiday period or you must purchase your admission.

2. If the line for the monorail is short, take the monorail; otherwise catch the ferry.

3. When you arrive at the Magic Kingdom, proceed through the entry turnstiles. Split your party up. Have one person go to the Hospitality House (across the square from City Hall) to make reservations for the 12:15 P.M. seating of *The Diamond Horseshoe Jamboree* (show and lunch). Have another person stop at City Hall for park maps and a copy of the daily entertainment schedule.

4. Regroup and move as fast as you can down Main Street to the

central hub. Because the Magic Kingdom uses two basic procedures when opening the park to the general public, you will probably encounter one of the following:

    a. The entire park will be open. If this is the case, proceed quickly to Space Mountain in Tomorrowland.

    b. Only Main Street will be open. In this case, turn right at the end of Main Street (before you reach the central hub), past the Plaza Ice Cream Parlor and the Plaza Restaurant, and stake out a place for your group at the entrance of the Plaza Pavilion. When the rope barrier is dropped at opening time, jog through the Plaza Pavilion and on to Space Mountain. Starting at the entrance to the Plaza Pavilion will give you about a 100-yard head start and an advantage over anyone coming from the central hub. Ride Space Mountain.

NOTE: If you are a Walt Disney World resort guest and enter the park on an early entry day, ride Space Mountain and see as much of Fantasyland as possible. As the time approaches for the park to open to the public, position yourself at the boundary of Fantasyland and Liberty Square. When the other lands open, head for Liberty Square. Pick up the Touring Plan at The Haunted Mansion (Step 10), skipping steps that direct you to attractions experienced during your early entry hour.

5. Go to Fantasyland, keeping the Grand Prix Raceway on your right, and ride 20,000 Leagues Under the Sea.

6. Exit 20,000 Leagues to the right and proceed to the courtyard of the castle. If you have small children in your party, let them ride Dumbo, the Flying Elephant.

7. While in Fantasyland, ride Snow White's Adventures.

8. Ride Peter Pan's Flight, also in Fantasyland.

9. Exiting Peter Pan to the left, cross the courtyard and ride It's a Small World.

10. Proceed to Liberty Square and experience The Haunted Mansion.

11. While in Liberty Square, visit *The Hall of Presidents*.

12. Your seating time should be approaching for *The Diamond Horseshoe Jamboree*. If you have enough time, go ahead and ride the Liberty Square Riverboat (the ride takes about 16 minutes plus whatever time you must wait to board—ask the attendant).

13. Enjoy *The Diamond Horseshoe Jamboree* and have lunch during the show.

> NOTE: At this point check your daily entertainment schedule to see if there are any parades or live performances which interest you. Make note of the times and alter the Touring Plan accordingly. Since you have already seen all the attractions that cause bottlenecks and have big lines, an interruption of the Touring Plan here will not cause you any problems. Simply pick up where you left off before the parade or show.

14. If you did not have time to ride the Liberty Square Riverboat before lunch and *The Diamond Horseshoe Jamboree*, ride now.
15. In Frontierland, take a raft to Tom Sawyer Island and explore.
16. After you leave Tom Sawyer Island, go to Adventureland and see the *Tropical Serenade (Enchanted Tiki Birds)*.
17. While in Adventureland, walk through the Swiss Family Treehouse.
18. This concludes the Touring Plan for the day. Enjoy the shops, see some of the live entertainment offerings, or revisit your favorite attractions until you are ready to leave.
19. If you leave the park at closing time, the monorail to the TTC will be mobbed. Either take the ferry or board a monorail to the Polynesian Resort and from there take the short walkway to the TTC. See note on page 282.

Day Two

1. Call (407) 824-4321 the day before you go for the official opening time.
2. Arrive at the Magic Kingdom's parking lot 50 minutes before the park's stated opening time. This will give you time to park and catch the tram to the TTC. Arrive an hour earlier than opening time if it is a holiday period.
3. If the line for the monorail is short, take the monorail; otherwise catch the ferry.
4. When you arrive at the Magic Kingdom, proceed through the entry turnstiles. Stop at City Hall for park maps and a copy of the daily entertainment schedule.

> NOTE: If you are a Walt Disney World resort guest and enter the park on an early entry day, revisit Space Mountain and enjoy

your favorite Fantasyland attractions. As the time approaches for the park to open to the public, position yourself at the boundary of Fantasyland and Liberty Square. When the other lands open, head for the Liberty Square waterfront and from there to Splash Mountain. Pick up the Touring Plan at Big Thunder Mountain Railroad (Step 6), skipping steps that direct you to attractions experienced during your early entry hour.

5. Proceed to the end of Main Street. If the entire park is open, head immediately for Frontierland and Splash Mountain. Otherwise, turn left past Refreshment Corner and position yourself in front of The Crystal Palace facing the walkway bridge to Adventureland. When the rope barrier is dropped, cross the bridge and turn left into Adventureland. Cut through Adventureland into Frontierland. Head straight for Splash Mountain and ride.

6. While in Frontierland, ride the Big Thunder Mountain Railroad, next door.

7. Return to Adventureland and ride the Jungle Cruise.

8. Exit the Jungle Cruise to the left. While in Adventureland, enjoy Pirates of the Caribbean.

9. Return to Frontierland and turn right to the *Country Bear Jamboree*.

10. After the show, exit left and catch the Walt Disney World Railroad to Mickey's Starland (the first stop).

11. Tour Mickey's House and proceed through Mickey's backdoor to *Mickey's Starland Show*, a live show featuring the Disney characters. After the show, you can exit the theater and visit Mickey in his dressing room, where he will pose with your group for photographs. If this interests you, see the Touring Tips for *Mickey's Starland Show* on pages 238–39.

12. Exit Mickey's Starland via the path to Fantasyland. In Fantasyland, see *Magic Journeys*.

NOTE: At this point check your daily entertainment schedule to see if there are any parades or live performances which interest you. Make note of the times and alter the Touring Plan accordingly. Since you have already seen all the attractions that cause bottlenecks and have big lines, an interruption of the Touring Plan here will not cause you any problems. Simply pick up where you left off before the parade or show.

13. Turn left after *Magic Journeys* and proceed to the Skyway. If the line is not too long, take the Skyway to Tomorrowland. If the wait seems prohibitive, walk to Tomorrowland via the Castle entrance and the central hub.

14. In Tomorrowland, if you are hungry, eat lunch at Tomorrowland Terrace or the Plaza Pavilion.

15. While in Tomorrowland, ride the WEDway PeopleMover.

16. Try the *Carousel of Progress*, also in Tomorrowland.

17. In Tomorrowland, also ride Dreamflight.

18. Proceed toward the central hub entrance to Tomorrowland and experience the *Mission to Mars*.

19. Walk across the street and view *American Journeys*.

20. This concludes the Touring Plan. Enjoy the shops, see some of the live entertainment offerings, or revisit your favorite attractions until you are ready to leave.

21. If you leave the park at closing time, the monorail to the TTC will be mobbed. Either take the ferry or board a monorail to the Polynesian Resort and from there take the short walkway to the TTC. See note on page 282.

PART FIVE: EPCOT Center

—— Comparing EPCOT Center and the Magic Kingdom ——

EPCOT Center is more than twice the physical size of the Magic Kingdom, and it has lines every bit as long as those waiting for the Jungle Cruise or Space Mountain. Obviously, visitors must come prepared to do a considerable amount of walking from attraction to attraction within EPCOT Center and a comparable amount of standing in line.

The size and scope of EPCOT Center also means that one can't really see the whole place in one day without skipping an attraction or two and giving other areas a cursory glance. A major difference between the Magic Kingdom and EPCOT Center, however, is that some of the EPCOT attractions can be either lingered over or skimmed, depending on one's personal interest. A good example is the General Motors' World of Motion pavilion consisting of two sections. The first section is a 15-minute ride while the second section is a collection of educational walk-through exhibits and mini-theaters. Nearly all visitors opt to take the ride, but many people, due to time constraints or lack of interest, bypass the exhibits.

Generally speaking, the rides at the Magic Kingdom tend to be designed to create an experience of adventure or fantasy. The experiences created in the EPCOT Center attractions tend to be oriented towards education or inspiration.

Some people will find that the attempts at education are superficial; others will want more entertainment and less education. Most visitors are somewhere in between, finding plenty of entertainment **and** education.

In any event, EPCOT Center is more of an adult place than the Magic Kingdom. What it gains in taking a futuristic, visionary, and technological look at the world, it loses, just a bit, in warmth, happiness, and charm.

As in the Magic Kingdom, we have identified several attractions in EPCOT Center as "not to be missed." But part of the enjoyment of a place like EPCOT Center is that there is something for everyone. If you go in a group, no doubt there will be quite a variety of opinions as to which attraction is "best."

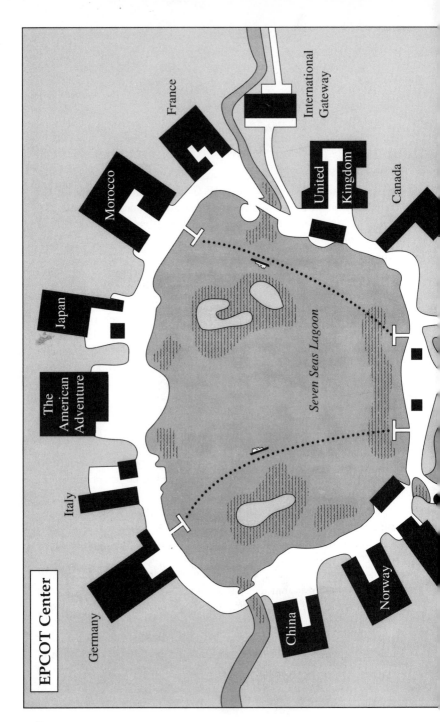

EPCOT Center

France

International Gateway

United Kingdom

Morocco

Canada

Japan

Seven Seas Lagoon

The American Adventure

Italy

Germany

China

Norway

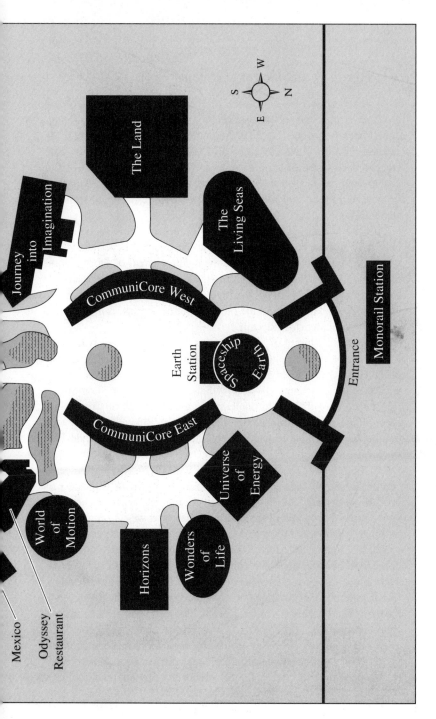

—— *Arriving and Getting Oriented* ——

Arriving at EPCOT Center by private automobile is easy and direct. The park has its own parking lot and, unlike the Magic Kingdom, there is no need to take a monorail or ferryboat to reach the entrance. Trams serve the entire EPCOT Center lot, or if you wish you can walk to the front gate. Monorail service does connect EPCOT Center with the Transportation and Ticket Center, the Magic Kingdom (transfer required), and with the Magic Kingdom resort hotels (transfer also required).

Like the Magic Kingdom, EPCOT Center has theme sections, but only two: Future World and World Showcase. The technological resources of major corporations and the creative talent of Disney combine in Future World, which represents a look at where man has come from and where he is going. World Showcase, featuring the distinctive landmarks, cuisine, and culture of a number of nations, is meant to be a sort of permanent world's fair.

From the standpoint of finding your way around, however, EPCOT Center is not at all like the Magic Kingdom. The Magic Kingdom is designed so that at nearly any location in the park you feel a part of a very specific environment—Liberty Square, let's say, or Main Street, U.S.A. Each of these environments is visually closed off from other parts of the park to preserve the desired atmosphere. It wouldn't do for the Jungle Cruise to pass the roaring blacktop of the Grand Prix Raceway, for example.

EPCOT Center, by contrast, is visually open. And while it seems strange to see a Japanese pagoda on the same horizon with the Eiffel Tower, in-park navigation is fairly simple. A possible exception is in Future World where the enormous east and west CommuniCore buildings effectively hide everything on their opposite sides.

While Cinderella Castle is the focal landmark of the Magic Kingdom, Spaceship Earth is the architectural symbol of EPCOT Center. This shiny, 180-foot "geosphere" is visible from almost every point. Like Cinderella Castle, it can help you keep track of where you are in the park. But because it's in a high-traffic location, and because it's not centrally located, it does not make a very good meeting place.

Any of the distinctively designed national pavilions make good meeting places, but be more specific than, "Hey, let's meet in Japan!" That may sound fun and catchy, but remember that the national pavilions are mini-towns with buildings, monuments, gardens, and plazas. You could wander around quite awhile "in Japan" without making connections with your group. Pick out a specific place in Japan, the sidewalk side of the pagoda, for example.

The EPCOT Acronym

It has become somewhat of a pastime among Walt Disney World employees and guests to create new and amusing definitions for the letters E.P.C.O.T. The official translation, of course, is:

Experimental **P**rototype **C**ommunity **O**f **T**omorrow

Readers and Disney employees have shared these *un*official versions:

Every **P**erson **C**omes **O**ut **T**ired

Every **P**arent **C**arries **O**ut a **T**oddler

Every **P**ocketbook **C**omes **O**ut **T**rashed

Economic **P**rivation **C**ity of **O**rlando **T**axbase

More Information and Help Galore— WorldKey Information Service

Whether you need more information or assistance or not, you should know about the innovative WorldKey Information Service. It not only may be useful as you visit EPCOT Center, it will also give you some experience dealing with what may be one of the common video systems of the future.

WorldKey is a network of interactive video display terminals—televisions that react when you touch certain parts of the screen.

The WorldKey system, developed by the Bell System and the Walt Disney Company, Inc., will provide you with up to 40 minutes of information about EPCOT Center, showing maps and pictures, and describing attractions, restaurants, entertainment, guest services, and shops.

Be patient with the WorldKey and it will guide you, step by step, through an explanation of how to use the system—in English or in Spanish (French and German are to be added later). Stick with the program through at least a few steps and you can use the WorldKey to contact an attendant. Via two-way television and hands-free two-way speakers, the WorldKey attendant can answer your questions, make hotel or restaurant reservations, and help find lost children, among other things.

Because the WorldKey system is so novel, a lot of visitors "play" with it as though it were just another video game. For most people this play is actually an educational experience. They are using what could become one of the data retrieval systems of tomorrow. They are learning about touch-sensitive screens. (You don't need to press, by the way; sometimes the system reacts even before your finger touches the screen.)

But whether people play with the WorldKey or put it to work, they usually end up walking away from the screen without completing the WorldKey program and setting it up for the next user. If people get frustrated with the WorldKey it's usually because they walked up to it while it was in the middle of showing the last user what he asked to see.

If, as opposed to finding a program in progress left from a previous user, you initiate the program, the WorldKey will quickly show you, step by step, how to use the system.

If you wish to speak to an attendant, work through the program until a prompt for an attendant is displayed on the screen. Touch the screen as indicated and soon one of the WorldKey attendants will come "live" onto the screen, ready to communicate with you.

Future World

Gleaming, futuristic structures of immense proportions leave little in doubt concerning the orientation of this, the first encountered theme area of EPCOT Center. The thoroughfares are broad and punctuated with billowing fountains, reflected in the shining facades of space-age architecture. Everything, including the bountiful landscaping, is clean and sparkling to the point of asepsis and seemingly bigger than life. Pavilions dedicated to man's past, present, and future technological accomplishments form the perimeter of the Future World area with the Spaceship Earth and its flanking CommuniCores East and West standing preeminent front and center.

Most of EPCOT Center services are concentrated in Future World in the Entrance Plaza near the main gate. Earth Station, directly behind the geodesic sphere, is the EPCOT Center equivalent of City Hall in the Magic Kingdom

—— Future World Services ——

EPCOT Center's service facilities in Future World include the following:

Wheelchair & Stroller Rental	Inside the main entrance and to the left toward the rear of the Entrance Plaza
Banking Services	At the Sun Bank just inside the entrance on the far left
Currency Exchange	At the Sun Bank
Storage Lockers	Turn right at Spaceship Earth (lockers are cleaned out every night)
Lost & Found	Outside the main entrance and to the far right
Live Entertainment and Parade Information	At Earth Station directly behind Spaceship Earth

Lost Persons	At Earth Station and at the Baby Center on the World Showcase side of the Odyssey Restaurant
Dining Reservations	At Earth Station
Walt Disney World & Local Attraction Information	At Earth Station
First Aid	Next to the Baby Center on the World Showcase side of the Odyssey Restaurant
Baby Center/Baby Care Needs	On the World Showcase side of the Odyssey Restaurant

SPACESHIP EARTH

Type of Ride: Educational journey through past, present, and into the future

When to Go: Before 9:10 A.M. or after 4 P.M.

Special Comments: If lines are long when you arrive, try again after 4 P.M.

Author's Rating: One of EPCOT's best; ★★★★½

Overall Appeal by Age Group:

Pre-school	Grade School	Teens	Young Adults	Over 30	Senior Citizens
★★★★	★★★★½	★★★★½	★★★★½	★★★★½	★★★★½

Duration of Ride: About 16 minutes

Average Wait in Line per 100 People Ahead of You: 3 minutes

Assumes: Normal operation

Loading Speed: Moderate to fast

DESCRIPTION AND COMMENTS   This Bell System ride spirals through the 17-story interior of EPCOT Center's premier landmark, taking visitors past AudioAnimatronics scenes depicting man's developments in communications, from cave painting to printing to television to space communications and computer networks. The ride is compelling and well done as you ascend the geosphere but, to us, a little disappointing on the way back down. Even so, it's a masterpiece and is thus accorded a "not to be missed" rating.

TOURING TIPS   Because of its location near EPCOT Center's main entrance, Spaceship Earth is literally inundated with arriving guests throughout the morning. If you are among the first guests in the park, go ahead and ride. Otherwise, it might be better to postpone Spaceship Earth until later in the day, say, after 4 P.M.

As you face the entrance to Spaceship Earth, you will notice that the direct walkway to the entrance runs between two labyrinthine queuing areas under the cover of the sphere. If these queuing areas are in use, bypass Spaceship Earth for the time being. If, on the other hand, these areas are nearly empty, feel free to hop in line. Because Spaceship Earth loads continuously and expeditiously, if the line runs only along the right side of the sphere you will be accommodated in less than 15 minutes.

EARTH STATION

DESCRIPTION AND COMMENTS   Not an attraction as such. Earth Station is situated at the base of the geosphere and serves as the exit of Spaceship Earth. It also serves as EPCOT Center's primary guest relations and information center. Attendants staff information booths and a number of WorldKey terminals are available. If you have spent any time in the Magic Kingdom, Earth Station is EPCOT Center's version of City Hall.

TOURING TIPS   If you wish to eat in one of the EPCOT Center sit-down restaurants, you can make your reservations from Earth Station through a WorldKey Information Service attendant (instead of running to the restaurant itself and standing in line for reservations, which is another alternative). In the morning, all of the WorldKey screens in Earth Station are tuned to restaurant reservationists. All you have to do is march up to the terminal and tell the reservationist where you want to eat. See the description of the WorldKey system, page 311, and the section dealing with eating in EPCOT Center, page 352.

COMMUNICORE

Type of Attraction: Multifaceted attraction featuring static and "hands-on" exhibits relating to energy, communications, information processing, and future EPCOT developments

When to Go: On your second day at EPCOT or after you have seen all the major attractions

Special Comments: Most exhibits demand time and participation to be rewarding; not much gained here by a quick walk-through

Author's Rating: Interesting on the whole, though not particularly compelling; *Rollercoaster* (you design your own roller coaster with the assistance of a computer) in EPCOT Computer Central (CommuniCore East) is our pick of the litter; ★★½

Overall Appeal by Age Group:

Pre-school	Grade School	Teens	Young Adults	Over 30	Senior Citizens
★★½	★★★	★★½	★★★	★★★	★★★

DESCRIPTION AND COMMENTS The name stands for "Community Core," and it consists of two huge, crescent-shaped, glass-walled structures housing industry-sponsored walk-through and "hands-on" exhibits, restaurants, and gift shops. The Disney people like to describe it as a "twenty-first-century village square where the town crier is an array of computer-fed, interactive video screens and high technology electronics libraries."

TOURING TIPS CommuniCore (two buildings: east and west) provides visitors an opportunity to sample a variety of technology in a fun, "hands-on" manner through the use of various interactive communication devices. Some of the exhibits are quite intriguing while others are a little dry. We observed a wide range of reactions by visitors to the many CommuniCore exhibits and can only suggest that you form your own opinion. In terms of touring strategy, we suggest you spend time in CommuniCore on your second day at EPCOT Center. If you only have one day, visit sometime during the evening if you have time. Be warned, however, that CommuniCore exhibits are almost all technical and educational in nature and may not be compatible with your mood or level of energy toward the end of a long day of touring. Also be advised that you cannot get much of anything out of a quick walk-through of CommuniCore; you have to play with the equipment to understand what is going on.

Attractions in CommuniCore East include:

EPCOT Computer Central

DESCRIPTION AND COMMENTS Touch-sensitive video terminals show users through simple and entertaining games how computers are used in design and control.

TOURING TIPS   See comments in CommuniCore Touring Tips.

Travelport

DESCRIPTION AND COMMENTS   This American Express exhibit in CommuniCore East has "vacation stations" equipped with touch-sensitive video terminals similar to those in the WorldKey system. If you work with a terminal you can see different types of vacations in different geographical areas.

TOURING TIPS   See comments in CommuniCore Touring Tips.

Energy Exchange

DESCRIPTION AND COMMENTS   There are also touch-sensitive video terminals in this Exxon exhibit, permitting users to tap into information about a variety of energy topics. Stationary displays are devoted to specific energy sources—solar, coal, nuclear, oil, and others. Visitors can use some of the devices to demonstrate the generation and expenditure of energy.

TOURING TIPS   See comments in CommuniCore Touring Tips.

Electronic Forum

DESCRIPTION AND COMMENTS   This section of CommuniCore consists of World News Center, which has TV monitors carrying live news broadcasts from around the world. At Future Choice Theater visitors can participate in an on-going opinion poll by pushing buttons built into the armrests of their seats. Responses appear on the theater screen so guests can see how their opinions stack up against those of other visitors.

TOURING TIPS   See comments in CommuniCore Touring Tips.

Backstage Magic

DESCRIPTION AND COMMENTS   The show, including a televised pre-show, provides an understandable introduction to computers, including a look at the EPCOT Center Computer Control Room. Special effects and a Disney electronic character named "I/O" help to sugarcoat the technical information.

TOURING TIPS   This show is produced in a relatively small theater, so there is almost always a 10–20 minute wait in line. We rate *Backstage*

Magic a solid ★★★ and recommend that you see it on your second day at EPCOT Center.

Attractions in CommuniCore West include:

FutureCom

DESCRIPTION AND COMMENTS   A Bell System exhibit with a variety of electronic games demonstrating facets of telecommunications. Another part of the exhibit demonstrates video teleconferencing, putting visitors face-to-face via two-way television with an attendant. Still another section has touch-sensitive video terminals that enable guests to "call up" information on any U.S. state and its current events.

TOURING TIPS   See additional comments in CommuniCore Touring Tips.

Expo Robotics

DESCRIPTION AND COMMENTS   One of the newer and certainly one of the better and more fascinating of all CommuniCore exhibits, Expo Robotics is an active, fast-paced demonstration of advanced robotic applications. On stage, five robots demonstrate juggling and top spinning. Nearby, guests can have their portrait sketched by a robot, or have their photograph dramatically superimposed on a famous EPCOT postcard scene. The technician can make it appear, for instance, as if you are standing on top of Spaceship Earth (the big dome).

TOURING TIPS   See additional comments in CommuniCore Touring Tips.

EPCOT Outreach and Teacher's Center

DESCRIPTION AND COMMENTS   EPCOT Outreach consists of static displays illustrating various EPCOT projects and developments, and a library service that provides information on demand concerning any topic presented in either Future World or World Showcase. If you have used these services in the past, note that their location in CommuniCore West has been moved to the FutureCom area.

TOURING TIPS   This is where someone will try to answer that question you have been kicking around all day. If you are an educator with a group, special tour-enhancing handouts can be obtained here.

THE LIVING SEAS

Type of Attraction: Multifaceted attraction consisting of an underwater ride beneath a huge saltwater aquarium and a number of exhibits and displays dealing with oceanography, ocean ecology, and sea life

When to Go: Before 10 A.M. or after 3 P.M.

Special Comments: The ride is only a small component of this attraction. See description and touring tips below for information on the rest of the attraction.

Author's Rating: An excellent marine exhibit; ★★★½

Overall Appeal by Age Group:

Pre-school	Grade School	Teens	Young Adults	Over 30	Senior Citizens
★★★	★★★½	★★★½	★★★★	★★★★	★★★★

Duration of Ride: 3 minutes

Average Wait in Line per 100 People Ahead of You: 3½ minutes

Assumes: All elevators in operation

Loading Speed: Fast

DESCRIPTION AND COMMENTS   The Living Seas is one of the most ambitious Future World offerings. The focus is a huge, 200-foot diameter, 27-foot-deep main tank containing fish, mammals, and crustaceans in a simulation of a real ocean ecosystem. Scientists and divers conduct actual marine experiments underwater in view of EPCOT Center guests. Visitors can view the undersea activity through eight-inch-thick windows below the surface (including viewing windows in the Coral Reef Restaurant), and via a three-part adventure ride which is the featured attraction of The Living Seas. It consists of a movie dramatizing the link between the ocean and man's survival followed by a simulated elevator descent to the bottom of the tank. Here guests board gondolas for a three-minute voyage through an underwater viewing tunnel.

The fish population of The Living Seas has grown substantially, but the underwater ride is over before you have gotten comfortably situated in the gondola. No matter, the strength of this attraction lies in the dozen or so exhibits offered after the ride. Visitors can view aquaculture fish-breeding experiments, watch short films about various forms of sea life, and much more. You can stay as long as you wish in the exhibit area.

The Living Seas is a high-quality marine/aquarium exhibit, but is no substitute for visiting Sea World, an enormous marine life theme park every bit on a par in terms of quality, appeal, educational value, and entertainment with the Magic Kingdom, EPCOT Center, or Disney-MGM Studios.

TOURING TIPS   The exhibits at the end of the ride are the best part of The Living Seas. In the morning, these are often bypassed by guests trying to rush or stay ahead of the crowd. The Living Seas needs to be lingered over at a time when you are not in a hurry. We recommend seeing The Living Seas in the late afternoon or evening, or on your second day at EPCOT Center.

THE LAND

DESCRIPTION AND COMMENTS   The Land is in fact a huge pavilion sponsored by Nestle which contains three attractions (discussed next) and a number of restaurants. The Land is scheduled for a face lift in 1994 and may be closed for part of the year. When it reopens, it will feature an upgraded Listen to the Land boat ride, as well as new shows in the Harvest and Kabaret theaters.

TOURING TIPS   The Land is a good place for a fast-food lunch; if you are there to see the attraction, however, don't go during meal times.

Attractions in The Land include:

Listen to the Land

Type of Ride: A boat ride adventure through the past, present, and future of U.S. farming and agriculture

When to Go: Before 10:30 A.M. or after 7:30 P.M.

Special Comments: Take this ride early in the morning but save the other Land attractions for later in the day; located on the lower level of The Land pavilion

Author's Rating: Interesting and fun; ★★★★

Overall Appeal by Age Group:

Pre-school	Grade School	Teens	Young Adults	Over 30	Senior Citizens
★★★	★★★	★★★½	★★★★	★★★★★	★★★★★

Duration of Ride: About 12 minutes

Average Wait in Line per 100 People Ahead of You: 3 minutes
Assumes: 15 boats operating
Loading Speed: Moderate

DESCRIPTION AND COMMENTS   A boat ride which takes visitors through a simulated giant seed germination, past various inhospitable environments man has faced as a farmer, and through a futuristic, innovative greenhouse where real crops are being grown using the latest agricultural technologies. Inspiring and educational with excellent effects and a good narrative, this attraction should "not be missed."

TOURING TIPS   This "not to be missed" attraction should be seen before the lunch crowd hits The Land restaurants, i.e., before 10:30 A.M., or in the evening after 7:30 P.M.

If you really enjoy this ride, or if you have a special interest in the agricultural techniques demonstrated, consider taking the Harvest Tour. Free of charge, this 45-minute guided tour takes guests behind the scenes for an in-depth examination of advanced and experimental growing methods. Reservations for the Harvest Tour are made on a space available basis at the Guided Tour Waiting Area (to the far right of the restaurants on the lower level).

Kitchen Kabaret

Type of Show: AudioAnimatronic variety show about food and nutrition
When to Go: Before 11 A.M. or after 2 P.M.
Special Comments: Located on the lower level of The Land pavilion
Author's Rating: Lively and amusing; ★★★
Overall Appeal by Age Group:

Pre-school	Grade School	Teens	Young Adults	Over 30	Senior Citizens
★★★½	★★★½	★★★	★★★	★★★	★★★

Duration of Presentation: Approximately 13 minutes
Preshow Entertainment: None
Probable Waiting Time: Less than 10 minutes

DESCRIPTION AND COMMENTS   Disney AudioAnimatronic (robotic) characters in the forms of various foods and kitchen appliances take the stage in an educational musical revue, which tells the story of the basic food groups (protein, carbohydrates, etc.). It's a cute show with entertainment provided by such characters as Bonnie Appetit, the Cereal Sisters, and the comedy team of Mr. Hamm and Mr. Eggz.

Sometime in 1994 *Kitchen Kabaret* will be replaced by a new show highlighting the advantages of a balanced diet.

TOURING TIPS   One of the few light entertainment offerings at EPCOT Center. Slightly reminiscent of the *Country Bear Jamboree* in the Magic Kingdom (but not quite as humorous or endearing in our opinion). Though the theater is not large, we have never encountered any long waits at the *Kitchen Kabaret* (even during meal times). Nevertheless, we recommend you go before 11 A.M. or after 2 P.M.

Harvest Theater

Type of Show: Film exploring man's relationship with his environment
When to Go: Before 11 A.M. and after 2 P.M.
Author's Rating: Extremely interesting and enlightening; ★★★½
Overall Appeal by Age Group:

Pre-school	Grade School	Teens	Young Adults	Over 30	Senior Citizens
★★½	★★★	★★★½	★★★½	★★★★	★★★½

Duration of Presentation: Approximately 18½ minutes
Preshow Entertainment: None
Probable Waiting Time: 10–15 minutes

DESCRIPTION AND COMMENTS   This attraction features a 70mm Panavision film. The subject is the interrelationship of man and his environment, and demonstrates how easily man can upset the ecological balance. The film is superb in its production and not too heavy-handed in its sobering message.

TOURING TIPS   This extremely worthwhile film should be part of every visitor's touring day. Long waits are usually not a problem at the Harvest Theater.

JOURNEY INTO IMAGINATION

DESCRIPTION AND COMMENTS   Another multi-attraction pavilion, located on the west side of CommuniCore West and down the walk from The Land. Outside is an "upside-down waterfall" and one of our favorite Future World landmarks, the so-called "jumping water," a leap-frogging fountain that seems to hop over the heads of unsuspecting passersby.

TOURING TIPS   We recommend early morning or late evening touring. See the individual attractions for further specifics.

Attractions in Journey into Imagination include:

Journey into Imagination Ride

Type of Ride: Fantasy adventure
When to Go: Before 10:30 A.M. or after 6 P.M.
Author's Rating: Colorful but dull; ★★½
Overall Appeal by Age Group:

Pre-school	Grade School	Teens	Young Adults	Over 30	Senior Citizens
★★★★	★★★★	★★★	★★★	★★★	★★★

Duration of Ride: Approximately 13 minutes
Average Wait in Line per 100 People Ahead of You: 3 minutes
Assumes: 20 trains operating
Loading Speed: Moderate to fast

DESCRIPTION AND COMMENTS   This ride features two Disney characters—Figment, an impish purple dragon, and Dreamfinder, a red-bearded adventurer who pilots a contraption designed to search out and capture ideas. This ride, with its happy, humorous orientation, is one of the lighter and more fanciful offerings in the park. It is the favorite ride of some, while others find it dull and vacuous.

The Journey into Imagination ride stimulates varied responses (mostly polar) among our readers. A mother from Springfield, Missouri, who toured with her husband and children (ages 4, 7, and 10), tells us:

> Keep telling people that Journey into Imagination is boring. It is not worth a five minute wait. We voted it the most boring ride at WDW.

While a reader from Montreal, Quebec, says:

I don't agree with your rating for Journey into Imagination. You claimed it to be dull, but I find it warm, happy, and a great ride. I feel this should be on the "not to be missed" list.

TOURING TIPS This ride, combined with *Captain EO* in the same building, draws large crowds beginning about 10:45 A.M. We recommend riding before 10:30 A.M. or after 6 P.M.

The Image Works

Type of Attraction: Hands-on creative playground employing color, music, touch-sensation, and electronic devices

When to Go: Any time you please

Special Comments: You do not have to wait in the long line for the ride in this pavilion to gain access to The Image Works. Simply go through the open door just to the left of where the line for the ride is entering. You will not have a wait.

Author's Rating: A fun change of pace; be sure to see the Dreamfinder's School of Drama; ★★★

Overall Appeal by Age Group:

Pre-school	Grade School	Teens	Young Adults	Over 30	Senior Citizens
★★★	★★★½	★★★	★★★	★★★	★★★

Probable Waiting Time: No waiting required

DESCRIPTION AND COMMENTS This is a playground for the imagination utilizing light, color, sound, and electronic devices which can be manipulated by visitors. There's the Magic Palette, with a video-screen canvas and an electronic paintbrush. Especially fun is the Electronic Philharmonic, which enables visitors to conduct the brass, woodwind, percussion, and string sections of an orchestra by movements of the hand. (The secret is raising and lowering your hands over the labeled discs on the console. Don't try pressing the discs as if they were buttons. Pretend you're a conductor—raise a hand away from the disc labeled brass, for example, and you will get louder brass. Lower your hand toward the disc labeled woodwinds and you'll get less volume from the woodwinds section.)

Dreamfinder's School of Drama is the best of The Image Works offerings. Children volunteer to act in a short play augmented by video effects. A couple touring with their three-year-old writes:

Another favorite of his [the child] and mine [Mom] was the chance to perform in a Dreamfinder short story at the Image Works. In these stories the players stand in front of a large blue screen and watch themselves get inserted [by video] into a simple story. The process is the same as is used by a local [TV] weatherman, and the acting instructions are clear and easy: "run in place" or "duck down." Video-taping the large [video] screen makes a great souvenir—just don't dress in blue.

TOURING TIPS   There are quite a number of interesting things to do and play with here, far more than the representative examples we listed. If you have more than one day at EPCOT Center, save The Image Works for the second day. If you are on a one-day schedule, try to work it in during the evening or late afternoon.

Magic Eye Theater: Captain EO

Type of Show: 3-D rock and roll space fantasy film

When to Go: Before 11 A.M. or after 5 P.M.

Special Comments: Adults should not be put off by the rock music or sci-fi theme; they will enjoy the show as much as the kids

Author's Rating: An absolute hoot! Not to be missed; ★★★★

Overall Appeal by Age Group:

Pre-school	Grade School	Teens	Young Adults	Over 30	Senior Citizens
★★★½	★★★★½	★★★★½	★★★★	★★★★	★★★½

Duration of Presentation: Approximately 17 minutes

Preshow Entertainment: 8 minutes

Probable Waiting Time: 12 minutes (at suggested times)

DESCRIPTION AND COMMENTS   *Captain EO* is sort of the ultimate rock video. Starring Michael Jackson and directed by Francis Coppola, the 3-D space fantasy is more than a film; it is a happening. Action on the screen is augmented by lasers, fiber-optics, cannons, and a host of other special effects in the theater. There's not much of a story, but there's plenty of music and dancing performed by some of the most unlikely creatures ever to shake a tail feather.

TOURING TIPS   *Captain EO* draws large crowds. During the summer and holiday periods when there are large numbers of kids in the park, it's best to see *Captain EO* before 10:30 A.M.

THE WORLD OF MOTION

DESCRIPTION AND COMMENTS   Presented by General Motors, this pavilion is to the left of Spaceship Earth when you enter and down toward World Showcase from the Universe of Energy pavilion. The pavilion is home to It's Fun to Be Free, a ride, and to TransCenter, an assembly of stationary exhibits and mini-theater productions on the theme of transportation.

We receive a considerable volume of mail from readers who maintain that the World of Motion "is one big commercial" for General Motors. While we agree that the promotional hype is a little more heavy-handed than in most of the other business-sponsored attractions, we maintain that the World of Motion is one of the most creatively conceived and executed attractions in Walt Disney World.

Attractions in The World of Motion include:

It's Fun to Be Free

Type of Ride: AudioAnimatronic survey of the history of transportation
When to Go: Before noon and after 4 P.M.
Author's Rating: Not to be missed; ★★★★½
Overall Appeal by Age Group:

Pre-school	Grade School	Teens	Young Adults	Over 30	Senior Citizens
★★★½	★★★★	★★★★	★★★★	★★★★	★★★★

Duration of Ride: Approximately 14½ minutes
Average Wait in Line per 100 People Ahead of You: 2¾ minutes
Assumes: Normal operation
Loading Speed: Moderate to fast

DESCRIPTION AND COMMENTS   A "not-to-be-missed" attraction, this ride conducts visitors through a continuum of twenty-four Audio-Animatronics scenes depicting where and how man has traveled, and what the future has in store for travel. The detail-work in individual scenes is amazing and the tongue-in-cheek, humorous tone of the ride makes the history lesson more than tolerable.

TOURING TIPS   This ride has a large carrying capacity and an efficient loading system, keeping lines generally manageable. Many days you can hop on this ride any time you want. Its largest crowds build between noon and 4 P.M.

TransCenter

Type of Attraction: Exhibits and mini-theater productions concerning the evolution and future of transportation, particularly as relates to the automobile

When to Go: On your second day or after you've seen the major attractions

Special Comments: World of Motion has a separate entrance to the exhibit area, making visitation possible other than when you take the It's Fun to Be Free ride.

Author's Rating: Informative with a healthy dose of humor; ★★★

Overall Appeal by Age Group:

Pre-school	Grade School	Teens	Young Adults	Over 30	Senior Citizens
★★½	★★★	★★★	★★★	★★★	★★★

Probable Waiting Time: No waiting required if you enter through the rear entrance

DESCRIPTION AND COMMENTS   Most visitors enter TransCenter when they disembark from the ride described above, but there are separate doors on the east side of the pavilion for those who wish to visit the various exhibits without taking the ride. TransCenter is a walk-through attraction of 33,000 square feet, and deals with a wide range of topics relating to transportation. One major display demonstrates the importance of aerodynamics to fuel economy, while others evaluate the prospects of future power systems and explains why the industry is turning to robotic production techniques. Yet another display shows some advanced designs for the possible land, sea, and air conveyances of tomorrow.

TOURING TIPS   There's a lot to see here. How much you take in will be determined by your interest in the subject and the flexibility of your schedule. We like TransCenter on the second day of a two-day visit, or during the mid-afternoon if you enjoy this sort of display more than the offerings of World Showcase. Late evening after you have finished your "must list" is also a good time.

HORIZONS

Type of Ride: A look at man's evolving perception of the future
When to Go: Before 10:30 A.M. or after 3:30 P.M.
Author's Rating: Not to be missed; ★★★★
Overall Appeal by Age Group:

Pre-school	Grade School	Teens	Young Adults	Over 30	Senior Citizens
★★★★	★★★★	★★★★	★★★★½	★★★★½	★★★★½

Duration of Ride: Approximately 15 minutes
Average Wait in Line per 100 People Ahead of You: 4 minutes
Assumes: Normal operation
Loading Speed: Moderate to fast

DESCRIPTION AND COMMENTS   The General Electric pavilion takes a look back at yesterday's visions of the future, including Jules Verne's concept of a moon rocket and a 1930s preview of a neon city. Elsewhere guests visit FuturePort and ride through a family habitat of the next century, with scenes depicting apartment, farm, and underwater and space communities.

TOURING TIPS   The entire Horizons pavilion is devoted to a single, continuously loading ride, which has a large carrying capacity. This "not to be missed" attraction can be enjoyed almost any time of day without long waits in line. An exception occurs immediately following the conclusion of a Universe of Energy performance, when up to 580 patrons often troop over and queue up for Horizons en masse. If you chance to encounter this deluge or its aftermath, take a 15-minute break. Chances are when you return to Horizons you will be able to walk right in.

WONDERS OF LIFE

DESCRIPTION AND COMMENTS   Presented by the Metropolitan Life Insurance Company, this newest addition to the Future World family is a multifaceted pavilion dealing with the human body, health, and medicine. Housed in a 100,000-square-foot, gold-domed structure, Wonders of Life houses a variety of attractions focusing on the capabilities of the human body and the importance of keeping it fit.

Attractions in Wonders of Life include:

Body Wars

Type of Ride: Flight simulator ride through the human body

When to Go: As soon as possible after the park opens

Special Comments: Not recommended for pregnant women or those prone to motion sickness

Author's Rating: Absolutely mind-blowing, not to be missed; ★★★★½

Overall Appeal by Age Group:

Pre-school	Grade School	Teens	Young Adults	Over 30	Senior Citizens
★★★	★★★★½	★★★★★	★★★★	★★★★	★★★

Duration of Ride: 5 minutes

Average Wait in Line per 100 People Ahead of You: 4 minutes

Assumes: All simulators operating

Loading Speed: Moderate to fast

DESCRIPTION AND COMMENTS   This is a thrill ride through the human body, developed in the image of the Star Tours space simulation ride. The idea is that you are a passenger on a sort of miniature space capsule that is injected into a human body. Once inside the body your mission is to pick up a scientist who has been inspecting a splinter in the patient's finger. Before retrieval, however, the scientist gets sucked into the circulatory system and you end up chasing her all over the body in an attempt to rescue her. The simulator creates a vividly realistic experience as guests seem to hurtle at fantastic speeds through anatomical images. The sights are as mind-boggling as the ride is breathtaking in this "not to be missed" attraction.

TOURING TIPS   This is EPCOT Center's first and only thrill ride and is popular with all age groups. Ride first thing after the park opens or just before closing time. Be advised that Body Wars makes a lot of people motion sick and that it is not at all unusual for a simulator to be taken off-line to clean up some previous rider's mess. If you are at all susceptible to motion sickness we suggest you reconsider riding Body Wars. If you are on the ride and begin to get nauseated, fix your gaze on *anything* other than the screen, i.e., the floor, the ceiling, the walls. Without the visual effects, the ride itself is not rough enough to disturb most guests. If you do get queasy, there are rest rooms to your left as you get off the ride. As an aside, Star Tours, another simulator ride at the Disney-MGM Studios, is just as wild but makes very few people sick. If you successfully rode Star Tours, that does not necessarily mean Body Wars will not upset you. Conversely, if Body Wars made you ill, you cannot assume Star Tours will do the same.

While reader comments on Body Wars cover the spectrum, the following quotes are fairly representative:

> The only thing we won't do on this next trip is go on Body Wars in EPCOT. The line is so deceptive. We waited almost two hours and then it was only to get motion sickness and feel awful!

and:

> Body Wars did not measure up to all the hype and warnings. We expected Space Mountain with visual effects, and it wasn't even close. You Weenies!

and finally:

> Body Wars at EPCOT was great fun. We rode it twice and loved it. A little scary but exciting. Some of the other things seemed kind of boring after our ride here.

Motion sickness aside, Body Wars is incredibly intense, too intense for some, especially preschoolers and seniors. As one elderly gentleman confided, "Feeling sick at my stomach took my mind off being terrified."

Cranium Command

Type of Show: AudioAnimatronic character show about the brain

When to Go: Before 11 A.M. or after 3 P.M.

Author's Rating: Funny, outrageous, and educational. Not to be missed; ★★★★★

Overall Appeal by Age Group:

Pre-school	Grade School	Teens	Young Adults	Over 30	Senior Citizens
★★★★	★★★★★	★★★★★	★★★★★	★★★★★	★★★★★

Duration of Presentation: About 20 minutes

Preshow Entertainment: Explanatory lead-in to feature presentation

Probable Waiting Time: Less than 10 minutes at touring times suggested

DESCRIPTION AND COMMENTS *Cranium Command* is EPCOT Center's great sleeper attraction. Stuck on the backside of the Wonders of Life pavilion and far less promoted than Body Wars, many guests elect to bypass this most humorous of all EPCOT Center offerings. Disney characters called "Brain Pilots" are trained to operate human brains. The show consists of a day in the life of one of these Cranium Commanders as he tries to pilot his assigned brain (that of an adolescent boy). We do not know who designed this attraction, but EPCOT Center in particular, and Walt Disney World in general, could use a lot more of this type of humor.

TOURING TIPS The presentation kicks off with a preshow cartoon that is essential to understanding the rest of the show. If you arrive in the waiting area while the cartoon is in progress, make sure you see enough to understand the story line before going into the main theater.

The Making of Me

Type of Show: Humorous movie about human conception and birth
When to Go: Early in the morning or after 4:30 P.M.
Author's Rating: Well done; ★★★½
Overall Appeal by Age Group:

Pre-school	Grade School	Teens	Young Adults	Over 30	Senior Citizens
★★★	★★★	★★★½	★★★½	★★★	★★★

Duration of Presentation: 14 minutes
Preshow Entertainment: None
Probable Waiting Time: About 25 minutes or more unless you go early in the morning or after 4:30 P.M.

DESCRIPTION AND COMMENTS This funny, lighthearted and very sensitive movie about human conception, gestation, and birth was considered to be a controversial addition to the Wonders of Life pavilion. In point of fact, Disney audiences have received it well, with most guests agreeing that the material is tastefully and creatively presented. The plot is in the *Back to the Future* genre and has the main character going back in time to watch his parents date, fall in love, marry, and, yes, conceive and give birth to him. The sexual material is well handled with loving relationships given much more emphasis than plumbing. Parents of children under seven tell us that the sexual information presented went over their children's heads for the most part. For children a little older, however, the film seems to precipitate quite a few questions. You be the judge.

A gentleman from Cheshire, England, who believes (correctly) that Americans are sexually repressed, had this to say:

> By the standards of sex education programmes shown to English children of ages 8–9, *The Making of Me* seemed almost Mary Poppinish in tone. Certainly other Brits found your warnings over content quite puzzling.

The reader quoted above would have a great time living in my city (Birmingham, Alabama), where some of the local clergy harangued the city council for months to have Bermuda shorts welded onto the bare buttocks of a large statue depicting Vulcan at his forge.

TOURING TIPS   *The Making of Me* is an excellent film shown in a theater not much larger than a phone booth. It is our fervent hope that the Disney people will soon relocate this show to a larger, more suitable theater. At present, however, the diminutive size of the theater insures that there will be a long wait unless you go just after the park opens or during the very late afternoon and evening.

Fitness Fairgrounds

DESCRIPTION AND COMMENTS   Much of the pavilion's interior is devoted to an assortment of visitor participation exhibits, where guests can test their senses in a fun house, receive computer-generated health analyses of their personal lifestyles, work out on electronically sophisticated exercise equipment, and watch a video presentation called "Goofy About Health" (starring who else?).

TOURING TIPS   We recommend you save the Fitness Fair exhibits for your second day, or the end of your first day at EPCOT Center.

UNIVERSE OF ENERGY

Type of Attraction: Combination ride/theater presentation about energy

When to Go: Before 10:30 A.M. or after 4:30 P.M.

Special Comments: Don't be dismayed by large lines; 580 people disappear into the pavilion each time the theater turns over

Author's Rating: A creative combination of theater and ride; ★★★½

Overall Appeal by Age Group:

Pre-school	Grade School	Teens	Young Adults	Over 30	Senior Citizens
★★★	★★★	★★★½	★★★½	★★★½	★★★½

Duration of Presentation: Approximately 26½ minutes

Preshow Entertainment: 8 minutes

Probable Waiting Time: 20–40 minutes

DESCRIPTION AND COMMENTS   The AudioAnimatronic dinosaurs and the unique traveling theater make this Exxon pavilion one of the most popular in Future World. Since this is a theater with a ride component, the line does not move at all while the show is in progress. When the theater empties, however, a large chunk of the line will disappear as people are admitted for the next show. At this "not to be missed" attraction, visitors are seated in what appears to be a fairly ordinary theater while they watch an animated film on fossil fuels. Then, the theater seats divide into six 97-passenger traveling cars which glide among the swamps and reptiles of a prehistoric forest. The special effects include the feel of warm, clammy air from the swamp, the smell of sulphur from an erupting volcano, and the sight of red lava hissing and bubbling toward the passengers. The remainder of the performance utilizes some nifty cinematic techniques to bring you back to the leading edge of energy research and development.

The Universe of Energy is a real toss-up for kids. Preschoolers are sometimes frightened by the dinosaurs, and almost all kids (as well as many adults) are bored by the educational segments. Guest ratings for this attraction (per our surveys) have been dropping slowly, but steadily, over the past two years. The comments of a man from Greely, Colorado, are typical:

> The Universe of Energy was the most boring ride in all of WDW. The preshow is interesting and the dinosaurs were great, but to have to go through the extremely long presentation on energy just to see the dinosaurs is far from worth it. I actually fell asleep (and I love WDW).

TOURING TIPS   This attraction draws large crowds beginning early in the morning. Either catch the show before 10:30 A.M. or wait until after 4:30 P.M. Waits for the Universe of Energy are normally within tolerable limits, however, since the Universe of Energy can operate more than one presentation at a time.

World Showcase

The second theme area of EPCOT Center is World Showcase. Situated around picturesque World Showcase Lagoon, it is an ongoing world's fair, with the cuisine, culture, history, and architecture of almost a dozen countries permanently on display in individual national pavilions. The so-called pavilions, which generally consist of familiar landmarks and typically representative street scenes from the host country, are spaced along a 1.2-mile promenade which circles the impressive forty-acre Lagoon.

While most adults enjoy the World Showcase, many children find it boring. To make the World Showcase more interesting to children, the Camera Center in Future World sells Passport Kits for $7.95. Each kit contains a blank passport and stamps for all of the World Showcase countries. As the kids accompany their folks to each country, they tear out the appropriate stamp and stick it in the passport. The kit also contains some basic information on the respective countries, as well as a Mickey Mouse button. As I'm in the publishing business, myself, I can tell you that Disney has built a lot of profit margin into this little product, but I guess that's not the salient issue. More importantly, parents tell us the passport kit helps get the kids through the World Showcase with a minimum of impatience, whining, and fits.

For the footsore and weary, there are double-decker omnibuses to carry visitors around the promenade and boats to ferry guests across the lagoon (the lines at the bus stops tend to be pushy, however, and it's almost always quicker to walk than use the buses or the boats). Moving clockwise around the promenade, the nations represented are:

Mexico

DESCRIPTION AND COMMENTS Two pre-Columbian pyramids dominate the architecture of this exhibit. The first makes up the facade of the pavilion and the second overlooks the restaurant and plaza alongside the boat ride, El Rio del Tiempo, inside the pavilion.

TOURING TIPS   A romantic and exciting testimony to the charms of Mexico, this pavilion probably contains more authentic and valuable artifacts and objets d'art than any other national pavilion. Many people zip right past these treasures, unfortunately, without even stopping to look. The village scene on the interior of the pavilion is both beautiful and exquisitely detailed. We recommend seeing this pavilion before 11 A.M. or after 6 P.M.

Attractions in Mexico include:

El Rio del Tiempo

Type of Ride: Boat ride

When to Go: Before 11 A.M. or after 7:00 P.M.

Author's Rating: Light and relaxing; ★★½

Overall Appeal by Age Group:

Pre-school	Grade School	Teens	Young Adults	Over 30	Senior Citizens
★★★	★★★	★★★	★★★	★★★	★★★

Duration of Ride: Approximately 7 minutes (plus 1½-minute wait to disembark)

Average Wait in Line per 100 People Ahead of You: 4½ minutes

Assumes: 16 boats in operation

Loading Speed: Moderate

DESCRIPTION AND COMMENTS   El Rio del Tiempo, The River of Time, is a boat trip which winds among AudioAnimatronics and cinematic scenes depicting the history of Mexico from the ancient cultures of the Maya, Toltec, and Aztec civilizations to modern times. Special effects include fiber-optic projections that provide a simulated fireworks display near the end of the ride.

While the volcano at the entrance suggests great things to come, the ride is disappointing to many guests. Pleasant and relaxing, but not particularly interesting or compelling, El Rio del Tiempo is definitely not worth a long wait.

TOURING TIPS   El Rio del Tiempo tends to get crowded during the early afternoon. Try it in the morning or early evening.

Norway

DESCRIPTION AND COMMENTS   A very different addition to the World Showcase international pavilions, the Norwegian pavilion is complex, beautiful, and architecturally diverse. There is a courtyard surrounded by an assortment of traditional Scandinavian buildings including a replica of the 14th-century Akershus Castle, a wooden stave church, red-tiled cottages, and replicas of historic buildings representing the traditional designs of Bergen, Ålesund, and Oslo. Attractions in Norway include an adventure boat ride in the mold of Pirates of the Caribbean, followed by a movie about Norway, and, in the stave church, a gallery of art and artifacts. Located between China and Mexico, the Norway pavilion houses the Restaurant Akershus, a reservations/sit-down eatery featuring koldtboard (cold buffet) plus a variety of hot Norwegian fare. For those on the run there is an open-air cafe and a bakery. For shoppers there is an abundance of native handicrafts.

Attractions in Norway include:

Maelstrom

Type of Ride: Disney adventure boat ride
When to Go: Before 11:30 A.M. or after 4:30 P.M.
Author's Rating: One of EPCOT Center's most exciting rides, also
    one of its shortest; ★★★½
Overall Appeal by Age Group:

Pre-school	Grade School	Teens	Young Adults	Over 30	Senior Citizens
★★★★	★★★★	★★★★	★★★★	★★★★	★★★★

Duration of Ride: About 4½ minutes, followed by a five-minute film
    with a short wait in between; about 14 minutes for the whole
    show.
Average Wait in Line per 100 People Ahead of You: 4 minutes
Assumes: Twelve or thirteen boats operating
Loading Speed: Fast

DESCRIPTION AND COMMENTS   Guests board dragon-headed ships for an adventure voyage through the fabled rivers and seas of Viking history and legend. In one of Disney's shorter water rides, guests brave trolls, rocky gorges, waterfalls, and a storm at sea. A new-generation

Disney water ride, the Viking voyage assembles an impressive array of special effects, combining visual, tactile, and auditory stimuli in a fast-paced and often humorous odyssey. After the ride guests are shown a short (five-minute) film on Norway.

TOURING TIPS Ride Maelstrom before 11:30 A.M. or in the late afternoon. Sometimes several hundred guests from a recently concluded performance of the *Wonders of China* arrive at Maelstrom en masse. Should you encounter this horde, bypass Maelstrom for the time being.

People's Republic of China

DESCRIPTION AND COMMENTS A half-sized replica of the Temple of Heaven in Beijing (Peking) identifies this pavilion. Gardens and reflecting ponds simulate those found in Suzhou, and an art gallery features a "Lotus Blossom" gate and formal saddle roof line.

Pass through the Hall of Prayer for Good Harvest to see the Circle-Vision 360 motion picture, *Wonders of China*. Warm and appealing, the film serves as a brilliant introduction to the people and natural beauty of this little-known nation. Two restaurants have been added to the China pavilion since its opening, a fast-food eatery and a lovely, reservations-only, full-service establishment.

TOURING TIPS A truly beautiful pavilion, serene yet exciting. The movie, *Wonders of China*, plays in a theater where guests must stand, but can usually be enjoyed at any time during the day without much waiting. If you are touring the World Showcase in a counterclockwise rotation and plan to go next to Norway and ride Maelstrom, take up a viewing position on the far left of the theater (as you face the attendant's podium). After the show, make sure you are one of the first to exit the theater. Hustle over to Maelstrom as fast as you can to arrive ahead of the several hundred other *Wonders of China* patrons who will be right behind you.

Attractions in People's Republic of China include:

Wonders of China

Type of Show: Film essay on the Chinese people and country
When to Go: Any time
Special Comments: Audience stands throughout performance

Author's Rating: Charming and enlightening; ★★★½
Overall Appeal by Age Group:

Pre-school	Grade School	Teens	Young Adults	Over 30	Senior Citizens
★★★	★★★½	★★★½	★★★★½	★★★★½	★★★★

Duration of Presentation: Approximately 19 minutes
Preshow Entertainment: None
Probable Waiting Time: 10 minutes

Germany

DESCRIPTION AND COMMENTS   A clocktower adorned with boy and girl figures overlooks the platz, or plaza, which identifies the pavilion of the Federal Republic of Germany. Dominated by a fountain depicting St. George's victory over the dragon, the platz is encircled by buildings reflecting traditional German architecture. The focal attraction is the Biergarten, a full-service (reservations only) restaurant featuring German food and beer. Yodeling, German folk dancing, and oompah band music accompany the fare during the evening meal.

TOURING TIPS   The pavilion is pleasant and festive. Germany is recommended for touring at any time of the day.

Italy

DESCRIPTION AND COMMENTS   The entrance to the Italian pavilion is marked by the 105-foot campanile, or bell tower, said to be a mirror image of the tower that overlooks St. Mark's Square in Venice. To the left of the campanile is a replica of the fourteenth-century Doge's Palace, also a Venetian landmark. Other buildings are composites of architecture found throughout Italy. The style is Florentine, for example, for L'Originale Alfredo di Roma Ristorante. Visitors can watch pasta being made in this popular restaurant which specializes in Fettuccine all'Alfredo. The Italian pavilion even has a small Venetian island with gondolas tied to barber-pole-striped moorings at the edge of the World Showcase Lagoon.

TOURING TIPS   The streets and courtyards in the Italian pavilion are among the most realistic in World Showcase—you really feel as if you have been transplanted to Italy. Since there is no attraction (film, ride, etc.) at the Italian pavilion, touring is recommended for all hours.

The American Adventure

Type of Show: Patriotic mixed-media and AudioAnimatronic presentation on U.S. history

When to Go: Before noon and after 3:30 P.M.

Author's Rating: Possibly the best attraction at EPCOT Center (for Americans); not to be missed; ★★★★★

Overall Appeal by Age Group:

Pre-school	Grade School	Teens	Young Adults	Over 30	Senior Citizens
★★★	★★★★	★★★★	★★★★½	★★★★★	★★★★★

Duration of Presentation: Approximately 29 minutes

Preshow Entertainment: Voices of Liberty choral singing

Probable Waiting Time: 16 minutes

DESCRIPTION AND COMMENTS   The United States pavilion, generally referred to as the American Adventure for the historical production performed there, consists of (typically) a fast-food restaurant and a patriotic, AudioAnimatronics show.

The American Adventure is a composite of everything the Disney people do best. Situated in an imposing brick structure reminiscent of colonial Philadelphia, the production is a stirring, 29-minute rendition of American history narrated by the AudioAnimatronic figures of Mark Twain (who carries a smoking cigar) and Ben Franklin (who climbs a set of stairs to visit Thomas Jefferson). Behind a stage that's almost half the size of a football field is a 28 × 155–foot rear projection screen (the largest ever used) on which appropriate motion picture images are interwoven with the action occurring on stage. Updated and re-engineered in 1992, the American Adventure is "not to be missed."

TOURING TIPS   Large and patriotic, but not as interesting externally as most of the other pavilions. The Liberty Inn restaurant is a good place to obtain a quick nonethnic, fast-food meal.

The American Adventure is, in the opinion of our research team, the very best attraction at EPCOT Center. It usually plays to capacity audiences from around noon through 3:30 P.M., so try to see it early or late. Owing to the theater's large capacity, waiting during the busy times of the day would hardly ever approach an hour, and would probably average 25–40 minutes. Finally, because of its patriotic theme, *The American Adventure* is decidedly less compelling to non-Americans.

Japan

DESCRIPTION AND COMMENTS   The five-story, blue-roofed pagoda, inspired by a shrine built in Nara in the seventh century, sets this pavilion apart from its neighbors. A hill garden rises behind it with arrangements of waterfalls, rocks, flowers, lanterns, paths, and rustic bridges. The building on the right (as one faces the entrance) was inspired by the ceremonial and coronation hall on the Imperial Palace Grounds at Kyoto. It contains restaurants and a large retail store.

TOURING TIPS   A tasteful and elaborate pavilion which creatively blends simplicity, architectural grandeur, and natural beauty, Japan can be toured at any time of day.

Morocco

DESCRIPTION AND COMMENTS   The bustle of the market, narrow, winding streets, lofty minarets, and stuccoed archways re-create the romance and intrigue of Tangiers and Casablanca. Attention to detail makes Morocco one of the most exciting of the World Showcase pavilions. In addition to the bazaar, Morocco also features a museum of Moorish art and the Restaurant Marrakesh, which serves some unusual and difficult-to-find North African ethnic specialities.

TOURING TIPS   Since there is no ride or theater attraction in Morocco, it can be toured any time at your convenience.

France

DESCRIPTION AND COMMENTS   Naturally there is a replica of the Eiffel Tower (and a big one at that), but the rest of the pavilion is meant to reflect a more general ambience of France in the period 1870 to 1910, a period known as La Belle Epoque (the beautiful time). The sidewalk cafe and the restaurant are both very popular here, but so is the pastry shop. You won't be the first visitor to get the idea of buying a croissant to tide you over until you can obtain a decent meal.

Impressions de France is the name of an 18-minute movie which is projected over 200 degrees onto five screens. They let you sit down in France (compared to the standing theaters in China and Canada) to view a well-made film introduction to the people, cities, and natural wonders of France.

TOURING TIPS   This pavilion is rich in atmosphere because of its detailed street scenes and bygone era flavor.

The streets of the French pavilion are diminutive and become quite congested when visitors line up for the film. Waits in line can be substantial here, so we recommend viewing before 11 A.M. and after 6 P.M.

Attractions in France include:

Impressions de France

Type of Show: Film essay on the French people and country

When to Go: Before 11 A.M. and after 6 P.M.

Author's Rating: An exceedingly beautiful film; not to be missed; ★★★★

Overall Appeal by Age Group:

Pre-school	Grade School	Teens	Young Adults	Over 30	Senior Citizens
★★½	★★★½	★★★½	★★★★½	★★★★½	★★★★½

Duration of Presentation: Approximately 18 minutes

Preshow Entertainment: None

Probable Waiting Time: 12 minutes (at suggested times)

United Kingdom

DESCRIPTION AND COMMENTS   A variety of periods and facades, with attempts to create city, town, and rural atmospheres, are compressed into this pavilion, which is mostly shops. The Rose & Crown Pub & Dining Room is the only World Showcase full-service restaurant with dining on the water side of the promenade. A city square, with classic formal facade, copies a look found in London and Edinburgh. One street has a 1500s style thatched-roof cottage, a four-story timber and plaster building, a pre-Georgian plaster building, a formal Palladian exterior of dressed stone, and a city square with Hyde Park bandstand (whew!).

TOURING TIPS   There are no attractions here to create congestion, so tour at any time you wish. Reservations are not needed to enjoy the Pub section of the Rose & Crown Pub, making it a nice place to stop for a beer along about mid-afternoon.

Canada

DESCRIPTION AND COMMENTS   The cultural, natural, and architectural diversity of the United States' neighbor to the north is reflected in this large and impressive pavilion. 30-foot totem poles embellish an Indian village situated beneath the gables of a magnificent château-style hotel. Near the hotel is a rugged stone building said to be modeled after a famous landmark near Niagara Falls, reflective of Canada's British influence. Canada also has a fine film extolling its many national, cultural, and natural virtues. Titled *O Canada!* the film is very enlightening, and demonstrates the immense pride Canadians have in their beautiful country. Visitors leave the theater through Victoria Gardens, inspired by the famed Butchart Gardens of British Columbia.

TOURING TIPS   A large-capacity theater attraction (guests must stand) that sees fairly heavy late morning attendance since it is the first pavilion encountered as one travels counterclockwise around World Showcase Lagoon. We recommend late afternoon or early evening as the best time for viewing the film. Le Cellier, a restaurant serving cafeteria-style on the lower level of the Canadian pavilion, is the only non-fast-food restaurant in the World Showcase that does not require reservations.

Attractions in Canada include:

O Canada!

Type of Show: Film essay on the Canadian people and country

When to Go: Morning, late afternoon, or early evening

Special Comments: Audience stands during performance

Author's Rating: Makes you want to catch the first plane to Canada! ★★★½

Overall Appeal by Age Group:

Pre-school	Grade School	Teens	Young Adults	Over 30	Senior Citizens
★★½	★★★	★★★½	★★★★	★★★★½	★★★★½

Duration of Presentation: Approximately 18 minutes

Preshow Entertainment: None

Probable Waiting Time: 10 minutes

Not to Be Missed at EPCOT Center

World Showcase	*The American Adventure*
	IllumiNations
Future World	Spaceship Earth
	Listen to the Land
	Captain EO
	It's Fun to Be Free
	Body Wars
	Cranium Command
	Horizons

Live Entertainment
in EPCOT Center

Live entertainment in EPCOT Center is somewhat more diversified, as might be expected, than that of the Magic Kingdom. World Showcase provides almost unlimited potential for representative entertainment from the respective nations, and Future World allows for a new wave of creativity in live entertainment offerings.

Some information concerning the live entertainment on the day of your visit can be obtained from the information desk in the Earth Station lobby. Another source of information is the WorldKey Information Service. WorldKey usually has the answers, but it is not as direct as quizzing an attendant.

Listed below are some of the performers and performances you are likely to encounter.

Future World Brass	A roving brass band that marches and plays according to a more or less extemporaneous schedule near Spaceship Earth and at other Future World locations.
Disney Characters	The Disney characters, once believed to be inconsistent with the image of EPCOT Center, have now been imported in number. The Disney characters appear for breakfast at the Stargate Restaurant in Future World from 9 to 10 A.M., and at the Odyssey Restaurant and Showcase Plaza several times each day according to the daily live entertainment schedule available at Earth Station. The Disney characters are also featured in live shows on the American Gardens Stage and at the Showcase Plaza between Mexico and Canada.

American Gardens Stage	The site of EPCOT Center's premier live performances is near the American Adventure, facing World Showcase Lagoon, in a large amphitheater. Top talent imported from all over the world plays the American Gardens Stage on a limited engagement basis. Many shows highlight the music, dance, and costumes of the performer's home country. Other shows include the Disney characters.
IllumiNations	An after-dark show, consisting of music, fireworks, erupting fountains, special lighting, and laser technology performed on the World Showcase Lagoon when the park is open late. Not to be missed.
Around World Showcase	A variety of unscheduled, impromptu performances take place in and around the various pavilions of World Showcase. You may encounter a strolling mariachi group in Mexico, street actors in Italy, a fife-and-drum corps or a singing group (The Voices of Liberty) at the American Adventure, traditional songs and dances in Japan, comical street drama in the United Kingdom, white-faced mimes in France, and bagpipes in Canada. There is a street entertainment performance at most of the World Showcase pavilions about every half hour (though not scheduled *on* the hour or half hour).
Dinner & Lunch Shows	The restaurants in World Showcase serve up healthy portions of live entertainment to accompany the victuals. Examples of restaurant floorshow fare include folk dancing and a baskapelle band in Germany (dinner only), singing waiters in Italy and Germany, and belly dancers in Morocco. Restaurant shows are performed at dinner only in Italy, but at both lunch and dinner in Morocco. Reservations are required (see "Eating in EPCOT Center," page 352).

World Showcase
Lagoon

The World Showcase Lagoon provides the
stage for a number of shows during the course
of the day featuring boats, kites, hang glid-
ers, music, and a variety of other unlikely
combinations. Check the daily entertainment
schedule for times and details.

—— IllumiNations ——

IllumiNations is EPCOT Center's daily great outdoor spectacle, integrating fireworks, laser lights, neon, and music in a stirring tribute to the nations represented at the World Showcase. The climax of every EPCOT Center day, we rate IllumiNations as not to be missed.

Getting Out of EPCOT after IllumiNations
(Read This before Selecting a Viewing Spot)

A major consideration in picking your vantage point is how anxious you are to leave the park at the conclusion of the show. IllumiNations essentially ends the day at EPCOT Center. After Illumi-Nations, you will find nothing open except a couple of gift shops in Future World. Because there is nothing to do, everyone remaining in the park leaves at the same time. Needless to say, this creates a great snarl at Package Pick-up, the EPCOT Monorail Station, and the Disney bus stop. It also pushes the tram system to the limit, hauling guests to their cars in the EPCOT Center parking lot. Stroller return, however, is extraordinarily efficient and does not occasion any delay.

If you are staying at one of the EPCOT Resorts (Swan and Dolphin hotels, Yacht and Beach Clubs), we recommend watching IllumiNa-tions from somewhere in the southern (American Adventure) half of the World Showcase Lagoon, and then exiting through the International Gateway (between France and the United Kingdom). You can walk or take a tram back to your hotel from the International Gateway. If you have a car and are visiting EPCOT Center in the evening for dinner and IllumiNations, park at the Walt Disney World Yacht or Beach Club. After the show you can duck out the International Gateway and be on the road to your hotel in 15 minutes. If you are staying at any other Walt Disney World hotel, and do not have a car, the fastest way home is to join the mass exodus through the main gate following IllumiNations and then catch a bus or the monorail.

For those who have a car in the EPCOT lot, the situation is more problematic. If you want to beat the crowd, your only option is to find a viewing spot at the end of the World Showcase Lagoon nearest Future World (and the exits). Take off as soon as IllumiNations concludes,

347

and try to get out ahead of the crowd. Be forewarned, however, that thousands of people will be doing exactly the same thing. To get a good vantage point anywhere between Mexico and Canada on the southern end of the lagoon, you will have to stake out your spot a good 45–55 minutes before the show. Quite conceivably, you may squander more time holding down your spot before IllumiNations than you would if you watched from the less congested southern end of the Lagoon, and then took your chances with the crowd on departure.

More groups get separated, and more children lost, following Illumi-Nations than at any other time. In the summer, you literally will be walking among a throng of up to 30,000 people. If you are heading for the parking lot, you need to anticipate this congestion and preselect a meeting spot in the EPCOT Center entrance area. You can hook back up there in the event that someone gets separated from the group. The place we recommend is the Sun Bank, located *inside* the turnstiles to the far right as you head toward the exits. Everyone in your party should be told not to exit through the turnstiles until it has been verified that your group is together. It can be a real nightmare if the group gets split up and you don't know whether the others are inside or outside the park.

For those with cars, the main problem is just getting to it. Once there, traffic flows out of the parking lot pretty well. If you paid close attention to where you parked, you might consider blowing off the tram and walking. Be aware, however, that the parking lot is a pretty wild place this time of night. If you have children and decide to walk, hang on to them for all you're worth.

Good Locations for Viewing IllumiNations and Other World Showcase Lagoon Performances

The best place to be for any World Showcase Lagoon presentation is seated comfortably on the lakeside veranda of the Cantina de San Angel in Mexico. Come early (*at least* 70 minutes for Illumi-Nations) and relax with a cold drink or a snack while you wait for the show. There is also outdoor Lagoonside seating at the Rose & Crown Pub in the United Kingdom. Because of a small wall, the view is not quite as good as from the Cantina. On the bright side, however, you can often get a table on the Rose & Crown beer terrace within 30–40 minutes of showtime.

Because most guests are hot to run for the exits following a pre-

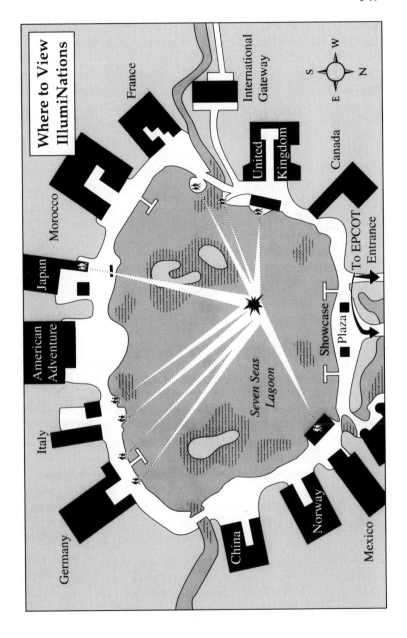

sentation, and because islands in the southern (American Adventure) half of the Lagoon block the view from some places, the most popular spectator positions are along the northern waterfront from Norway and Mexico on around to Canada and the United Kingdom. Although the northern end of the Lagoon unquestionably offers excellent viewing positions, it is usually necessary to claim a spot 35–60 minutes before IllumiNations begins. For those who are late finishing dinner, or anyone else who does not want to invest 45 minutes standing by a rail, here are some good viewing spots along the southern perimeter (moving counter clockwise from the United Kingdom to Germany) that often go unnoticed until 10–20 minutes before showtime:

1. *The Secret Park.* There is a wonderful waterside park, accessible from the United Kingdom, which is unknown to all but a few. To reach the park, walk toward France from the Rose & Crown Pub in the United Kingdom. As you pass near the end of the Pub, stay on the sidewalk and bear left. You will shortly find yourself in an almost private park, complete with benches and a perfect view of IllumiNations. En route to the park, you will see a roped-off back entrance to the terrace of the Pub. This is another good viewing spot (don't be shy about ducking under the rope). Following our 1992 edition, as sometimes happens, the "Secret Park" became somewhat less secret. A reader from Demotte, Indiana, wrote describing this improbable scene:

> We watched the Illuminations show from the "Secret Park" behind the British pub. It was a very good location and allowed us an easy exit after the show. On a humorous note, about ten minutes before the show was to begin, a lady came hiking down the path to the park with a copy of your guide in her hand. She became quite agitated when she saw that the area was full and exclaimed quite loudly, "I thought this place was a secret!" About half the people in place for the show held up copies of your book.

2. *International Gateway Island.* The pedestrian bridge across the canal near the International Gateway spans an island which offers great viewing spots. This island is much more obvious to passers-by than the secret park and normally fills up 20 minutes before showtime.

3. *Second-floor (Restaurant Level) Deck of the Mitsukoshi Building in Japan.* Though an oriental arch slightly blocks your line of sight, this second-floor covered deck offers a great vantage point. If

the weather is iffy, it is the most protected viewing area in the World Showcase, except for the Cantina de San Angel in Mexico.

4. *Gondola Landing at Italy.* An elaborate waterfront promenade offers excellent viewing positions for IllumiNations. Claim your spot at least 20 minutes before showtime.

5. *The Boat Dock opposite Germany.* Another good vantage point, the dock generally fills up 20 minutes before IllumiNations begins.

6. *Waterfront Promenade by Germany.* A good view is possible from a Lagoonside walkway extending about 90 feet from Germany toward China.

7. *The Magic Johnson Hedge.* Near the boat dock in Germany and next to the WorldKey Information kiosk is a tall, thick hedge. Viewing positions behind the hedge offer a great perspective for people over six feet tall or children on their parents' shoulders.

Do these suggestions work every time? No. A dad from San Ramon, California, had this to say:

> Your recommendations for IllumiNations didn't work out in the time frame you mentioned. People had the area staked out *two hours* ahead of time.

It should be noted that none of the above viewing locations are reserved for *Unofficial Guide* readers and, on busier nights, good spots are claimed early. Personally, we think it's a drag to hold down a slab of concrete for two hours in advance of IllumiNations. Most nights you can find an acceptable vantage point 15–30 minutes prior to the show. If IllumiNations is a top priority for you, however, and you want to be absolutely certain of nailing down a good viewing position, claim your place an hour or more before showtime.

Eating in EPCOT Center

We've been reviewing EPCOT Center's restaurants since the park opened in 1982 and have seen a lot of changes, most of them for the better. There is more variety now than ever before, and more choices for folks who do not want to take the time for a full-service, sit-down meal. The fast food is quite good, better than in the Magic Kingdom, and more of the full-service ethnic restaurants are now offering sampler platters to showcase the variety of their cuisine.

Where certain World Showcase restaurants were once timid about delivering an honest representation of the host nation's cuisine, we are now seeing bold ethnic menus—*mole* in Mexico, sushi in Japan, and couscous and bastila in Morocco. Some restaurants, however, still sacrifice ethnic authenticity to please the tastes of picky Americans, who, more than anyone, need their palates challenged (or do not need to be eating in ethnic restaurants).

Many EPCOT Center restaurants are overpriced, most conspicuously Nine Dragons (China) and the Coral Reef at The Living Seas pavilion. Chefs de France and Bistro de Paris (France), Restaurant Akershus (Norway), Biergarten (Germany), Restaurant Marrakesh (Morocco), and the San Angel Inn Restaurant (Mexico) represent a relatively good value through a combination of well-prepared food, ambience, and in the case of Germany, entertainment. If expense is an issue, have your main meal at lunch. The entrees are much the same as on the dinner menu, but the prices are significantly lower.

Making reservations for full-service restaurants still involves standing in line in the morning when you would rather be doing something else, and in most cases, abandoning your touring itinerary to hustle (usually from the opposite side of the park) to the restaurant to be seated. The restaurants are such an integral part of EPCOT Center, however, that we think it would be a mistake not to have a meal in at least one of them.

One of the most persistent problems for many exhausted EPCOT

Center diners is Disney's stopwatch efficiency. Unless you know how to slow down the service, you will literally be processed through your "fine dining" experience before you have a chance to catch your breath. This can be advantageous, of course, if you have small, fussy children in your party. If, however, you have spent an entire day hoofing all over the Isle of Walt, the last thing you need is the bum's rush.

If you want to relax and linger over your expensive meal, do not, repeat, do not, order your entire dinner at once. Place drink orders while you study the menu. If you would like a second drink, ask for it before you order. Next, order appetizers but tell the waiter you need more time to choose your main course. Order your entree only after the appetizers have been served. Feel free to dawdle over coffee and dessert.

— Getting a Handle on the World Showcase Restaurants —

Getting a reservation for a particular restaurant depends on its popularity and seating capacity, and, of course, the size of the crowd on the day of your visit. Each restaurant has seatings for both lunch and dinner.

Guests staying at Walt Disney World lodgings may make reservations one to three days in advance by dialing 56 (45 for campground guests). If you wish to make dining reservations prior to arriving at Walt Disney World (one to three days in advance), call (407) 824-3737. Reservations can likewise be made for restaurants at the Disney-MGM Studios and at the Magic Kingdom. Those guests who are lodging out of the World must make their reservations at EPCOT Center on the day of the meal.

For those who are making same-day reservations (during the busier times of the year), arrive at the entrance turnstiles, passport in hand, 45 minutes before EPCOT Center opens. On admission go quickly to Earth Station (the building at the base of the dome). Both lunch and dinner reservations can be made at the same time. Be prepared with alternatives for both restaurants and seatings in case your first choices are filled. If members of your group are susceptible to motion sickness and have elected to skip Body Wars, they might make the meal reservations while the remainder of the group rides. They can easily rejoin the group at the eastside entrance of Earth Station as you return from Body Wars en route to Spaceship Earth.

If you don't follow this plan, you might have a long wait in line to make reservations with no guarantee that anything will be available. On many days the World Showcase restaurants book solid for preferred seating times within an hour to an hour and a half of the park opening. Even if you get a reservation, you will have spent your most productive/crowd-free touring time in the process.

If you visit EPCOT Center during a quieter time of year, you do not need to be so compulsive about making dining reservations first thing in the morning. During slower periods, most restaurants have plenty of seats available. One notable exception is the San Angel Inn in Mexico which fills quickly because of its relatively small size.

If you follow one of our touring plans, you will be near the United States pavilion (The American Adventure) at noon. We suggest, therefore, a lunch reservation for 12:30 P.M. or 1 P.M. at nearby Germany. For dinner, we recommend reservations at the San Angel Inn in Mexico or Akershus in Norway. If you plan to eat your evening meal at the Coral Reef (in Future World), you may want to wait until after dinner to see the attraction itself.

If you blow it and arrive late but still want to eat in one of the World Showcase restaurants, here are some strategies that often pay off:

1. Go to a WorldKey Information terminal in or out of Earth Station (there are some located around the bridgeway connecting Future World to World Showcase) and use the system as described on page 311 to call up an attendant. Try to make a reservation.

2. If you can't get a reservation via WorldKey, go to the restaurant of your choice and apply at the door for a reservation. Sometimes only lunch reservations are taken at the door, but lunch and dinner menus are comparable if not the same. Just have your main meal at lunch.

3. If neither of the first two options works, go to the restaurant of your choice and ask the hostess to call you if she gets a cancellation. A reservation is held about 15–20 minutes before the vacancy is filled with "standby" diners. Very early and very late seatings have more "no shows."

4. If the options mentioned above do not pan out, you can often get

a table just by showing up at Restaurant Marrakesh (reservations often go unfilled because of American unfamiliarity with the cuisine). If Moroccan is too adventurous for you, try Le Cellier, a cafeteria in the Canadian pavilion, or The Land Grille Room in The Land pavilion (Future World), which is often overlooked at dinner time.

— EPCOT Center Dining for Families with Small Children —

EPCOT Center's restaurants offer an excellent (though not inexpensive) opportunity to introduce small children to the variety and excitement of ethnic food. No matter how fancy or formal an EPCOT restaurant looks or sounds, rest assured that the staff is well accustomed to wiggling, impatient, and often boisterous small children. Chefs de France, for example, may be the only French restaurant in the country where a majority of the clientele is clad in shorts and T-shirts, and where you can count on finding at least two dozen small diners formally attired in basic-black mouse ears. Bottom line: small children are the rule, not the exception, at EPCOT restaurants.

The restaurants that preschoolers enjoy most are the Biergarten in Germany, the San Angel Inn Restaurant in Mexico, and the Coral Reef Restaurant in the Living Seas pavilion in Future World. The Biergarten combines a rollicking and noisy atmosphere with good basic fare like roast chicken. A German oompah band provides entertainment (dinner only). Children often have the opportunity to participate in native Bavarian dances.

The San Angel Inn Restaurant is located in a simulated Mexican village marketplace. From the table, children can watch boats from the Rio del Tiempo attraction drift beneath a smoking volcano. Between chips, tacos, and other familiar items, there is usually no difficulty finding something picky children will eat. The Coral Reef, with tables set alongside viewing windows of the Living Seas aquarium, offers a satisfying mealtime diversion for children and adults alike. If your kids do not eat fish, the Coral Reef also serves chicken. The Biergarten and the San Angel Inn offer a good value, as well as good food. The Coral Reef, though overpriced, also serves very good food.

EPCOT Center restaurants understand how itchy children get when they have to sit for an extended period. Your server will keep the small ones supplied with crackers and rolls, and will get your dinner on the table much faster than in comparable restaurants elsewhere. Letters from readers suggest that being served too quickly (i.e., not having enough time to relax) is a much more frequent occurrence than having to wait a long time. Finally, most EPCOT Center restaurants have special children's menus, and all have booster seats and highchairs.

If you are on hand when the park opens, and intend to rent a stroller, the best strategy is for one parent to run ahead to Earth Station (just behind the big dome) and make dining reservations while the other obtains the stroller.

—— *The Restaurants of EPCOT Center* ——

While eating at EPCOT Center can be a consummate hassle, it is likewise true that an afternoon in the World Showcase section of EPCOT Center without a dinner reservation is something like not having a date on the day of the prom. Each pavilion has a beautifully seductive ethnic eatery, offering the hungry tourist the gastronomic delights of the world. To tour one after another of these exotic foreign settings and not partake is almost beyond the limits of willpower.

In all honesty, the food in some of the World Showcase restaurants is not very compelling, but the overall experience is exhilarating. And if you fail to dine in the World Showcase, you will miss out on one of EPCOT Center's more delightful features.

In our opinion there is no logical correlation between price, quality, and popularity of the World Showcase restaurants. Our researchers, for example, found L'Originale Alfredo di Roma Ristorante (Italy) sometimes disappointing despite the fact it is almost always one of the first two restaurants to fill its seatings. To help you make your choice, a data summary of each World Showcase restaurant requiring reservations (plus Le Cellier in Canada) is presented below. We have also assigned each restaurant a star, quality, and value rating. Turn to pages 141–45 for a detailed explanation of our rating system. All full-service restaurants have children's menus.

Canada

Le Cellier (no reservations required)
This is the only cafeteria-style restaurant in the World Showcase and represents a tasty and economical choice for those who want a nicer meal but do not have reservations elsewhere.

Time to go: Lunch—before 11:30 and after 2:00
Dinner—before 5:30 and after 8:00
Entree Prices: Lunch, $7–17   Dinner, $9–18

United Kingdom

Rose & Crown Pub & Dining Room   ★★★   83/C

Seating Capacity: 152

Popularity: More popular for lunch. About the fifth to book for dinner, owing more to its small size than to its popularity.

Critic's Rating: Hearty, but simple food; try fish and chips, a shepherd's pie, or the mixed grill, washed down with Bass ale or Guinness-Harp beer on tap. Stop and refresh yourself on a hot (or cold) afternoon with a round at the cozy bar.

Atmosphere: Excellent, warm pub interior with an unparalleled view of the World Showcase Lagoon.

Entree Prices: Lunch, $8–12   Dinner, $10–21

Entertainment: Madrigal music with lute.

Comments: Fish and chips, steak and kidney pie, roast beef, and other basic pub fare make up the menu here. Waitresses are saucy in the best English tradition and add immeasurably to the dining experience.

France

Chefs de France   ★★★   84/D

Seating Capacity: 162

Popularity: Usually the third restaurant to fill its reservations.

Critic's Rating: Palatable, but lacks the style and diversity of a good French restaurant.

Atmosphere: Elegant and bright, but not intimate or romantic.

Entree Prices: Lunch, $8–15   Dinner, $9–22

Entertainment: None.

Comments: An understandable menu and cooperative wait staff make it easy for those not familiar with the cuisine. The fare, however, lacks the variety, imagination, and subtlety normally associated with fine French dining. Though well thought of in the Orlando area, Les Chefs would have a hard time attracting customers in Paris, Nice, or even New York.

Bistro de Paris ★★★½ 89/C

Seating Capacity: 150

Popularity: Very popular. Many patrons make reservations here by mistake, thinking they are scheduling Chefs de France.

Critic's Rating: The better of the two French restaurants.

Atmosphere: Bright and bustling.

Entree Prices: Dinner, $20–25

Entertainment: None.

Comments: Usually not open for lunch. Bistro de Paris offers hearty French provincial fare, competently prepared. Try one of the dishes that combines French preparation with fresh Florida seafood.

Morocco

Restaurant Marrakesh ★★★ 81/C

Seating Capacity: 250

Popularity: Normally the seventh or eighth restaurant to fill its reservations.

Critic's Rating: Different, usually good; portions sometimes skimpy.

Atmosphere: Colorful and exotic.

Entree Prices: Lunch, $10–14 Dinner, $14–25

Entertainment: Belly dancing and a Moroccan band.

Comments: Interesting fare, almost impossible to find except in the largest U.S. cities. Because Moroccan food is unfamiliar to most visitors, Marrakesh sometimes has tables available for walk-ins. Try the tagine chicken or the lamb kabob.

Japan

Mitsukoshi Restaurants: Teppanaki Dining Room ★★★½ 88/C
Tempura KiKu ★★★ 83/C

Seating Capacity: Teppanyaki Dining Room, 160; Tempura Kiku, 27

Popularity: Normally the sixth or seventh restaurant to fill its reservations.

Critic's Rating: Eschews traditional Japanese fare for teppan table cooking a la Benihana of Tokyo chain restaurants. In the Matsu No Ma Lounge, however, good sushi can be had at reasonable prices.

Atmosphere: Enchanting stained wood and paper walls; traditional Japanese surroundings.

Entree Prices: Lunch, $9–19   Dinner, $15–29

Entertainment: Provided by the chopping, juggling teppan chefs.

Comments: While this restaurant offers some of the best teppan dining you will find in the United States, it has missed a wonderful opportunity to introduce the diversity and beauty of authentic Japanese cuisine to the American public. In addition to Teppanyaki, there is Tempura Kiku, a small separate dining room specializing in tempura. Finally, be aware that diners at the teppan tables (large tables with a grill in the middle) commonly are seated with other parties.

Italy

L'Originale Alfredo di Roma Ristorante   ★★★½   **86/D**

Seating Capacity: 254

Popularity: Usually the first or second restaurant to fill its seatings.

Critic's Rating: Overrated and definitely overpriced. Our guess is that many diners feel more familiar with Italian food than with the other ethnic cuisines available at EPCOT Center, thus making Alfredo's popular beyond its ability to deliver.

Atmosphere: Elegant, bright, with beautiful murals adorning several walls.

Entree Prices: Lunch, $10–22   Dinner, $16–25

Entertainment: Wonderfully talented singing waiters and waitresses erupting in a profusion of song, including Italian opera and traditional tunes. Unfortunately, these six-decibel blasts are delivered at the singer's convenience rather than the diner's. If it's quiet, intimate conversation you crave, choose another restaurant.

Comments: Choosing from Alfredo's menu is like walking through a mine field. Some dishes are excellent (calamari), others are not so good (antipasto misto). The Fettucine Alfredo is excellent, but a little rich and heavy for a main course. Most of the veal dishes, as well as the Osso Buco are competent. Pasta with seafood is hit or miss, as is seafood in general. Most of the other pasta entrees are well done and dependable.

Germany

Biergarten ★★★ 81/C

Seating Capacity: 360

Popularity: Usually the fifth or sixth to book its reservations.

Critic's Rating: Food is good. The dinner show is fun and rousing, and the overall atmosphere is festive.

Atmosphere: The largest of the reservation restaurants. Multiple tiers of diners surround a stage where yodelers, dancers, and a German band perform at each scheduled dinner seating. The beer flows freely and diners join in the singing, making the Biergarten a happy, delightful place to dine.

Entree Prices: Lunch, $9–11 Dinner, $15–21

Entertainment: Yodelers, dancers, singers, and a German band (evenings only).

Comments: Best bets are the wursts and the spitted chicken. While the combination plate suits most American palates, Germans will find the sauerbraten wimpy. Because of the size of the Biergarten, there is an above-average chance of getting in without a reservation as a "standby."

China

Nine Dragons Restaurant ★★½ 74/F

Seating Capacity: 250

Popularity: Usually the sixth or seventh restaurant to fill its reservations.

Critic's Rating: Chinese food at expensive prices.

Entertainment: None.

Atmosphere: Traditional Chinese.

Entree Prices: Lunch, $9–18 Dinner, $10–23

Comments: The food at Nine Dragons has improved significantly and it is now possible to eat family style, as is the custom in China and most traditional Chinese restaurants. Unfortunately, Nine

Dragons remains inferior both in terms of quality and selection to Orlando's independent Chinese restaurants. If you do not want to leave Walt Disney World (and you don't mind spending a wad), try Sum Chows at the Walt Disney World Dolphin.

Norway

Restaurant Akershus   ★★★½   89/B

Seating Capacity: 200

Popularity: Steadily growing as word spreads of its quality.

Critic's Rating: The most interesting menu in Walt Disney World.

Atmosphere: Scandinavian, bright and scrubbed, clean and cheery.

Buffet Price: Lunch, $11, kids $5   Dinner, $17, kids $9

Entertainment: None.

Comments: A beautiful cold and hot buffet features salmon, herring, various Norwegian salads, and a variety of meats. Hearty, adventurous eating. One of the best of the World Showcase restaurants.

Mexico

San Angel Inn Restaurant   ★★★½   87/D

Seating Capacity: 158

Popularity: Usually the third or fourth restaurant to fill its reservations.

Critic's Rating: Excellent, though expensive, Mexican food.

Atmosphere: Superb, truly romantic. You sit beneath the stars in a re-creation of a small village on the banks of the Rio del Tiempo with the jungle and an Aztec pyramid in the background.

Entree Prices: Lunch, $8–15   Dinner, $12–26

Entertainment: None.

Comments: Delightful menu goes beyond the normal Mexican fare, offering regional and special dishes that are very difficult to find in the U.S. Try the chicken *mole*. Very expensive for Mexican food, particularly if you order standard stuff like enchiladas.

Future World Reservation Restaurants

Future World restaurants are primarily fast-food establishments. There are, however, two exceptions, and both are worthy competitors of the World Showcase ethnic restaurants in terms of food quality, atmosphere, and menu creativity. What's more, they are sometimes forgotten in the great morning reservations rush.

The Land Pavilion

The Land Grille Room   ★★★   **82/C**

Seating Capacity: 232

Popularity: Most popular at lunch. Often overlooked for dinner.

Critic's Rating: Good food and creative menu. A good choice for finicky eaters and beef-and-potato lovers.

Atmosphere: Elegant revolving platform which overlooks rain forest, prairie, and farm scenes along the Listen to the Land boat-ride route. Unexpectedly intimate and romantic.

Entree Prices: Breakfast, $5–11   Lunch, $8–20
        Dinner, $14–22

Entertainment: None.

Comments: A nice change of pace. The menu features nicely prepared American food, served in large portions. The only full-service restaurant in EPCOT Center that serves breakfast.

Living Seas Pavilion

Coral Reef Restaurant   ★★★★   **90/D**

Seating Capacity: 250

Popularity: Popular because of its novelty and fresh seafood specialty. Often the first to fill its reservations.

Critic's Rating: Fresh seafood creatively prepared; excellent.

Atmosphere: Diners eat fresh seafood and are surrounded by even fresher (live) seafood. Very interesting.

Entree Prices: Lunch, $11–36   Dinner, $18–38

Entertainment: Diners view fish in the main tank of The Living Seas through floor-to-ceiling underwater windows.

Comments: Though it has taken awhile for the Coral Reef to live up to its potential, the restaurant now serves food worthy of its elegant venue. Fresh seafood, competently prepared, beautifully presented, and enhanced by delicate (and sometimes exotic) sauces, makes the Coral Reef a standout among seafood restaurants.

While everything is very expensive, you can't beat the Coral Reef for its good seafood and incredible atmosphere. When you make your reservation, ask for a table in the first three rows.

Alternatives and Suggestions for Eating in EPCOT Center

Listed below are some suggestions for any dauntless, epicurean adventurer who is determined to eat at EPCOT Center:

1. Do not stand in lines at restaurants unless absolutely necessary. Use the WorldKey terminals (calling up an attendant) to make your reservations. If you are staying at a Walt Disney World lodging or campground property make your reservation by phone before you come.

2. For fast-food meals, EPCOT Center is like the Magic Kingdom; eat before 11 A.M. or after 2 P.M. The Odyssey Restaurant and the Liberty Inn at the American Adventure pavilion move people through pretty speedily, and sometimes you can get served in a reasonable time in The Land pavilion (the latter being a bit more iffy). The Land is a cut above the average, as are many of the counter service restaurants in the World Showcase.

If you want to sample the ethnic diversity of the World Showcase without eating in the reservations-only restaurants, we recommend:

Norway	Kringla Bakeri og Kafé for pastries, open-face sandwiches, and Ringnes beer (our favorite)
Germany	Sommerfest, for bratwurst and Becks beer
Japan	Matsu No Ma Lounge, for sushi and sashimi
France	Boulangerie Pätisserie, for French pastries
United Kingdom	Rose & Crown Pub for Guinness-Harp and Bass beers and ales

3. Review the "Alternatives and Suggestions for Eating in the Magic Kingdom," page 260. Many tips for the Magic Kingdom also apply to EPCOT Center.

Shopping in EPCOT Center

The shops in Future World seem a little out of place, the atmosphere being too visionary and grandiose to accommodate the pettiness of the bargain table. Similarly, it obviously has been difficult to find merchandise consistent with the surroundings. Expressed differently, what is available for purchase in Future World is generally available at a lot of other places. Exceptions include EPCOT and Disney trademark souvenirs, as well as robotically created T-shirts and portraits at Expo Robotics in Communicore West.

The World Showcase shops add a lot of realism and atmosphere to the street scenes of which they are part. Much of the merchandise is overpriced and is readily available elsewhere. On the other hand, some of the shops in the World showcase really are special. In the United Kingdom, visit the Queen's Table (fine china); in China, Yong Feng Shangdian (crafts, rugs, carvings, furniture); in Japan, Mitsukoshi Department Store (porcelain, bonsai trees, pearls straight from a live oyster).

If you do not want to haul your purchases around, have the salesperson forward them to Package Pick-up where they can be collected when you leave the park. Be sure to specify whether you will be departing through the main entrance or through the International Gateway. Allow three hours from time of purchase for your goods to reach the pick-up facility.

Behind the Scenes Tours in EPCOT Center

Interested adults (16 and over) can book guided walking tours exploring respectively the architecture of the international pavilions of EPCOT Center (Hidden Treasures of World Showcase), and/or Walt Disney World's gardens (Gardens of the World), horticulture, and landscaping. Each tour lasts three-and-a-half hours. Cost is about $20, plus an EPCOT Center admission ticket. For reservations call (407) 354-1855.

A shorter tour along similar lines is the Harvest Tour, which takes guests behind the scenes to tour the vegetable gardens in The Land pavilion of EPCOT Center. The tour requires same-day reservations made on the lower level of The Land (to the far right of the fast-food windows). There is no charge for the Harvest Tour, which lasts 30–45 minutes.

Traffic Patterns in EPCOT Center

After admiring for many years the way traffic is engineered at the Magic Kingdom, we were somewhat amazed at the way EPCOT Center was laid out. At the Magic Kingdom, Main Street, U.S.A., with its many shops and eateries, serves as a huge gathering place when the park opens and subsequently funnels visitors to the central hub; from there, equally accessible entrances branch off to the various lands. Thus the crowds are first welcomed and entertained (on Main Street) and then distributed almost equally to the respective lands.

At EPCOT Center, by contrast, Spaceship Earth, the park's premier architectural landmark and one of its featured attractions, is situated just inside the main entrance. When visitors enter the park they invariably and almost irresistibly head right for it. Hence crowds tend to bottleneck as soon as the park opens less than 75 yards from the admission turnstiles. For those in the know, however, the congestion at Spaceship Earth provides some excellent opportunities for escaping waits at other rides and shows in the Future World section of EPCOT Center.

Early-morning crowds are contained in the Future World half of EPCOT Center for the simple reason that most of the rides and shows are located in Future World. Except for Spaceship Earth, and Body Wars in the Wonders of Life pavilion, distribution of visitors to the various Future World attractions is fairly equal. Before the opening of the Wonders of Life pavilion, attractions on the west side of Future World (The Living Seas, The Land, Journey into Imagination) drew larger crowds. With the addition of Body Wars and the other Wonders of Life attractions, traffic is now more evenly distributed.

Between 9 A.M. and 11 A.M., there are more people entering Future World via the entrance than departing Future World into World Showcase. Attendance continues building in Future World until sometime between noon and 2 P.M. World Showcase attendance builds rapidly with the approach of the midday meal. Exhibits at the far end of World Showcase Lagoon report playing to full-capacity audiences from about noon on through 6:30–7:30 P.M.

The central focus of World Showcase in the eyes of most visitors is its atmosphere, featuring international landmarks, romantic street scenes, quaint shops, and ethnic restaurants. Unlike the Magic Kingdom with its premier rides and attractions situated along the far perimeters of its respective lands, World Showcase has only two major entertainment draws (Maelstrom in Norway, and *The American Adventure*). Thus, where the Magic Kingdom uses its super attractions to draw and distribute the crowds rather evenly, EPCOT Center's cluster of premier attractions in Future World serves to hold the greater part of the crowd in the smaller part of the park. There is no compelling reason to rush to the World Showcase. The bottom line in Future World is a crowd that builds all morning and into the early afternoon. The two main sections of EPCOT Center do not approach equality in attendance until the approach of the evening meal. It should be stated, however, that evening crowds in World Showcase do not compare with the size of morning and midday crowds in Future World. Attendance throughout EPCOT Center is normally lighter in the evening.

An interesting observation at EPCOT Center from a crowd-distribution perspective is the indifference of repeat visitors relative to favoring one attraction over another. At the Magic Kingdom repeat visitors make a mad dash for their favorite ride and their preferences are strong and well defined. At EPCOT Center, by contrast, many returning tourists indicate that (with the possible exceptions of Body Wars and *The American Adventure*) they enjoy the major rides and features "about the same." The conclusion suggested here is that touring patterns at EPCOT Center will be more systematic and predictable (i.e., by the numbers, clockwise, counterclockwise, etc.) than at the Magic Kingdom.

While some guests leave EPCOT Center in the early evening, the vast majority troop out en masse following IllumiNations. Upwards of 30,000 people head at the same time for the parking lot and monorail station.

Closing time at EPCOT Center does not precipitate congestion similar to that observed when the Magic Kingdom closes. One primary reason for the ease of departure from EPCOT Center is that its parking lot is adjacent to the park as opposed to being separated by a lake as at the Magic Kingdom. At the Magic Kingdom, departing visitors bottleneck at the monorail to the Transportation and Ticket Center and main parking lot. At EPCOT Center you can proceed directly to your car.

EPCOT Center
Touring Plans

The EPCOT Center Touring Plans are field-tested, step-by-step itineraries for seeing all of the major attractions at EPCOT Center with a minimum of waiting in line. They are designed to keep you ahead of the crowds while the park is filling in the morning and to place you at the less crowded attractions during EPCOT Center's busier hours of the day. They assume that you would be happier doing a *little* extra walking as opposed to a lot of extra standing in line.

Touring EPCOT Center is much more strenuous and demanding than touring the Magic Kingdom. To begin with, EPCOT Center is about twice as large as the Magic Kingdom. Secondly, and unlike the Magic Kingdom, EPCOT Center has essentially no effective in-park transportation system; wherever you want to go, it's always quicker and easier to walk. Where visitors arriving at the Magic Kingdom disperse rather evenly, visitors arriving at EPCOT Center tend to cluster. Spaceship Earth forms immense lines ten minutes after opening, while the rest of the park is virtually empty. The Touring Plans will assist you in avoiding crowds and bottlenecks on days of moderate to heavy attendance, but cannot lessen the distance you will have to walk. Wear comfortable shoes and be prepared for a lot of hiking. On days of lighter attendance, when crowd conditions are not a critical factor, the Touring Plans will serve primarily to help you organize your tour.

Touring Plans provided for EPCOT Center include the following:

- EPCOT Center One-Day Touring Plan
- Author's Selective EPCOT Center One-Day Touring Plan
- EPCOT Center Two-Day Touring Plan

Touring Plan Clip-out Pocket Outlines. For your convenience, we have prepared outline versions of all the Touring Plans presented in this guide. The Pocket Outline versions present the same touring itineraries as the detailed Touring Plans, but with vastly abbreviated directions. First, select the Touring Plan which is most appropriate for your party, then familiarize yourself with the detailed version of the Touring Plan. Once you understand how the Touring Plan works, clip out the Pocket Outline version of your selected Touring Plan from the back of this guide, and carry it with you as a quick reference when you visit the theme park.

—— *EPCOT Center Touring Plans and Small Children* ——

EPCOT Center is educationally oriented and considerably more adult in tone and presentation than the Magic Kingdom. Most younger children enjoy EPCOT Center if their visit is seven hours or less in duration, and if their tour emphasizes the Future World section of the park. Younger children, especially grade-school children, find the international atmosphere of the World Showcase exciting but do not have the patience for much more than a quick walk-through. While we found touring objectives of adults and younger children basically compatible in Future World, we noted that children tired quickly of World Showcase movies and shows, and tried to hurry their adult companions.

If possible, we recommend that adults touring with children eight years old and younger use the Two-Day Touring Plan (page 383) or the Author's Selective One-Day Touring Plan (page 379). The Two-Day Touring Plan is comprehensive but divides the tour into two less arduous visits. The Author's Selective One-Day Touring Plan includes only EPCOT Center's very best attractions (according to the author) and is, therefore, shorter and less physically demanding. Adults with small children following the One-Day Touring Plan should consider bypassing movies in Canada and China where the audience must stand. Also, be sure to review EPCOT Center attractions in the Small Child Fright Potential Chart on pages 180–83.

At EPCOT Center, sometimes less is more. Our bet is that you and your small children will better enjoy the day if you leave the park after lunch for a swim and a nap. We consider this rest break critical to having a happy and successful day, and recommend it even for families lodging outside of Walt Disney World. If you are following one of our Touring Plans, simply break it off right after lunch and go back to your hotel. Resist the temptation to rest in the park unless your children are small enough to take a good long nap in a stroller. When you return refreshed to EPCOT Center in the late afternoon, visit any attractions in Future World that you missed while following the Touring Plan in the morning.

—— *A Word About the International Gateway* ——

The International Gateway is a secondary entrance to EPCOT Center situated between the United Kingdom and France in the World Showcase section of the park. The purpose of the International Gateway is to provide easy access by tram or foot to guests lodging at the Walt Disney World Swan and Dolphin hotels, or Disney's Yacht and Beach Club Resorts. While offering much in the way of convenience to the guests in these hotels, the location of the International Gateway in the World Showcase area of the park mitigates time-efficient touring.

First thing in the morning, particularly if you are on a tight schedule, you should begin touring from the EPCOT Center main entrance. The attractions you want to see before the park gets crowded are all near the front gate in the Future World area. If, for whatever reasons, you elect to enter at opening time from the International Gateway, it will take 10–13 minutes to walk at a normal pace from the Gateway to Spaceship Earth or the Wonders of Life pavilion. Disney World hotel and campground guests using the International Gateway should make their EPCOT Center dining reservations by phone at least one day, though no more than two days, in advance by dialing 56 (45 for campground guests).

—— *Preliminary Instructions for All*
EPCOT Center Touring Plans ——

On days of moderate to heavy attendance follow the Touring Plans exactly; do not deviate from them except:

1. When you do not want to experience an attraction called for on the Touring Plans—simply skip that step and proceed to the next.

2. When you encounter an extremely long line at an attraction called for by the Touring Plans—the central idea is to avoid crowds, not join them. Crowds build and dissipate throughout the day for a variety of reasons. The Touring Plans anticipate recurring crowd patterns but cannot predict spontaneously arising situations (Spaceship Earth breaking down, for instance, with the hundreds of people standing in line suddenly descending on the nearby Universe of Energy). If a line is ridiculously long, simply skip that step and move on to the next; you can always come back later and give it another try.

Park Opening Procedures

Your success during your first hour of touring will be affected somewhat by the particular opening procedure the Disney people use that day.

EPCOT Center almost always opens a half hour before the official opening time, using one of two basic opening procedures:

1. Some days, usually when attendance is expected to be heavy, all of EPCOT Center opens at once. If this is the case, go directly to Earth Station (adjoining the big sphere on the far side) and make restaurant reservations for lunch and/or dinner. After making your reservations, set out on the Touring Plan of your choice.

2. On other days, only Spaceship Earth (the ride in the sphere) and Earth Station (where you make restaurant reservations) will be open when guests are admitted to the park. If this is the case, ride Spaceship Earth after you make your dining reservations, then line up as follows:

a. If you are going to Body Wars in the Wonders of Life pavilion first, proceed to Communicore East (to the left of Earth Station as you exit Spaceship Earth). When the rest of the park opens, pass through CommuniCore East, taking the first exit to the left, and proceed directly to the Wonders of Life pavilion.

b. If you are going to Listen to the Land boat ride in The Land pavilion first, proceed to Communicore West (to the right of Earth Station as you exit Spaceship Earth). When the rest of the park opens, pass through Communicore West, taking the second exit to the right, and walk directly to The Land pavilion.

Making Your EPCOT Center Restaurant Reservations

If you are a Walt Disney World resort hotel or campground guest, you can make EPCOT Center restaurant reservations from one to three days in advance. Dial 55 for same-day reservations and 56 for advance reservations (45 for campground guests). You can also make reservations one to three days in advance from home (or en route) by calling (407) 824-4500.

If you are not a Walt Disney World lodging or campground guest, or did not make reservations in advance, you can make same-day reservations for EPCOT Center restaurants when you arrive at the park. When admitted at the main entrance, proceed to Earth Station, adjoining the giant sphere on the far side. Here an attendant will direct you to one of many two-way television monitors to make your reservations for lunch and dinner. Simply look into the monitor and state your preference, for instance, "I would like reservations for four persons for lunch at 12:30 in Germany." If you want to eat a meal in France, which has more than one restaurant, you will be asked to specify the restaurant by name. Though France is not on our list of top recommendations, we prefer Bistro de Paris over Chefs de France for most entrees.

Lunch Situation A. If your group is small (four persons or less) and you follow one of our Touring Plans walking at a moderately fast pace throughout the morning, this is approximately where you will be during the lunch hours:

If You Want to Eat at	*You Will Be Near*
11:00–11:30 A.M.	Mexico, Norway, China
11:30–12:00 noon	Norway, China, Germany

12:00–12:30 P.M.	China, Germany, Italy
12:30–1:00 P.M.	Germany, Italy, Japan
1:00–1:30 P.M.	Italy, Japan, Morocco, France
1:30–2:00 P.M.	Morocco, France, United Kingdom
2:00–2:30 P.M.	France, United Kingdom, Canada
	(no reservations required)

Lunch Situation B. If your group is large (five or more persons), **or** you follow one of our Touring Plans walking at a leisurely pace throughout the morning, this is approximately where you will be during the lunch hours:

If You Want to Eat at	*You Will Be Near*
11:00–11:30 A.M.	Mexico, Norway
11:30–12:00 noon	Mexico, Norway, China
12:00–12:30 P.M.	Norway, China, Germany
12:30–1:00 P.M.	China, Germany, Italy
1:00–1:30 P.M.	Germany, Italy, Japan
1:30–2:00 P.M.	Italy, Japan, Morocco
2:00–2:30 P.M.	Japan, Morocco, France

Author's Recommendation for Lunch: Regardless of whether you are moving fast or slow, we recommend lunch in Mexico or Norway.

Author's Recommendation for Dinner: You can eat your evening meal in any of EPCOT Center's restaurants without interrupting the sequence and efficiency of the Touring Plans. We recommend a 7 P.M. reservation when it gets dark early and an 8 P.M. reservation during the late spring, summer, and early fall. The timing of the reservation is important if you want to see IllumiNations, EPCOT Center's nightly grand laser and fireworks spectacular, held over the World Showcase Lagoon shortly after dark.

Our suggestions for dinner include the premier restaurants in Norway, Mexico, Germany, and Morocco. We also like sashimi at the Matsu No Ma Lounge in Japan followed by dinner in the Tempura Kiku Restaurant. If you are hot for some good seafood, make reservations at the Coral Reef Restaurant in Future World. Finally, if you are a picky eater, or simply prefer American cuisine, try The Land Grille Room (Land pavilion), also in Future World.

Before You Go

1. Call (407) 824-4321 the day before you go for the official opening time.

2. Purchase admission prior to your arrival. You can either order tickets through the mail before you leave home or buy them at the Disney Store in your local mall, the Walt Disney World Information Center off I-75 near Ocala (north of Orlando), the Disney Store in the Orlando airport, or at Walt Disney World lodging properties.

3. Make lunch and dinner reservations before arriving at EPCOT Center. If you are staying in Walt Disney World, dial 56 (45 for campground guests) to make EPCOT Center lunch and dinner reservations one to three days in advance. If you want to make reservations before checking into your hotel, call (407) 824-4500.

4. Become familiar with the park opening procedures (described above) and read over the Touring Plan you've chosen so you have an understanding of what you are likely to encounter.

—— EPCOT Center One-Day
Touring Plan ——

FOR: **Adults and children eight years or older.**
ASSUMES: Willingness to experience all major rides and shows.

Be forewarned that this plan requires a lot of walking and some backtracking; this is necessary to avoid long waits in line. A little extra walking and some early morning hustle will save you from two to three hours of standing in line. Note also that you might not complete the tour. How far you get will depend on how quickly you move from attraction to attraction, how many times you pause for rest and food, how quickly the park fills, and what time the park closes.

This Touring Plan is not recommended for families with children under eight years of age. If you are touring with young children and have only one day, use the Author's Selective EPCOT Center One-Day Touring Plan. Break off after lunch to go to your hotel for a swim and a nap, and then return to the park in the late afternoon. If you can allocate two days to EPCOT Center, use the EPCOT Center Two-Day Touring Plan.

1. Arrive 45–50 minutes prior to the park's official opening time. Wait to be admitted.

2. When admitted to the park, move quickly (jog if you are up to it—but do not run) around the left side of Spaceship Earth to Earth Station (the round building directly behind and adjoining the big sphere) to make lunch and dinner reservations. If you do not wish to make lunch or dinner reservations, or have made them already by phone, skip ahead to Step 3.

3. If only Spaceship Earth and Earth Station are open when you are admitted to the park, go ahead and ride Spaceship Earth after making your restaurant reservations. When you exit Spaceship Earth into the lobby of Earth Station, turn left and proceed to Communicore East. When the rest of the park opens, pass through Communicore East and bear left through the first exit; go on to the Wonders of Life pavilion.

If the entire park is open, make your restaurant reservations, then head directly to the Wonders of Life pavilion by way of Communicore East.

4. In the Wonders of Life pavilion, ride Body Wars. Body Wars, incidentally, has quite a track record for making people sick. Be sure to check our Touring Tips on pages 329–30 before riding. Save the other attractions at the Wonders of Life pavilion for later. If you do not want to ride Body Wars, skip ahead to Step 5.

5. If you have not already experienced Spaceship Earth, try it now. When you arrive the line may appear long. If the line forms *outside* the curb and runs along rope and pole barriers, go ahead and ride. If, in addition to rope and pole barriers along the curb, the line *also* winds through a maze of permanent chrome barriers situated *inside* the curb, skip Spaceship Earth for the moment.

6. Go next to The Land pavilion and ride Listen to the Land. Save other attractions in The Land for later and move directly to Step 7.

7. Leave The Land and turn to the right. Proceed to the Journey into Imagination pavilion and ride Journey into Imagination.

8. Exit the ride, but do not go back outside; follow the corridor to the Magic Eye Theater and see *Captain EO*.

9. After *Captain EO*, leave the Journey into Imagination pavilion and take the first available path to Communicore West. Cut through Communicore West, proceed across the plaza, and pass through Communicore East. Exiting Communicore East on the far side, proceed to the World of Motion pavilion.

10. Experience the World of Motion ride. Do not linger too long in the exhibit area at the end of the ride.

11. Bear left after exiting the World of Motion exhibit area, and bear left again on the path that leads to the Odyssey Restaurant. Cut through the Odyssey Restaurant to the World Showcase.

12. Turn left and proceed around the World Showcase Lagoon clockwise. Stop at Mexico and experience El Rio del Tiempo boat ride. The ride is located in the far left corner of the interior courtyard and is not very well marked. If you make any purchases, consign them to Package Pick-up for collection when you leave the park.

13. As you leave the Mexican pavilion continue left to Norway. Ride Maelstrom.

    NOTE: Be aware of the time in respect to your lunch reservations. Simply break off the Touring Plan and go to the restaurant when the time comes. After lunch pick up the Touring Plan where you left off.

14. Continue left around the World Showcase Lagoon to China. See *Wonders of China*.

15. Continue on to Germany and Italy. There are no attractions at either pavilion. If you do not have a restaurant reservation, Sommerfest (fast food) at Germany serves tasty bratwurst, soft pretzels, desserts, and Beck's beer on draft.

16. Continue the clockwise circuit to the American Adventure pavilion. See the show. Once again, if you do not have restaurant reservations, the Liberty Inn (on the left side of the American Adventure) offers fast food: hamburgers, hot dogs, chicken breast sandwiches.

17. Resuming your stroll, visit Japan and Morocco. If you make any purchases, consign them to Package Pick-up for collection when you leave the park.

18. Go left from Morocco to France. See the film *Impressions de France*.

19. Go next to the United Kingdom.

20. Turn left as you leave the United Kingdom and visit Canada. See the film *O Canada!*

21. Return to Future World via the central plaza and cut through Communicore East to Horizons. Ride.

22. Following Horizons, bear right and return to the Wonders of Life pavilion. See *Cranium Command*. Note that the preshow is essential in understanding the main attraction.

23. Exit the Wonders of Life and go right to the Universe of Energy. Do not be dismayed if the line looks long. This production swallows up almost 600 people every 15 minutes.

    NOTE: Be aware of the time in respect to your dinner reservations. Simply break off the Touring Plan and go to the restaurant when the time comes. After dinner, check your daily entertainment schedule for the showtime of IllumiNations, EPCOT Center's superb laser and fireworks spectacular. This is not to be missed; give yourself at least a half hour after dinner to find a good viewing spot along the perimeter of the World Showcase Lagoon. For additional information on the best viewing spots, see pages 348–51.

24. After Universe of Energy, pass back through Communicore East. If you missed Spaceship Earth in the morning, ride it now. Otherwise, cut through the lobby of Earth Station and proceed to Communicore West and Step 25.

25. Taking the first exit to the right, go next to The Living Seas. For maximum efficiency, try to be one of the last people to enter the theater (where you sit), from the preshow area (where you stand). Take a seat as close to the end of a middle row as possible. This will put you in position to be first on the ride that follows the theater presentation. After the ride, enjoy the various exhibits of Sea Base Alpha.

26. Leave The Living Seas to the right and return to The Land. See the *Kitchen Kabaret* and/or the film shown in the Harvest Theater.

27. If there is still time before closing and you have some energy left, stroll the streets of the World Showcase nations or check out the exhibits in CommuniCores East and West. Of special note is Expo Robotics in CommuniCore West. Another fun exhibit is The Image Works upstairs in the Journey into Imagination pavilion.

28. Unless a special holiday schedule is in effect, everything at EPCOT Center (except for a few shops in Future World) closes after IllumiNations. Thirty thousand people bolt for the exits at the same time. Suggestions for coping with this mass exodus can be found on page 347.

— Author's Selective EPCOT Center One-Day Touring Plan —

FOR: **All parties.**

ASSUMES: A willingness to experience major rides and shows.

This Touring Plan is selective and includes only the very best EPCOT Center has to offer according to the author. The absence of a particular attraction in the itinerary should not be construed as negative relative to the attraction's worth.

Families with children under eight using this Touring Plan are encouraged to review EPCOT Center attractions in the Small Child Fright Potential Chart on pages 180–83. We recommend that you rent a stroller for any child small enough to fit in one, and that you take your small children back to the hotel for a nap after lunch. If you can allocate two days to see EPCOT Center, we suggest trying the EPCOT Center Two-Day Touring Plan.

1. Arrive 45–50 minutes prior to the park's official opening time. Wait to be admitted.

2. When admitted to the park, move quickly (jog if you are up to it—but do not run) around the left side of Spaceship Earth to Earth Station (the round building directly behind and adjoining the big sphere) to make lunch and dinner reservations. If you do not wish to make lunch or dinner reservations, or have made them already by phone, skip ahead to Step 3.

3. If only Spaceship Earth and Earth Station are open when you are admitted to the park, go ahead and ride Spaceship Earth after making your restaurant reservations. When you exit Spaceship Earth into the lobby of Earth Station, turn left and proceed to Communicore East. When the rest of the park opens, pass through Communicore East and bear left through the first exit; go on to the Wonders of Life pavilion.

    If the entire park is open, make your restaurant reservations, then head directly to the Wonders of Life pavilion by way of Communicore East.

4. In the Wonders of Life pavilion, ride Body Wars. Body Wars, incidentally, has quite a track record for making people sick. Be

sure to check our Touring Tips on pages 329–30 before riding. Save the other attractions at the Wonders of Life pavilion for later. If you do not want to ride Body Wars, skip ahead to Step 5.

5. If you have not already experienced Spaceship Earth, try it now. When you arrive the line may appear long. If the line forms *outside* the curb and runs along rope and pole barriers, go ahead and ride. If, in addition to rope and pole barriers along the curb, the line *also* winds through a maze of permanent chrome barriers situated *inside* the curb, skip Spaceship Earth for the moment.

6. Go next to The Land pavilion and ride Listen to the Land. Skip the other attractions in The Land for later and move directly to Step 7.

7. Leave The Land and turn right to Journey into Imagination. Enter via the doors on the upper left side of the building. Follow the corridor to the Magic Eye Theater and see *Captain EO*.

8. After *Captain EO*, leave the Journey into Imagination pavilion and take the first available path to Communicore West. Cut through Communicore West, proceed across the plaza, and pass through Communicore East. Exiting Communicore East on the far side, proceed to the World of Motion pavilion.

9. Experience the World of Motion ride. Do not linger too long in the exhibit area at the end of the ride.

10. Bear left after exiting the World of Motion exhibit area, and bear left again on the path that leads to the Odyssey Restaurant. Cut through the Odyssey Restaurant to the World Showcase.

11. Turn left and proceed around the World Showcase Lagoon clockwise. Visit the interior courtyard at Mexico, but skip the boat ride. If you make any purchases, consign them to Package Pick-up for collection when you leave the park.

12. Continue left to Norway. Ride Maelstrom.

13. Continue left around the World Showcase Lagoon to China. See *Wonders of China*.

   NOTE: Be aware of the time in respect to your lunch reservations. Simply break off the Touring Plan and go to the restaurant when the time comes. After lunch pick up the Touring Plan where you left off.

14. Walking clockwise around the World Showcase Lagoon, visit

Germany and Italy. There are no attractions at either pavilion. If you do not have a restaurant reservation, Sommerfest (fast food) at Germany serves tasty bratwurst, soft pretzels, desserts, and Beck's beer on draft.

15. Continue the clockwise circuit to the American Adventure pavilion. See the show. Once again, if you do not have restaurant reservations, the Liberty Inn (on the left side of the American Adventure) offers fast food: hamburgers, hot dogs, chicken breast sandwiches.

16. Resuming your stroll, visit Japan and Morocco. If you make any purchases, consign them to Package Pick-up for collection when you leave the park.

17. Leave Morocco and go to France. See the film *Impressions de France*.

18. Go next to the United Kingdom.

19. Turn left as you leave the United Kingdom and visit Canada. The film *O Canada!* is quite good, but the audience must stand. Optional.

20. Return to Future World via the central plaza and cut through Communicore East to Horizons. Ride.

21. Following Horizons, bear right and return to the Wonders of Life pavilion. See *Cranium Command*. Note that the preshow is essential in understanding the main attraction.

22. Exit the Wonders of Life and go right to the Universe of Energy. Do not be dismayed if the line looks long. This production swallows up almost 600 people every 15 minutes.

NOTE: Be aware of the time in respect to your dinner reservations. Simply break off the Touring Plan and go to the restaurant when the time comes. After dinner, check your daily entertainment schedule for the showtime of IllumiNations, EPCOT Center's superb laser and fireworks spectacular. This is not to be missed; give yourself at least a half hour after dinner to find a good viewing spot along the perimeter of the World Showcase Lagoon. For additional information on the best viewing spots, see pages 348–51.

23. After Universe of Energy, pass back through Communicore East. If you missed Spaceship Earth in the morning, ride it now. Otherwise, cut through the lobby of Earth Station and proceed to Communicore West and Step 24.

24. Taking the first exit to the right, go next to The Living Seas. For maximum efficiency, try to be one of the last people to enter the theater (where you sit), from the preshow area (where you stand). Take a seat as close to the end of a middle row as possible. This will put you in position to be first on the ride that follows the theater presentation. After the ride, enjoy the various exhibits of Sea Base Alpha.

25. This concludes the Touring Plan. If you have any time or energy left, visit attractions you missed or shop until time for IllumiNations. Unless a special holiday schedule is in effect, everything at EPCOT Center (except for a few shops in Future World) closes after IllumiNations. Thirty thousand people bolt for the exits at the same time. Suggestions for coping with this mass exodus can be found on page 347.

—— EPCOT Center Two-Day Touring Plan ——

FOR: **All parties.**

This Touring Plan is for EPCOT Center visitors who wish to tour EPCOT Center comprehensively over a two-day period. Day One takes advantage of early morning touring opportunities, while Day Two begins in the late afternoon and continues until the park closes.

Families with children under eight using this Touring Plan are encouraged to review EPCOT Center attractions in the Small Child Fright Potential Chart on pages 180–83. We recommend that you rent a stroller for any child small enough to fit in one. We also suggest that you break off Day One no later than 2:30 P.M. in order to return to your hotel for rest. If you missed attractions called for in Day One of the Plan, add them to your itinerary on Day Two.

Day One

1. Arrive 45–50 minutes prior to the park's official opening time. Wait to be admitted.
2. When admitted to the park, move quickly (jog if you are up to it—but do not run) around the left side of Spaceship Earth to Earth Station (the round building directly behind and adjoining the big sphere) to make lunch and dinner reservations. If you do not wish to make lunch or dinner reservations, or have made them already by phone, skip ahead to Step 3.
3. If *only* Spaceship Earth and Earth Station are open when you are admitted to the park, go ahead and ride Spaceship Earth after making your restaurant reservations. When you exit Spaceship Earth into the lobby of Earth Station, turn left and proceed to Communicore East. When the rest of the park opens, pass through Communicore East and bear left through the first exit; go on to the Wonders of Life pavilion.

    If the entire park is open, make your restaurant reservations, then head directly to the Wonders of Life pavilion by way of Communicore East.
4. In the Wonders of Life pavilion, ride Body Wars. Body Wars,

incidentally, has quite a track record for making people sick. Be sure to check our Touring Tips on pages 329–30 before riding. Save the other attractions at the Wonders of Life pavilion for later. If you do not want to ride Body Wars, skip ahead to Step 5.

5. While at the Wonders of Life, see *The Making of Me*.

6. If you have not already experienced Spaceship Earth, try it now. When you arrive the line may appear long. If the line forms *outside* the curb and runs along rope and pole barriers, go ahead and ride. If, in addition to rope and pole barriers along the curb, the line *also* winds through a maze of permanent chrome barriers situated *inside* the curb, skip Spaceship Earth for the moment.

7. Go next to The Land pavilion and ride Listen to the Land. Save other attractions in The Land for later and move directly to Step 8.

8. Leave The Land and go to the right. Proceed to the Journey into Imagination pavilion and ride Journey into Imagination.

9. Exit the ride, but do not go back outside; follow the corridor to the Magic Eye Theater and see *Captain EO*.

10. After *Captain EO*, leave the Journey into Imagination pavilion and take the first available path to Communicore West. Cut through Communicore West, proceed across the plaza, and pass through Communicore East. Exiting Communicore East on the far side, proceed to the World of Motion pavilion.

11. Experience the World of Motion ride. Do not linger too long in the exhibit area at the end of the ride.

12. Bear left after exiting the World of Motion exhibit area, and bear left again on the path that leads to the Odyssey Restaurant. Cut through the Odyssey Restaurant to the World Showcase.

13. Turn left and proceed around the World Showcase Lagoon clockwise. Stop at Mexico and experience El Rio del Tiempo boat ride. The ride is located in the far left corner of the interior courtyard and is not very well marked. If you make any purchases, consign them to Package Pick-up for collection when you leave the park.

14. On exiting the Mexican pavilion, continue left to Norway. Ride Maelstrom.

NOTE: Be aware of the time in respect to your lunch reservations. Simply break off the Touring Plan and go to the restaurant when the time comes. After lunch pick up the Touring Plan where you left off.

15. Continue left around the Lagoon to China. See *Wonders of China*.

16. Walking clockwise around the World Showcase Lagoon, visit Germany and Italy. There are no attractions at either pavilion. If you do not have a restaurant reservation, Sommerfest (fast food) at Germany serves tasty bratwurst, soft pretzels, desserts, and Beck's beer on draft.

17. Continue the clockwise circuit to the American Adventure pavilion. See the show. Once again, if you do not have restaurant reservations, the Liberty Inn (on the left side of the American Adventure) offers fast food: hamburgers, hot dogs, chicken breast sandwiches.

18. Resuming your stroll, visit Japan and Morocco. If you make any purchases, consign them to Package Pick-up for collection when you leave the park.

19. Go left from Morocco to France. See the film *Impressions de France*.

20. This concludes the Touring Plan for Day One. Attractions and pavilions not included today will be experienced tomorrow. If you are full of energy and wish to continue touring, follow the EPCOT Center One-Day Touring Plan, starting at Step 18. If you've had enough, you can either exit through the International Gateway or head out through the main entrance. To reach the main entrance without hoofing around the World Showcase Lagoon, catch a boat at the dock near Morocco.

Day Two

1. Enter EPCOT Center at about 3 P.M. Pick up a daily entertainment schedule and a park map at Earth Station.

2. While at Earth Station make dinner reservations, if you have not done so by phone. Since it will be well past the usual time for making reservations, you will have to summon a reservationist by using the WorldKey information service terminals (see page 311).

    You can eat your evening meal in any of EPCOT Center's restaurants without interrupting the sequence and efficiency of the Touring Plan. We recommend a 7 P.M. reservation when it gets dark early and an 8 P.M. reservation during the late spring, summer, and early fall. The timing of the reservation is important if you want to see IllumiNations, EPCOT Center's nightly grand laser and fireworks spectacular, held over the World Showcase Lagoon shortly after dark.

If your preferred restaurants and seatings are filled, try for a reservation at Morocco or Norway. Because the delightful ethnic dishes of these countries are not well known to most Americans, it is often possible to get a reservation late in the day.

3. Go to The Living Seas. For maximum efficiency, try to be one of the last people to enter the theater (where you sit) from the preshow area (where you stand). Take a seat as close to the end of a middle row as possible. This will put you in position to be first on the ride which follows the theater presentation. After the ride, enjoy the various exhibits of Sea Base Alpha.

4. Exit The Living Seas to the right and return to The Land. See the *Kitchen Kabaret* or the film in the Harvest Theater, a wonderful film that examines the necessity of man living in harmony with the land.

5. Leave The Land and backtrack to Spaceship Earth (the big sphere) and ride. If you experienced Spaceship Earth on Day One of the Touring Plan, skip ahead to Step 6.

6. Pass through CommuniCore East, taking the first exit to the left, and proceed to the Universe of Energy. See the show.

7. Exit to the left and proceed to the Wonders of Life pavilion. See *Cranium Command*. Be sure to catch the preshow.

8. Exit Wonders of Life to the left and proceed next door to Horizons. Ride.

NOTE: Be aware of the time in respect to your dinner reservations. Simply break off the Touring Plan and go to the restaurant when the time comes. After dinner, check your daily entertainment schedule for the showtime of IllumiNations, EPCOT Center's superb laser and fireworks spectacular. This is not to be missed; give yourself at least a half hour after dinner to find a good viewing spot along the perimeter of the World Showcase Lagoon. For additional information on the best viewing spots, see pages 348–51.

9. Leave Future World and walk counterclockwise around the World Showcase Lagoon to Canada. See *O Canada!*

10. Turn right as you leave Canada and visit the United Kingdom.
11. This concludes the Touring Plan. Enjoy your dinner and Illumi-Nations. If you have time, shop or revisit your favorite attractions.
12. Unless a special holiday schedule is in effect, everything at EPCOT Center (except for a few shops in Future World) closes after IllumiNations. Thirty thousand people bolt for the exits at the same time. Suggestions for coping with this mass exodus can be found on page 347.

PART SIX: The Disney-MGM Studios, Universal Studios Florida, and Sea World

Disney-MGM Studios

And Now for Something Completely Different (Again)

Several years ago, the Disney folks decided they wanted to make movies for adults. Figuring that Snow White wouldn't share the set with Bette Midler mouthing four-letter words, they cranked up a brand new production company to handle the adult stuff. Results have been impressive; a complete rejuvenation with new faces and tremendous creativeness, and an amazing resurgence at the box office.

So, as a new era of Disney film and television success began to crest, what better way to showcase and promote their product than with an all-new motion-picture and television entertainment park at Walt Disney World?

The MGM Connection

To broaden the appeal and to lend additional historic impact, Disney obtained the rights to use the MGM (Metro-Goldwyn-Mayer) name, the MGM film library, MGM motion picture and television titles, excerpts, costumes, music, sets, and even Leo, the MGM logo lion. Probably the two most readily recognized names in the motion picture industry, Disney and MGM in combination showcase more than 60 years of movie history.

Comparing Disney-MGM Studios to the Magic Kingdom and EPCOT Center

Such a comparison appears to be an "apples and oranges" proposition at first glance. The Magic Kingdom has modeled most of its attractions from Disney movie and TV themes; EPCOT Center has pioneered attractions and rides as vehicles for learning. Looking more closely, however, there are numerous similarities. Like EPCOT Center, the Disney-MGM Studios is at once fun and educational, and as in the Magic Kingdom, the themes for the various rides and shows are drawn from movies and television. All three parks rely heavily on Disney special effects and AudioAnimatronics (robotics) in their entertainment mix.

The Disney-MGM Studios is about the same size as the Magic Kingdom and about one-half as large as the sprawling EPCOT Center. Unlike the other parks, however, Disney-MGM Studios is a working motion picture and television production facility. This means, among other things, that more than half of the entire Studios area is controlled access, with guests permitted only on tours and accompanied by guides, or restricted to observation walkways.

When EPCOT Center opened in 1982, Disney patrons expected a futuristic version of the Magic Kingdom. What they got was humanistic inspiration and a creative educational experience. Since then, the Disney folks have tried to inject a little more magic, excitement, and surprise into EPCOT Center. But remembering the occasional disappointment of those early EPCOT Center guests, Disney planners have fortified the Disney-MGM Studios with megadoses of action, suspense, surprise, and, of course, special effects. If you are interested in the history and technology of the motion picture and television industries, there is plenty of education to be had. However, if you feel lazy and just want to be entertained, the Disney-MGM Studios is a pretty good place to be.

—— *How Much Time to Allocate* ——

A guest really has to scurry to see all of EPCOT Center or the Magic Kingdom (some say it can't be done) in one day. The Disney-MGM Studios are more manageable. There is less walking and much less ground to cover by foot. Trams transport guests throughout much of the back lot and working areas, and the attractions in the open-access parts are concentrated in an area about the size of Main Street and Tomorrowland put together. There will be a day, no doubt, as the Disney-MGM Studios develops and grows, when you will need more than a day to see everything without hurrying. For the time being, however, the Studios are a nice one-day outing.

Because it is smaller, however, the Disney-MGM Studios is more affected by large crowds. Likewise, being the newest Disney theme park, large crowds can be considered the norm for the foreseeable future. To help you avoid the crowds we have developed Touring Plans for the Disney-MGM Studios which will keep you a step ahead of the mob and minimize any waits in line. Even when the park is heavily attended, however, you can see most everything in a day.

—— *The Disney-MGM Studios in the Evening* ——

Because the Disney-MGM Studios can be seen in two-thirds of a day, most guests who arrive in the morning run out of things to do by 3:30 or 4 P.M., and leave the park. Their departure greatly diminishes the crowd and makes the Studios an ideal park for evening touring. Lines for almost all attractions except *The Voyage of the Little Mermaid* are short and manageable, and the park is cooler and more comfortable. Productions at the *Indiana Jones Epic Stunt Spectacular* and the Backlot Theater are infinitely more enjoyable during the evening than in the sweltering heat of the day. And, finally, there is Sorcery in the Sky, thought by many of our readers to be the most spectacular fireworks show at Walt Disney World. A drawback to touring the Studios at night is there will not be much activity on the production soundstages or the Animation Building. Another problem is you might get stuck eating dinner at the Studios. If you've got to eat, try Mama Melrose's for full-service dining or the Hollywood & Vine Cafeteria.

—— *Arriving and Getting Oriented* ——

The Disney-MGM Studios has its own pay parking lot and is also serviced by shuttle bus from the Transportation and Ticket Center, from EPCOT Center, and from Walt Disney World hotels. In addition, many of the larger "out-of-the-World" hotels shuttle guests to the Studios. If you drive, Walt Disney World's ubiquitous trams will arrive to transport you to the ticketing area and entrance gate.

As you enter, Guest Services will be on your left, serving as a park headquarters and information center similar to City Hall in the Magic Kingdom and Earth Station at EPCOT Center. Check here for a schedule of live performances, lost persons, lost objects, emergencies, and

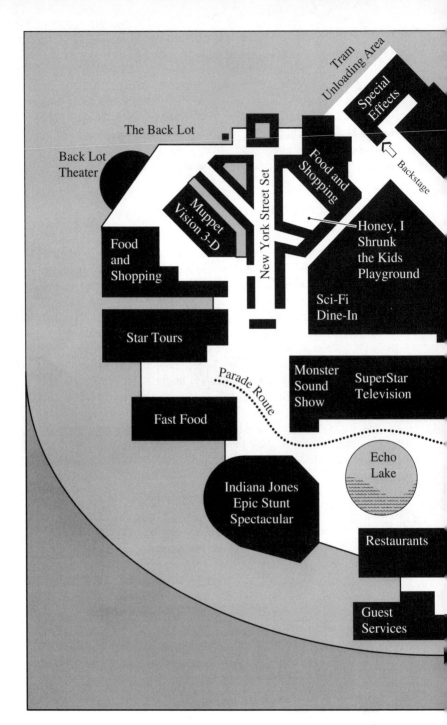

Tram
Unloading Area

Special
Effects

The Back Lot

Backstage

Back Lot
Theater

Food and
Shopping

Muppet
Vision 3-D

New York Street Set

Honey, I
Shrunk
the Kids
Playground

Food
and
Shopping

Sci-Fi
Dine-In

Star Tours

Parade Route

Monster
Sound
Show

SuperStar
Television

Fast Food

Echo
Lake

Indiana Jones
Epic Stunt
Spectacular

Restaurants

Guest
Services

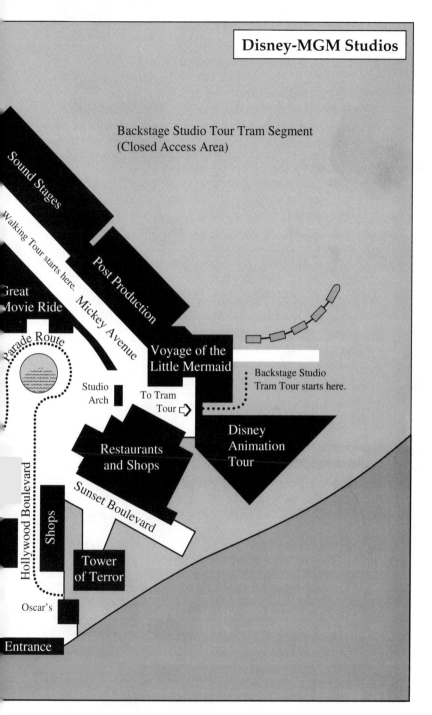

Disney-MGM Studios

Backstage Studio Tour Tram Segment
(Closed Access Area)

Sound Stages

Walking Tour starts here.

Post Production

Great Movie Ride

Mickey Avenue

Parade Route

Voyage of the Little Mermaid

Studio Arch

To Tram Tour

Backstage Studio Tram Tour starts here.

Disney Animation Tour

Restaurants and Shops

Hollywood Boulevard

Sunset Boulevard

Shops

Tower of Terror

Oscar's

Entrance

general information. If you have not been provided with a map of the Studios, pick one up here. To the right of the entrance you will find lockers, strollers, and wheelchair rentals.

For the sake of orientation, about one-half of the entire complex is set up as a theme park. As at the Magic Kingdom you enter the park and pass down a main street; only this time it's Hollywood Boulevard of the 1920s and 30s. At the end of Hollywood Boulevard is a replica of Hollywood's long-famous Chinese Theater. While not as imposing as Cinderella Castle or EPCOT Center's Spaceship Earth, the Theater is nevertheless Disney-MGM Studios' focal landmark and serves as a good spot to meet if your group gets separated.

The open-access (theme park) areas of the Studios complex are at the theater end of Hollywood Boulevard, off Sunset Boulevard (branching off Hollywood Boulevard to the right), and around a lake off to the left of the Boulevard as you face the theater. Attractions in this section of the Studios are rides and shows, which you can experience according to your own tastes and timetable. The remainder of the Disney-MGM Studios consists of the working sound stages, technical facilities, wardrobe shops, administrative offices, animation studios, and back lot sets; these are accessible to visitors by foot, or by a combination tram and walking Studio Tour.

—— *What to See* ——

As in our coverage of the Magic Kingdom and EPCOT Center, we have identified certain attractions as "not to be missed." We suggest, however, that you try everything. Usually exceeding your expectations, and always surprising, Disney rides and shows are rarely what you would anticipate.

—— *Chalk Board with Waiting Times* ——

As a courtesy, the Disney-MGM Studios provide a large chalk board which lists the current waiting times for all Disney-MGM attractions. Updated continuously throughout the day, the chalk board is situated on Hollywood Boulevard near The Hollywood Brown Derby restaurant.

In the early morning, well-intended Disney employees will try to direct you to the *Indiana Jones Epic Stunt Spectacular,* saying, "Go now or you will have a long wait." If you are on hand when the park opens, simply ignore them and stick to the Touring Plan. A Detroit woman reported the following:

> My older sister and family went to [Disney-] MGM. They got there and were encouraged by Disney people to go to a different show other than your plan. They did and ended up waiting in line for everything.

Open-Access Movie Theme Park

Hollywood Boulevard

Hollywood Boulevard is a palm-lined re-creation of Hollywood's main drag during the city's golden age. Architecture is streamlined *moderne* with art deco embellishments. Most of the theme park's service facilities are located here, interspersed with numerous shops and eateries. Shoppers can select from among Hollywood and movie-related souvenir items to one-of-a-kind collectibles obtained from studio auctions and estate sales. Disney trademark items are, of course, also available.

In addition to the services and commercial ventures, trolleys transport guests who want a lift from the park entrance to the Chinese Theater at the end of the Boulevard, and characters from Hollywood's heyday, as well as roving performers, entertain passers-by. The Boulevard also serves as the site for daily parades and other happenings.

Hollywood Boulevard Services

Most of the park's service facilities are housed along Hollywood Boulevard, including the following:

Wheelchair & Stroller Rental	To the right of the entrance at Oscar's Super Service
Banking Services	An automated bank teller can be found to the right of the entrance turnstiles (outside the park). Only American Express cards and Cirrus system credit cards (look for the Cirrus logo on the back of your card) will work.
Storage Lockers	Rental lockers are located to the right of the main entrance on Hollywood Boulevard on the left side of Oscar's.
Lost & Found	Lost & Found is in the Guest Services Building to the left of the entrance on Hollywood Boulevard.

Live Entertainment/ Parade Information	Available at Guest Services
Lost Persons	Lost persons can be reported at Guest Services
Walt Disney World & Local Attraction Information	At Guest Services
First Aid	At Guest Services
Baby Center/Baby Care Needs	At Guest Services. Oscar's sells baby food and other necessities.
Film	At the Darkroom on the right side of Holly- wood Boulevard just beyond Oscar's

Sunset Boulevard (opens fall 1994)

Sunset Boulevard is a major new addition to the Disney-MGM Studios. Located near The Hollywood Brown Derby restaurant, Sunset Boulevard provides another venue for dining, shopping, and street entertainment. The new thoroughfare is evocative of 1940's Hollywood in theme and architecture.

The Twilight Zone Tower of Terror (opens fall 1994)

Type of Attraction: Disney mixed-media adventure ride
When to Go: Before 10 A.M. and after 5 P.M.
Special Comments: Not to be missed
Author's Rating: Attraction not open at press time
Overall Appeal by Age Group: Attraction not open at press time
Duration of Ride: About 11 minutes
Average Wait in Line per 100 People Ahead of You: 4 minutes
Assumes: All elevators operating
Loading Speed: Fast

DESCRIPTION AND COMMENTS   The Tower of Terror is a new species of thrill ride in the Disney repertoire, though it borrows elements from The Haunted Mansion at the Magic Kingdom. The idea is that you are touring a once famous Hollywood hotel gone to ruin. As at Star Tours, the queuing area serves to integrate the guests into the story as they pass through the hotel's once opulent public rooms and lobby.

The ride vehicle, one of the hotel's elevators, takes the guests for a floor-by-floor tour of the thirteen-story haunted hostelry. En route, guests are subjected to the full range of Disney special effects as they encounter various unexpected horrors and optical illusions. The climax of the adventure occurs when the elevator reaches the top floor (13, of course) and the elevator cable snaps.

Though the sensation of the final plunge is calculated to give thrill-seekers something to sink their teeth into, the attraction is really about its extraordinary visual and audio effects. In any event, our speculation at press time is the attraction has great potential for terrifying small children and rattling the dentures of more mature visitors. If the Tower of Terror is open when you visit and you have teenagers in your party, use them as experimental probes. If they report back that they really liked the Tower of Terror, run in the opposite direction as fast as you can.

TOURING TIPS   As Walt Disney World's most ambitious and hyped new attraction of 1994, you can bet that the Tower of Terror will be mobbed. If it is open when you visit, try to ride early in the morning.

The Great Movie Ride

Type of Attraction: Disney mixed-media adventure ride

When to Go: Before 10 A.M. and after 5 P.M.

Special Comments: Elaborate, with several surprises; not to be missed

Author's Rating: ★★★★

Overall Appeal by Age Group:

Pre-school	Grade School	Teens	Young Adults	Over 30	Senior Citizens
★★★★	★★★★	★★★★	★★★★½	★★★★½	★★★★½

Duration of Ride: About 19 minutes

Average Wait in Line per 100 People Ahead of You: 2 minutes

Assumes: All trains operating

Loading Speed: Fast

DESCRIPTION AND COMMENTS   Entering through a re-creation of Hollywood's Chinese Theater, guests board vehicles for a fast-paced tour through soundstage sets from such classic films as *Casablanca*, *The Wizard of Oz*, *Aliens*, *Raiders of the Lost Ark*, and many more. Each set is populated with new-generation Disney AudioAnimatronics (robots) as well as an occasional human, all assisted by a variety of dazzling special effects. Disney's largest and most ambitious ride-through attraction, The Great Movie Ride encompasses 95,000 square feet and showcases some of the most famous scenes in filmmaking history. Life-sized AudioAnimatronic sculptures of such stars as Gene Kelly, John Wayne, James Cagney, Julie Andrews, and Harrison Ford inhabit the largest sets ever constructed for a Disney ride.

TOURING TIPS The Great Movie Ride is a Disney-MGM feature attraction which draws large crowds (and lines) from the moment the park opens. An interval-loading, high-capacity ride, lines disappear quickly. Even so, waits can exceed an hour after mid-morning (as an aside, actual waits usually run about one-third shorter than the time posted on the "Waiting Sign." If the sign indicates an hour wait, your actual wait will probably be around 40 minutes).

SuperStar Television

Type of Attraction: Audience participation television production
When to Go: After 10 A.M.
Author's Rating: Well-conceived; not to be missed; ★★★½
Overall Appeal by Age Group:

Pre-school	Grade School	Teens	Young Adults	Over 30	Senior Citizens
★★★½	★★★★★	★★★★★	★★★★½	★★★★½	★★★★½

Duration of Presentation: 30 minutes
Preshow Entertainment: Participants selected from guests waiting in the preshow area
Probable Waiting Time: 10–20 minutes

DESCRIPTION AND COMMENTS Audience volunteers (conscriptees) participate in a television production where special effects are used to integrate the actions of the amateurs with footage of well-known stars of past and current TV shows. The combined result, a sort of video collage where the volunteers miraculously end up in the footage with the stars, is broadcast on large-screen monitors above the set. The outcome, always rated in laughs, depends on how the volunteers respond to their dramatic debut.

TOURING TIPS The theater seats 1,000 persons, so it is not usually difficult to get in. If you want to be in the production, however, it is essential that you enter the preshow holding area at least 15 minutes before the next performance. Participants for the show are more or less drafted by a casting director from among guests of both genders and from all age groups. Those who stand near the director and those who are distinctively (outlandishly?) attired seem to be selected most often.

Star Tours

Type of Attraction: Space flight simulation ride

When to Go: First hour and a half the park is open

Special Comments: Expectant mothers or anyone prone to motion sickness are advised against riding. The ride is too intense for many children under 8.

Author's Rating: Disney's absolute best, anytime, anyplace; not to be missed; ★★★★★

Overall Appeal by Age Group:

Pre-school	Grade School	Teens	Young Adults	Over 30	Senior Citizens
★★★★★	★★★★★	★★★★★	★★★★★	★★★★★	★★★★★

Duration of Ride: Approximately 7 minutes

Average Wait in Line per 100 People Ahead of You: 5 minutes

Assumes: All simulators operating

Loading Speed: Moderate to fast

DESCRIPTION AND COMMENTS   This attraction is so amazing, so real, and so much fun that it just makes you grin and giggle. It is the only Disney ride anywhere for which we have voluntarily waited 45 minutes in line, not once, but three times in succession. The attraction consists of a ride in a flight simulator modeled after those used in the training of pilots and astronauts. Guests, supposedly on a little vacation outing in space, are piloted by a droid (android, a.k.a. humanoid, a.k.a. robot) on his first flight with real passengers. Mayhem ensues almost immediately, the scenery flashes by at supersonic speed, and the simulator bucks and pitches. You could swear you were moving at light speed. After several minutes of this, the droid somehow gets the spacecraft landed and you discover you are about ten times happier than you were before you boarded. Speaking strictly for the research team, we would like to see a whole new generation of Disney rides on the order of Star Tours.

TOURING TIPS   This one ride is worth your admission to Disney-MGM Studios. Except for the 40 minutes or so following opening, lines will be long all day. If you are not present during the first hour and a half, expect a long wait. If you have small children (or anyone else) who are apprehensive about this attraction, ask the attendant about switching off (see page 187).

The Monster Sound Show

Type of Attraction: Audience participation show demonstrating sound effects

When to Go: Before 11 A.M. or after 5 P.M.

Author's Rating: Funny and informative; ★★★½

Overall Appeal by Age Group:

Pre-school	Grade School	Teens	Young Adults	Over 30	Senior Citizens
★★★½	★★★★½	★★★★½	★★★★½	★★★★½	★★★★½

Duration of Presentation: 12 minutes

Preshow Entertainment: David Letterman and Jimmy McDonald video

Probable Waiting Time: 15–30 minutes except during the first half hour the park is open

DESCRIPTION AND COMMENTS A live show where guests are invited on stage for a crash course in becoming sound-effects technicians. The results of their training, always funny, are played back at the end of the show for the audience to enjoy.

TOURING TIPS Because the theater is relatively small, long waits (mostly in the hot sun) are common here. Another thing: the *Sound Show* is periodically inundated by guests coming from a just-concluded performance of SuperStar Television or the *Indiana Jones Epic Stunt Spectacular*. This is not the time to get in line. Wait at least 20 minutes and try again.

Being chosen for participation in *The Monster Sound Show* is pretty much a function of luck. There is not much beyond being accidentally in the right place at the right time to enhance your chances for getting picked.

Indiana Jones Epic Stunt Spectacular

Type of Attraction: Movie stunt demonstration and action show

When to Go: First morning show or last evening show

Special Comments: Performance times posted on a sign at the entrance
to the theater

Author's Rating: Done on a grand scale; ★★★★

Overall Appeal by Age Group:

Pre-school	Grade School	Teens	Young Adults	Over 30	Senior Citizens
★★★★½	★★★★★	★★★★★	★★★★½	★★★★½	★★★★½

Duration of Presentation: 30 minutes

Preshow Entertainment: Selection of "extras" from audience

Probable Waiting Time: None

DESCRIPTION AND COMMENTS   Coherent and educational, though
somewhat unevenly paced, the production showcases professional stunt
men and women who demonstrate various dangerous stunts with a
behind-the-scenes look at how it's all done. The sets, props, and special effects are incredible.

TOURING TIPS   The Epic Stunt Theater holds 2,000 people but, owing
to the popularity of the presentation, generally plays to capacity audiences. On busy days, we recommend you attend the first scheduled
performance in the morning (usually about 30–45 minutes after opening). Because the park has not yet become crowded, you should be able
to walk into the early show with no wait, and will probably be seated
even if you arrive a couple of minutes late. After the first show, all
bets are off. For subsequent performances, you might end up waiting
as long as an hour.

If you miss the first scheduled performance, your fallback plan is to
check the line for the second performance exactly 30 minutes before
showtime. If the line reaches the green dinosaur by the lake, you will
probably not be admitted to the next show. If the line does not extend
that far, go ahead and queue up; you'll most likely be admitted. Should
you wish to ensure that you get into the second show, hop in line 40
minutes (ugh!) prior to showtime. If you plan to tour during the late
afternoon and evening, try attending the last scheduled performance of
the day.

As a footnote, the Disney people could relieve much of the congestion and discomfort of waiting in the hot sun by simply allowing guests
to walk into the theater and sit down. Sea World follows this practice
with all of their stadium shows, much to their guests' appreciation.

Backlot Theater

Type of Attraction: Live Hollywood-style musical, usually featuring the Disney characters; performed in an open-air theater

When to Go: In the evening

Special Comments: Performance times are listed in the daily entertainment schedule

Author's Rating: Excellent; ★★★★½

Overall Appeal by Age Group:

Pre-school	Grade School	Teens	Young Adults	Over 30	Senior Citizens
★★★★½	★★★★½	★★★★½	★★★★½	★★★★½	★★★★½

Duration of Presentation: 25 minutes

Preshow Entertainment: None

Probable Waiting Time: None

DESCRIPTION AND COMMENTS *Backlot Theater* combines Disney characters with singers and dancers in upbeat and humorous Hollywood musical productions. The Beauty and the Beast show, in particular, is outstanding. Unfortunately, the audience must sit in the wilting Florida sun. During the summer, most guests cannot make it through an entire performance. The landscaping department has planted some nice sycamore trees, but the trees won't be large enough to provide much shade for a couple of years. As a mother from Conroe, Texas, described it:

> Beauty & the Beast was shown in the [Backlot] Theater, and while I'm sure the presentation was great, we were too busy trying to fan ourselves and the bleachers were burning our rear ends.

From Palmyra, Pennsylvania, another mom sent in this opinion:

> [Regarding] the [Backlot] Theater, the seating layout is terrible. We were all the way in the back and it was impossible to see past the row in front of us. Kids were standing and blocking the view because they couldn't see. A complete waste of time, though I am sure *Beauty and the Beast* must have been wonderful.

The theater was moved in 1993 from its previous address on Hollywood Boulevard to its current obscure location. To reach the theater, proceed to the "park" end of the New York Street set and bear left.

TOURING TIPS   Unless you visit during a cooler time of year, try to see this show in the evening. Sometimes the production is so popular, as is *Beauty and the Beast*, that you might have to show up 20–50 minutes in advance to get a seat.

The Voyage of the Little Mermaid

Type of Attraction: Musical stage show featuring characters from the Disney movie *The Little Mermaid*

When to Go: Before 9:30 A.M. or just before closing

Author's Rating: Romantic, lovable, and humorous in the best Disney tradition; ★★★★★

Overall Appeal by Age Group:

Pre-school	Grade School	Teens	Young Adults	Over 30	Senior Citizens
★★★★★	★★★★★	★★★★½	★★★★½	★★★★★	★★★★★

Duration of Presentation: 15 minutes

Preshow Entertainment: Taped ramblings about the decor in the preshow holding area

Probable Waiting Time: Before 9:30 A.M., 30 minutes; after 9:30 A.M., 50–90 minutes

DESCRIPTION AND COMMENTS   *The Voyage of the Little Mermaid* is a real winner, appealing to every age group. Cute without being silly or saccharine, as well as infinitely lovable, the *Little Mermaid* show is the most tender and romantic entertainment offered in any Disney theme park. A simple and engaging story, an impressive mix of special effects, and some memorable Disney characters make *The Voyage of the Little Mermaid* a "not-to-be-missed" attraction.

TOURING TIPS   Because it is well done and situated at a busy pedestrian intersection, *The Voyage of the Little Mermaid* plays to capacity crowds all day. Unless you make the first or second show of the day, you will probably have to wait an hour or more. If you plan to spend an evening (as well as a morning) at the Disney-MGM Studios, see the first *Little Mermaid* show and save the *Indiana Jones Epic Stunt Spectacular* for evening viewing. If you try to see the first morning production of *Indiana Jones* and then head for the *Little Mermaid*, you can expect a wait of 45–75 minutes for the latter.

In our Touring Plan we recommend attending the first showing of the *Little Mermaid*, and then hot-footing it over to the first performance of *Indiana Jones*. On most days, the first *Little Mermaid* show will conclude about one minute before *Indiana Jones* is scheduled to begin. Because the first *Indiana Jones* performance is seldom full, however, you will be admitted even if you arrive a little late. Don't sweat missing the first couple of minutes of *Indiana Jones*. It's nothing you can't live without.

When you enter the preshow lobby for the *Little Mermaid*, position yourself near the doors on the left. When the doors open, go into the theater, pick a row of seats, and let about six to ten people enter the row ahead of you. This is necessary because an important section of the stage cannot be seen from the last six seats on the far side of the theater. The strategy here is twofold: to obtain a good seat and be close to the exit doors.

Jim Henson's MuppetVision 3-D

Type of Attraction: 3-D movie starring the Muppets
When to Go: Before noon and after 3 P.M.
Author's Rating: Uproarious, not to be missed; ★★★★½
Overall Appeal by Age Group:

Pre-school	Grade School	Teens	Young Adults	Over 30	Senior Citizens
★★★★½	★★★★★	★★★★½	★★★★½	★★★★½	★★★★½

Duration of Presentation: 17 minutes
Preshow Entertainment: Muppets on television
Probable Waiting Time: 12 minutes

DESCRIPTION AND COMMENTS *MuppetVision 3-D* provides a total sensory experience, with the wild 3-D action augmented by auditory, visual, and even tactile special effects in the theater. If you are tired and hot, this presentation will make you feel brand new. Not to be missed.

TOURING TIPS Watch out for huge throngs of people arriving en masse from just concluded performances of the *Indiana Jones Epic Stunt Spectacular*. If you encounter a long line, chalk it up to bad timing and try again later.

Honey, I Shrunk the Kids Movie Set
Adventure Playground

Type of Attraction: Small, but elaborate, playground
When to Go: Before 10:30 A.M. or after dark
Author's Rating: Great for small children, expendable for adults; ★★½
Overall Appeal by Age Group:

Pre-school	Grade School	Teens	Young Adults	Over 30	Senior Citizens
★★★★½	★★★★	★★	★★½	★★★	★★½

Duration of Presentation: Varies
Average Wait in Line per 100 People Ahead of You: 20 minutes

DESCRIPTION AND COMMENTS   This attraction is an elaborate playground, particularly appealing to kids 11 and younger. The idea is that you have been "miniaturized" (i.e., shrunk) and have to make your way through a yard full of 20-foot-tall blades of grass, giant ants, lawn sprinklers, and other oversized wonders.

TOURING TIPS   Honey, I Shrunk the Kids is strictly a playground for children. It is imaginative and has tunnels, slides, rope ladders, and a variety of oversized props. All surface areas are padded, and Disney personnel are on hand to help keep children in some semblance of control. While this Movie Set Adventure Playground undoubtedly looked good on paper, the actual attraction has problems that are hard to "miniaturize." First, it's not nearly large enough to accommodate the number of kids who would like to play. Only 240 people are allowed "on the set" at any one time, and many of these are supervising parents or other curious adults who hopped in line for the attraction without knowing what they were waiting for. By 10:30 or 11 A.M., the play area is full to capacity with seven to ten dozen waiting outside (none too patiently) to be admitted.

This brings us to the second major flaw: the absence of any provision for getting people to leave. Once inside, kids can play as long as their parents allow. This results in an uneven flow of traffic through the playground, and extremely long waits for those outside in line. If it were not for the third flaw, that the attraction is poorly ventilated, and is as hot and sticky as an Everglades swamp, there is no telling when anyone would leave.

If you wish your children to experience Honey, I Shrunk the Kids, get them in and out before 11 A.M. (preferably before 10:30 A.M.). By late morning this attraction is way too hot and crowded for anyone to enjoy. You can access the playground via the New York back lot set, or through the Backstage Plaza fast-food and retail area.

Teenage Mutant Ninja Turtles

Type of Attraction: Short stage show and autograph session

When to Go: At your convenience according to the daily entertainment schedule

Author's Rating: Great for small children, totally expendable for adults; ★½

Overall Appeal by Age Group:

Pre-school	Grade School	Teens	Young Adults	Over 30	Senior Citizens
★★★★½	★★★★	★★	★½	★	★½

Duration of Presentation: 2½ minute show followed by 10 minutes of autographing

Average Wait in Line per 100 People Ahead of You: Street theater; no waiting, except for autographs.

DESCRIPTION AND COMMENTS   Located at the far end of the New York Street area, the *Teenage Mutant Ninja Turtles* show is performed about 12 times each day. Showtimes are listed in the daily entertainment schedule. There is no seating and no shade. The audience must stand in the sweltering sun throughout. Fortunately for everyone, however, the production is mercifully short; so short, in fact, that if you arrive three minutes late you will have missed it! Essentially the Turtles drive up in their customized van, prance around, and do a few choreographed ninja moves on stage. Apparently this short burst of activity so exhausts the Turtles that a longer or more elaborate performance is out of the question. After the show, each Turtle mans (turtles?) an assigned station and signs autographs. While to adults the Turtles look exactly alike, most kids are able to identify them.

TOURING TIPS   What can I say? None of this Turtle stuff makes sense unless you are under 12 or a Samurai herpetologist. Because the audience stands, small children can't see a thing unless they are right up front. The real event seems to be the autograph party (where each Turtle stakes out a different corner of the square and holds court). Savvy kids, ignoring the show altogether, line up in advance at the appropriate corner to get their favorite Turtle's autograph. The only people in front of the stage are uninitiated kids and totally confused adults. And so it goes.

If your children desire to participate in this autograph ritual, get them in line at the appropiate corner about ten minutes before showtime. If they complain that they can't see the show from the autograph line, just remind them that Disney is weird and nothing here is *supposed* to make sense. Donatello, for some reason, usually has the shortest line. Raphael's line affords the best view of the show. After about ten minutes, a nonterrapin cast member herds the Turtles back to their van. Kids left without autographs are admonished to get in line earlier next time.

New York Street Back Lot

Type of Attraction: Walk-through back lot movie set
When to Go: Any time
Author's Rating: Interesting with great detail; ★★★★
Overall Appeal by Age Group:

Pre-school	Grade School	Teens	Young Adults	Over 30	Senior Citizens
★★★	★★★★	★★★★	★★★★	★★★★	★★★★

Duration of Presentation: Varies
Average Wait in Line per 100 People Ahead of You: No waiting

DESCRIPTION AND COMMENTS   This part of the Studios' back lot was previously accessible to tourists only on the tram segment of the Backstage Tour. Now guests can walk around the elaborate New York street set and appreciate its rich detail at their leisure. A second benefit of opening this part of the Studios to pedestrian traffic is it creates a little more elbow room, relieving some of the congestion in the Hollywood Boulevard and Echo Lake areas.

TOURING TIPS   Because there is never a wait to enjoy the New York back lot set, save it until you have seen those attractions which develop long lines.

Studio Tours

Disney-MGM Studios Animation Tour

Type of Attraction: Walking tour of the Disney Animation Studio
When to Go: Before 11 A.M. and after 5 P.M.
Author's Rating: Next to Star Tours, this is our favorite Disney-MGM
attraction; not to be missed; ★★★★½
Overall Appeal by Age Group:

Pre-school	Grade School	Teens	Young Adults	Over 30	Senior Citizens
★★★★	★★★★	★★★★	★★★★★	★★★★★	★★★★★

Duration of Presentation: 36 minutes
Preshow Entertainment: Gallery of animation art in waiting area
Average Wait in Line per 100 People Ahead of You: 7 minutes

DESCRIPTION AND COMMENTS   Disney-MGM Studios Animation Tour
is where, for the first time, the public is invited to watch Disney artists
at work. Since Disneyland opened in 1955, Walt Disney Productions
has been petitioned by its fans to operate an animation studio tour.
Finally, after a brief three-and-a-half decade wait, an admiring public
can watch artists create beloved Disney characters.

The Animation Tour more than exceeds expectations. Much more
than watching a few artists at work, the tour is dynamic, fast-paced,
educational, and most of all, fun. Upon entering the Animation Building, most guests spend a few minutes waiting in a gallery of Disney
animation art. Use your waiting time to enjoy this combination of art
and animation history. From the gallery, guests enter a theater where
an eight-and-one-half minute introductory film on animation is shown.
Starring Walter Cronkite and Robin Williams as your Animation Tour
hosts, the film is an absolute delight.

After the film, guests enter the working studio, where they view
artists and technicians at work through large plate glass viewing windows. Arranged according to the sequence of creation for an animated

production, each work station and task is explained by hosts Walter and Robin via video monitors mounted in each area. Starting with story and character development, guests work sequentially through animation (where the characters are brought to life in rough art), to clean up (where the rough art is refined to finished line drawing), to effects and backgrounds (where backgrounds for the characters are developed), to photocopying, where drawings are transferred from paper to plastic cels prior to being finished with ink and paint. Finally the cels are photographed, put together, and edited.

Having completed the walk-through of the working studio, guests gather in another holding area and view a multi-monitor video presentation in which the Disney animators share their personal perspectives on the creative process. While serving the functional purpose of keeping guests occupied and entertained while awaiting the conclusion of the tour, the presentation is especially warm and endearing, and very worthwhile in its own right.

Finally, guests are seated in a commodious theater to enjoy a concluding film. Pulling together all the elements of animation production, the film features clips from many Disney animation classics.

TOURING TIPS Because the Animation Tour is a relatively small-volume attraction, lines begin to build on busy days by mid-morning. Try to line up for the Animation Tour before 11 A.M.

After the introductory film, when you enter the working part of the studio, feel free to stay and watch as long as you like. The Cronkite/Williams narrative (on video monitors in each work area) rolls along in sequence at a fairly brisk pace, and most guests try to keep up. Since at each work station the video repeats about every two to three minutes, you can let the better part of your 160-person tour group work past you while you hang out at the first station. Then take your time, watching the artists and technicians as long as you wish. You will most likely catch up with your group. If you don't, no big deal; enjoy the conclusion of the tour with the next group.

Backstage Studio Tour

Type of Attraction: Combination tram and walking tour of modern film and video production

When to Go: Any time

Author's Rating: One of Disney's better efforts; efficient, compelling, informative, fun; not to be missed; ★★★★★

Overall Appeal by Age Group:

Pre- school	Grade School	Teens	Young Adults	Over 30	Senior Citizens
★★★★½	★★★★½	★★★★	★★★★½	★★★★	★★★★

Duration of Presentation: About 1 hour and 15 minutes overall; 15 minutes for the tram segment, and an hour for the walking segment called *Inside the Magic*

Special Comments: You can discontinue the tour, if you wish, following the tram segment

Preshow Entertainment: Musicians in the entrance plaza and a video in the tram boarding area

Average Wait in Line per 100 People Ahead of You: 2 minutes

Assumes: 16 tour departures per hour

Loading Speed: Fast

DESCRIPTION AND COMMENTS Approximately two-thirds of the Disney-MGM Studios is occupied by a working film and television facility where throughout the year actors, artists, and technicians work on various productions. Everything from TV commercials, specials, and game shows to feature motion pictures are produced here. Visitors to the Disney-MGM Studios can avail themselves of a veritable "behind-the-scenes" education in the methods and technologies of motion picture and television production. The vehicle for this learning experience is a comprehensive tour of the working studios.

At the end of Hollywood Boulevard, to the right of the Chinese Theater (The Great Movie Ride), guests enter the limited-access area through an ornate studio gate (a sort of art deco version of the Arc de Triomphe) leading into a large plaza. In the plaza lines form for the Backstage Studio Tour on the left and for the Animation Tour (described earlier) on the right.

The Tram Segment

As the anchor (though perhaps not the most popular) attraction at Disney-MGM, the Backstage Studio Tour is fast-paced, informative, and well-designed. Divided into riding and walking segments, the tour begins aboard the ever-faithful tram. Departing (on busy days) about once every four minutes, the tour winds among various production and shop buildings and thence to the elaborate back lot sets.

The Backstage Studio Tour stops first at the wardrobe and crafts shops. Here costumes are designed, created, and stored, as are sets and props. From the tram, viewing through large picture windows, guests watch craftsmen at work.

From the shops the tour proceeds to the winding streets of the back lot where western desert canyons and New York City brownstones exist side by side with modern suburban residential streets. The highlight of the back lot tour for many is the passage through Catastrophe Canyon, a special-effects adventure that includes a thunderstorm, an earthquake, an oil-field fire, and a flash flood.

The tram portion of the tour terminates at the Backstage Plaza, where guests can avail themselves of rest rooms, food, and shopping (if they desire) before commencing the walking part of the tour. To reach the starting point of the walking segment, follow the large, pink rabbit footprints out of the tram unloading area.

The Walking Segment: Inside the Magic

Taking the walking segment of the Backstage Studio Tour immediately following the tram segment is not mandatory. You can take a break after getting off the tram, and return to finish the walking tour anytime you wish. However, there is something to be said for the educational continuity of experiencing the segments back-to-back, not to mention the convenience.

First stop is a special-effects water tank where technicians explain the mechanical and optical tricks that "turn the seemingly impossible into on-screen reality." Included here are rain effects, a naval battle, and a storm at sea. The waiting area for this part of the tour features a display of miniature navy vessels used in the filming of famous war movies.

Next guests enter a Special Effects Workshop where the arts of enlargement, miniaturization, stop-frame photographic animation, and other technical mysteries are demonstrated and explained.

After Special Effects it's on to the Soundstages, where specially designed and soundproofed observation platforms allow unobtrusive viewing of ongoing productions. After the guide explains the basics of whatever productions are in progress (if any), guests view a video which explores the technical and artistic aspects of soundstage work.

Next guests enjoy a four-minute movie, *The Lottery*, starring Bette Midler, that was produced in its entirety at the Disney-MGM Studios. In addition to being amusing, *The Lottery* provides an example of a finished production. At the next stop guests inspect the sets and props used in *The Lottery* and watch a video explaining how the film was produced. After all of the behind-the-scenes secrets are revealed, guests walk among the sets, props, and special-effects equipment for a closer inspection.

At this juncture guests continue the tour into Post Production where sound, computer effects, and editing are examined. Post Production, in keeping with the foregoing parts of the tour, is interesting and worth seeing. At the conclusion of Post Production, guests are shown previews of new Disney/Touchstone film releases.

TOURING TIPS   Do not be discouraged if the line for the tram segment appears long when you arrive. Trams depart (on busy days) about every four minutes and each tram can hold as many as 200 guests. During warm weather months, the most comfortable time of day to take the tram portion of the backstage tour is the evening. A drawback to this is most of the behind-the-scenes workers have gone home. Their absence, however, only affects a small part of the tour.

You will almost never have to wait longer than 15 minutes to join the tour for the walking segment.

Not to Be Missed at the Disney-MGM Studios

Star Tours
Backstage Studios Tour
Animation Tour
Indiana Jones Epic Stunt Spectacular
The Great Movie Ride
MuppetVision 3-D
The Voyage of the Little Mermaid
The Twilight Zone Tower of Terror

Live Entertainment at the Disney-MGM Studios

Until 1993, live entertainment, parades, and special events were not as fully developed or as elaborate at the Disney-MGM Studios as at the Magic Kingdom or EPCOT Center. With the introduction of Aladdin's Royal Caravan parade and the Beauty and the Beast stage show, the Disney-MGM Studios joined the big leagues. These outstanding performances, coupled with the Sorcery in the Sky fireworks spectacular, give the Studios a live entertainment repertoire every bit as compelling as that offered by the other parks.

Aladdin's Royal Caravan

A daytime parade that (until fall 1994) begins at the main entrance end of Hollywood Boulevard and circles in front of The Great Movie Ride. From there it passes in front of Superstar Television and *The Monster Sound Show* and eventually winds up by Star Tours. After the Sunset Boulevard section of the park opens in the fall of 1994, the parade will enter Hollywood Boulevard from Sunset Boulevard.

The parade features huge inflated versions of the characters from Disney's animated feature *Aladdin*, as well as stilt walkers, floats, bands, and acrobats. Colorful, creative, and totally upbeat, Aladdin's Royal Caravan may be Disney's most entertaining daytime parade.

Staged one to three times a day, the parade brings pedestrian traffic to a standstill along its route and makes moving from one part of the park to another problematic. If you are anywhere along the parade route when the Caravan gets underway, your best bet is to stay put and enjoy it. Unlike Magic Kingdom parades, there are no unusually good or frequently over-

417

looked vantage points for *Aladdin*. One of the better places to view the parade is from the steps of Superstar Television. To claim this prime turf, however, you must stake out your spot at least 25–30 minutes in advance.

Backlot Theater

This amphitheater near the end of the New York Street scene is the stage for a variety of production reviews, usually featuring music from movies and Disney characters. Performance times are posted in front of the theater and are listed in the daily entertainment schedule.

Disney Characters

In addition to appearing at the Backlot Theater, Disney characters, particularly Mickey, Minnie, and Roger Rabbit, can be found in the Studio Courtyard. They're usually in front of the Animation Building, in the Backstage Plaza, or along Mickey Avenue (which runs next to the soundstages).

Jim Henson's Muppet Characters

The Muppet characters, including Kermit and Miss Piggy, ham it up, sign autographs, and pose for photos a couple of times each day. Check your daily entertainment schedule. The site of all this activity is hidden on the backside of *MuppetVision 3-D*. The easiest way to get there is to proceed through Muppet Square to Mama Melrose's Ristorante Italiano and turn right.

Mickey Mouse Club

The Mickey Mouse Club is taped on one of the Studios' Soundstages. Inquire at the Guest Services Building if you would like to join the audience. In addition to the taping, cast members participate in casual conversation on the stage of the Backlot Theater. Conversation time is listed in the daily entertainment schedule.

Star Today

Some days there is a visiting celebrity at the Studios. In addition to riding in a motorcade on Hollywood Boulevard, the star appears at various locations, and sits for interviews, etc.

To find out if a star is on site, inquire at the Guest Services Building at the entrance end of Hollywood Boulevard.

Sorcery in the Sky
Fireworks

An excellent fireworks show based on the exploits of Mickey Mouse in his role as the Sorcerer's apprentice in *Fantasia*. Held daily at closing time when the park stays open after dark. Watch the show from anywhere along Hollywood Boulevard.

Street Entertainment

Street entertainment is provided along Hollywood and Sunset Boulevards in the form of jugglers and other roving performers. The Studios has its own modest marching band and a tuba quartet, both of which play in the Hollywood Boulevard, Studio Courtyard, and Echo Lake Area. While not exactly street entertainment, a piano player performs daily at the Backstage Plaza.

Eating at Disney-MGM Studios

Dining in the Disney-MGM Studios is more interesting than in the Magic Kingdom and less ethnic than at EPCOT Center. Disney-MGM has four reservations-recommended restaurants, The Hollywood Brown Derby, the 50's Prime Time Cafe, the Sci-Fi Dine-In Theater Restaurant, and Mama Melrose's Ristorante Italiano. Additional restaurants are planned for the new Sunset Boulevard section of the park which opens in fall 1994. To help you make your choice, we have also assigned each restaurant a star, quality, and value rating. Turn to pages 141–42 for a detailed explanation of our rating system.

The Hollywood Brown Derby   ★★★   82/D

Seating Capacity: 250

Popularity: Fills its reservations early every day

Critic's Rating: The Brown Derby receives a passing grade. The food does not knock you off your feet, but it is good. Presentation is very nice, service is good.

Fare: Cobb salad, fresh seafood, veal, chicken, pasta, desserts, full bar

Atmosphere: Nicely appointed, but somewhat cavernous. Interesting, but not what you would call intimate or romantic. Line drawing caricatures of movie stars decorate the walls.

Entree Prices: Lunch, $10–16   Dinner, $15–24

Entertainment: None

Reservations: Make reservations at the door of the restaurant, the Restaurant Reservations Desk on Hollywood Boulevard, or, for Walt Disney World lodging and campground guests only, dial 56 (45 for campground guests) at least one day, but no more than three days, in advance. If you want to try the Brown Derby and do not have reservations, try walking in at about 3–4 P.M.

Comments: This, the flagship restaurant of Disney-MGM Studios, shares its rest rooms with the enormous, 560-seat, fast-food Soundstage Restaurant around the corner. Even at 3 or 4 P.M. on a busy day, female diners must wait in line to use the rest room. If you encounter such a line, the Catwalk Bar (upstairs from the Brown Derby and Soundstage restaurants) has its own rest rooms which are usually not as crowded.

50's Prime Time Cafe/Tune In Lounge ★★ 64/D

Seating Capacity: 226

Popularity: Fills its seatings early each day

Critic's Rating: Marginally improved, but still inconsistent

Fare: Meatloaf, pot roast, chicken, and other homey fare

Atmosphere: This is like eating out in your own kitchen, 50's style

Entree Prices: Lunch, $7–16 Dinner, $11–20

Entertainment: Vintage sitcoms on TV

Reservations: Make reservations at the door of the restaurant, the Restaurant Reservations Desk by the Brown Derby on Hollywood Boulevard, or for Walt Disney World lodging and campground guests only, dial 56 (45 for campground guests) at least one day, but no more than three days, in advance. If you want to try the 50's Prime Time Cafe and do not have reservations, try walking in at about 3–4 P.M.

Comments: We get a lot of mail from readers who like the 50's Prime Time Cafe. Most say the food is good, the portions large, and that it is easy finding something the kids like. We, unfortunately, cannot concur in that opinion. By our evaluation the food is bland, more resembling the fare served in an elementary school cafeteria than in someone's home. The pot roast, for instance, is apparently cooked by itself without the usual onions, potatoes, and carrots. Tableside it is served with mashed potatoes.

While we enjoy the ambiance of the 50's Prime Time Cafe, and particularly like watching the old sitcom clips, we cannot recommend having a meal there. Our suggestion for participating in the scene (without enduring a bland meal) is to make late afternoon or evening reservations and just order dessert. The ice cream desserts are pretty decent.

Sci-Fi Dine-In Theater Restaurant ★½ 59/D

Seating Capacity: 250

Popularity: Fills its seatings early each day

Critic's Rating: The draw here is the entertainment, not the food

Fare: Burgers, salads, sandwiches, children's box lunches

Atmosphere: Like eating in your car at a 50's drive-in movie

Entree Prices: Lunch, $7–12   Dinner, $11–20

Entertainment: Cartoons and clips of vintage horror and sci-fi movies such as *The Attack of the 50-foot Woman*, *Robot Monster*, and *Son of the Blob*. Also shown are lurid previews, proclaiming "See a sultry beauty in the clutches of a half-crazed monster! See the world's battle for survival!" To make the experience complete, old drive-in trailers plugging the concession stand are intermingled with the clips, cartoons, and previews. All told, you can watch for about 45 minutes without seeing anything repeated.

Reservations: Make reservations at the door of the restaurant, the Restaurant Reservations Desk by the Brown Derby on Hollywood Boulevard, or for Walt Disney World lodging and campground guests only, dial 56 (45 for campground guests) at least one day, but no more than three days, in advance. If you want to try the Sci-Fi Dine-In and do not have reservations, try walking in at 11 A.M. or at about 3 P.M.

Comments: You sit in little cars in a large building where it is always night, and watch vintage film clips as you eat. Free popcorn is served before your meal by waiters on roller skates. The food is pretty dismal. We recommend making a late afternoon or late evening reservation and ordering only dessert. In other words, think of the Sci-Fi as an attraction (which it is) as opposed to a restaurant (which it is not).

Mama Melrose's Ristorante Italiano ★★★ 82/C

Seating Capacity: 250

Popularity: Would be more popular but for its out-of-the-way location

Critic's Rating: Thumbs up!

Fare: Italian with a California twist

Atmosphere: Big-city neighborhood Italian restaurant of the 30's

Entree Prices: Lunch, $8–16   Dinner, $10–25

Entertainment: None

Reservations: Make reservations at the door of the restaurant, the
Restaurant Reservations Desk by the Brown Derby on Hollywood
Boulevard, or for Walt Disney World lodging and campground
guests only, dial 56 (45 for campground guests) at least one day,
but no more than three days, in advance. Because of its out-
of-the-way location, you can sometimes just walk into Mama
Melrose's, especially in the evening.

Comments: Mama Melrose's is by far the most relaxing restaurant at
the Disney-MGM Studios, sporting a worn, ethnic neighborhood
look that is as comfortable as an old sweatshirt. The newest full-
service restaurant at Disney-MGM, Mama Melrose's is getting
better all the time. Pasta and seafood combos are excellent, as
are salads and most of the designer pizzas. Bread is served in the
traditional style with olive oil.

—— *Other Disney-MGM Studios Restaurants* ——

A cut below the headliner restaurants is the Cafeteria of the Stars
featuring baby-back ribs, steaks, prime rib, rotisserie chicken, and a
variety of salads. Lunch entrees run $6–11, with dinner running $8–15.
Beer and wine are available.

For the masses, the Studios provides several bulk loaders: the 560-
seat Soundstage Restaurant, the 600-seat Backlot Express, and a number of small sandwich and pastry vendors. Menu offerings are varied
and interesting, running the gamut from down-home cooking to California *nouvelle cuisine*. Beer and wine can be purchased at the Soundstage and Backlot Express.

The Disney-MGM Studios has three bars, the large Catwalk Bar,
upstairs over the Soundstage Restaurant; the Tune In Lounge (part of
the 50's Prime Time Cafe); and the pleasant, old neighborhood bar at
Mama Melrose's Ristorante Italiano.

Shopping at Disney-MGM Studios

Shops throughout the park carry movie-oriented merchandise and, of course, lots of Disney trademark souvenir items. Most of the shopping is concentrated on Hollywood Boulevard and features movie nostalgia goodies ranging from Jujubes (if you are over 40, you still probably have some stuck in your teeth) to black-and-white postcards of the stars.

Unusual shops include Sights and Sounds where guests can record a music video (direction and backup music are provided) and the Animation Gallery, which is located in the Animation Building and markets reproductions of "cels" from animated features and other animation art. Sid Cahuenga's near the main entrance sells vintage movie posters and celebrity autographs. Mickey's of Hollywood on Hollywood Boulevard is the place to buy Disney trademark merchandise.

Disney-MGM Studios One-Day Touring Plan, for Visitors of All Ages

Because it offers a smaller number of attractions, touring Disney-MGM Studios is not as complicated as touring the Magic Kingdom or EPCOT Center. In addition, all Disney-MGM rides and shows are essentially oriented to the entire family, thus eliminating differences of opinion regarding how to spend the day. Where in the Magic Kingdom Mom and Dad want to see *The Hall of Presidents*, Big Sis is revved up to ride Space Mountain, and the preschool twins are clamoring for Dumbo, the Flying Elephant, at Disney-MGM Studios the whole family can pretty much see and enjoy everything together.

Since there are numerically fewer attractions at Disney-MGM than at the other parks, the crowds are more concentrated. If a line seems unusually long, ask a Disney-MGM attendant what the estimated wait is. If the wait is too long try the same attraction again while a show at the Epic Stunt Theater is in progress or while some special event is going on. All of these activities serve to draw people away from the lines.

The Disney-MGM Studios One-Day Touring Plan assumes a willingness to experience all major rides and shows. Be forewarned that Star Tours, The Great Movie Ride, the Tower of Terror (opens fall 1994), and the Catastrophe Canyon segment of the Backstage Studios Tram Tour are sometimes frightening to children under eight years old. Star Tours, additionally, can be upsetting to anyone prone to motion sickness. When following the Touring Plan, simply skip any attraction you do not wish to experience.

Before You Go

1. Call (407) 824-4321 the day before you go for the official opening times.

425

2. Purchase your admission prior to arrival. You can either order tickets through the mail or buy them at a local Disney Store before you leave home. You can also buy them at the Walt Disney World Information Center off I-75 near Ocala if you are driving. If you arrive by plane, purchase your admission at the Disney Store in the Orlando airport or at a Walt Disney World resort hotel.

3. If you are lodging at a Walt Disney World hotel or campground, make lunch and dinner reservations (if desired) before your arrival. Dial 56 (45 for campground guests) at least one day, but no more than three days, in advance to make Disney-MGM lunch and dinner reservations. You can make your restaurant reservations from home or en route by calling (407) 824-4500.

At the Disney-MGM Studios

1. Arrive at the park 40 minutes before the official opening time. Review a daily entertainment schedule. Wait at the entrance turnstiles to be admitted.

    On your daily entertainment schedule, check out the times for the first performances of *Voyage of the Little Mermaid* and the *Indiana Jones Epic Stunt Spectacular*. During the busier times of the year, the first performance of *The Little Mermaid* will usually begin about 15 minutes *before* the first showing of *Indiana Jones*. Your objective is to see the first performance of each of these productions.

2. When you are admitted to the park (which may be at the official opening time or 30 minutes prior to the official opening time), walk straight down Hollywood Boulevard until it broadens into a large, roughly circular plaza. Pass through the studios arch to the right of the plaza and turn left to *Voyage of the Little Mermaid*. Get in line. As an aside, Disney cast members may try to direct you to *Indiana Jones* as you proceed down Hollywood Boulevard. Though they are well meaning, stick to the plan.

    When admitted inside the lobby, stand close to the doors on the right. When the doors open, go into the theater, choose a row of seats, and then let six to ten people enter the row before you enter (you cannot see all of the stage from the last six seats on the far side). This strategy will give you a good view of the stage and also put you in a perfect position to be one of the first to exit at the conclusion of the show.

NOTE: On days when the official opening time is 9 A.M., the gates almost always open at 8:30 A.M., with the first performance of *The Little Mermaid* at 9 A.M. If you are literally one of the first through the turnstiles at 8:30 A.M., and if your whole party is capable of warp speed, you might be able to ride Star Tours before going to *The Little Mermaid*. Basically you've got about 19 minutes to hustle to Star Tours, ride, and get back to *The Little Mermaid* before the 9 A.M. show fills up. It can be done, but you've got to be very fast. Incidentally, on days when guests are admitted on the hour (instead of on the half hour), the first showing of *The Little Mermaid* will be 15 minutes after the hour. When this schedule is in operation, head directly to *The Little Mermaid*.

3. At the conclusion of *The Little Mermaid*, the exit doors to your left will open automatically. This is when you really have to hustle. On most days, the first performance of *Indiana Jones* is scheduled to begin at almost exactly the same time the first showing of *The Little Mermaid* concludes. What you want to do is to zip over to the Stunt Spectacular Stadium and catch that first show. Because the first show is almost never full, the Disney attendants will admit you even if you arrive four or five minutes late (there is nothing in those first few minutes that you can't afford to miss).

   To get to the stadium, bear right on exiting *The Little Mermaid* and pass back through the studios arch into the big circular plaza. Cut directly across the plaza until you see a lake. Proceed around the lake counterclockwise and you will see the stadium up some stairs on your right. When you enter the stadium, turn right and proceed to the farthest section of seats on the top right. You will be able to see fine and will be in a great position to be one of the first to exit after the show. Enjoy the *Indiana Jones Epic Stunt Spectacular*.

4. At the conclusion of *Indiana Jones*, proceed quickly through the nearby exit. Turn left and hustle over to Star Tours. Ride.

5. After riding Star Tours, walk back in the direction of *Indiana Jones* and turn left to return to the large circular plaza. In the ornate Chinese Theater facing the plaza, experience The Great Movie Ride.

6. We do not include a full-service restaurant meal as part of this Touring Plan. If you want to try one of Disney-MGM's better

restaurants, make your reservations now. Reservations can be made at the door of the restaurant of your choice or, on some days, at the Restaurant Reservations Desk on Hollywood Boulevard. Walt Disney World lodging and campground guests can make reservations by dialing 56 (45 for campground guests) at least one day, but no more than three days, in advance.

7. After The Great Movie Ride, the park's greatest potential bottlenecks are behind you and you can slow your pace. Next, backtrack through the studios arch (toward *The Little Mermaid*) and continue across the square to the Animation Building to the rear and right. Take the Animation Tour. If you are in need of a rest room, you will find them at the *left* rear of the same square.

8. Exit to the right on leaving the Animation Building and bear right again to the tram loading area of the Backstage Studio Tour. Board a tram and enjoy.

9. When you get off the tram, continue through the shopping and concession area. Pass the Honey, I Shrunk the Kids playground. (If you have small children in your party, you might consider stopping here for a while if the playground is not crowded.) Save the walking part of the Backstage Tour (*Inside the Magic*) for later. Exit onto the New York Street set and bear left.

10. Continue toward the fake skyscrapers and turn right into Muppet Square. See *MuppetVision 3-D*.

11. After *MuppetVision 3-D*, head back past Star Tours and turn left into the Echo Lake area. Check out the line at *The Monster Sound Show*. This attraction is often inundated following a performance of *Indiana Jones* nearby. If *The Monster Sound Show* has a long line when you arrive, chalk it up to bad timing and try again later.

12. After *The Monster Sound Show*, bear right and return to the New York Street set. Turn right at Honey, I Shrunk the Kids playground, cross the concession area, and proceed to the origination point of the walking segment of the Backstage Tour. Continue the tour.

13. After the walking tour, you will have seen everything except SuperStar Television and, possibly, *The Monster Sound Show*. Catch one or both at your convenience.

14. See the Studio Showcase near Muppet Square. Tour Hollywood Boulevard. Consult your daily entertainment schedule for parades, special events, and performances at the Theater of the Stars.

15. This concludes the Touring Plan. Eat, shop, enjoy live entertainment, or revisit your favorite Disney-MGM attraction as desired. When you're ready to leave the park, walk (the Disney-MGM parking lot is not all that big) or take a tram to your car.

If The Tower of Terror Is Open During Your Visit

1. See *The Little Mermaid*
2. See *The Indiana Jones Stunt Spectacular*
3. See the Tower of Terror
4. Take The Great Movie Ride
5. Ride Star Tours
6. See *MuppetVision 3-D*
7. Take the Animation Tour
8. Take the Backstage Studio tram tour
9. Take the walking segment of the Backstage Tour (*Inside the Magic*)
10. See *The Monster Sound Show*
11. See *Superstar Television*
12. Enjoy parades, live performances, and special events

The New Old Kid on the Block: Universal Studios Comes to Florida

Universal City Studios, Inc. has been running a studios tour and movie-theme tourist attraction for·more than 25 years, predating all of the Disney parks except Disneyland. In the early 1980s, Universal announced plans to build a studios/theme park complex in Florida. While Universal labored over its new project, however, the Disney organization jumped into high gear and rushed its own studios/theme park onto the market, beating out Universal by a year and a half.

Universal Studios Florida opened its doors to the public in June of 1990. At that time it was almost four times the physical size of the Disney-MGM Studios (Disney-MGM having expanded somewhat subsequently), with much more of the total facility accessible to the visiting public. Like its sister facility in Hollywood, Universal Studios Florida is spacious, beautifully landscaped, meticulously clean, and delightfully varied in its entertainment offerings. Yet, in certain important, almost critical ways, the Florida complex is quite different from Universal Studios Hollywood.

Universal Studios Hollywood is one of the most well-conceived and well-executed tourist attractions in the world. It accommodates large numbers of guests with practically no waiting in line. While Disneyland, several miles away, was testing new techniques in queuing management (how to keep guests happy standing in a line for 45 minutes), Universal Studios was operating a park where lines were the exception, not the rule.

After buying admission to Universal Studios Hollywood, each guest is assigned a reservation for the Tram Tour, a well-paced, multi-segmented tour of Universal's famed film and television studios. Educational, dramatic, and exciting, the Tour is a clinic in television and motion picture art and is the feature attraction of the park. Guests are relieved of the drudgery of waiting in line for the tour by simply showing up at the embarkation point at their appointed reservation time. Many surprises are built into the tour, including an attack by "Jaws," an earthquake, and an encounter with King Kong. In addition to being a wonderful experience, the Tram Tour is also easy on the feet.

All other attractions at Universal Studios Hollywood are extra-large theaters featuring various movie- and TV-theme presentations which are performed according to a show schedule (provided to each guest on admission). Once again there are no lines. As showtime approaches, guests simply enter the empty theater and take a seat, first come first serve. No lines, no standing, no bother, plus you get to wait for the show sitting down in the theater.

As Universal Studios Hollywood has engineered one of the most guest-considerate and stress-free theme attractions in the world, it is only logical to expect that Universal Studios would build on these same proven, successful techniques when designing a second generation mega-attraction in Florida. Right? Think again.

Incredibly, at Universal Studios Florida, the Universal planners and designers trashed most of the formats and techniques which made the Hollywood park so exceptional, electing instead to develop an attraction in the Disney style with hours of waiting and miles of walking. In Hollywood, Universal created a superior product by going in a different direction, marching to their own beat. In Florida, unfortunately, Universal has tried to "out Disney" Disney, and the results have been mixed.

Gone in Florida is the all-encompassing tram tour, and the much appreciated reservation system. Gone, also, is any sort of integrated educational presentation on movie and television production. True, there are individual shows on costuming and make-up, set construction, special effects, film making, and post production, but it is unlikely that each patron will see them all or that the presentations will be viewed in any sort of logical sequence. Worst, in California a guest gets all the above during the Tram Tour with no wait; in Florida a guest must wait in line for each different show.

Then, there are the rides. In Hollywood, there is one ride, the Tram Tour. Everything, from earthquakes to avalanches to an attack by "Jaws," happens while you ride the tram. At Universal Studios Florida the rides are more in the Disney mold, i.e., totally separate ride/adventure experiences. On the bright side, the Universal Florida rides are exciting and innovative, and as with many Disney rides, focus on familiar and/or beloved motion picture characters or situations.

On Universal Studios Florida's E.T. ride, you escape the authorities on a flying bike and leave the earth for a visit to E.T.'s home planet. In Kongfrontation, King Kong tears up a city with you in it. In Jaws, the persistent great white makes a heart-stopping assault on your small boat, and in Earthquake, The Big One, special effects create the most realistic earthquake simulation ever produced. The Funtastic World of Hanna-Barbera places you in a bucking rocket simulator for a high-speed chase with Yogi Bear and the Flintstones. Finally, guests ride in a Delorean cum time machine in yet another chase, this one based on the film *Back to the Future*.

While many of these rides represent prototypical state-of-the-art technology and live up to their advance billing in terms of excitement, creativity, uniqueness, and special effects, they unfortunately lack the capacity to handle the number of guests who frequent major Florida tourist destinations. If a ride has great appeal, but can accommodate only a small number of guests per ride or per hour, long lines will form. It is not unusual for the wait to exceed an hour and a quarter for the E.T. ride, and 50 minutes for the Hanna-Barbera ride.

Happily, most of the shows and theater performances at Universal Studios Florida are situated in good-sized theaters which accommodate large numbers of people. Since most performances run continuously waits usually do not exceed twice the performance time of the show (about 40 minutes). Many shows are multi-segmented, with the audience moving to three or more staging areas during the course of the presentation.

—— *Arriving and Getting Oriented* ——

Universal Studios Florida is located on Kirkman Road, accessible from I-4 via exits 29 or 30B. The parking lot holds about 7,000 cars and is filled each day starting with those areas closest to the gate. A tram transports guests to the ticket booths and entrance. One-Day and Two-Day Tickets are available (including tax) at about $37 and $59 respectively for adults, $30 and $47 for children (3 to 9).

Universal Studios Florida is laid out in an upside down "L" configuration. Beyond the main entrance, a wide boulevard stretches past a number of rides and shows down to a New York City back lot set. Branching off this major pedestrian thoroughfare to the right are five streets which access other areas of the studios and which ultimately intersect a promenade circling a large lake.

The park is divided into six sections: The Front Lot, Production Central, New York, Hollywood, San Francisco/Amity, and Expo Center. Where one section begins and another ends is a little blurry, but no matter. Guests orient themselves by the major rides, sets, and landmarks, and will refer, for instance, to "New York," "the waterfront," "over by E.T.," or "by Mel's Diner." Overall, the area of Universal Studios Florida open to guest visitation is about the same size as EPCOT Center.

Universal Studios Florida offers all the services and amenities you would expect from a major theme park including: stroller and wheelchair rental, lockers, diaper-changing and infant-nursing facilities, car assistance, and foreign language assistance. Most of the studios are accessible to disabled guests and TDD's are available to the hearing impaired. Almost all of the Universal Studios Florida services are located in The Front Lot, just inside the main entrance.

In an earlier edition of the *Unofficial Guide* we listed the Universal Studios Florida information number as (407) 636-8000. In preparing this edition we routinely called to verify the number and reached the following recorded message: "Hello, you have reached the Universal Studios Florida dyslexic hot line. If you dialed '636-' instead of '363-' 8000, you have reached the right number."

Sorry to contribute to the confusion, guys. The correct number for information is (407) 363-8000.

—— *Universal Studios Florida Attractions* ——

The Funtastic World of Hanna-Barbera

Type of Attraction: Flight simulation ride
When to Go: First thing in the morning
Special Comments: Very intense for some preschoolers
Author's Rating: A delight for all ages; ★★★½
Overall Appeal by Age Group:

Pre- school	Grade School	Teens	Young Adults	Over 30	Senior Citizens
★★★★	★★★★½	★★★★	★★★★	★★★★	★★★★

Duration of Ride: 4½ minutes with 3½ minute preshow
Loading Speed: Moderate to slow

Universal Studios Florida

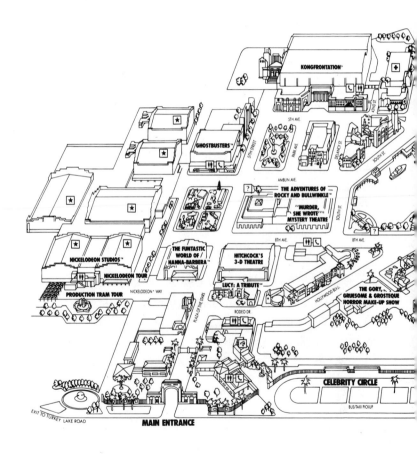

KONGFRONTATION

GHOSTBUSTERS

5TH AVE

PARK AVE

DELANCY ST.

SOUTH ST

5TH STREET

AMBLIN AVE.

THE ADVENTURES OF
ROCKY AND BULLWINKLE

''MURDER,
SHE WROTE''
MYSTERY THEATRE

SOUTH ST

NICKELODEON STUDIOS

NICKELODEON TOUR

THE FUNTASTIC
WORLD OF /
HANNA-BARBERA

8TH AVE.

8TH AVE.

HITCHCOCK'S
3-D THEATRE

PRODUCTION TRAM TOUR

NICKELODEON WAY

LUCY: A TRIBUTE

THE GORY,
GRUESOME & GROSTEQUE
HORROR MAKE-UP SHOW

PLAZA OF THE STARS

RODEO DR.

HOLLYWOOD BLVD.

CELEBRITY CIRCLE

BUS/TAXI PICKUP

EXIT TO TURKEY LAKE ROAD

MAIN ENTRANCE

434

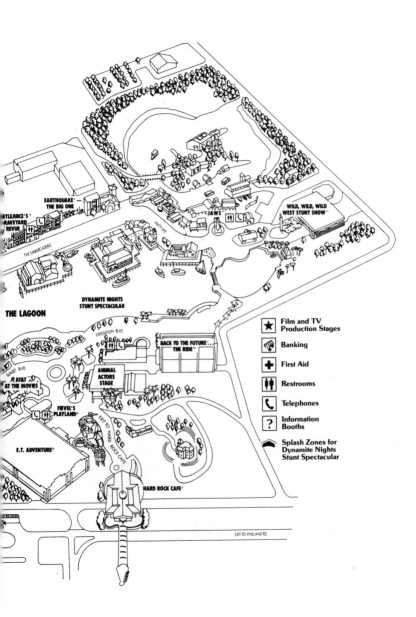

EARTHQUAKE™
THE BIG ONE

BEETLEJUICE'S™
GRAVEYARD
REVUE

THE EMBARCADERO

AMITY AVE

JAWS™

WILD, WILD, WILD
WEST STUNT SHOW™

DYNAMITE NIGHTS
STUNT SPECTACULAR

THE LAGOON

EXPOSITION BLVD.

SUNSET BLVD.

AT&T
AT THE MOVIES

BACK TO THE FUTURE™...
THE RIDE™

ANIMAL
ACTORS
STAGE

FIEVEL'S
PLAYLAND™

EXIT TO HARD ROCK CAFE™

E.T. ADVENTURE™

HARD ROCK CAFE™

EXIT TO VINELAND RD.

★ Film and TV
Production Stages

Banking

✚ First Aid

Restrooms

Telephones

? Information
Booths

Splash Zones for
Dynamite Nights
Stunt Spectacular

DESCRIPTION AND COMMENTS   A flight simulation ride in the same family as Disney's Star Tours and Body Wars, except that all the visuals are cartoons. Guests accompany Yogi Bear in a high-speed chase to rescue a child snatched by kidnappers.

TOURING TIPS   This wild, funny, and thoroughly delightful ride is also unfortunately a cycle ride (the whole ride must shut down during loading and unloading). Consequently large lines build early in the day and move very slowly. Ride first thing in the morning.

"Alfred Hitchcock: The Art of Making Movies"

Type of Attraction: Mini-course on filming action sequences and a testimonial to the talents of Alfred Hitchcock

When to Go: After you have experienced all the rides

Special Comments: May frighten small children

Author's Rating: A little slow moving, but well done; ★★★½

Overall Appeal by Age Group:

Pre-school	Grade School	Teens	Young Adults	Over 30	Senior Citizens
★★½	★★★	★★★½	★★★½	★★★½	★★★½

Duration of Presentation: 40 minutes

Probable Waiting Time: 22 minutes

DESCRIPTION   Guests view a film collage featuring famous scenes from Hitchcock films (including some unreleased 3-D footage), and then exit to an adjoining sound stage where the stabbing scene from *Psycho* is recreated using professional actors and audience volunteers. Finally guests move to a third area where the technology of filming action scenes on a sound stage is explained. The Hitchcock "greatest hits" film is disjointed and pretty confusing, unless you have a good recollection of the movies and scenes highlighted. The sound stage reenactment of the shower scene from *Psycho* is both informative and entertaining, as are the special sets and film techniques demonstrated in the third staging area.

TOURING TIPS   Because of its location just beyond the main entrance, the lines for the Hitchcock attraction appear long, but usually disappear quickly. In any event, we recommend you let the morning crowds clear and postpone seeing this attraction until just before you leave the park in the evening.

Nickelodeon Studios Walking Tour

Type of Attraction: Behind-the-scenes guided tour
When to Go: When Nickelodeon shows are in production (usually weekdays)
Author's Rating: ★★★
Overall Appeal by Age Group:

Pre-school	Grade School	Teens	Young Adults	Over 30	Senior Citizens
★★½	★★★	★★★	★★★	★★★	★★★

Duration of Tour: 36 minutes
Probable Waiting Time: 30–45 minutes

DESCRIPTION AND COMMENTS   This walking tour of the Nickelodeon studio examines set construction, sound stages, wardrobe, props, lighting, video production, and special effects. While a lot of the same information is presented more creatively in the "Alfred Hitchcock," "Murder, She Wrote," and Horror Make-up Show productions, the Nickelodeon Tour is specifically tailored to kids. Not only are they made to feel supremely important on this tour, their opinions are used to shape future Nickelodeon programming.

A new addition to the tour which adds some much needed zip is "Game Lab," where guests preview strange games being tested for possible inclusion on Nickelodeon. The Game Lab segment ends with a lucky child getting "slimed." If this ritual is unknown to you, consult your children.

TOURING TIPS   While grade schoolers, in particular, enjoy this tour, it is pretty expendable for everyone else. Go on a second day at the Studios, or a second visit. If Nickelodeon is not in production, forget it entirely.

Production Tram Tour

Type of Attraction: Guided tram tour of the various outdoor sets
When to Go: Late in the afternoon
Special Comments: Not comparable to the Disney-MGM Studios tram tour
Author's Rating: Interesting; ★★½

Overall Appeal by Age Group:

Pre-school	Grade School	Teens	Young Adults	Over 30	Senior Citizens
★★	★★	★★	★★½	★★½	★★½

Duration of Tour: 20 minutes

Probable Waiting Time: Varies widely

DESCRIPTION AND COMMENTS   The tram tour offers guests an informative, effortless way to see the various sets on the back lot. Though you see essentially the same sights when you tour the park on foot, the background provided by the tram tour guide enhances your understanding and appreciation of the sets and props.

TOURING TIPS   We like the tram tour, if the wait to board is short. The tram tour offers a good general orientation to the studios, but is not the best way to use your time early in the morning. Try it late in the afternoon if you are interested in learning more about the sets.

"Ghostbusters"

Type of Attraction: Theater presentation featuring special effects from *Ghostbusters*

When to Go: Should be your first show after experiencing all of the rides

Special Comments: A limited potential for frightening young children

Author's Rating: Upbeat and fun with great special effects; ★★★★

Overall Appeal by Age Group:

Pre-school	Grade School	Teens	Young Adults	Over 30	Senior Citizens
★★★★	★★★★½	★★★★½	★★★★½	★★★★	★★★★

Duration of Presentation: 15 minutes

Probable Waiting Time: 26 minutes

DESCRIPTION AND COMMENTS   An elaborate set from *Ghostbusters* is used to demonstrate a variety of incredible special effects. Light-hearted and fast-paced with lots of humor, *Ghostbusters* has been improved with the addition of a new story line and an excellent preshow. The whole production is punctuated by the catchy rock theme from the movie.

TOURING TIPS   This is a fun show that draws big crowds. Enjoy "Ghostbusters" in the morning, after you've experienced the rides. Note that the entrance to "Ghostbusters" is not very well marked. Look for the "Ghostbusters" sign hanging over the sidewalk, and duck into the first open door to its right.

Kongfrontation

Type of Attraction: Themed adventure ride
When to Go: Before 11 A.M.
Special Comments: May frighten small children
Author's Rating: Not to be missed; ★★★★★
Overall Appeal by Age Group:

Pre-school	Grade School	Teens	Young Adults	Over 30	Senior Citizens
★★★½	★★★★★	★★★★★	★★★★	★★★★	★★★★

Duration of Ride: 4½ minutes
Loading Speed: Moderate

DESCRIPTION AND COMMENTS   One of Universal Studios Florida's headliner attractions, guests board an aerial tram for a ride from Manhattan to Roosevelt Island. En route news reaches the group that the giant ape has escaped. The tram passes evidence of Kong's path of destruction, and finally encounters the monster himself. In the course of the journey, King Kong demolishes buildings, uproots utility poles, swats helicopters, and hurls your tram car to the ground.

TOURING TIPS   A truly amazing piece of work; not to be missed. Ride in the morning following The Funtastic World of Hanna-Barbera, Back to the Future, and E.T. Adventure.

The Gory Gruesome & Grotesque Horror Make-up Show

Type of Attraction: Theater presentation on the art of make-up
When to Go: After you have experienced all the rides
Special Comments: May frighten small children
Author's Rating: A gory knee-slapper; ★★★★

Overall Appeal by Age Group:

Pre-school	Grade School	Teens	Young Adults	Over 30	Senior Citizens
★★★	★★★★	★★★★	★★★½	★★★½	★★★½

Duration of Presentation: 25 minutes
Probable Waiting Time: 20 minutes

DESCRIPTION AND COMMENTS   A lively, well-paced look at how make-up artists create film monsters, realistic wounds, severed limbs, and other unmentionables. In addition to being one of the funnier and more upbeat presentations at Universal Studios, the *Horror Make-up Show* also presents a wealth of fascinating information. Overall, it is an excellent and enlightening, if somewhat gory, introduction to the blood and guts art of cinema monster-making.

TOURING TIPS   Exceeding most guest's expectations, the *Horror Make-up Show* is the "sleeper" attraction of Universal Studios. Presented in a tongue-in-cheek style, humor transcends the gruesome effects, and most folks (including preschoolers) take all the blood and guts in stride. It's usually not too hard to get into, so enjoy the *Horror Make-up Show* after you've had your fill of rides.

"Murder, She Wrote" Mystery Theater

Type of Attraction: A multi-sequence mini-course on the post production techniques of sound effects, editing, background music, and dubbing.

When to Go: After you have experienced all the rides

Special Comments: A nice air-conditioned break during the hottest part of the day

Author's Rating: Well presented; ★★★½

Overall Appeal by Age Group:

Pre-school	Grade School	Teens	Young Adults	Over 30	Senior Citizens
★★	★★½	★★★	★★★½	★★★★	★★★½

Duration of Presentation: 40 minutes
Probable Waiting Time: 20 minutes

DESCRIPTION AND COMMENTS   Guests move from theater to theater in this multi-sequence introduction to post production technology. The presentation consists of editing, dubbing, and adding sound effects to a climactic scene from "Murder, She Wrote." Members of the audience are recruited to assist with the sound effects and voice-overs.

TOURING TIPS Informative, worthwhile, and often hilarious, "Murder, She Wrote" does a good job of making fairly technical information understandable. In spite of the name, there is nothing here which will intimidate small children. We recommend enjoying the show during the heat of the day.

Earthquake, the Big One

Type of Attraction: Combination theater presentation and theme adventure ride
When to Go: In the morning, after Kongfrontation and Jaws
Special Comments: May frighten small children
Author's Rating: Not to be missed; ★★★★½
Overall Appeal by Age Group:

Pre-school	Grade School	Teens	Young Adults	Over 30	Senior Citizens
★★★	★★★★★	★★★★★	★★★★½	★★★★½	★★★★½

Duration of Presentation: 20 minutes
Loading Speed: Moderate

DESCRIPTION AND COMMENTS Guests view a film on how miniatures are used to create special effects in earthquake movies, followed by a demonstration of how miniatures, blue screen, and matte painting are integrated with live-action stunt sequences (starring audience volunteers) to achieve a realistic final product. Next, guests board a subway from Oakland en route to San Francisco, and experience a simulated earthquake. Special effects range from fires and runaway trains to exploding tanker trucks and tidal waves. This ride is one of Universal's more compelling efforts. Not to be missed.

TOURING TIPS Experience Earthquake in the morning, after you've gone on all the other rides.

Jaws

Type of Attraction: Theme adventure boat ride
When to Go: Before 11:30 A.M.

Special Comments: Recently reopened
Author's Rating: ★★★★

DESCRIPTION AND COMMENTS The original Jaws ride never operated dependably, and was ultimately closed and dismantled. A new ride, in which guests on an excursion boat encounter and do battle with the great white shark, was opened in the summer of 1993.

TOURING TIPS Try to ride before 11:30 A.M. *Note:* You will get wet riding Jaws.

Back to the Future

Type of Attraction: Flight simulator thrill ride
When to Go: First thing in the morning, after Hanna-Barbera and
E.T. Adventure
Special Comments: Very rough ride; may induce motion sickness.
Must be 3' 10" tall to ride. Switching off option available (see
page 187).
Author's Rating: Not to be missed if you have a strong stomach;
★★★★★

Overall Appeal by Age Group:

Pre-school	Grade School	Teens	Young Adults	Over 30	Senior Citizens
†	★★★★★	★★★★★	★★★★★	★★★★	★★½

† Sample size too small for an accurate rating
Duration of Ride: 4½ minutes
Loading Speed: Moderate

DESCRIPTION AND COMMENTS This attraction is to Universal Studios Florida what Space Mountain is to the Magic Kingdom: the most popular thrill ride in the park. Guests in Doc Brown's lab get caught up in a high-speed chase through time that spans a million years. An extremely intense simulator ride, Back to the Future is similar to Star Tours and Body Wars at Walt Disney World, but is a whole lot rougher and more jerky. Though the storyline of the adventure doesn't make much sense, the visual effects are wild and powerful. The guest vehicles (Delorean time machines) in the Back to the Future ride are much smaller than those of Star Wars and Body Wars, so the ride feels more like a personal adventure (and less like a group experience). In a survey of 84 tourists who had experienced simulator rides in both Universal Studios and Disney World, riders under 35 preferred Back to the Future to the Disney attractions by a seven-to-four margin. Older riders, however, stated a two-to-one preference for Star Tours over either Back to the Future or Body Wars. The remarks of a Mount Holly, New Jersey, woman are typical: "Our favorite [overall] attraction was Back to the Future at Universal. Comparing it to Star Tours and Body Wars, it was more realistic because the screen surrounds you."

TOURING TIPS As soon as guests are allowed into the park, there is a veritable stampede in the direction of Back to the Future. Interestingly, the initial onslaught is followed by a 20–30 minute hiatus during which new arrivals at Back to the Future drop off sharply. By riding the Funtastic World of Hanna-Barbera first, and E.T. Adventure second, you allow the first wave of people to process through Back to the Future. When you ultimately arrive at Back to the Future, you should fall conveniently between those who were on hand when the park opened and a second wave of less compulsive guests. If you visit Universal Studios on a Saturday, there are a lot of locals in the park; ride Hanna-Barbera first, Back to the Future second, and E.T. third. One final note: sitting in the rear seat of the car makes the ride more realistic.

E.T. Adventure

Type of Attraction: Theme adventure ride

When to Go: Before 10 A.M.

Special Comments: This ride was renovated and greatly improved in 1992

Author's Rating: ★★★★

Overall Appeal by Age Group:

Pre-school	Grade School	Teens	Young Adults	Over 30	Senior Citizens
★★★★½	★★★★½	★★★★	★★★★	★★★★	★★★★

Duration of Ride: 4½ minutes

Load Speed: Moderate

DESCRIPTION AND COMMENTS Guests board a bicycle-like conveyance to escape with E.T. from earthly law enforcement officials, and then journey to E.T.'s home planet. An attraction similar to Peter Pan's Flight in the Magic Kingdom, only longer with more elaborate special effects, and a wilder ride.

TOURING TIPS   Most preschoolers and grade school children love E.T. We thought it worth a 20–30 minute wait, but nothing longer. Lines build quickly for this attraction after 9:45 A.M., and waits can extend to more than two hours on busy days. Ride in the morning, right after Hanna-Barbera. Guests who balk at the idea of sitting on the bicycle can ride in a comfortable gondola. A Columbus, Ohio, mother wrote this about horrendous lines at E.T.: "The line for E.T. took two hours! The rest of the family waiting outside thought that we had gone to E.T.'s planet for real."

Animal Actors Stage

Type of Attraction: Trained animals stadium performance
When to Go: After you have experienced all the rides
Author's Rating: Warm and delightful; ★★★½
Overall Appeal by Age Group:

Pre-school	Grade School	Teens	Young Adults	Over 30	Senior Citizens
★★★★	★★★★	★★★★	★★★★	★★★★	★★★★

Duration of Presentation: 20 minutes
Probable Waiting Time: 25 minutes

DESCRIPTION AND COMMENTS   A humorous presentation demonstrating how animals are trained for film work. Well-paced and informative, the show features cats, dogs, monkeys, birds, and other creatures. Sometimes the animals do not behave as expected, but that's half the fun.

TOURING TIPS   We would like this show better if guests were simply allowed to enter the theater at their leisure and sit down. As it is, everyone must stand in line waiting to be admitted. Presented about ten times daily, the *Animal Actors Stage* schedule is listed in the daily entertainment guide. See the show whenever it is convenient; get in line about 15 minutes before showtime.

Dynamite Nights Stunt Spectacular

Type of Attraction: Simulated stunt scene filming

When to Go: At your convenience; check the daily entertainment schedule

Special Comments: Viewing is more comfortable at the night show

Author's Rating: Well done; ★★★★

Overall Appeal by Age Group:

Pre-school	Grade School	Teens	Young Adults	Over 30	Senior Citizens
★★★	★★★★½	★★★★½	★★★★½	★★★★	★★★★

Duration of Presentation: 20 minutes

Probable Waiting Time: None

DESCRIPTION AND COMMENTS   Performed each day on the Lagoon. In this show, stunt men demonstrate a variety of spectacular stunts and special effects. The plot involves lawmen trying to intercept and apprehend drug smugglers. Our main problem with this presentation is that the Lagoon is so large it is somewhat difficult to follow the action.

TOURING TIPS   On par with Disney-MGM's stunt show, the Universal Studios version is staged on a huge open Lagoon with the audience taking up positions along the encircling rail. There is no waiting in line, but if you want to nail down a really good vantage point you need to stake out your position about 25 minutes before showtime. This can make for some heavy-duty sweating if you attend a daytime show. The best viewing spots are along the docks at Lombard's Landing and Chez Alcatraz restaurants on the waterfront, across the street from Earthquake.

Wild, Wild, Wild West Stunt Show

Type of Attraction: Stunt show with a western theme

When to Go: After you've experienced all the rides, go at your convenience

Author's Rating: Solid and exciting; ★★★★

Overall Appeal by Age Group:

Pre-school	Grade School	Teens	Young Adults	Over 30	Senior Citizens
★★★★½	★★★★★	★★★★½	★★★★	·★★★★	★★★★

Duration of Presentation: 16 minutes
Probable Waiting Time: None

DESCRIPTION AND COMMENTS   A wild west stunt show with shoot-outs, fist fights, horse tricks, and high falls, staged about 10 times daily in a 2,000 seat, covered stadium. The pace is quick, the stunts are exciting and well executed, and unlike the stunt show performed on the Lagoon, the action is easy to follow.

TOURING TIPS   Go whenever convenient. Showtimes are listed in the daily entertainment guide. During the summer, the stadium is more comfortable after dusk.

Fieval's Playland

Type of Attraction: Children's play area with water slide and stage show

When to Go: Any time

Author's Rating: A much needed attraction for preschoolers; ★★★★

Overall Appeal by Age Group:

Pre-school	Grade School	Teens	Young Adults	Over 30	Senior Citizens
★★★★	★★★★	★★★	★★★	★★★	★★★

Probable Waiting Time: 20–30 minutes for the water slide; otherwise, no waiting at all.

DESCRIPTION AND COMMENTS   Fieval's Playland is an imaginative children's play area where oridinary household items are reproduced on a giant scale, as a mouse would experience them. Preschoolers and grade-schoolers can climb nets, walk through a huge boot, splash in a sardine can fountain, seesaw on huge spoons, or climb onto a cow skull. Though most of Fieval's Playland is reserved for preschoolers, a water slide raft ride is open to guests of all ages.

TOURING TIPS   You can walk right into Fieval's Playland without having to wait in line and you can stay as long as you want. Younger children love the oversized household items, and there is enough to keep teens and adults busy while the little ones let off steam. The water slide is open to all ages, but is extremely slow in loading and accommodates only 300 riders per hour. With an average wait in line of 20–30 minutes, we do not think the 16-second raft ride is worth the trouble. In addition, your chances of getting soaked are high. A major shortcoming of the entire attraction is its lack of shade. Visiting the play area during the heat of the day is not advised.

Beetlejuice's Graveyard Review

Type of Attraction: Rock and roll stage show
When to Go: At your convenience
Author's Rating: Outrageous; ★★★★
Overall Appeal by Age Group:

Pre-school	Grade School	Teens	Young Adults	Over 30	Senior Citizens
★★★★	★★★★½	★★★★½	★★★★	★★★★	★★★½

Duration of Presentation: 16 minutes
Probable Waiting Time: None

DESCRIPTION AND COMMENTS   The *Graveyard Review* is a high-powered rock and roll stage show starring Beetlejuice, Frankenstein, the Bride of Frankenstein, the Wolfman, Dracula, and the Phantom of the Opera. In addition to some fine vintage rock, the show features some of the most exuberant choreography to be found on any stage, and some impressive sets and special effects.

TOURING TIPS   Mercifully, this attraction has been moved under cover. See the show at your convenience.

The Adventures of Rocky and Bullwinkle

Type of Attraction: Live character stage show
When to Go: Early evening, or at night when it is cooler
Author's Rating: A reunion with old friends; ★★★½
Overall Appeal by Age Group:

Pre-school	Grade School	Teens	Young Adults	Over 30	Senior Citizens
★★★★	★★★★	★★★½	★★★	★★★★	★★★½

Duration of Presentation: 15 minutes
Probable Waiting Time: None

DESCRIPTION AND COMMENTS   This show reminds you how funny cartoons used to be. If you are a Rocky (the Flying Squirrel) and Bullwinkle (the Moose) fan, its the same old stuff, i.e., bad guys Boris and Natasha presenting bombs disguised as food, trophies, and the like to Rocky and Bullwinkle. The show is a little unevenly paced, but funny with good special effects. As with the cartoon, the humor operates on one level for children, and on another level with puns and double-entendres for adults.

TOURING TIPS   Universal has a habit of locating new live productions in temporary bleachers exposed to the sun. Rocky and Bullwinkle, unfortunately, is no exception. Try to see the show when the weather is cooler, or after sunset.

Lucy, a Tribute

Type of Attraction: Walk-through exhibit
When to Go: Any time
Author's Rating: A touching remembrance; ★★★
Overall Appeal by Age Group:

Pre-school	Grade School	Teens	Young Adults	Over 30	Senior Citizens
★	★	★★	★★★	★★★	★★★

Probable Waiting Time: None

DESCRIPTION AND COMMENTS   This exhibit depicts the life and career of comedienne Lucille Ball, with emphasis on her role as Lucy Ricardo in the long-running television series "I Love Lucy." Well designed and informative, the attraction succeeds admirably in recalling the talent and temperament of the beloved redhead.

TOURING TIPS   See the Lucy exhibit during the hot, crowded midafternoon, or alternatively, on your way out of the park. An adult could easily spend 15–30 minutes here. Children, on the other hand, tend to get restless after a couple of minutes.

Street Scenes

Type of Attraction: Elaborate outdoor sets for making films
When to Go: Any time
Special Comments: You will see most sets without special effort as you tour the park
Author's Rating: One of the park's great assets; ★★★★★

Overall Appeal by Age Group:

Pre-school	Grade School	Teens	Young Adults	Over 30	Senior Citizens
★★★	★★★★½	★★★★½	★★★★½	★★★★★	★★★★★

Probable Waiting Time: No waiting

DESCRIPTION AND COMMENTS   Unlike the Disney-MGM Studios, all of Universal Studios Florida's back lot sets are open to guest inspection. Sets include New York City streets, San Francisco's waterfront, a New England coastal town, the house from *Psycho*, Rodeo Drive and Hollywood Boulevard, and a Louisiana bayou, among others.

TOURING TIPS   You will see most of the sets as you walk through the park during your visit. If you want to learn more about them, however, take the Production Tram Tour which loads in the Production Central area outside the Nickelodeon soundstage.

—— Disney-MGM Studios vs. Universal Studios Florida ——

Nearly half of Disney-MGM Studios is off limits to guests except by guided tour, but virtually all of Universal Studios Florida is open to patron exploration. Unlike Disney-MGM, Universal Florida's open area includes the entire back lot, where guests can walk at their leisure among the many and varied sets.

Universal hammers on the point that it is a working motion picture and television studio first, and only incidentally a tourist attraction. Whether this assertion is a point of pride with Universal or an apology to the tourist is unclear. It is true, however, that guests are more likely to see movie or television production in progress at Universal Florida than at Disney-MGM. On any given day, several production crews will be shooting on the Universal back lot sets in full view of any guests who care to watch.

Universal Studios Florida is so large, and because almost all of it is open to the public, most of the crowding and congestion so familiar in the streets and plazas of Disney-MGM is eliminated. At Universal Studios Florida there is plenty of elbow room.

The quality of the attractions is excellent at both parks, though the Disney-MGM rides and attractions are generally engineered to move people more efficiently. This advantage is somewhat offset, however, by the fact that there are more rides and shows at Universal. At Disney-MGM Studios there are four rides, six covered theater shows, two walking tours, two walk-through attractions, and two uncovered outdoor productions. At Universal Studios Florida there are five rides (six, when Jaws comes back on line), nine covered theater shows, one tram tour, one walking tour, and three uncovered outdoor productions.

Amazingly, and to the visitor's advantage, each of these parks offers a completely different product mix, so there is little or no redundancy for a person who visits both. Disney-MGM and Universal Florida each offer a good exposure to the cinematic arts, though Disney-MGM's presentations are crisper, better integrated, and more coherent.

Stunt shows are similar at both parks. The Disney version (for which guests sometimes endure long waits) and the *Wild, Wild, Wild West*

Stunt Show (where guests do not have to wait at all) are both staged in 2,000-seat stadiums that allow a good view of the action. The *Dynamite Nights Stunt Spectacular* at Universal Studios is staged in a large Lagoon with patrons simply taking up viewing positions along the railing. The Lagoon (which provides a realistic setting) is so large that sometimes the action is hard to see or follow. All three shows have their moments, and the two stadium shows are fairly informative. In the final analysis, Universal Studios gets the call in the stunt department, offering more variety with considerably shorter waits.

Our recommendation is to try one of the studios. If you enjoy one, you will probably enjoy the other. If you have to choose between the studios, consider the following:

1. **Touring Time.** If you tour efficiently, it takes about five to seven hours to see the Disney-MGM Studios (including a lunch break). Because Universal Studios Florida is larger, and contains more (and often less efficiently engineered) rides and shows, touring time, including one meal, runs about seven to ten hours.

2. **Convenience.** If you are lodging along International Drive, I-4's northeast corridor, the Orange Blossom Trail (US 441), or in Orlando, Universal Studios Florida will be closer. If you are lodging along US 27, FL 192, or in Kissimmee or Walt Disney World, the Disney-MGM Studios will be more convenient.

3. **Endurance.** Universal Studios Florida is larger and requires more walking than Disney-MGM, but it is also much less congested so the walking is easier. Wheelchairs are available, as is handicapped access, at both parks.

4. **Cost.** Both parks cost about the same for admission, food, and incidentals. All attractions are included in the price of admission.

5. **Best Days to Go.** Tuesdays, Mondays, Thursdays, and Fridays (except on holiday weekends) are the best days to visit Universal Studios Florida. Saturdays, Sundays, Fridays, and Tuesdays are the best days for visiting the Disney-MGM Studios during the busier times of the year. During the off-season, visit the Disney-MGM Studios on Fridays, Tuesdays, Mondays, and Thursdays.

6. **When to Arrive.** For Disney-MGM, arrive with your ticket in hand 40 minutes before the official opening time. For Universal Studios, arrive about 35 minutes before the official opening time.

7. ***Small Children.*** Both Disney-MGM Studios and Universal Studios Florida are relatively adult entertainment offerings. By our reckoning, half the rides and shows at Disney-MGM, and about two-thirds of the rides and shows at Universal Studios Florida, have a significant potential for frightening small children.

8. ***Food.*** In general, the food is much better at Universal Studios.

One-Day Touring Plan for Universal Studios Florida

This plan is for all visitors. If there is a ride or show listed which you prefer not to experience, simply skip that step in the plan and proceed to the next. Try to move from attraction to attraction quickly and, if possible, not stop for lunch until after Step 10.

The Hard Rock Cafe is a fun place for lunch or dinner if you enjoy rock 'n' roll. The food is good (though they sometimes over-cook their burgers) and the service, once you are seated, is usually efficient. If you go, get your hand stamped for reentry (the restaurant is technically located outside of the park), and be prepared for a wait. We arrived at the Hard Rock at 3 P.M. on a Wednesday and had to wait in 4 different lines for a total of 35 minutes before being seated. On another occasion, at 8 P.M. on a Thursday, we waited in 11 different lines (no kidding! and all in the same restaurant) for a total of an hour and a half before getting a table.

Touring Plan

1. Call (407) 363-8000 the day before your visit for the official opening time.
2. On the day of your visit, eat breakfast and arrive at Universal Studios Florida 35 minutes before opening time.
3. At the front gate, purchase your admission and line up at the turnstile. Be sure to pick up a map and the daily entertainment schedule. Ask the ticket seller, or any other attendant, whether the Jaws ride is operating and inquire if any rides or shows are closed that day. Adjust the Touring Plan accordingly.
4. When the park opens move quickly to The Funtastic World of Hanna-Barbera, a rocket simulation ride.
5. After the Hanna-Barbera ride, take a right on Hollywood Boulevard, first passing Mel's Diner (on your left) and then Cafe La Bamba on your right; go through the Central Park set into the Expo Center section of the park.
6. Ride the E.T. Adventure (if touring on a Saturday, ride Back to the Future and then E.T.)

7. Exit E.T. and head back toward the Lagoon, keeping *Animal Actors Stage* on your right. Ride Back to the Future.

8. After Back to the Future, walk around the Lagoon, keeping the water on your right, and enter the New York section of the park. Go to Kongfrontation and ride.

9. Following Kongfrontation, return to the waterfront and pass into the San Francisco/Amity set. If Jaws is operating, ride Jaws first and then Earthquake. If Jaws is not on line, proceed directly to Earthquake. If you want a good sit-down meal for lunch or dinner, Lombard's Landing across from Earthquake is a great choice. Make reservations now while you are in the area. For other eating alternatives, see Step 11.

10. If you are still in one piece after the Flintstones, a bike ride to another galaxy, a shark attack, an earthquake, and an encounter with King Kong, you may as well take on some ghosts. Cross the Gramercy Park set in New York and see "Ghostbusters." The line will appear long, but should move quickly as guests are admitted inside.

11. This is a good time for lunch if you have not already eaten. Cafe La Bamba in the Hollywood area offers a good Mexican buffet, and Mel's Diner nearby has good milkshakes. The International Food Bazaar next to Back to the Future serves gyros, bratwurst, pizza, and other ethnic goodies. A good, but often overlooked eatery is the Studio Stars Restaurant across the street from the prop "Boneyard" and down a block from "Alfred Hitchcock." This restaurant features California cuisine and also serves a buffet. In the New York area we like Louie's Italian Restaurant for pizza, calzone, and salads; and the outrageous sandwiches and pastries which are the specialty of the Beverly Hills Boulangerie near the park's main entrance. If you are in the mood for a more relaxed, upscale dining experience, the nicest restaurant in the park is Lombard's Landing on the waterfront (across the street from Earthquake). In addition to prime rib and creative seafood entrees, Lombard's also serves a truly exceptional hamburger at a fair price. Finally, there is the Hard Rock Cafe. Serving good food to the accompaniment of vintage rock music, the Hard Rock is a cultural institution.

12. At this point you have six major attractions left to see:

(1) *The Gory Gruesome & Grotesque Horror Make-up Show*
(2) "Murder, She Wrote" Mystery Theater

(3) *Animal Actors Stage*

(4) *Dynamite Nights Stunt Spectacular*

(5) *Wild, Wild, Wild West Stunt Show*

(6) "Alfred Hitchcock: The Art of Making Movies"

Animal Actors Stage and the two stunt shows are performed several times each day, as listed in the daily entertainment schedule. Plan the remainder of your itinerary according to the next listed showtimes for these presentations. The *Horror Make-up Show* and "Murder, She Wrote" Mystery Theater (situated on opposite sides of Mel's Diner) run continuously, and can be worked into your itinerary as time permits. Save "Alfred Hitchcock" for your last attraction as you leave the park.

13. We have not included the Nickelodeon Studios Tour or the Production Tram Tour in the Touring Plan. If you have school age children in your party, you might consider taking the Nickelodeon tour late in the evening or on a second day at the park. Try the tram tour second to last before "Alfred Hitchcock."

14. This concludes the Touring Plan. Spend the remainder of your day at Universal Studios Florida revisiting your favorite rides and shows, or inspecting any of the sets and street scenes you may have missed earlier. Also check your daily entertainment schedule for any live performances. Street entertainment at Universal Studios includes Beetlejuice Dead in Concert, The Blues Brothers, and *The Adventures of Rocky and Bullwinkle*, all performed in the New York and San Francisco areas.

A Word About Sea World

Many dozens of readers have written requesting that we provide some coverage of Sea World. OK. In brief, here's what you need to know (for any additional information, call (407) 363-2613):

Sea World is a world-class marine life theme park located near the intersection of I-4 and the Bee Line Expressway. Admission (including tax) is about $35 for adults and $29 for children (3 to 9). Parking is $4 per car, $6 per RV or camper. It takes about six to eight hours to see everything, but you can see the big deal stuff in five hours or less.

Sea World is approximately the size of the Magic Kingdom, and requires about the same amount of walking. Most attractions are accessible to nonambulatory disabled persons.

In terms of size, quality, and creativity, Sea World is unequivocally on a par with the three major theme parks in Walt Disney World. Unlike Walt Disney World, however, Sea World primarily features stadium shows or walk-through exhibits. This means that you will spend about 90 percent less time waiting in line during eight hours at Sea World than you would for the same length visit at a Disney park.

Because lines, with one or two exceptions, are not much of a problem at Sea World, you can tour at almost any time of day. We recommend that you start your tour at about 3:30 or 4 P.M. (when the park is open until 9 P.M. or later). Many of the day's early guests will have departed by this hour, and you will be able to enjoy the various outdoor attractions in the relative cool of late afternoon and evening. If you eat at Sea World, try the Smokehouse for barbecue.

Most of Sea World's shows operate according to a daily entertainment schedule which is printed conveniently on a placemat sized map of the park. The four featured shows are:

The Shamu Killer Whale Show

The Sea Lion and Otter Show

The Atlantis Water Ski Show

The Whale and Dolphin Discovery Show

When you arrive, develop your touring itinerary around these four shows. One of the first things you will notice as you check out the performance times is that the shows are scheduled in a way that make it almost impossible to see the productions back-to-back in sequence. The Shamu show, for instance, might run from 5 to 5:25 P.M. Ideally, you would like to bop over to the Sea Lion and Otter Show which begins at 5:30 P.M. Unfortunately, however, five minutes is not enough time to exit Shamu Stadium and walk all the way across the park to the Sea Lion & Otter Stadium. Sea World, of course, planned it this way so you would spend more time in the park.

It is possible to catch the Shamu show and the Sea Lion and Otter Show in succession by sitting near an exit at Shamu Stadium and leaving just a minute or two early (while the performers are taking their bows). Getting a couple of minutes head start on the crowd and hustling directly to the Sea Lion & Otter Stadium will get you seated just as the show is beginning.

If you are going to a show in Shamu Stadium or at the Atlantis Water Ski Stadium, don't worry about arriving late. Both of these stadiums are huge, so you will almost certainly get a seat. Plus, there is not much in the first few minutes of either show that you can't afford to miss. Same with the Whale and Dolphin Discovery Show. For the Sea Lion and Otter Show, however, the beginning is really good, so try to be on time.

Below is a list rating Sea World attractions:

★★★★½	Terrors of The Deep (shark & eels exhibit)
★★★★½	Penguin Encounter (penguin and puffin exhibit)
★★★★	Manatees: The Last Generation (manatee exhibit)
★★★★	Shamu Killer Whale Show
★★★★	Sea Lion and Otter Show
★★★★	Mission: Bermuda Triangle (simulation ride)
★★★★	Atlantis Water Ski Show
★★★½	Tropical Reef (reef fish aquarium exhibit)
★★★	Hawaiian Rhythms (Polynesian dance and music)

★★★   Nautilus Showplace (acrobatic or dance performance)

★★★   Shamu's Happy Harbor (children's play area)

★★½   Sea World Theater (Sea World propaganda and dancing fountains)

There are also stand-alone exhibits featuring dolphins, sting rays, manatees, harbor seals, pelicans, spoonbills, and flamingos, as well as a tidal pool and tropical rain forest.

PART SEVEN:
The Water Theme Parks

Typhoon Lagoon

Designed to be the ultimate swimming theme park, Typhoon Lagoon is four times the size of River Country, Walt Disney World's first splash-and-sun attraction. Nine water slides and streams, some as long as 400 feet, drop from the top of a 100-foot-high man-made mountain. Landscaping and an "aftermath of a typhoon" theme impart an added adventurous touch to the wet rides. Features include the world's largest inland surf facility, with waves up to six feet in height in a lagoon large enough to "encompass an oceanliner," and a saltwater snorkeling pool where guests can swim around with a multitude of real fish.

Beautifully landscaped, Typhoon Lagoon is entered through a misty rain forest emerging into a ramshackle tropical town where concessions and services are situated. Disney special effects make every ride an odyssey as swimmers encounter bat caves, lagoons and pools, spinning rocks, dinosaur bone formations, and countless other imponderables.

Typhoon Lagoon provides water adventure for all age groups. Activity pools for young children and families feature geysers, tame slides, bubble jets, and fountains. For the older and more adventurous there are two speed slides, three corkscrew body slides, and three tube/rapids rides (plus one children's rapids ride) plopping off Mount Mayday. For slower metabolisms there is Castaway Creek, a scenic, relaxed, meandering, 2,100-foot-long tube ride that winds through a hidden grotto and a rain forest. And, of course, for the sedentary, there is usually plenty of sun to sleep in.

What sets Typhoon Lagoon apart from other water parks is not so much its various slides, but the Disney attention to detail in creating an integrated adventure environment. The eye (as well as the body) is deluged with the strange, the exotic, the humorous and the beautiful. In point of fact, faster, higher, and wilder slides and rapid rides can be found elsewhere. But no other water park comes close to Typhoon Lagoon in diversity, variety, adventure, and total impact.

Typhoon Lagoon has its own 1,000-car pay parking lot and can

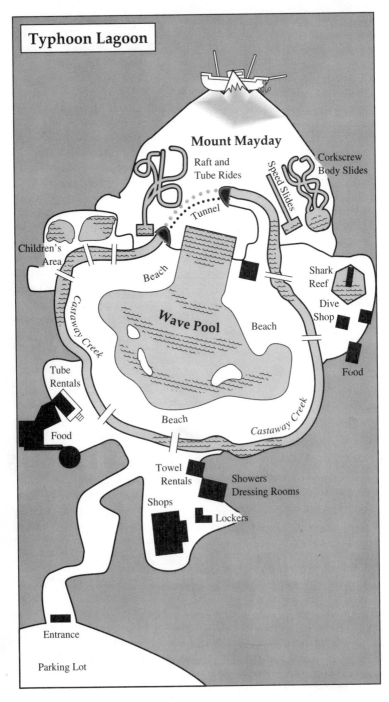

Typhoon Lagoon

Mount Mayday

Raft and Tube Rides

Corkscrew Body Slides

Speed Slides

Tunnel

Children's Area

Beach

Wave Pool

Beach

Shark Reef

Dive Shop

Castaway Creek

Tube Rentals

Food

Beach

Castaway Creek

Food

Towel Rentals

Showers Dressing Rooms

Shops

Lockers

Entrance

Parking Lot

also be reached by shuttle bus from Walt Disney World and Walt Disney World Village hotels and campgrounds. There are no lodging accommodations at Typhoon Lagoon.

Finally, Typhoon Lagoon is expensive, about $21 a day for adults and $17 a day for children 3–9. Children under three are admitted free. If you enjoy all the features of Typhoon Lagoon, the admission cost is a fair value. If, however, you are going primarily for the slides, you will have only two early morning hours to enjoy the slides before the waiting lines become prohibitive.

Typhoon Lagoon Touring Tips

When it comes to water slides, unfortunately, modern traffic engineering bows to old-fashioned queuing theory. It's one person, one raft, or one tube at a time, and the swimmer "on deck" cannot go until the person preceding him is safely out of the way. Thus the hourly carrying capacity of a slide is nominal compared to the continuously loading rides of EPCOT Center and the Magic Kingdom. Since a certain interval between swimmers is required for safety, the only way to increase capacity is to increase the number of slides and rapids rides.

The best way to avoid standing in lines is to visit Typhoon Lagoon on a day when it is less crowded. Because of the park's popularity among Florida locals, weekends can be tough. We recommend going on a Monday or Tuesday when most other tourists will be visiting the Magic Kingdom, EPCOT Center, or the Disney-MGM Studios, and the locals will be at work. Fridays are also a good bet since auto travelers commonly use this day to get a start on their trip home. Sunday morning is also a good time to go. Be forewarned, however, that during the summer and holiday periods, Typhoon Lagoon fills to capacity and closes its gates by about 11 A.M. To give you an idea of what "crowded" means at Typhoon Lagoon, we quote a reader from Newbury Park, California:

> The only disappointment we had at WDW was Typhoon Lagoon. While WDW was quite uncrowded, Typhoon Lagoon seemed choked with people. I'd hate to see it on a really crowded day. Even the small slides had lines greater than thirty minutes. They weren't worth half the wait. Castaway Creek might have been relaxing, but I found it to be a continuous traffic jam. I [also] would have enjoyed the snorkeling area except we were forced to go through at warp speed. After half a day we returned to the

Yacht Club where Stormalong Bay provided much more pleasant water recreation.

If your schedule is flexible, the best time of all to enjoy Typhoon Lagoon is from midafternoon to late in the day when the weather has cleared after a storm. The Lagoon usually closes during bad weather. If the storm is prolonged, most guests in the park go back to their hotel. When Typhoon Lagoon reopens after the inclement weather has passed, you can almost have the place to yourself.

If you are mostly interested in the slides, and are willing to sacrifice exotic landscaping for less congestion and more elbow room, try Water Mania on US 192 south of I-4. Water Mania is cheaper, too.

Typhoon Lagoon Touring Plan

Though large and elaborate, Typhoon Lagoon actually has fewer slides than Wet 'n Wild (its main Orlando area competitor) and on crowded days long lines can develop for the chutes coming off Mount Mayday. Thus to have a great day and beat the crowd, we recommend the following:

1. **Getting Information.** Call (407) 824-4321 the night before you go to inquire when the park opens.

2. **To Picnic or Not to Picnic.** Decide whether or not you want to bring a picnic lunch. Guests are permitted to bring lunches and beverage coolers to Typhoon Lagoon. No alcoholic beverages are allowed. Glass containers of all kinds (including mayonnaise, mustard, peanut butter, and pickle jars) are likewise forbidden.

3. **Getting Started.** Get up early, have breakfast, and arrive at Typhoon Lagoon a half hour before opening time. If you have a car, we recommend driving instead of taking a Walt Disney World bus.

4. **Attire.** We suggest that you wear your bathing suit under shorts and a T-shirt so you do not need to use lockers or dressing rooms. Lockers are available and come in small and large sizes for a $5 or $7 per day rental fee, respectively, of which $2 is refundable when you return your key. The lockers are roomy enough for one person or a couple, but will not accommodate an entire family. Though you can access your locker freely all day, it should be noted that the lockers are not conveniently located. Finally, you are not allowed to leave stuff in the locker overnight.

   Be sure to wear shoes. The footpaths at Typhoon Lagoon are relatively easy on bare feet, but there is a lot of ground to cover. If you have tender feet, we recommend wearing your shoes as you move around the park, taking them off whenever you raft, slide, or go into the water.

5. **What to Bring.**   Things you will need include a towel, suntan lotion, and of course money. Since wallets and purses just get in the way, lock them safely in your trunk, carrying your money in a plastic bag along with your Walt Disney World hotel ID (if you have one). Though no place is completely safe, our folks felt very comfortable hiding our plastic money bags among our chaise lounges, coolers, and swimming paraphernalia once we settled in. Nobody disturbed our stuff and our cash was much easier to access than if we had had to run across the park to a locker. If you are really carrying a wad or you tend to worry about money anyway, get the locker.

6. **What Not to Bring.**   Personal swim gear (fins, masks, rafts, etc.) are not allowed in Typhoon Lagoon. Everything you will need is either provided or available to rent. If you forget your towel, you can rent one. If you forget your swimsuit or lotion, these can be purchased. Personal flotation devices (life jackets) are available free of charge at High & Dry Towels. To obtain a PFD you must leave a $25 deposit which is held until the equipment is returned. The same service is available at River Country.

7. **Admissions.**   Purchase your admission about a half hour before opening time. If you are staying at a Walt Disney World lodging property, you may be entitled to an admission discount so bring your hotel or campground ID. For guests on an extended stay at Walt Disney World, unlimited admission to Typhoon Lagoon is included in several of the Be Our Guest and Super Duper Pass admission packages.

8. **Getting Oriented.**   Typhoon Lagoon is a circular park with the surf lagoon right in the middle. In terms of a clock face, you enter at the six o'clock position, and Mount Mayday (with the boat on top) is straight across the lagoon at twelve o'clock. A narrow canal, Castaway Creek, carves a wide circle around the lagoon and its adjoining beach area. Shark Reef, all the slides and raft rides, the children's area, and all services and concessions are situated around the outside perimeter of Castaway Creek. As you enter, tube rentals are to your left at seven o'clock, dressing rooms and lockers are to your right at four o'clock.

9. ***Tube Rental.*** When the park opens, walk straight ahead until you get to Castaway Creek. Turn left (without crossing) and head for the tube rental shack. Rent a tube for bobbing in Typhoon Lagoon. Rental tubes can also be used on Mayday Falls and Keekhaul Falls, eliminating the need for you to stand in a separate line at the Falls to pick up a loaner tube.

NOTE: Rafting in the lagoon has been discontinued. The lagoon now alternates between "bobbing" waves (small, non-breaking waves) and large, breaking waves for body surfing. During body surfing periods, tubes are not allowed in the lagoon.

A $1 deposit is required per renter (the person who signs the rental agreement). Thus, Mom can plunk down one deposit and rent tubes for the whole family. We recommend a tube for each member of the family over four years of age. Single (one person) tubes rent for $5 a day and double (two person) tubes for $10 a day. Swim fins for body surfing are also available at $1 an hour.

As you might expect, signing rental agreements and checking out equipment is a little time-consuming. That is why you want to rent your tube first thing. If you decide to wait, thinking to save a few bucks on the rental fee, you will probably find yourself in a long slow line. If you want to be super-efficient, have one person in your party rent tubes while others pick a nesting spot.

Many readers have written complaining that their tubes were stolen by other guests. If this should happen, you will be issued another tube at no charge, but of course will have to suffer the inconvenience. We recommend taking a length of rope and tying your tube(s) to a chair or chaise lounge. This of course is essentially a symbolic gesture, but one that will keep all but the most brazen away from your tube(s).

10. ***Lockers, Dressing Rooms, Towel Rental, Rest Rooms.*** These are situated to the right of the entrance, back upstream along Castaway Creek.

11. ***Getting Settled In.*** Establish your base for the day. There are many, many beautiful sunning and lounging spots scattered around Typhoon Lagoon. The breeze is best along the beaches of the lagoon (surf pool). If there are children under six in your

party, you might choose an area to the left of Mount Mayday (with the ship on top) near the children's swimming area.

Arriving early, you can just about have your pick. There are flat lounges (unadjustable) and chairs (better for reading). There are grass shelters for those who prefer shade and even a few hammocks. Our research crew of seven staked out an area that had a shelter plus some sunny beach on the breezy side of the lagoon. There were picnic tables nearby.

The best spectator sport at Typhoon Lagoon is the surfing action in the lagoon. The second-best thing to being out there yourself is watching the zany antics of the other guests. With this in mind, you might choose a nesting spot with a good unobstructed view of the surf pool.

If you are a locker person, set up camp on the right side of the lagoon, along the beach. This will make it more convenient to visit your money.

12. **Shark Reef.**   After settling in and stowing away your rented rafts for later use, walk around the right side of the lagoon to Shark Reef where you can snorkel in a saltwater pool with some live fish. Fins, mask, snorkel, and wetsuit vest are provided at no charge in the wooden building flanking the diving pool. Having obtained proper equipment (no forms or money involved), you are directed to take a shower and then to report to a snorkeling instructor. After a few minutes of instruction, you swim approximately 60 feet to the other side of the pool. You are not allowed to paddle about aimlessly, but must traverse the pool more or less directly.

Shark Reef is fun early in the morning. Equipment collection, shower, instruction, and, finally, the quick swim can be accomplished without too much hassle. Also, owing to the small number of guests present, the attendants are more flexible about lingering in the pool and minor departures in your charted course.

Later, as crowds build, it becomes increasingly difficult and time-consuming to provide the necessary instruction. The result: platoons of would-be frogmen (should I say "frogpersons"?), zippily attired in their diving regalia, all restlessly awaiting their snorkeling lesson. Guests are formed into impromptu classes with the entire class briefed, and subsequently launched, together. What takes four or five minutes shortly after opening can take over an hour by 11 A.M.

By far the most prevalent and exotic species to be viewed in the pool are the dual-finned *homo sapiens*. Other denizens of the deep include small, colorful tropical fish, some diminutive rays, and a few very small leopard and hammerhead sharks. In terms of numbers, it would be unusual to swim the length of the pool and not see some fish. On the other hand, you are not exactly bumping into them all the time either.

It is very important to fit your diving mask on your face so that it seals around the edges. Brush hair away from your forehead and take a couple of sniffs with your nose, once the mask is in place, to create a vacuum. Be advised that mustaches often prevent the mask from sealing properly. The first indication that your mask is not correctly fitted will be saltwater in your nose.

If you do not want to swim around with fish early in the morning or fight crowds later in the day, you can avail yourself of an underwater viewing chamber, accessible anytime without waiting, special equipment, showers, instruction, or water in your nose.

13. ***Body Slides.*** Moving counterclockwise around the surfing lagoon in the direction of Mount Mayday, go next to the body slides on the right side of the mountain. Here you will find three corkscrew slides, the Storm Slides, and two steep speed slides called Humunga Kowabunga.

The corkscrew slides are pretty good, twisting off the mountain through arches in the rock and terminating in a pool. One line feeds all three slides. While each corkscrew is a little bit different, they all have pretty much the same feel.

The aggravating thing about the Storm Slides is the walkway to reach them. Obviously designed to handle a line of several hundred waiting guests, the concourse winds and dips all over the side of the mountain. For most folks it is sufficiently arduous to simply scale the vertical distance from pool level to the top of the slide. The walkway does not simply ascend to the top, but instead undulates, dropping down two steps for every three steps up, so that you must climb almost twice as many steps as would ordinarily be necessary to attain the same height.

Humunga Kowabunga (located next to the Storm Slides)

offers dual-speed slides dropping about three stories at a pitch just short of vertical. While there is no minimum height requirement for the Storm Slides, riders for Humunga Kowabunga must be four feet tall. Pregnant women and those with back problems and various other health deficits are warned against riding any of the body slides.

We recommend riding each of the three Storm Slides once and then trying the speed slide (which looks worse than it is). If you want to sample remaining park attractions before the lines get heavy, this is about all the time you can afford to spend here.

Coach's Note: To go as fast as possible on a body slide, cross your legs at the ankles and cross your arms over your chest. When you take off, arch your back so that almost all your weight is on your shoulder blades and heels (the less contact with the surface, the less resistance). You can steer by shifting most of your upper body weight onto one shoulder blade. For max speed, weight the shoulder blade on the outside of each curve. If you want to go slow (what's the point?), distribute your weight equally as if you were lying on your back in bed.

14. *Raft Rides.* From the body slides continue counterclockwise, passing via a tunnel through Mount Mayday. On the left side of the mountain are three so-called raft rides: Gangplank Falls, Mayday Falls, and Keelhaul Falls.

Of the three, only Gangplank Falls actually involves rafts; the other two use inner tubes. All three are nicely done but are relatively tame as flume rides go. Each courses down a convoluted spillway replete with waves, eddies, chutes, and reversal currents. On Gangplank Falls, guests share round inflatable rafts resembling children's backyard wading pools. A sign at the entrance to the queueing area indicates a three-person minimum to ride. If your party numbers less, not to worry. Simply proceed to the loading point where an attendant will team you up with others.

On Mayday and Keelhaul Falls, you ride single-person inner tubes instead of a raft. Of the two, Mayday Falls is the more exciting, Keelhaul Falls being almost tame. Minimum height for Mayday and Keelhaul is four feet. There is no height requirement for Gangplank Falls.

15. ***Repeat Rides.*** Having completed the raft rides, you will have experienced all of Typhoon Lagoon's attractions which develop lines. If you arrived early and kept up a good pace you should be able to repeat some of your favorite rides without a prohibitive wait. In any event, now is the time to try. The park will only become more crowded as the day goes on.

16. ***Options.*** By the time you finish repeating your favorite slides the park will have become noticeably (if not impossibly) more crowded. Fortunately, the two remaining untried Typhoon Lagoon features, Typhoon Lagoon surf pool and Castaway Creek, accommodate large numbers with no waiting. Expressed differently, you can structure your own schedule from this point on. The only lines you will encounter will be for food. If you are worn out, relax on Castaway Creek, curl up in a hammock, or grab a bite. If you are still full of energy, head for the surf pool.

17. ***Surf Pool.*** The surf lagoon (along with the beautiful landscaping) is what makes Typhoon Lagoon truly special. We have to tell you that you will experience larger waves in the Typhoon Lagoon surf pool than most folks have ever encountered in the ocean. The surf machine puts out a wave about every 90 seconds (just about how long it takes to get back in position if you caught the previous wave). Perfectly formed and ideal for riding, each wave is about five to six feet tall from trough to crest. Before you throw yourself into the fray, watch two or three waves from some vantage point onshore. Since each wave breaks in almost the same spot you can get a feel for position and timing. Observing the technique of other surfers will help also.

The best way to ride the waves is to swim out about three-fourths of the way to the wall at the wave machine end of the surf pool. When the wave comes (you will both feel and hear it), swim vigorously toward the beach, attempting to position yourself one-half to three-fourths of a body length below the breaking crest. The waves are so perfectly engineered that they will either carry you forward or bypass you (unlike an ocean wave, they will not slam you down).

The primary hazard in the surf pool is collision with other

surfers and swimmers. If you are surfing, the best way to avoid collision is to paddle out pretty far (as described above) so that you will be at the top of the wave as it breaks. This tactic eliminates the possibility of anyone landing on you from above while assuring maximum forward visibility and steerage for collision avoidance with those between you and the beach. A corollary to all this is that the worst place to swim is in the area where the wave actually breaks. As you look up you will see a six-foot wall of water carrying eight-dozen screaming surfers bearing down on you at 90 miles an hour. This is the time to remember every submarine movie you've ever seen . . . Dive! Dive! Dive!

When the surf pool changes to bobbing waves, it's time to grab your tube. If you do not have a tube, you can still have fun swimming or floating in the gentle waves, but you will feel like the only kid on the team without a uniform. It's only five bucks a day; just do it.

Finally, an additional warning: Typhoon Lagoon surf has an uncanny knack for loosening watchbands, stripping jewelry, and sucking stuff out of your pockets. Don't take anything out there except your swimsuit (and hold on to it).

18. ***Castaway Creek.***   Castaway Creek is a great idea. It is a long, long tranquil inner-tube ride that gives the impression that you are doing something while you are being sedentary. For wimps, wussies, and exhausted people of all ages, Castaway Creek is the answer to a prayer. Flowing ever so slowly around the whole park, through caves and beneath waterfalls, past gardens, shipwrecks, and bridges, Castaway Creek offers a relaxing, foot-saving alternative for touring the park.

Castaway Creek can be reached from a number of put-in/take-out points distributed around its circumference. There are never any lines; just wade out into the creek and plop into one of the inner-tubes floating by. Ride the gentle current all the way around or get out at any exit. If you lay back and go with the flow, it will take about 30–35 minutes to float the full 2,100-foot circuit.

As you might anticipate, there will be other guests on whom the subtlety of Castaway Creek will be lost. They will be the ones racing, screaming, and splashing. Let them pass, stopping in place for a few moments if necessary to put some distance between yourself and them.

19. ***Children's Swimming Area.*** To the left of the raft rides is Ketchakiddie Creek, a delightful children's swimming area featuring mild slides, bubble jets, waterfalls, and a variety of "hands-on" play structures. Spacious and attractive, Ketchakiddie is designed to stimulate young imaginations as well as young bodies.

20. ***Lunch.*** If you did not bring a picnic lunch, you can of course purchase food. Portions are adequate to generous, quality is comparable to chain fast food, and prices are (as you would expect) a bit high.

21. ***More Options.*** If you are really a water puppy, you might consider returning to your hotel for a little heat-of-the-day siesta and returning to Typhoon Lagoon for some early evening swimming. Special lighting after dusk makes Typhoon Lagoon an enchanting place to be. Crowds also tend to be lighter in the evening. If you leave the park and want to return, be sure to hang on to your admission ticket and have your hand stamped. If you are staying in a hotel serviced by Walt Disney World buses, older kids can return on their own to Typhoon Lagoon, giving Mom and Dad a little private quiet time.

River Country

River Country is aesthetically among the best of the water theme parks—beautifully landscaped and immaculately manicured with rocky canyons and waterfalls skillfully blended with white sand beaches. The park is even situated to take advantage of the breeze blowing in from Bay Lake. For pure and simple swimming and splashing, River Country gets high marks. For its slides, however, River Country does not begin to compete with its big sister, Typhoon Lagoon, or with its nearby competitors. Where Wet 'n Wild (on International Drive) features in excess of 16 major slides and tube rides, River Country has one tube ride and two corkscrew-style slides. Few slides and many swimmers add up to long lines. If slides are your thing, and you are allergic to long lines, hit River Country as soon as it opens in the morning or alternatively in the hour before closing. You can come and go throughout the day simply by obtaining a reentry stamp.

Sunbathers will enjoy River Country, particularly if they position themselves near the lakefront to take advantage of any cooling breeze. Be forewarned, however, that the chaise lounges are basically flat with the head slightly elevated, and do not have adjustable backs. For a comfortable reading position or for lying on your stomach, therefore, they leave a great deal to be desired.

Access to River Country by car is a hassle. First you are directed to a parking lot, where you leave your car, gather your personal belongings and wait for a Disney bus to transport you to the water park. The ride is rather lengthy, and pity the poor soul who left his bathing suit in the car (a round-trip to retrieve it will take about a half hour). In the morning, because the bus from the parking lot to River Country is very crowded, we suggest catching the Pioneer Hall bus (which loads at the same place in the parking lot) and then walking over to River Country.

There are no lodging accommodations at River Country. Food is available or you can pack in a picnic lunch to enjoy in River Country's picturesque, shaded lakeside picnic area. Access is by bus from the Transportation and Ticket Center (junction and transfer point for the EPCOT Center and Magic Kingdom monorails) or from the River Country parking lot on Vista Boulevard (see map, page 86). River Country can also be reached by boat from any of the Bay Lake or Seven Seas Lagoon resort hotels. Combination passes, which include both River Country and Discovery Island, are available and represent the best buy for anyone interested in the minor Disney theme parks. For guests staying at Walt Disney World for five or more days, the 5-Day Super Duper Pass includes unlimited admission to both River Country and Typhoon Lagoon.

—— Orlando/Kissimmee Area Water Theme Parks ——

Just for the record, if you are into water theme parks, here's how the area's offerings compare:

	Typhoon Lagoon	River Country	Water Mania	Wet 'n Wild
Theme presentation	Yes	Yes	No	No
Beautiful scenery/landscaping	Yes	Yes	No	No
Large general swimming area	Yes	Yes	Yes	Yes
Children's swimming area	Yes	Yes	Yes	Yes
Snorkeling pool	Yes	No	No	No
Wave pool	Yes	No	Yes	Yes
Vertical-drop thrill slide	2	No	2	2
Graduated-drop thrill slide	No	No	2	2
Corkscrew body slide	3	2	3	4
Corkscrew tube/raft/mat slide	No	No	1	6
Whitewater rapids ride	3	1	1	2
Tranquil/scenic tube ride	1	No	1	1
Knee waterski	No	No	No	Yes
Surfing wave	No	No	Yes	No

Typhoon Lagoon vs. Wet 'n Wild and Water Mania

Wet 'n Wild has Typhoon Lagoon and Water Mania beat in the slide department. Wet 'n Wild has more slides, wilder slides, and more direct ramps and walkways, which cuts down travel time back up to the top. The headliner at Wet 'n Wild is the Black Hole, where guests descend on a two-person tube down a totally enclosed corkscrew slide. The Black Hole is a wet version of Space Mountain only much darker. Our research team thinks this is the single most exciting slide offered at any Florida swimming theme park. Water Mania has a similar slide called the Abyss that is almost pitch black. The newest thrill slide is the Bomb Bay, introduced at Wet 'n Wild in 1993. Guests are dropped from a compartment resembling a bomb bay down a 79°-angle chute.

Water Mania, on US 192 south of I-4, edges out Typhoon Lagoon in the slide department and is less crowded than either of its competitors. In addition, Water Mania is the only water park to offer a stationary wave for surfing.

Typhoon Lagoon wins hands down in landscaping and aesthetic beauty, and has the best surf pool of the three parks. Each of the parks has an outstanding water activity area for small children. All three parks feature unique attractions. Wet 'n Wild has a ride in which guests kneel on water skis, Typhoon Lagoon has Shark Reef where guests snorkel among live fish, and Water Mania has its surfing wave.

Prices for one-day admission are about the same at Wet 'n Wild and Typhoon Lagoon, and a little cheaper at Water Mania. Also, discount coupons are often available in local visitor magazines for Water Mania and Wet 'n Wild.

Wet 'n Wild stays open until 11 P.M. during the summer; Typhoon Lagoon and Water Mania generally close between 5 P.M. and 8 P.M. We think the late closing time is a great plus for Wet 'n Wild. Warm Florida nights are a great time to enjoy a water theme park. There is less waiting for slides and the pavement is cooler on your feet. Not only that, Wet 'n Wild features live music in the evenings at its Wave Pool Stage. To top it off, admission prices at Wet 'n Wild are discounted 50 percent after 5 P.M. on days when the park is open late.

PART EIGHT: Night Life In and Out of Walt Disney World

Walt Disney World at Night

The Disney folks contrive so cleverly to exhaust you during the day that the mere thought of night activity sends most visitors into anaphylactic shock. For the hearty and the nocturnal, however, there is a lot to do in the evenings at Walt Disney World.

In the Parks

At EPCOT Center the major evening event is IllumiNations, a mixed-media laser and fireworks show at the World Showcase Lagoon. Showtime is listed on the daily entertainment and special events schedule.

In the Magic Kingdom there are the ever-popular evening parade(s) and Fantasy in the Sky fireworks. Consult the daily entertainment schedule for performance times.

The Disney-MGM Studios feature a laser and fireworks spectacular called Sorcery in the Sky on nights when the park is open late. Consult the daily entertainment schedule for showtimes.

At the Hotels

Waterside at the Polynesian Resort is the Bay Lake and Seven Seas Lagoon Floating Electrical Pageant. For something more elaborate, consider one of the dinner theaters described on the next page. Finally, if you want to go honky-tonkin', many of the hotels at the Disney Hotel Plaza (adjacent to Walt Disney World Village) have lively bars with rock bands and other entertainment.

At Fort Wilderness Campground

A campfire program is conducted each night at the Fort Wilderness Campground. Open only to Walt Disney World resort guests, the event begins with a sing-along led by Disney characters Chip and Dale, and progresses to cartoons and a Disney feature movie. There is no charge.

At Pleasure Island

Pleasure Island, Walt Disney World's nighttime entertainment complex, features seven nightclubs for one admission price. Dance to rock or country, or take in a showbar performance, or see a movie. Pleasure Island is located in Walt Disney World Village and is accessible from the theme parks and from the Transportation and Ticket Center by shuttle bus. For a detailed description of Pleasure Island, plus Touring Plan, see page 487.

At Disney's Boardwalk (no opening date set)

Disney's Boardwalk will be situated along the walkway connecting EPCOT Center with the Swan Hotel. Modeled after the Coney Island and Atlantic City boardwalks in their days of glory, Disney's version features game arcades, amusement park rides for all ages, bright lights, music, and food. Disney's Boardwalk will be accessible on foot from EPCOT Center or from any of the EPCOT Center resort hotels (Swan, Dolphin, Yacht Club, Beach Club) and by bus from other Walt Disney World destinations. Guests who walk over from EPCOT Center after IllumiNations can catch a bus directly back to the EPCOT Center parking lot to retrieve their car at the conclusion of the evening.

—— Walt Disney World Dinner Theaters ——

There are several dinner theater shows each night at Walt Disney World. Reservations can be made on the day of the show at any of the resort hotels, or by calling (407) 824-8000. Visitors with reservations for a Walt Disney World lodging property can make reservations prior to arrival by calling the same number. Getting reservations for *Broadway at the Top* and *Polynesian Revue* presentations is not too tough. Getting a reservation to the *Hoop Dee Doo Revue* is a trick of the first order.

Broadway at the Top

Broadway at the Top, situated atop the Contemporary Resort Hotel, features a creative menu with entrees such as roast duck, shrimp brochette and steak combination, seafood catch of the day, prime rib, and veal with sausage. Unlike most other dinner theaters, the pace is unhurried and the menu provides plenty of variety. The food is good and nicely presented, and the service is excellent.

The entertainment consists of dinner music and dancing to a live orchestra (playing primarily easy-listening standards), followed by a lively stage show featuring showtunes from Broadway and limited choreography. The presentation is professional and straightforward, but not particularly imaginative or compelling. *Broadway at the Top* appeals to a more mature audience and we do not recommend the show for children under twelve. Cost is about $49 per person plus drinks and tips. Gentlemen are required to wear jackets (but not ties).

The Polynesian Revue

Presented nightly at the Polynesian Resort, the evening consists of a "Polynesian style" all-you-can-eat meal followed by south seas island native dancing. The dancing is interesting and largely authentic, and the dancers are comely but definitely PG in the Disney tradition. We think that the show has its moments and the meal is adequate, but that neither is particularly special. Cost per adult is about $33. If you really enjoy this type of entertainment, and experience a problem getting a reservation for the Polynesian Revue, Sea World presents a similar dinner and show each evening.

A well-traveled, married couple from Fond du Lac, Wisconsin, described the Polynesian Revue this way:

> The Polynesian Revue was a beautiful presentation, better than some shows we have seen in Hawaii! The food, however, lacked in all areas.

Also at the Polynesian Resort's Luau Cove is *Mickey's Tropical Revue*, where Disney characters are tossed into the regular entertainment show. This show starts at 4:30 P.M. when it is too early to be hungry and too hot to be sitting around outdoors. Cost is about $29 for adults, $23 for juniors (12–20), and $14 for children (3–11).

Hoop Dee Doo Revue

This show, presented nightly at Pioneer Hall at Fort Wilderness Campgrounds, is by far the most popular of the Disney dinner shows. The meal, served family-style, consists of barbequed ribs, fried chicken, corn on the cob, and baked beans, along with chips, bread, salad, and dessert. Though the quality has slipped a bit, most of the fare is satisfactory (albeit greasy). Portions are generous and service is excellent.

The show consists of western dancehall song, dance, and humor, much in the mold of the *Diamond Horseshoe Jamboree* in the Magic Kingdom, only longer. The cast is talented, energetic, and lovable, each one a memorable character. Between the food, the show, and the happy, appreciative audience, the *Hoop Dee Doo Revue* is a delightful way to spend an evening. Cost is about $35 for adults, $26 for juniors, and $18 for children.

Now for the bad news. The *Hoop Dee Doo Revue* is sold out months in advance to guests who hold lodging reservations at Walt Disney World properties. If you plan to stay at one of the Walt Disney World hotels, try making your *Hoop Dee Doo* reservations when you book your room. If you have already booked your lodging call as far in advance as possible. For those with accommodations outside of Walt Disney World:

1. Call (407) 824-2748 thirty days prior to visiting. If that does not work:

2. Call (407) 824-2748 at 9 A.M. each morning while you are at Walt Disney World to make a same-day reservation. There are three performances each night, and for all three combined, only three to twenty-four people, total, will be admitted on same-day reservations. If no reservations are available:

3. Show up at Pioneer Hall (no easy task in itself unless you are staying in the Campgrounds) 45 minutes before showtime (early and late shows are your best bets) and put your name on the standby list. If someone with reservations fails to show, you may be admitted.

If you go to the *Hoop Dee Doo Revue*, with or without reservations, give yourself plenty of time to get there. The experience of a Houston, Texas, reader makes the point well:

We had 7:30 P.M. reservations for the Hoop Dee Doo Revue, so we left [Disney-] MGM just before 7:00 and drove directly to Fort Wilderness. Two important things to note: First, the road direction signs at WDW are terrible. I would recommend a day-light orientation drive upon arrival, except that there are so many ways to get confused that one might be lulled into a false sense of security. Second, when we got to Fort Wilderness, we had great difficulty determining where Pioneer Hall was and how to get there. I accosted several people and found a man who could tell us where we were on the map, and that a bus was the only way to get to Pioneer Hall. I would recommend leaving for Pioneer Hall one hour before your show reservations. Boredom is not nearly so painful as anxiety (reservations are held until fifteen minutes after the stated time).

A California dad had this tip to offer:

> To go to the Hoop Dee Doo at Fort Wilderness, take the boat from the Magic Kingdom rather than any bus. This [is] contrary to the "official" directions. The boat dock is a short walk from Pioneer Hall [in Fort Wilderness], while the bus goes to the [main] Fort Wilderness parking lot where one has to transfer to another bus to Pioneer Hall.

If all of this sounds too much like work, try the show at *Fort Liberty*, a non-Disney attraction on FL 192. Call (407) 351-5151 for reservations.

— *Other Area Dinner Theater Options* —

There are more than a dozen dinner theaters within 20 minutes of Walt Disney World. Of these, *Fort Liberty* is a good substitute for the *Hoop Dee Doo Revue*. *Medieval Times*, featuring mounted knights in combat, is fun and most assuredly different, and *King Henry's Feast* is a fun variety show on the theme of King Henry's birthday celebration. The food at all three of these dinner theaters is both good and plentiful and all three shows are highly recommended. Cost per adult is around $30–34, but discount coupons are readily available at brochure racks and in local tourism periodicals found in motel lobbies. *Fort Liberty* and *King Henry* reservations can be made by calling (407) 351-5151. Call (407) 239-0214 for *Medieval Times*.

A fourth dinner theater, *Mardi Gras*, stages a better Broadway-style show than Disney's *Broadway at the Top* does. The food at *Mardi Gras*, however, is not up to that of *Broadway at the Top*. Then again, neither is the price of admission ($32 at *Mardi Gras*, $49 at *Broadway at the Top*). At *Broadway at the Top* you can enjoy a great view and the tables are roomy. At *Mardi Gras* there is no view, and guests are literally packed at the tables. For information or reservations for *Mardi Gras* call (407) 351-5151.

A relative newcomer among dinner shows is *Arabian Nights*, located on US 192 east of I-4 on the way to Kissimmee. A prime rib dinner is featured here along with a show that could be called, "Everything You Ever Wanted to Know about Horses." The tab for adults is about $32. The phone number for information and reservations is (407) 239-9223.

Pleasure Island

Pleasure Island, which opened in 1989, is a six-acre nighttime entertainment complex situated on a man-made island in Walt Disney World Village. The complex consists of seven theme nightclubs, a ten-theater movie complex, restaurants, and shops. While some of the restaurants and shops are open during the day, Pleasure Island does not really come alive until after 7 P.M. when the nightclubs open.

Admission Options.   One admission (about $13) entitles a guest to enjoy all seven nightclubs (the Baton Rouge Lounge on the Empress Lilly steamboat is not part of Pleasure Island per se, but is so close that we include it in our discussion and Touring Plan as an eighth club). Guests younger than 18 years old must be accompanied by a parent after 7 P.M. Unlimited seven-day admission to Pleasure Island is also included in the 5-Day Super Duper Pass.

Alcoholic Beverages.   Guests not recognizably older than 21 are required to provide proof of their age if they wish to purchase alcoholic beverages. To avoid repeated checking as the patron moves from club to club, a color-coded wristband indicating eligibility status is provided. All the nightclubs on Pleasure Island serve alcohol. Those under 21, while allowed in all of the clubs except Mannequins and STRAX, are not allowed to purchase alcoholic beverages. Finally, and gratefully, you do not have to order any drinks at all. You can go into any club, enjoy the entertainment, and never buy that first beer. You won't be hassled a bit.

Dress Code.   Casual is in. Shirts and shoes are required.

New Variations on an Old Theme.   The single-admission nightclub complex was originated in Florida at Orlando's Church Street Station, still very much alive and well in historic downtown Orlando. Starting fresh, the Disney folks have been able to eliminate some of the

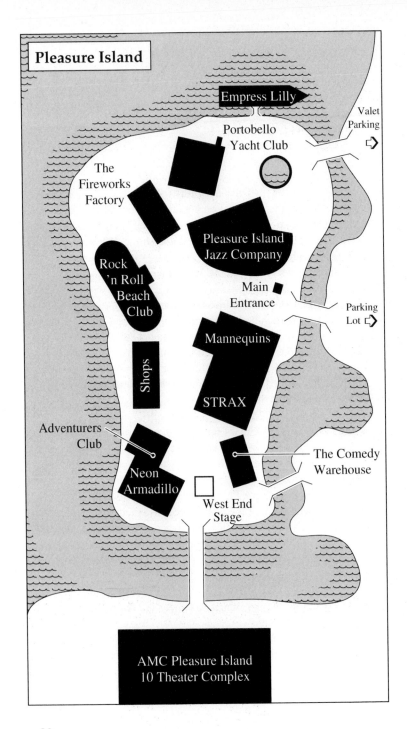

Pleasure Island

Empress Lilly

Valet Parking

Portobello Yacht Club

The Fireworks Factory

Pleasure Island Jazz Company

Rock 'n Roll Beach Club

Main Entrance

Parking Lot

Shops

Mannequins

STRAX

Adventurers Club

Neon Armadillo

The Comedy Warehouse

West End Stage

AMC Pleasure Island 10 Theater Complex

problems which have haunted Church Street Station and a lot of other nightspots over the years.

Summertime, and the Parking Is Easy.   To begin, Pleasure Island has its own vast parking lot so, unlike Church Street downtown, parking is easy. Pleasure Island's parking lot is confusing, however, unnecessarily convoluted, and not well-marked. If you drive, study all landmarks and other identifying objects near your parking space so you will be able to locate your car when you are ready to leave.

Good News for the Early to Bed Crowd.   If you are not nocturnal by nature or if you are tired from a long day in the theme parks, you do not have to wait until 11 or 12 P.M. for the Disney nightspots to get revved up. There is no waiting till the wee hours for Pleasure Island to hit its stride. All bands, dancers, comedians, and showmen come on like gangbusters from the very beginning of the evening. For *real* night people, it feels weird to be dancing to "Shout" at 8:15 P.M. But that's the way it is at Pleasure Island; there are no "best sets" or grand finales.

It's Possible to Visit All the Clubs in One Night.   Where a performance in most nightclubs might be an hour or more in duration, at Pleasure Island the performances are shorter but staged more frequently. This allows a guest to move around from club to club without missing much. Since you can experience the essence of a given club pretty quickly, there is no need to hang around for two or three drinks just to see what is going on. This format enables a guest to have a complete and satisfying experience in a brief time and then, if desired, to move on to sample another club.

The music clubs (Rock & Roll Beach Club, STRAX, Neon Armadillo, Baton Rouge Lounge, Mannequins, and Jazz Company) go nonstop. Sometimes there are special performances within the context of on-going club entertainment. The Adventurers Club and the Comedy Warehouse offer scheduled shows. All shows are of short duration, leaving plenty of time to sample other Pleasure Island offerings.

We are very high on Pleasure Island. The cover is a little pricey and the drinks are not cheap, but the entertainment is absolutely top-notch. And if you arrive by 9 P.M., you will have time to sample all of the clubs.

We get a lot of mail from couples in their 30s and 40s arguing

Pleasure Island's merits (or lack thereof). The following quotes are representative. A reader from Bettendorf, Iowa, states:

> I would not spend the money to go to Pleasure Island again. It is quite obvious that Disney is interested in the 21–30 year-old crowd here. There were many people our age (38) and older looking for something to do and not finding it. The Adventurer's Club is the only real Disney creation on the island. Walt Disney World crosses all age brackets and I expected the same from Pleasure Island. What a disappointment! I think you need to go back to the drawing board on your evaluation of Pleasure Island (and so does Disney).

A central Texas couple, however, had this to say:

> Your description, even with the statement that you are high on Pleasure Island, didn't prepare my wife and me for what a great place it is. Perhaps our expectations were moderate, but we thought it was an absolute blast, and we are neither under 40 nor club hounds.

Sorry, Invited Guests Only. From time to time, particularly during the early evening (before 9 P.M.), certain Pleasure Island clubs are reserved for private parties and declared temporarily off-limits to paying guests.

Pleasure Island First Timers' Touring Plan

This itinerary is for first-time visitors to Pleasure Island who want to check out all of the clubs.

1. Arrive by 6:30 or 7 P.M. if you intend on eating at a Pleasure Island restaurant. If you eat before you go, try to arrive by 9 P.M.

2. Purchase your admission or enter using your 5-Day Super Duper Pass.

3. *Comedy Warehouse.* Bearing left from the admission windows, proceed to the Comedy Warehouse. If a show is scheduled to begin within a half hour, browse the shops (some are great entertainment in their own right) until about ten minutes before showtime. Then head back to the Comedy Warehouse for the show. If showtime is more than 30 minutes off, check out the country and bluegrass music at the Neon Armadillo, located pretty much across the street from the Comedy Warehouse. Use your own judgment about whether you have time to buy a drink. Return to the Comedy Warehouse ten minutes before showtime.

4. *Adventurers Club.* After the show at the Comedy Warehouse, cross the street to the Adventurers Club. Another comedy presentation may be underway; check the posted schedule. Patterned after a rather stuffy English gentlemen's club, the Adventurers Club is a two-story turn-of-the-century affair with big armchairs, walls covered with animal heads (some of which talk), and other artifacts.

   Many guests will stroll through the Adventurers Club, inspect the ridiculous decor, and then leave, not realizing that they missed anything. The main attraction at the Adventurers Club is a show in the club's private library. About once every 30 or 40 minutes all the guests present will be ushered into the library for a show. Nobody informs the guests that a show is upcoming; they either must hang around long enough to be invited in, or alternately intuit that with Disney, what you see isn't what you get.

When you arrive at the Adventurers Club, ask an attendant when the next show in the library will be starting. If showtime is 20 minutes or less away, go on in and have a drink. If it's a long while until the next show, the Neon Armadillo is right next door.

5. *Neon Armadillo Music Saloon.*   Located next door to the Adventurers Club, what you see here is definitely what you get: first-class country and bluegrass music. If you have not spent some time here counting down to showtime for one of the comedy presentations, go ahead and visit the Neon Armadillo now.

6. *STRAX.*   When Pleasure Island opened in 1989 this club was an under-21 club called Videopolis East. For various reasons (fights and teenage gang conflicts), it was closed and reopened as Cage. Cage was targeted to older (over 21) rockers, but never really achieved much of an identity. Now enter STRAX, a so-called 70s club featuring the music of Iron Butterfly, Led Zeppelin, The Doors, and Grand Funk Railroad, any one of which would have sent Walt Disney into anaphylactic shock. The decor during our last visit were the same steel beams, catwalks, and metal mesh that imbued the previous incarnations with such charm. A new theme is planned, but nobody seems to know what it will be. Stay tuned. At STRAX, as at Mannequins, you must be 21 to enter.

7. *Mannequins Dance Palace.*   Backtrack toward Pleasure Island's front entrance to Mannequins. Mannequins is a ritzy, contemporary rock dance club with incredible lighting and special effects. Music for dancing is recorded but the sound system is superb. Those under 21 are not permitted in Mannequins.

8. *The Pleasure Island Jazz Company.*   Located across the walkway from the entrance of Mannequins, this is the next nightspot on the Touring Plan. The Jazz Company is the newest of the Pleasure Island clubs and occupies a space previously used as a food court and a private party room. The club features live jazz and blues and hosts jam sessions with local musicians.

9. *Rock & Roll Beach Club.*   The next stop is the Beach Club,

featuring oldies and current rock. The bands here are always first-rate and they raise the roof beginning early in the evening. A variety of games are available for those who do not wish to dance.

10. **West End Stage.** The West End Stage, while not a club, is the most happening place on Pleasure Island. Live rock bands play under the stars in the plaza, with the Neon Armadillo and the Adventurers Club on one side and the Comedy Warehouse on the other. The bands are, without exception, super as are the lighting and sound systems. The high stage provides excellent visibility. Performances at the West End Stage run four times each night. Drinks are available from street vendors.

11. **Baton Rouge Lounge.** The last club on the itinerary is the Baton Rouge Lounge situated on the stern of the main deck of the Empress Lilly riverboat. Located at the far end of Pleasure Island, the Empress Lilly can be reached by walking out the main entrance and turning left, then turning left again, crossing back over the canal. The Baton Rouge Lounge features light musical comedy or folk and is a great place to mellow out after the hard-driving music of the other clubs. It should be pointed out that technically the lounge is not part of Pleasure Island and you do not have to buy a Pleasure Island admission to enter.

12. **Pleasure Island Restaurants.** There has been a lot of attention paid to menu creation at Pleasure Island's eateries. Unfortunately, most of the fun is in the anticipation, the real item not quite living up to its billing.

The Empress Room on the Empress Lilly is the island's flagship restaurant and its best. Serving Continental cuisine, the Empress Room is pricey and reservations are required. Call (407) 828-3900 to make reservations. Coats are required for gentlemen. Our dining experiences at the Empress Room were mediocre until last year, when to our delight, we found the fare significantly improved.

In addition to the Empress Room, there are two somewhat less sumptuous dining rooms on the Empress Lilly (Steerman's Quarters and the Fisherman's Deck), each serving steak and seafood as well as New Orleans specialties. Attire at these latter is more casual, reservations are taken but not required, and prices are somewhat more reasonable. With these restaurants, however, the riverboat ambience is a decided winner over the table fare. There is no entertainment in any of the Empress Lilly eateries.

Onshore, across from the riverboat, is the Portobello Yacht Club, which serves seafood, pasta, and pizza. Casual yet stylish, the Portobello does a credible job with its Northern Italian fare. On the down side, we get mixed messages from our readers on this restaurant—most complain it is overpriced.

The Fireworks Factory specializes in barbeque, with several types of ribs available. Slaw and cornbread are some of the best we have had anywhere. Appetizers (catfish, buffalo wings, barbequed shrimp) are disappointing. If you stick to ribs and chicken and skip the appetizers, you can have a good meal here.

If you want to eat dinner at a Pleasure Island full-service restaurant, we recommend arriving by 6:30 P.M. and eating early or waiting until after 10:00 P.M. An alternative, of course, is to eat sandwiches and munchies in the clubs. It is not necessary to buy any sort of club admission to eat at Pleasure Island restaurants. Many of the restaurants are open during the day as well as in the evening.

13. ***Pleasure Island Shopping.*** Pleasure Island features some shops which are entertainment attractions in themselves. At Cover Story, guests don costumes prior to being photographed for the mock cover of a major magazine. Want to see yourself on the cover of *Cosmo*? Here's the place. In a similar vein, Super-Star Studio provides the opportunity to star in your own music video. Props, including keyboard, drums, and guitar are available. Video technicians record your lip sync (or you can actually sing), varying camera angles and making you look good. Post Production adds background to your tape for added realism. Work alone or make up a whole group with your friends. If you do not want your own magazine cover or rock video, drop in and watch others; it's a hoot of the first order.

It is not necessary to pay any sort of admission to shop at Pleasure Island during the day. In the evening, however, all of Pleasure Island except the restaurants is gated.

Pleasure Island vs. Church Street Station

Both Pleasure Island and Church Street Station are worthwhile attractions. Pleasure Island has a plastic, trendy, brand-new (translate Disney) feel. Church Street Station is situated in a restored city block of historic old Orlando adjacent to the railroad tracks. Both sites have their strong points, but architecturally Church Street is much more interesting.

As discussed previously, parking is a minor problem at Church Street, but no problem at all (if you can remember where you parked) at Pleasure Island.

Performances are longer and fewer in number at Church Street making it much more difficult than at Pleasure Island to see all the shows covered in your admission. Also, the timing of performances (starting and ending times) at Church Street mitigates against getting from one show to another or getting a good seat. Pleasure Island's comedy clubs feature shorter shows performed more frequently, and the music clubs run pretty much continuously, so that making the rounds is no particular problem.

Rock music and dancing is more diversified at Pleasure Island with the addition of the 70s club STRAX. Guests can now enjoy classic rock at the Beach Club and on the West End Stage, 70s rock at STRAX, and contemporary rock and new disco at Mannequins. Church Street Station offers only two rock venues, but both are outstanding. The Orchid Garden Ballroom features some of the best live oldies rock in the area, while Phineas Phogg's offers Top-40 music and dancing.

When it comes to country music and dancing, as good as the Neon Armadillo is, it cannot compare to Church Street's rollicking Cheyenne Saloon & Opera House. Comedy is good at both places, although different.

Church Street is a more adult night complex. The humor is bawdier, the crowd older, and you don't have to check out the wristband of the girl by the bar to know she's over 21.

Food is a toss-up. Both places serve both good and undistinguished fare at an upscale price. You just have to ask the right questions and pick your way carefully through the menus.

Church Street admission is about $17 per adult (including sales tax); a bit pricey compared to Pleasure Island's $15.

For additional information, call:
Church Street Station: (407) 422-2434
Pleasure Island: (407) 934-7781

Readers' Questions to the Author

Q: When you do your research, are you admitted to the parks free? Do the Disney people know you are there?

A: We pay the regular admission and usually the Disney people do not know we are on site. Similarly, both in and out of Walt Disney World, we pay for our own meals and lodging.

Q: How often is The Unofficial Guide *revised?*

A: We publish a new edition once a year, but make minor corrections every time we go to press, about three times a year on average.

Q: I have an old 1991 edition of the Unofficial Guide. *How much of the information [in it] is still correct?*

A: Veteran travel writers will acknowledge that five to eight percent of the information in a guidebook is out of date by the time it comes off the press! Walt Disney World is always changing. If you are using an old edition of the *Unofficial Guide*, descriptions of attractions still existing should be generally accurate. However, many other things change with every edition, particularly the Touring Plans and the hotel and restaurant reviews. Finally, and obviously, older editions of the *Unofficial Guide* do not include new attractions or developments.

Q: How many people have you surveyed for your Age Group Ratings on the attractions?

A: Since the publication of the first edition of the *Unofficial Guide* in 1985, we have interviewed or surveyed just over 9,000 Walt Disney World patrons. Even with such a large survey population, however, we continue to have difficulty with certain age groups. Specifically, we would love to hear from seniors about their experiences with Splash Mountain, Big Thunder Mountain, Space Mountain, Star Tours, the Tower of Terror, and Body Wars.

Q: Do you stay in Walt Disney World? If not, where do you stay?

A: We do stay at Walt Disney World lodging properties from time to time, usually when a new hotel opens. Since we began writing about Walt Disney World in 1982 we have stayed in over 45 different properties in various locations around Orlando, Lake Buena Vista, and Kissimmee. During our last visit we stayed at the Dixie Landings Resort and liked it very much.

Q: I laughed at the "When to Go" suggestions [for the attractions]. Too many were before 10 A.M. and after 5 P.M. What are we supposed to do between 10 A.M. and 5 P.M.?

A: Our best advice is to go back to your hotel and take a nice nap. More in keeping with the spirit of your question, however, the attractions with the shortest waits between 10 A.M. and 5 P.M. are as follows:

Magic Kingdom	*Tropical Serenade*
	Tom Sawyer Island
	The Hall of Presidents
	Liberty Square Riverboat
	Magic Journeys
	It's a Small World
	Mickey's Starland Show
	Grandma Duck's Petting Farm
	Mission to Mars
	American Journeys
	Dreamflight
	WEDway PeopleMover
	Carousel of Progress
EPCOT Center	CommuniCore East
	CommuniCore West
	Universe of Energy
	Cranium Command
	Horizons
	Harvest Theater
	Kabaret Theater
	Image Works
	Wonders of China
	The American Adventure
	O Canada!

Disney-MGM Studios

– Backstage Studio Tour (tram segment)
– *Inside the Magic* (backstage tour walking segment)

– Superstar Television
– New York Street set
– Animation Tour
– *The Monster Sound Show*

Q: I don't think the food at Walt Disney World is bad at all. Could it be that you are just overly picky?

A: I will acknowledge that there is certainly more mediocre food at Walt Disney World than "bad" food. As for my orientation, I target the restaurant reviews in this guide to readers with discriminating palates, in other words, to those actively seeking the most satisfying dining experience available. And, yes, I am picky, particularly at the prices we pay for food at Walt Disney World.

Q: You go on and on about how much trouble it is to eat in the Magic Kingdom and how mediocre the food is, but never make any constructive recommendations for how to improve the situation.

A: One way to provide dining variety, simplify service, and speed customer processing is to operate a buffet. Guests pay one fixed price on entering, eliminating the need to key in different menu items, and then serve themselves. Instead of a Mom or Dad placing different orders for every member of the family, Mom just walks up to the cashier and says, "Two adults and three kids, please." Many of the Las Vegas casinos operate huge buffets, efficiently serving several thousand patrons every meal. One casino operates four individual, double-sided, serving stations (i.e., eight serving lines) in their buffet, allowing almost 400 people to be serving themselves at once.

Q: When my wife and I were shopping for a Walt Disney World guidebook, I picked up your book and my wife picked up another Disney guide almost exactly the same size, but less expensive. To make a long story short, we couldn't agree so we bought both. When we got home, I noticed that even though the books were the same size the Unofficial Guide *had almost twice as many pages. How could this be?*

A: Different paper stocks have different bulks. It's an old trick in the publishing business, especially with fiction, to print a short book on bulky paper to make it look more substantial, i.e., bigger. The size of the type in a book is important, too. The book you mentioned in your letter has large type, with about a maximum of 1800 characters per page. The *Unofficial Guide* uses smaller type and packs 2700 characters on a page. As a consumer advocate, I'd be the last person to argue that more is better, but by doing a little math (mutiplying the page count by the number of characters per page), I figured out that the *Unofficial Guide* has almost 2½ times more content than the Disney guide your wife selected.

Q: What is your favorite Florida attraction?

A: What attracts me (as opposed to my favorite attraction) is Juniper Springs, a stunningly beautiful canoeing stream about an hour north of Orlando in the Ocala National Forest. Originating as a limestone aquifer, crystal clear water erupts from the ground and begins a ten-mile journey to the creek's mouth at Lake George. Winding through palm, cypress, and live oak, the stream is more exotic than the Jungle Cruise, and alive with birds, animals, turtles, and alligators. Put in at the Juniper Springs Recreation Area on FL 40, 36 miles east of Ocala. The seven-mile trip to the FL 19 bridge takes about four and a half hours. Canoe rentals and shuttle service are available at the recreation area. Phone (904) 625-2808 for information.

Q: Why are there no photographs of the theme parks in the Unofficial Guide*?*

A: Disney has copyrighted many identifiable buildings and structures in Walt Disney World. Any recognizable photo of Walt Disney World which we publish without Disney's permission, even if we take the picture with our own camera, could constitute copyright infringement, according to Disney's legal representatives. Walt Disney World will not grant the *Unofficial Guide* permission to publish photographs because of its relationship with Steve Birnbaum's *Official Guide to Walt Disney World*.

Readers' Comments

A reader from Georgetown, Massachussetts, writes:

In particular I do not agree with your stance on day guests using the Walt Disney World transportation system—particularly your suggestion that people insist they have a right to ride the monorail to the Polynesian Resort in order to access the Ticket & Transportation Center parking lot more quickly. As we have chosen to stay on Disney property, we do not complain that we could have gotten cheaper accommodations elsewhere. We are willing to expend more money and [for] that reason are accorded some privileges not extended to persons who have chosen less expensive accommodations off Disney World property.

On another subject, a mother from Savannah, Georgia, ventures this opinion:

The final point I would like to address is babies and small children; nothing adds to the stress of a long, hot day like the sound of crying and screaming. Even our four-year-old noticed that "those babies don't like it here." If for some reason this is the *only* time you will *ever* be able to come to Walt Disney World, I guess there is no getting around it, but in reality it would be a good idea to wait until the kids are old enough to handle the place. There is a lot more to consider than the idea that the baby would like seeing Mickey Mouse.

A Bloomington, Indiana, couple had this to say:

My wife and I are 42 yrs. old. We took your advice on taking an afternoon break. That 2–3 hours rest time back at the Disney Inn kept us refreshed for our entire stay. I think without the afternoon breaks we would have missed more and enjoyed less.

Similarly, a Michigan woman stated:

We were so glad we took the nap advice. At first we thought no way, but then thought about it and it was such good advice. I think the adults needed it more than the kids. We were all ready and willing for our afternoon naps, and had a great time when we returned [to the theme park].

A British school principal offered this advice about touring in early June:

On Fridays in June just about half of the 11–15 year olds in Florida seem to be taken to the Magic Kingdom as an end of term treat. I particularly enjoyed talking to the teachers, being a Head myself, but I am sure that many visitors would regard these hoards with trepidation, particularly if they arrived at 10 A.M. as we did. It was our only late start and we paid the price.

A woman from Brooklyn, New York, struck a defiant note on behalf of readers with bad backs:

On big rides, you mention the heart caution and pregnancy warning but not back trouble. One of our [group] had to miss all the big ones.

And, finally, our favorite from a mother living in Sudbury, Suffolk, England:

When the Touring Plan worked so well on our first day at EPCOT, I wanted to jump up and down and shout Hallelujah (but being British I didn't!).

And so it goes.

Index

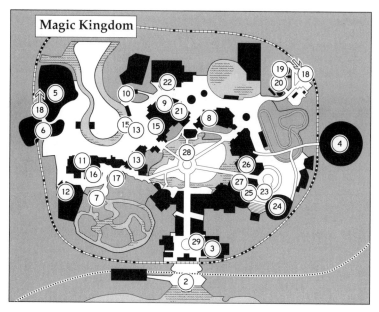

Magic Kingdom

Magic Kingdom
One-Day Touring Plan, for Adults
Pocket Outline Version
For the detailed version of this Touring Plan, see page 279.
(Interrupt the Touring Plan for *The Diamond Horseshoe Jamboree*.)

1. Arrive at TTC 50 minutes prior to opening.
2. Take the monorail or ferry to park entrance.
3. Make reservations for 12:15 P.M. *Diamond Horseshoe* show.
4. As soon as Tomorrowland opens, ride Space Mountain.
5. Go to Frontierland via the central hub. Ride Big Thunder Mountain.
6. Ride Splash Mountain.
7. Ride the Jungle Cruise.
8. Ride Snow White's Adventures.
9. Ride Peter Pan's Flight.
10. See The Haunted Mansion.
11. Return to Frontierland. See the *Country Bear Jamboree*.
12. Ride Pirates of the Caribbean.
13. If you have time before the *Diamond Horseshoe* show, ride the Liberty Square Riverboat first.

14. If you do not have *Diamond Horseshoe* reservations, eat lunch.
15. In Liberty Square, ride the riverboat and see *The Hall of Presidents*.
16. See *Tropical Serenade*.
17. See the Swiss Family Treehouse.
18. Back in Frontierland, take the railroad to Mickey's Starland.
19. See *Mickey's Starland Show*.
20. Meet Mickey at his Hollywood Theater.
21. See *Magic Journeys*.
22. Ride It's a Small World.
23. Ride the PeopleMover.
24. See the *Carousel of Progress*.
25. Ride Dreamflight.
26. See the *Mission to Mars*.
27. See *American Journeys*.
28. See live performances.
29. Browse along Main Street.
30. Depart Magic Kingdom.

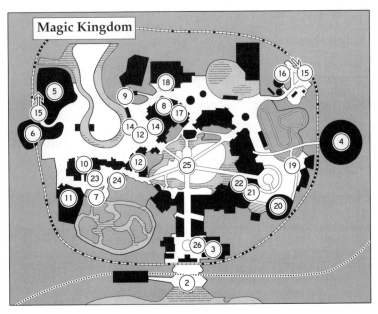

Magic Kingdom
Author's Selective One-Day Touring Plan, for Adults
Pocket Outline Version

For the detailed version of this Touring Plan, see page 283.

(Interrupt the Touring Plan for *The Diamond Horseshoe Jamboree*.)

1. Arrive at the TTC 50 minutes prior to opening.
2. Take the monorail or ferry to park entrance.
3. Make reservations for the 12:15 P.M. *Diamond Horseshoe* show.
4. As soon as Tomorrowland opens, ride Space Mountain.
5. Go to Frontierland via the central hub. Ride Big Thunder Mountain.
6. Ride Splash Mountain.
7. Ride the Jungle Cruise.
8. Ride Peter Pan's Flight.
9. See The Haunted Mansion.
10. See the *Country Bear Jamboree*.
11. Ride Pirates of the Caribbean.
12. If you have time before the *Diamond Horseshoe* show, ride the Liberty Square Riverboat first.
13. If you do not have *Diamond Horseshoe* reservations, eat lunch.
14. Ride the riverboat and see *The Hall of Presidents*.
15. Take the railroad from Frontierland to Mickey's Starland.
16. See *Mickey's Starland Show*.
17. See *Magic Journeys* in Fantasyland.
18. Ride It's a Small World.
19. Go to Tomorrowland.
20. See the *Carousel of Progress*.
21. Ride Dreamflight.
22. See *American Journeys*.
23. See *Tropical Serenade*.
24. See the Swiss Family Treehouse.
25. Enjoy live entertainment.
26. Browse along Main Street.
27. Depart Magic Kingdom.

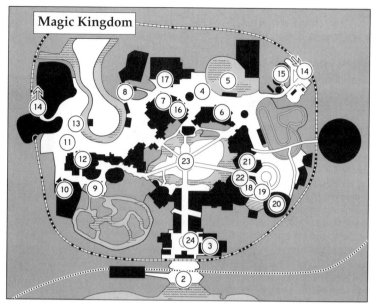

Magic Kingdom
One-Day Touring Plan, for Parents with Small Children
Pocket Outline Version
For the detailed version of this Touring Plan, see page 287.
Review the Small Child Fright Potential Chart on pages 180–182.

1. Arrive at the TTC 50 minutes prior to opening.
2. Take the monorail or ferry to park entrance.
3. Make reservations for the 12:15 P.M. *Diamond Horseshow* show.
4. When Fantasyland opens, ride Dumbo. (See the detailed version of this plan for special instructions on early entry days.)
5. Ride 20,000 Leagues Under the Sea.
6. Ride Mr. Toad's Wild Ride.
7. Ride Peter Pan's Flight.
8. See The Haunted Mansion.
9. Ride the Jungle Cruise.
10. Ride Pirates of the Caribbean.
11. Go to Frontierland.
12. If you have time before the *Diamond Horseshoe* show, see the *Country Bear Jamboree* first.

13. Explore Tom Sawyer Island.
14. Take the railroad to Mickey's Starland.
15. See *Mickey's Starland Show* and meet Mickey.
16. In Fantasyland, see *Magic Journeys.*
17. Ride It's a Small World.
18. Go to Tomorrowland. Ride Dreamflight.
19. Ride the PeopleMover.
20. See *Carousel of Progress.*
21. See *Mission to Mars.*
22. See *American Journeys.*
23. Enjoy live entertainment.
24. Browse along Main Street.
25. Depart Magic Kingdom.

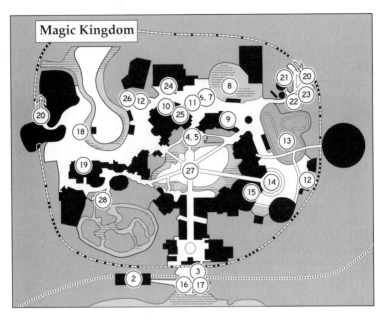

Magic Kingdom
Dumbo-or-Die-in-a-Day Touring Plan, for Parents with Small Children
Pocket Outline Version

For the detailed version of this Touring Plan, see page 291.
Review the Small Child Fright Potential Chart on pages 180–182.
(Interrupt the Touring Plan for lunch, rest, and dinner.)

1. Arrive at the TTC 50 minutes prior to opening.
2. Take the monorail to the park entrance.
3. Rent a stroller (if needed).
4. Go to King Stefan's in the castle.
5. At the castle, make dinner reservations.
6. Ride Dumbo.
7. Ride Dumbo again.
8. Ride 20,000 Leagues Under the Sea.
9. Ride Mr. Toads Wild Ride.
10. Ride Peter Pan's Flight.
11. Ride Cinderella's Carrousel.
12. Ride the Skyway to Tomorrowland.
13. Ride the Grand Prix Raceway.
14. Ride Starjets.
15. Ride Dreamflight.
16. Return to your hotel for lunch and a nap.

17. Return to the Magic Kingdom.
18. In Frontierland, go to Tom Sawyer Island.
19. See the *Country Bear Jamboree.*
20. Take the train to Mickey's Starland.
21. See *Mickey's Starland Show* and meet Mickey.
22. Visit the petting farm.
23. Enjoy the playground.
24. If you have time before dinner, ride It's a Small World.
25. After dinner, see *Magic Journeys.*
26. In Liberty Square, see The Haunted Mansion.
27. Watch the evening parade.
28. In Adventureland, ride the Jungle Cruise.
29. Repeat favorite attractions.
30. Depart Magic Kingdom.

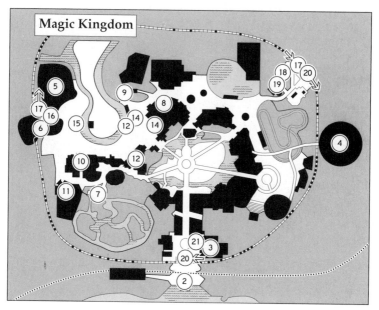

Magic Kingdom
Two-Day Touring Plan A, for When the Park Is Open Late
Pocket Outline Version

For the detailed version of this Touring Plan, see page 295.
(Interrupt the Touring Plan for *The Diamond Horseshoe Jamboree*.)

Day One

1. Arrive at the TTC 50 minutes prior to opening.
2. Take the monorail or ferry to park entrance.
3. Make reservations for the 12:15 P.M. *Diamond Horseshoe* show.
4. As soon as Tomorrowland opens, ride Space Mountain.
5. Go to Frontierland via the central hub. Ride Big Thunder Mountain.
6. Go next door and ride Splash Mountain.
7. Go to Adventureland and ride the Jungle Cruise.
8. Ride Peter Pan's Flight in Fantasyland.
9. Go to Liberty Square. See The Haunted Mansion.
10. Return to Frontierland. See the *Country Bear Jamboree*.

11. In Adventureland, ride Pirates of the Caribbean.
12. If you have time before the *Diamond Horseshoe* show, ride the Liberty Square Riverboat.
13. If you don't have *Diamond Horseshoe* reservations, eat lunch.
14. In Liberty Square, ride the riverboat and see *The Hall of Presidents*.
15. In Frontierland, explore Tom Sawyer Island.
16. Go to the Frontierland Train Station.
17. Take the train to Mickey's Starland.
18. See *Mickey's Starland Show*.
19. Visit Mickey at the Hollywood Theater.
20. Take the train to Main Street.
21. Browse along Main Street.
22. Depart the Magic Kingdom.

525

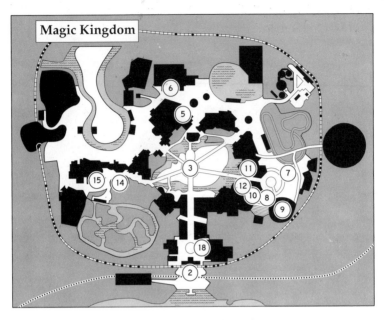

Magic Kingdom
Two-Day Touring Plan A, for When the Park Is Open Late
Pocket Outline Version
For the detailed version of this Touring Plan, see page 298.

Day Two

1. Arrive at the TTC 50 at 2:00 P.M. in order to see the afternoon parade.
2. Take the monorail or ferry to park entrance.
3. Watch the parade.
4. Make dinner reservations if you want to eat in the park.
5. In Fantasyland, see *Magic Journeys.*
6. Ride It's a Small World.
7. Go to Tomorrowland.
8. Ride the PeopleMover.
9. See the *Carousel of Progress.*
10. Ride Dreamflight.
11. See *Mission to Mars.*
12. See *American Journeys.*
13. Eat dinner.
14. Go to Adventureland. Explore the Swiss Family Treehouse.
15. See *Tropical Serenade.*
16. Try any rides you missed.
17. Repeat favorite attractions.
18. Browse along Main Street.
19. Depart the Magic Kingdom.

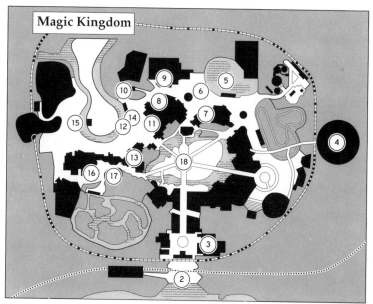

Magic Kingdom
Two-Day Touring Plan B, for Morning Touring
and for When the Park Closes Early
Pocket Outline Version

For the detailed version of this Touring Plan, see page 300.
(Interrupt the Touring Plan for *The Diamond Horseshoe Jamboree.*)

Day One

1. Arrive at the TTC 50 minutes prior to opening.
2. Take the monorail or ferry to park entrance.
3. Make reservations for the 12:15 P.M. *Diamond Horseshoe* show.
4. As soon as Tomorrowland opens, ride Space Mountain.
5. Ride 20,000 Leagues Under the Sea.
6. Ride Dumbo.
7. Ride Snow White's Adventures.
8. Ride Peter Pan's Flight.
9. Ride It's a Small World.
10. In Liberty Square, see The Haunted Mansion.

11. See *The Hall of Presidents.*
12. If you have time before the *Diamond Horseshoe,* ride the Liberty Square Riverboat first.
13. Eat lunch at the *Diamond Horseshoe.*
14. Ride the riverboat if you missed it before lunch.
15. In Frontierland, explore Tom Sawyer Island.
16. In Adventureland, see *Tropical Serenade.*
17. See the Swiss Family Treehouse.
18. Enjoy live entertainment.
19. Depart the Magic Kingdom.

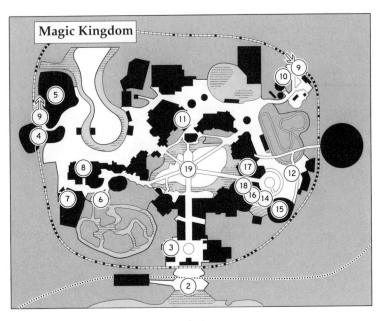

Magic Kingdom
Two-Day Touring Plan B, for Morning Touring
and for When the Park Closes Early
Pocket Outline Version
For the detailed version of this Touring Plan, see page 302.

Day Two

1. Arrive at the TTC 50 minutes prior to opening.
2. Take the monorail or ferry to park entrance.
3. Pick up a daily entertainment schedule.
4. In Frontierland, ride Splash Mountain.
5. Ride Big Thunder Mountain Railroad.
6. In Adventureland, ride the Jungle Cruise.
7. Ride Pirates of the Caribbean.
8. Back in Frontierland, see *Country Bear Jamboree.*

9. Take the train to Mickey's Starland.
10. See *Mickey's Starland Show* and visit Mickey.
11. Go to Fantasyland. See *Magic Journeys.*
12. Go to Tomorrowland.
13. Eat lunch.
14. Ride the PeopleMover.
15. See the *Carousel of Progress.*
16. Ride Dreamflight.
17. See *Mission to Mars.*
18. See *American Journeys.*
19. Enjoy live entertainment.
20. Depart the Magic Kingdom.

EPCOT Center
One-Day Touring Plan
Pocket Outline Version

For the detailed version of this Touring Plan, see page 375.
(Interrupt the Touring Plan for lunch, dinner, and IllumiNations.)

1. Arrive 45 minutes before the official opening time.
2. Go to Earth Station and make restaurant reservations.
3. Ride Spaceship Earth, if the rest of the park is not open. If the whole park is open, ride Body Wars first.
4. Ride Body Wars in the Wonders of Life pavilion.
5. Ride Spaceship Earth, now, if you missed it earlier.
6. Ride Listen to the Land.
7. Ride Journey into Imagination.
8. See *Captain EO.*
9. Walk to the opposite side of Future World.
10. Ride the World of Motion.
11. Go to the World Showcase.
12. Ride El Rio del Tiempo in Mexico.
13. Ride Maelstrom in Norway.
14. See *Wonders of China.*
15. Visit Italy and Germany.
16. See *The American Adventure.*
17. Visit Japan and Morocco.
18. See the film in France.
19. Visit the United Kingdom.
20. See *O Canada!*
21. Return to Future World. Ride Horizons.
22. See *Cranium Command.*
23. Visit the Universe of Energy.
24. Ride Spaceship Earth, if you missed it earlier.
25. See The Living Seas.
26. See the two shows you missed earlier at The Land pavilion.
27. Enjoy IllumiNations.
28. Depart EPCOT Center.

EPCOT Center

EPCOT Center
Author's Selective One-Day Touring Plan
Pocket Outline Version

For the detailed version of this Touring Plan, see page 379.
(Interrupt the Touring Plan for lunch, dinner, and IllumiNations.)

1. Arrive 45 minutes prior to official opening time.
2. Go to Earth Station and make restaurant reservations.
3. Ride Spaceship Earth, if the rest of the park is not open. If the whole park is open, ride Body Wars first.
4. Ride Body Wars in the Wonders of Life pavilion.
5. Ride Spaceship Earth, now, if you missed it earlier.
6. Ride Listen to the Land.
7. See *Captain EO*.
8. Walk to the opposite side of Future World.
9. Ride the World of Motion.
10. Go to the World Showcase.
11. Visit Mexico.
12. Ride Maelstrom in Norway.
13. See *Wonders of China*.
14. Visit Italy and Germany.
15. See *The American Adventure*.
16. Visit Japan and Morocco.
17. See the film in France.
18. Visit the United Kingdom.
19. See *O Canada!*
20. Return to Future World. Ride Horizons.
21. See *Cranium Command.*
22. Visit the Universe of Energy.
23. Ride Spaceship Earth, if you missed it earlier.
24. See The Living Seas.
25. Enjoy Illuminations.
26. Depart EPCOT Center.

EPCOT Center

EPCOT Center
Two-Day Touring Plan
Pocket Outline Version

For the detailed version of this Touring Plan, see page 383.
(Interrupt the Touring Plan for lunch)

Day One

1. Arrive 45 minutes before the official opening time.
2. Go to Earth Station and make restaurant reservations.
3. Ride Spaceship Earth, if the rest of the park is not open. If the whole park is open, ride Body Wars first.
4. Ride Body Wars in the Wonders of Life pavilion.
5. See the *Making of Me.*
6. Ride Spaceship Earth, now, if you missed it earlier.
7. Ride Listen to the Land.
8. Ride Journey into Imagination.
9. See *Captain EO.*
10. Go to the World of Motion pavilion.
11. Ride World of Motion.
12. Go to the World Showcase.
13. Ride El Rio del Tiempo in Mexico.
14. Ride Maelstrom in Norway.
15. See *Wonders of China.*
16. Visit Italy and Germany.
17. See *The American Adventure.*
18. Visit Japan and Morocco.
19. See the film in France.
20. Depart EPCOT Center.

EPCOT Center

EPCOT Center
Two-Day Touring Plan
Pocket Outline Version

For the detailed version of this Touring Plan, see page 385.
(Interrupt the Touring Plan for dinner and IllumiNations.)

Day Two

1. Arrive at EPCOT at 3 P.M.
2. Go to Earth Station and make dinner reservations.
3. Go to The Living Seas.
4. See the two shows you missed at The Land.
5. Ride Spaceship Earth, if you missed it yesterday.
6. Visit the Universe of Energy.
7. See *Cranium Command*.
8. Ride Horizons.
9. See *O Canada!*
10. Visit the United Kingdom.
11. Enjoy Illuminations.
12. Depart EPCOT Center.

EPCOT Center

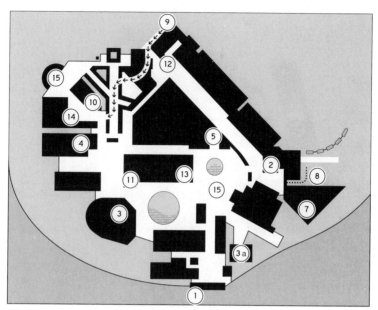

Disney-MGM Studios
One-Day Touring Plan
Pocket Outline Version

For the detailed version of this Touring Plan, see page 425.
(Before you go, check detailed itinerary for park opening procedures.)

1. Arrive 40 minutes before official opening time.
2. See *Voyage of the Little Mermaid.*
3. Hustle to *Indiana Jones.*
3a. (If the Tower of Terror is open, ride after *Indiana Jones* and then proceed to Step 4.)
4. Ride Star Tours.
5. Ride The Great Movie Ride.
6. Make meal reservations, if desired.
7. Take the Animation Tour.
8. Take the tram segment of the Backstage Tour.
9. Get off the tram and walk up New York Street.
10. See *MuppetVision 3-D.*
11. See *The Monster Sound Show.*
12. Take the walking segment of the Backstage Tour (*Inside the Magic*).
13. See SuperStar Television.
14. See the Studio Showcase.
15. Enjoy live entertainment.
16. Depart the Studios.

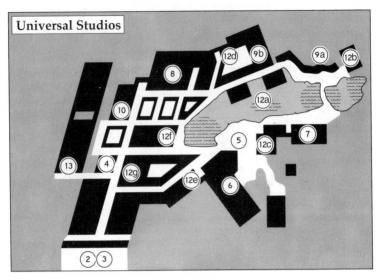

Universal Studios

Universal Studios
One-Day Touring Plan
Pocket Outline Version

For the detailed version of this Touring Plan, see page 453.

1. Call (407) 363-8000 the day before your visit for the official opening time.
2. Arrive 35 minutes before opening time.
3. Ask if any rides are closed.
4. When admitted, ride Hanna-Barbera.
5. Go to the Expo Center section of the park.
6. Ride E.T. Adventure.
7. Ride Back to the Future.
8. Ride Kongfrontation.
9. Ride Jaws, if open (9a); then ride Earthquake (9b).
10. See *Ghostbusters*.
11. This is a good time for lunch.
12. See the *Stunt Spectacular* (12a), the *Wild West Stunt Show* (12b), the *Animal Actors Stage* (12c), and *Beetlejuice* (12d), as convenient according to the daily entertainment schedule. As time permits, work the *Horror Make-up Show* (12e), and *Murder, She Wrote* (12f), which run continuously, into your schedule. See *Alfred Hitchcock* (12g) last.
13. If you are with grade-school age children, see Nickelodeon Studios.
14. See any live shows you may have missed.

Unofficial Guide **Reader Survey**

If you would like to express your opinion about Walt Disney World or this guidebook, complete the following survey and mail it to:

> *Unofficial Guide* Reader Survey
> P.O. Box 43059
> Birmingham, AL 35243

Inclusive dates of your visit _____

Did you have a car? _____   Hometown _____ State _____

Members of your party:	Person 1	Person 2	Person 3	Person 4	Person 5
Gender (M or F)	____	____	____	____	____
Age	____	____	____	____	____

Magic Kingdom:

	Person 1	Person 2	Person 3	Person 4	Person 5
Favorite Attraction	____	____	____	____	____
Next Favorite Attraction	____	____	____	____	____
Most Disappointing	____	____	____	____	____

EPCOT Center:

	Person 1	Person 2	Person 3	Person 4	Person 5
Favorite Attraction	____	____	____	____	____
Next Favorite Attraction	____	____	____	____	____
Most Disappointing	____	____	____	____	____

Disney-MGM Studios:

	Person 1	Person 2	Person 3	Person 4	Person 5
Favorite Attraction	____	____	____	____	____
Next Favorite Attraction	____	____	____	____	____
Most Disappointing	____	____	____	____	____

Where did you stay? _____

Concerning accommodations, on a scale with 100 best and 0 worst, how would you rate:

    The quality of your room? _____   Value for the money? _____

Did you return to your room for rest during the day? _____

On a scale with 100 best and 0 worst, rate how the Touring Plans worked:

    Magic Kingdom Touring Plan: Rating _____ Name of Plan _____

    EPCOT Center Touring Plan: Rating _____ Name of Plan _____

    Disney-MGM Studios Touring Plan: Rating _____

    Universal Studios Florida Touring Plan: Rating _____

    Typhoon Lagoon Touring Plan: Rating _____

    Pleasure Island Touring Plan: Rating _____

Favorite Restaurant in Walt Disney World _____

Most Disappointing Restaurant in Walt Disney World _____

Favorite Restaurant out of Walt Disney World _____

Most Disappointing Restaurant out of Walt Disney World _____
_____

Did you buy this guide: Before leaving? _____ While on your trip? _____

How did you hear about this guide?

    Loaned or recommended by friend _____ Radio or TV talk show_____

    Newspaper or magazine feature or review _____

    Bookstore salesperson_____ Just picked it out on my own_____

What other guidebooks did you use? _____
_____

On the 100 best and 0 worst scale, how would you rate them? _____
_____

Using the same scale, how would you rate the *Unofficial Guide?* _____

Comments about your Walt Disney World vacation or about the *Unofficial Guide:* _____
_____
_____
_____
_____
_____
_____
_____
_____

Walt Disney World Restaurant Survey

Tell us about your Walt Disney World dining experiences. Listed below are the theme park full-service restaurants followed by the resort hotel restaurants on the next page. Beside each restaurant is a thumbs-up and thumbs-down symbol. If you enjoyed the restaurant enough that you would like to eat there again, circle the thumbs-up symbol. If not, circle the thumbs-down symbol.

Theme Park Full-Service Restaurants (in alphabetical order):

Akershus	Norway: EPCOT	👍	👎
Alfredo di Roma Ristorante	Italy: EPCOT	👍	👎
Biergarten	Germany: EPCOT	👍	👎
Bistro de Paris	France: EPCOT	👍	👎
Chefs de France	France: EPCOT	👍	👎
Coral Reef Restaurant	Living Seas: EPCOT	👍	👎
Hollywood Brown Derby	Disney-MGM Studios	👍	👎
King Stefan's Banquet Hall	Magic Kingdom	👍	👎
Land Grille Room	Land Pavilion: EPCOT	👍	👎
Liberty Tree Tavern	Magic Kingdom	👍	👎
Mama Melrose's Ristorante	Disney-MGM Studios	👍	👎
Marrakesh	Morocco: EPCOT	👍	👎
Nine Dragons Restaurant	China: EPCOT	👍	👎
(50's) Prime Time Cafe	Disney-MGM Studios	👍	👎
Rose & Crown	United Kingdom: EPCOT	👍	👎
San Angel Inn	Mexico: EPCOT	👍	👎
Sci-Fi Dine-In Restaurant	Disney-MGM Studios	👍	👎
Tempura Kiku	Japan: EPCOT	👍	👎
Teppanyaki Dining Room	Japan: EPCOT	👍	👎
Tony's Town Square Restaurant	Magic Kingdom	👍	👎

See following page for Walt Disney World hotel restaurants.

Walt Disney World Hotel Restaurants (in alphabetical order):

American Vineyards............. Hilton..................................... 👍 👎
Ariel's...............................Beach Club Resort.................. 👍 👎
Arthur's 27.........................Buena Vista Palace................. 👍 👎
Baskervilles.........................Grosvenor Resort.................... 👍 👎
Benihana...........................Hilton..................................... 👍 👎
Boatwright's Dining Hall.......Dixie Landings Resort............. 👍 👎
Bonfamille's Cafe.................Port Orleans Resort................. 👍 👎
Cape May Cafe.................... Beach Club Resort.................. 👍 👎
Captain Jack's Oyster Bar...... Disney Village Marketplace...... 👍 👎
Chef Mickey's..................... Disney Village Marketplace...... 👍 👎
Contemporary Cafe...............Contemporary Resort.............. 👍 👎
Coral Isle Cafe....................Polynesian Resort................... 👍 👎
Crockett's Tavern.................Fort Wilderness...................... 👍 👎
Empress Room.................... Empress Lilly Riverboat.......... 👍 👎
Fireworks Factory................Pleasure Island....................... 👍 👎
Fisherman's Deck................ Empress Lilly Riverboat.......... 👍 👎
Flagler's.............................Grand Floridian...................... 👍 👎
Garden Gallery....................Disney Inn............................. 👍 👎
Garden Grove Cafe...............WDW Swan.......................... 👍 👎
Grand Floridian Cafe............ Grand Floridian...................... 👍 👎
Harry's Safari Bar & Grill   WDW Dolphin....................... 👍 👎
Minnie Mia's Italian Eatery....Disney Village Marketplace...... 👍 👎
Narcoossee's.......................Grand Floridian...................... 👍 👎
Olivia's Cafe...................... Vacation Club Resort.............. 👍 👎
The Outback........................Buena Vista Palace................. 👍 👎
Palio..................................WDW Swan.......................... 👍 👎
Papeete Bay Verandah...........Polynesian Resort................... 👍 👎
Plaza Diner......................... Hotel Royal Plaza................... 👍 👎
Pompano Grill......................Disney Village....................... 👍 👎
Portobello Yacht Club.......... Pleasure Island...................... 👍 👎
Ristorante Carnevale............ WDW Dolphin....................... 👍 👎
Steerman's Quarters..............Empress Lilly Riverboat.......... 👍 👎
Sum Chows.........................WDW Dolphin....................... 👍 👎
Victoria and Albert's.............Grand Floridian...................... 👍 👎
Yachtsman Steakhouse.......... Yacht Club Resort.................. 👍 👎